Mac OS X for Unix Geeks

FOURTH EDITION

Mac OS X for Unix Geeks

Brian Jepson, Ernest E. Rothman, and Rich Rosen

O'REILLY®

Beijing · Cambridge · Farnham · Köln · Sebastopol · Tokyo

Mac OS X for Unix Geeks, Fourth Edition

by Brian Jepson, Ernest E. Rothman, and Rich Rosen

Published by O'Reilly Media, Inc., 1005 Gravenstein Highway North, Sebastopol, CA 95472.

O'Reilly books may be purchased for educational, business, or sales promotional use. Online editions are also available for most titles (*http://safari.oreilly.com*). For more information, contact our corporate/institutional sales department: 800-998-9938 or *corporate@oreilly.com*.

Editor: Isabel Kunkle
Production Editor: Sarah Schneider
Copyeditor: Rachel Head
Proofreader: Sarah Schneider

Indexer: Ellen Troutman Zaig
Cover Designer: Karen Montgomery
Interior Designer: David Futato
Illustrator: Robert Romano

Printing History:

September 2008:	Fourth Edition.
May 2005:	Third Edition. Originally published under the title *Mac OS X Tiger for Unix Geeks*.
February 2004:	Second Edition. Originally published under the title *Mac OS X Panther for Unix Geeks*.
October 2002:	First Edition.

ISBN: 978-0-596-52062-5

[LSI]   [2011-05-20]

1305553533

Table of Contents

Part II.   Building Applications

Preface

Once upon a time, Unix came with only a few standard utilities. If you were lucky, it included a C compiler. When setting up a new Unix system, you'd have to crawl the Net looking for important software: Perl, *gcc*, *bison*, *flex*, *less*, Emacs, and other utilities and languages. That was a lot of software to download through a 28.8-Kbps modem. These days, Unix distributions come with many more features, and more and more users are gaining access to a wide-open pipe.

Free Linux distributions pack most of the GNU tools onto a CD-ROM, and now commercial Unix systems are catching up. Solaris comes with a companion CD of free software including a big selection of GNU utilities, and just about every flavor of Unix (including Mac OS X) now includes Perl. Mac OS X also comes with many tools, most of which are open source and complement the tools associated with Unix.

This book serves as a bridge for Unix developers and system administrators who've been lured to Mac OS X because of its Unix roots. When you first launch the Terminal application, you'll find yourself at home in a Unix shell. However, Apple's credo is "Think Different," and you'll soon find yourself doing things a little differently. Some of the standard Unix utilities you've grown accustomed to may not be there, */etc/passwd* and */etc/group* have been supplanted with something called Directory Services, and when it comes to developing applications, you'll find that things like library linking and compiling have a few new twists to them.

Despite all the beauty of Mac OS X's Aqua interface, you'll find that some things are different on the Unix side. But rest assured, the changes are easy to deal with if you know what to do. This book is your survival guide for taming the Unix side of Mac OS X.

Audience for This Book

This book is aimed at Unix developers—a category that includes programmers who have switched to Linux from a non-Unix platform—as well as web developers who spend most of their time in ~/*public_html* over an *ssh* connection, and experienced Unix hackers. In catering to such a broad audience, we've chosen to include some material that advanced users might consider basic. However, this choice makes the book accessible to all Unix programmers who've switched to Mac OS X as their operating system of choice, whether they have been using Unix for 1 year or 10. If you are coming to Mac OS X with no Unix background, we suggest that you start with *Learning Unix for Mac OS X Tiger* by Dave Taylor (O'Reilly) to get up to speed with the basics.

Organization of This Book

This book is divided into four parts. Part I helps you map your current Unix knowledge to the world of Mac OS X. Part II discusses compiling and linking applications. Part III takes you into the world of Fink and covers packaging. Part IV discusses using Mac OS X as a server and provides some basic system management information. Appendix A provides useful reference information.

Here's a brief overview of what's in the book.

Part I, Getting Around

This part of the book orients you to Mac OS X's unique way of expressing its Unix personality.

Chapter 1, Inside the Terminal
> This chapter provides you with an overview of the Terminal application, including a discussion of the differences between the Terminal and the standard Unix *xterm*.

Chapter 2, Searching and Metadata
> This chapter introduces Spotlight, a subsystem for searching your Mac. In this chapter, you'll learn how to access this powerful metadata store from the command line.

Chapter 3, Files and Filesystems
> Here you'll learn about the layout of the Mac OS X filesystem, with descriptions of key directories and files.

Chapter 4, Startup
> This chapter describes the Mac OS X boot process, from when the Apple icon first appears on your display to when the system is up and running.

Chapter 5, Directory Services
> This chapter gets you started with Mac OS X's powerful Directory Services system, which replaces or complements the standard Unix flat files in the */etc* directory.

Chapter 6, Printing
> This chapter explains how to set up a printer under Mac OS X and shows you around CUPS, the open source printing engine under Mac OS X's hood.

Chapter 7, The X Window System and VNC
> In this chapter, you'll learn how to install and work with the X Window System and how to use both built-in Mac OS X and third-party tools for establishing VNC connections between Mac OS X and other Unix systems.

Chapter 8, Third-Party Tools and Applications
> This chapter introduces some third-party applications that put a new spin on Unix features, such as SSH/SFTP frontends, TEX applications, the statistical package R, and multimedia-related applications.

Chapter 9, Dual-Boot and Beyond
> Mac OS X isn't the only operating system you can run on your Mac. In this chapter, you'll learn how you can run many operating systems on your Mac, perhaps even two or three at a time.

Part II, Building Applications

Although Apple's C compiler is based on the GNU Compiler Collection (GCC), there are important differences between compiling and linking on Mac OS X and on other platforms. This part of the book describes these differences.

Chapter 10, Compiling Source Code
> This chapter describes the peculiarities of the Apple C compiler, including using macros that are specific to Mac OS X, working with precompiled headers, and configuring a source tree for Mac OS X.

Chapter 11, Libraries, Headers, and Frameworks
> Here we discuss building libraries, linking, and miscellaneous porting issues you may encounter with Mac OS X.

Part III, Working with Packages

There are several packaging options for software that you compile, as well as for software you obtain from third parties. This part of the book covers software packaging on Mac OS X.

Chapter 12, Fink
> In this chapter you'll learn all about Fink, a package management system and porting effort that brings many open source applications to Mac OS X.

Chapter 13, MacPorts
> MacPorts offers another way to install lots of open source software on your Mac. You'll learn all about it in this chapter.

Chapter 14, Creating and Distributing Installable Software
> This chapter describes the native package formats used by Mac OS X, as well as packaging options you can use to distribute applications.

Part IV, Serving and System Management

This part of the book talks about using Mac OS X as a server and discusses system administration.

Chapter 15, Using Mac OS X As a Server
> In this chapter, you'll learn about setting up your Macintosh to act as a server, selectively letting traffic in (even through a Small Office/Home Office firewall such as the one found in the AirPort base station), setting up Postfix, and setting up and configuring MySQL and PostgreSQL.

Chapter 16, System Management Tools
> This chapter describes commands for monitoring system status and configuring the operating system.

Chapter 17, Other Programming Languages: Perl, Python, Ruby, and Java
> This chapter describes the versions of Perl, Python, Ruby, and Java that ship with Mac OS X, as well as optional modules that can make your experience much richer.

Appendix

The appendix includes reference information that will be useful to newcomers.

Appendix A
> If you are totally new to Mac OS X, this appendix will get you up to speed with the basics of its user interface. It also introduces terminology that we use throughout the book.

Xcode Tools

This book assumes that you have installed the Xcode tools, which include the latest version of Apple's port of *gcc*. If you bought a boxed version of Mac OS X Tiger or Leopard, you can find the installer for Xcode in the *Xcode* folder on the same DVD that you used to install Mac OS X. Boxed versions of earlier releases of Mac OS X included Xcode on a separate CD-ROM. If you'd like to be absolutely sure that you have the latest versions of the tools, they are available to Apple Developer Connection (ADC) members at *http://connect.apple .com*.

Where to Go for More Information

Although this book will get you started with the Unix underpinnings of Mac OS X, there are many online resources that can help you get a better understanding of Unix for Mac OS X:

Apple's Open Source mailing lists page
> This page leads to all the Apple-hosted Darwin mailing lists and includes links to list archives.
>
> > *http://developer.apple.com/darwin/mail.html*

The Darwin project
> Darwin is a complete Unix operating system for x86 and PowerPC processors. Mac OS X is based on the Darwin project. Spend some time at the project's web page to peek as deep under Mac OS X's hood as is possible.
>
> > *http://www.opensource.apple.com/darwinsource/*

Fink
> Fink is a collection of open source Unix software that has been ported to Mac OS X. It is based on the Debian package management system and includes utilities to easily mix precompiled binaries and software built from source. Fink also includes complete GNOME and KDE desktop distributions.
>
> > *http://fink.sourceforge.net*

MacPorts
> MacPorts (formerly known as DarwinPorts), a project of OpenDarwin, is an open source community-based project that provides a unified porting system for Darwin, Mac OS X, FreeBSD, and Linux. At the time of this writing, it includes thousands of ports, including the GNOME desktop system. The MacPorts project is hosted by Apple, Inc.
>
> > *http://www.macports.org*

MacOSXHints
> MacOSXHints presents a collection of reader-contributed tips, along with commentaries from people who have tried the tips. It includes an extensive array of Unix tips.

http://www.macosxhints.com

Stepwise

Before Mac OS X, Stepwise was the definitive destination for OpenStep and WebObjects programmers. Now Stepwise provides news, articles, and tutorials for Cocoa and WebObjects programmers.

http://www.stepwise.com

VersionTracker

VersionTracker keeps track of software releases for Mac OS X and other operating systems.

http://www.versiontracker.com

MacUpdate

MacUpdate also tracks software releases for Mac OS X.

http://www.macupdate.com

FreshMeat's Mac OS X section

FreshMeat catalogs and tracks the project history of thousands of applications (mostly open source).

http://osx.freshmeat.net

Conventions Used in This Book

The following typographical conventions are used in this book:

Italic

Used to indicate new terms, URLs, filenames, file extensions, directories, commands and options, modules, and Unix utilities. For example, a path in the filesystem will appear in the text as */Applications/Utilities*.

`Constant width`

Used to show functions, variables, keys, attributes, the contents of files, or the output from commands.

`Constant width bold`

Used in examples to show commands or other text that should be typed literally by the user.

`Constant width italic`

Used in examples and commands to show text that should be replaced with user-supplied values, and to highlight comments in command output.

Menus/Navigation

Menus and their options are referred to in the text as File→Open, Edit→Copy, etc. Arrows are also used to signify a navigation path when

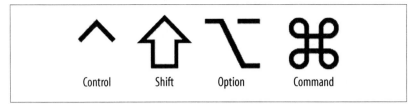

| Control | Shift | Option | Command |

Figure P-1. These symbols, which appear in Mac OS X's menus, are used for issuing keyboard shortcuts so you can quickly work with an application without having to use the mouse

using window options; for example, System Preferences→Accounts→*username*→Password means that you should launch System Preferences, click the icon for the Accounts preference panel, select the appropriate username, and then click on the Password pane within that panel.

Pathnames

Pathnames are used to show the location of a file or application in the filesystem. Directories (or *folders* for Mac and Windows users) are separated by a forward slash. For example, if you're told to "...launch the Terminal application (*/Applications/Utilities*)," it means you can find the Terminal application in the *Utilities* subfolder of the *Applications* folder.

$, #

The dollar sign ($) is used in some examples to show the user prompt for the *bash* shell; the hash mark (#) is the prompt for the *root* user.

Menu symbols

When looking at the menus for any application, you will see some symbols associated with keyboard shortcuts for particular commands. For example, to open a document in Microsoft Word, you could go to the File menu and select Open (File→Open), or you could issue the keyboard shortcut ⌘-O.

Figure P-1 shows the symbols used in the various menus to denote a keyboard shortcut.

Rarely will you see the Control symbol used as a menu command option; it's more often used in association with mouse-clicks to emulate a right-click on a two-button mouse or for working with the *bash* shell.

 This icon signifies a tip, suggestion, or general note.

This icon indicates a warning or caution.

Comments and Questions

Please address comments and questions concerning this book to the publisher:

O'Reilly Media, Inc.
1005 Gravenstein Highway North
Sebastopol, CA 95472
800-998-9938 (in the United States or Canada)
707-829-0515 (international/local)
707-829-0104 (fax)

To comment or ask technical questions about this book, send email to:

bookquestions@oreilly.com

We have a website for the book, where we list examples, errata, and any plans for future editions. The site also includes a link to a forum where you can discuss the book with the author and other readers. You can access this site at:

http://www.oreilly.com/catalog/9780596520625/

For more information about books, conferences, Resource Centers, and the O'Reilly Network, see the O'Reilly website at:

http://www.oreilly.com

Safari® Books Online

 When you see a Safari® Books Online icon on the cover of your favorite technology book, that means the book is available online through the O'Reilly Network Safari Bookshelf.

Safari offers a solution that's better than e-books. It's a virtual library that lets you easily search thousands of top tech books, cut and paste code samples, download chapters, and find quick answers when you need the most accurate, current information. Try it for free at *http://safari.oreilly.com*.

Acknowledgments from the Previous Editions

This book builds on the first edition of *Mac OS X for Unix Geeks*, for which we had help from a number of folks. Thanks to:

- The folks at Apple, for technical review and handholding in so many tough spots!
- Erik Ray, for some early feedback and pointers to areas of library linking pain.
- Simon St.Laurent, for feedback on early drafts and for prodding us toward more Fink coverage.
- Chris Stone, for tech review and helpful comments on the Terminal application.
- Tim O'Reilly, for deep technical and editorial help.
- Brett McLaughlin, for lots of great technical comments as well as helpful editorial ones.
- Brian Aker, for detailed technical review and feedback on Unixy details.
- Chuck Toporek, for editing, tech review, and more.
- Elaine Ashton and Jarkko Hietaniemi, for deeply detailed technical review and help steering the book in a great direction.
- Steven Champeon, for detailed technical review and help on Open Firmware and the boot process.
- Simon Cozens, for technical review and for pushing us toward including an example of how to build a Fink package.
- Wilfredo Sanchez, for an immense amount of detail on everything, and for showing us the right way to do a startup script under Jaguar. His feedback touched nearly every aspect of the book, and without it there would have been gaping holes and major errors.
- Andy Lester, Chris Stone, and James Duncan Davidson, for reviewing parts of the book and pointing out spots that needed touching up.

Acknowledgments from Brian Jepson

Thanks to Nathan Torkington, Rael Dornfest, and Chuck Toporek for helping shape and launch the previous editions of this book, and to Ernie Rothman and Rich Rosen for making it a reality with me. Thanks also to Charles Stephen Edge, Jr., for his helpful tech review of the manuscript. A big thanks to Isabel Kunkle, our editor, who helped us launch this new edition, keep it on track, and get it into your hands. Thanks also to readers of the previous edition who wrote to us asking for a new edition. Your encouragement means a lot!

I'd especially like to thank my wife, Joan, and my stepsons, Seiji and Yeuhi, for their support and encouragement through my late-night and weekend writing sessions, and for their patience throughout the unusual experiments I inflicted upon the home network and various computers during the writing and research of this book.

Acknowledgments from Ernest E. Rothman

I would first like to thank Brian Jepson, who conceived this book and was generous enough to invite me to participate in its development, and Rich Rosen, for joining us first as a technical reviewer and later as a coauthor. I would like to express my gratitude to Charles Stephen Edge, Jr., for his many useful comments as technical reviewer, and to our editor Isabel Kunkle, for editing, encouragement, patience, and kindness. I am also grateful to the visionary folks at Apple, Inc., for producing and constantly improving Mac OS X, and to the developers who spend a great deal of time writing applications and posting helpful insights on newsgroups, mailing lists, websites, and blogs. Finally, I am very grateful to my lovely wife, Kim, for her love, patience, and encouragement, and to my Newfoundland dogs, Max Bear and Joseph, for their love and patience. Both Max and Joseph were at my side for most of the time that I worked on the book, but my beloved Max (4/19/2002–5/5/2008) passed away suddenly before its completion. He will be forever in my heart.

Acknowledgments from Rich Rosen

First, my thanks to Brian Jepson and Ernie Rothman for giving me this opportunity to work with them on this book. Thanks also to Isabel Kunkle, for providing all sorts of help and guidance throughout this process, and to Charles Stephen Edge, Jr., for keeping us honest and making sure everything we said made sense.

On a personal note, my gratitude goes out to Leon Shklar, for providing me with so many great opportunities at the most opportune times, and to Dave Makower, for his steadfast friendship and his wealth of Mac knowledge. Likewise, I'm grateful to Igor Novgorodtsev for allowing me to borrow his copy of the Tiger edition of this book when I needed it.

Thanks to my parents, Arthur and Toby, for their lifelong support and encouragement. Most of all, I thank my wife, Celia, for nourishing my ears, my eyes, my heart, and my soul.

## PART I

Getting Around

This part of the book orients you to Mac OS X's unique way of expressing its Unix personality. You'll start out with a quick overview of the Terminal application—Mac OS X's Unix interface—and then go on to learn more about Spotlight and searching, the filesystem, startup processes, and more. You'll also see how to run Linux on your Mac, as well as how to run Mac OS X on x86 PCs.

Chapters in this part of the book include:

Chapter 1, *Inside the Terminal*
Chapter 2, *Searching and Metadata*
Chapter 3, *Files and Filesystems*
Chapter 4, *Startup*
Chapter 5, *Directory Services*
Chapter 6, *Printing*
Chapter 7, *The X Window System and VNC*
Chapter 8, *Third-Party Tools and Applications*
Chapter 9, *Dual-Boot and Beyond*

Inside the Terminal

The first order of business when exploring a new flavor of Unix is to find the command prompt. In Mac OS X, you won't find the command prompt in the Dock or on a Finder menu. Instead, you'll need to use the Terminal application, located in */Applications/Utilities*. Inside the Terminal, Unix users will find a familiar command-line environment. In this chapter we'll describe the Terminal's capabilities, comparing them to the corresponding functionality of X11 terminal emulators such as *xterm* when appropriate. We'll also highlight key features of some alternatives to the Terminal. The chapter concludes with a synopsis of the *open* command, which you can use to launch native Mac OS X applications from the Terminal, and a quick look at a freeware application that allows you to open a Terminal window from a Finder window.

Mac OS X Shells

Mac OS X comes with the Bourne Again SHell (*bash*) as the default user shell and also includes the TENEX C shell (*tcsh*), the Korn shell (*ksh*), and the Z shell (*zsh*). *bash*, *ksh*, and *zsh* are compatible with *sh*, the original Bourne shell. When *tcsh* is invoked through the *csh* link, it behaves much like *csh*. Similarly, */bin/sh* is a hard link to *bash*, which also reverts to traditional behavior when invoked through this link (see the *bash* manpage for more information).

The version of *bash* that ships with Mac OS X is, according to its manpage, a conformant implementation of the Shell and Utilities portion of the IEEE POSIX Standard 1003.1 specification. Invoking *bash* with the *--posix* command-line option changes the default behavior of *bash* to comply with the POSIX 1003.1 standard in cases where the default behavior differs from this standard.

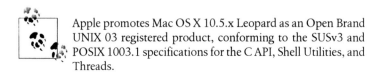 Apple promotes Mac OS X 10.5.x Leopard as an Open Brand UNIX 03 registered product, conforming to the SUSv3 and POSIX 1003.1 specifications for the C API, Shell Utilities, and Threads.

If you install additional shells, you should add them to the */etc/shells* file. To change the Terminal's default shell, see "Customizing the Terminal" later in this chapter. To change a user's default shell (used for both the Terminal and remote console logins), see "Modifying a user" in Chapter 5.

The Terminal and xterm Compared

There are several differences between Mac OS X's Terminal application and the *xterm* and *xterm*-like applications common to Unix systems running the X Window System:

- You cannot customize the characteristics of the Terminal with command-line switches such as *-fn*, *-fg*, and *-bg*. Instead, you must use the Terminal Inspector or the Terminal Preferences.

- Unlike *xterm*, in which each window corresponds to a separate process, a single master process controls the Terminal. However, each shell session is run as a separate child process of the Terminal. You can force a separate instance of some applications, including Terminal, by using the *open* command with the *-n* and *-a* switches, as described later in this chapter.

- A selection made in the Terminal is not automatically put into the clipboard. You use ⌘-C to copy and ⌘-V to paste. Even before you press ⌘-C, the selected text is contained in a location called the *pasteboard*. One similarity between the Terminal and *xterm* is that selected text can be pasted in the same window with the middle button of a three-button mouse (or with Shift-⌘-V). If you want to paste selected text into another window, you must drag and drop it with the mouse or use copy and paste. The operations described in "The Services Menu," later in this chapter, also use the pasteboard.

- The value of $TERM is xterm-color when running under Terminal (it's set to xterm under *xterm* by default).

- Pressing Page Up or Page Down scrolls the Terminal window, rather than letting the running program handle it. Use Shift-Page Up or Shift-Page Down if you want a character-mode program to receive those keystrokes.

- Terminal makes full use of Input Manager and CoreText, Mac OS X's native text and graphics rendering engines, to fully support non-English languages and to make everything faster and smoother.

If you need an *xterm*, you can have it: simply type *xterm* in the Terminal and press Enter, and the X11 environment will start up along with an *xterm* window. See Chapter 7 for more information about the X Window System.

 Beginning with Leopard, the X11 package is installed by default. In earlier releases of Mac OS X, however, the X11 package was available as an optional installation. So, if you're installing an earlier release of Mac OS X, you can either install X11 by selecting to "customize" your installation of Mac OS X, or you can install X11 from the installation DVD at a later time.

There are also Mac OS X-native applications that offer alternatives to Apple's Terminal, such as Terminator and iTerm (both freeware applications). We'll have more to say about these programs later in this chapter.

Enabling the root User

By default, the Mac OS X *root* user account is disabled, so you have to use *sudo* to perform administrative tasks. Even the most advanced Mac OS X users should be able to get by with *sudo*, and we suggest that you do not enable the *root* user account. However, if you must enable the *root* user account in Leopard, start Directory Utility (*/Applications/Utilities*), click the lock to authenticate yourself, and select Edit→Enable Root User. In earlier Mac OS X releases, you can enable the *root* user account by starting NetInfo Manager (*/Applications/Utilities*), clicking the lock to authenticate yourself, and selecting Security→Enable Root User. Though we do not recommend it, you can run a login (*sh*) shell as root, even if the *root* user is not enabled, by entering the command *sudo -i*. You can also run an alternative shell, say *tcsh*, as *root* with the command *sudo /bin/tcsh*. Alternatively, you can run a default shell process with administrative privileges with the *sudo -s* command.

Using the Terminal

If you haven't launched the Terminal, don't open it just yet. First, drag Terminal's application icon from the *Utilities* subdirectory of the *Applications* folder, and park it in the Dock so you'll have quick access to it when you need to access the command line. (If you have launched it, drag its Dock icon to a different location along the Dock, or Control/right-click it and choose "Keep

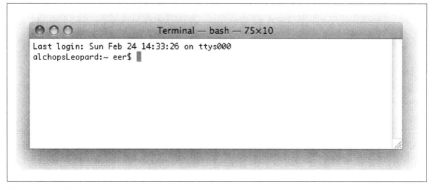

Figure 1-1. The Terminal window

in Dock"). Now you've got the Terminal right where you can find it quickly. To launch the Terminal, click its icon in the Dock once.

> The full path to the Terminal is */Applications/Utilities/Termi nal.app*, although the Finder by default hides the *.app* extension. *Terminal.app* is not a binary file. Like all *.app* applications, it's a Mac OS X *bundle*: a folder that contains a collection of files, including the binary and support files for the Terminal's user interface.
>
> You can Control-click (or right-click) on the Terminal in the Finder and select Show Package Contents to see what's inside. You can also use the Unix commands *ls* and *cd* to explore the directory */Applications/Utilities/Terminal.app/*.

After the Terminal starts, a Terminal window appears. It shows the last login, the *tty* name (the name of the Unix device for standard input), and a *bash* prompt. By default, the prompt consists of your computer name, a colon, and the current directory followed by a space, your username, and the $ character, as shown in Figure 1-1.

If you'd like to be greeted by a banner message each time you open a new Terminal window, you'll have to create or edit the */etc/motd* file (this file already existed in Mac OS X releases prior to Leopard). Regardless of whether you want to create an *motd* file or just change the message contained in an existing *motd* file, you'll need administrative privileges to edit the file. The *sudo vi /etc/motd* command can be used to open the file in the *vi* editor as the superuser. You'll need to be an administrative user to use *sudo*. When you execute a command preceded by *sudo*, you'll be prompted for your password.

The first user you create while installing Mac OS X is an administrative user, but you can also check the box marked "Allow user to administer this computer" when you create new users in System Preferences→Accounts.

Launching Terminal Windows

One difference *xterm* users will notice is that there is no obvious way to launch a new Terminal window with user-specified settings from the command line. For example, the Mac OS X Terminal has no simple equivalent to the following commands:

```
xterm &
xterm -e -fg green -bg black -e pine -name pine -title pine &
```

Instead, you create a new Terminal window by pressing ⌘-N or selecting Shell→New Window→Basic (or one of the other settings) from the menu bar. It is also possible to open a new Terminal window (or tab) with the help of *osascript*, which is a command-line program for executing AppleScript code. For example, the shell script (*nw*) shown in Example 1-1 opens a new Terminal window.

Example 1-1. A script to open a new Terminal window

```
#!/bin/sh
# Script nw opens a new Terminal window
osascript <<EOF
tell app "System Events"
  keystroke "n" using command down
end tell
EOF
```

This shell script uses *osascript* to invoke AppleScript, which in turn interacts with System Events to achieve the effect of pressing ⌘-N. (In principle, this script should work when executed from other terminal emulators, provided that they make use of the ⌘-N keystroke to open new windows. For example, it works just as well with iTerm.)

You could also command the Terminal application directly. It supports the AppleScript verb "do script". If you give it a blank script, it will just open a new window, as shown in Example 1-2.

Example 1-2. Another script to open a new Terminal window

```
#!/bin/sh
# Script: nw2
# Opens a new Terminal window
osascript <<EOF
tell app "Terminal"
```

```
    do script ""
end tell
EOF
```

The menu bar selection Shell→New Window offers a mix of choices, which include: several predefined settings as well any custom settings you have defined. Of these, one menu option will have "⌘-N" next to it. That option will open a new window with your default settings for Terminal. The predefined settings include Basic, Grass, Homebrew, Novel, Ocean, Pro, and Red Sands, and they differ in their text, background color, and other attributes. Later, we'll discuss how you can create your own settings.

> To cycle between open Terminal windows, you can use the same keystroke that most other Mac OS X applications use: ⌘-`. You can also switch between windows by pressing ⌘-Right Arrow or ⌘-Left Arrow, by using the Window menu, or by using the Terminal's Dock menu (Control-click or right-click on the Terminal Dock icon). You can also jump to a particular Terminal window with ⌘-*number* (see the Window menu for a list of numbers). To cycle through tabs, use ⌘-{ or ⌘-}, or ⌘-Shift-Right Arrow or Left Arrow.

As an alternative to creating a new Terminal window, you can create a new Terminal tab within the current Terminal window by pressing ⌘-T or selecting Shell→New Tab→Basic (or some other setting from the list) from the menu bar. Terminal tabs may be opened with different predefined settings, just like Terminal windows. For example, you may have a Basic tab and a Homebrew tab in the same Terminal window. You can rearrange the order of tabs within a Terminal window by dragging a tab with your mouse, just as you can with Safari or Firefox tabs. You can also move an active tab to a new window by selecting Window→Move Tab to New Window from the menu bar. Alternatively, you can move a tab to a new window by dragging it with your mouse onto the desktop, provided that the tab is not the active one in the window. And, should you decide that you have too many open Terminal windows, you can merge all of them into one Terminal window as tabs by selecting Window→Merge All Windows from the menu bar. In that case, each open Terminal window will become a tab in a single window. Figure 1-2 shows several tabs within the same Terminal window, with the rightmost tab active.

You can customize startup options for new Terminal windows by creating a new setting, and if you'd like, you can export the new settings to *.terminal* files. Those files can subsequently be imported into your other Macs that are running Leopard or sent to other users. See "Exporting and Importing Terminal Settings" later in this chapter for more details.

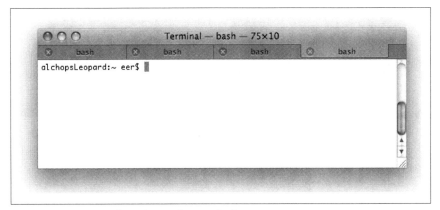

Figure 1-2. A Terminal window with several tabs

Double-clickable shell scripts

Executable shell scripts are double-clickable in Mac OS X. That is, when you double-click any executable script in the Finder, a new Terminal window will open to run the script. The new window will open with Terminal's default settings. However, you can stuff the shell script full of *osascript* commands to set the Terminal window's characteristics after it launches. The *osascript* command lets you run AppleScript from the command line. Example 1-3 shows a shell script that sets the size and title of the Terminal window and then launches the *vim* editor.

Example 1-3. Launching the vim editor

```
#!/bin/sh
# Script RunVim
osascript  <<EOF
tell app "Terminal"
  set number of rows of first window to 34
  set number of columns of first window to 96
  set custom title of first window to "Vim Editor"
end tell
EOF
vim $@
```

As with any shell script, you'll need to make it executable before you can run it. For example, to make *RunVim* executable, you would issue the following *chmod* command:

```
chmod +x RunVim
```

You can assign a custom-made icon to your shell scripts. To change a script's icon, use the following procedure:

1. Copy the desired icon to the clipboard.
2. Select your script in the Finder and open the Get Info window (⌘-I). The file's icon appears in the upper-left corner.
3. Click the current icon so that it is highlighted, and use the Paste option (Edit→Paste or ⌘-V) to paste the new icon over it.
4. Close the Get Info window by typing ⌘-W. The pasted icon is now associated with the script.

To add the shell script application to the Dock, locate the application in the Finder and drag its icon to the Dock. Now you can click on the script's Dock icon to invoke the script. You can also drag the executable's icon to the Places section of the Finder's Sidebar, although this section of the Finder is intended primarily for quick access to frequently visited folders.

The Contextual Menu

Users familiar with the X Window System know that right-clicking an *xterm* window opens a terminal-related contextual menu. Mac OS X's Terminal also has a contextual menu that can be accessed by Control-clicking (or right-clicking, if you have a two- or three-button mouse). In Tiger, the Terminal contextual menu includes the choices Copy, Paste, Paste Selection, Paste Escaped Text, Select All, Clear Scrollback, Send Break (equivalent to Control-C), Send Hard Reset, Send Reset, and Window Setting. Each of these items also has a keyboard shortcut. In Leopard, the contextual menu choices are limited to Search in Spotlight, Search in Google, Look Up in Dictionary, Copy, Paste, and Show Inspector. The contextual menu items from Tiger's Terminal are available as various menu bar items in Leopard.

Customizing the Terminal

As noted earlier, you can customize many attributes of Terminal windows (and tabs) through the Terminal application's Preferences. In this section, we'll discuss tweaking the Terminal's Preferences and some on-the-fly customizations you can make.

Preferences

Terminal's Preferences are organized into four panes: Startup, Settings, Window Groups, and Encodings. In the Encodings preference pane, you can select various encodings required for a wide variety of languages. The other three groups of preferences require further discussion.

Startup

Under the Startup preference pane, you can configure Terminal so that when it starts, either a new window with a particular setting is opened, or a window group (see the upcoming section "Window groups") is opened. The other item you can configure in the Startup preference pane is listed under "Shells open with". One choice is the system login utility (*/usr/bin/login*), and the other selection is the complete path of some specific command, such as an alternative shell. This is similar to the "Run command" option that's available on the Shell tab for a particular Terminal setting, but the choice you make in "Shells open with" affects all Terminal settings unless you've specified a "Run command" and also deselected the "Run inside shell" option in the setting. (Otherwise, the "Run command" is fed into your shell of choice.)

 You can change the default shell in the Terminal Preferences, but this change applies only to Terminal (i.e., it will not affect the login shell used for remote or console logins). Changing a user's default shell is covered in "Modifying a user" in Chapter 5.

Settings

Though we briefly discussed some of the options available in the Settings preference pane earlier, let's now take a closer look. The predefined settings are listed in the left subwindow of the Settings pane, and the options associated with each setting are accessible via a set of tabs in the right subwindow. The options are organized into five categories: Text, Window, Shell, Keyboard, and Advanced. Table 1-1 summarizes the options available on each tab.

Table 1-1. Options for Terminal settings

Tab	Options
Text	*Font*: Choose your font.
	Text: Enable and disable attributes such as antialiasing, bold fonts, blinking text, American National Standards Institute (ANSI) colors, and bright colors for bold text.
	Cursor: Select a cursor style and color, and turn blinking on or off.
Window	*Title*: Specify your own window title and indicate whether to include in that title the active process name, shell command name, setting name, tty name, dimensions, and command key.
	Background: Set the color and opacity (no background image).
	Window size: Set the number of rows and columns.
	Scrollback: Set the size of the scrollback buffer (the number of rows of previous input and output you can scroll upwards to review).

Tab	Options
Shell	*Startup*: Choose a command to run on startup (for example, an alternate shell).
	When the shell exits: Specify an action to take when the shell exits (e.g., when you type *logout* or *exit*). Choices include "Close the window," "Close if the shell exited cleanly," and "Don't close the window."
	Prompt before closing: Indicate when to prompt when closing a Terminal window. Choices include "Always," "Never" (the default), or "Only if there are processes running other than [those in the specified list]."
Keyboard	This tab controls key mappings for function, arrow, page up/down, and other keys.
Advanced	Declare your terminal (i.e., set the terminal type variable, $TERM) as ansi, dtterm, rxvt, vt52, vt100, vt102, xterm, or xterm-color (the default); have the Delete key send a Control-H; escape non-ASCII input; paste newlines as carriage returns (on by default); enforce strict VT-100 keypad behavior; scroll to the bottom on input; toggle the audible and visual bells; and set the international character encoding.

In pre-Leopard releases, one configurable option was "Option-click to position cursor." If you enabled this feature, you were able to Option-click with the mouse to position the cursor in Terminal applications such as *vim* or Emacs (saving you many keystrokes when you needed to move the insertion point). This option also worked over a remote login session, if the behavior was supported by the remote host's terminal capabilities. Beginning in Leopard, the Option-click behavior is the default behavior.

Window groups

There are situations in which you will want to routinely have several Terminal windows and tabs open, each having its own process and attributes. For example, you might be editing a file with *vim* in one window and running *octave* in another, with both windows having black backgrounds and white text. At the same time, you might be monitoring some output file using *tail* in another Terminal window, this one having a fixed size of 80 rows×80 columns and displaying black text on a white background. If this setup is one that you use frequently, you're in luck: you can save the time that it normally takes you to get things going by saving that set of Terminal windows as a *window group*.

Before you can establish a window group, you'll need to define a setting (under the Settings preference pane) corresponding to each window that will be in the window group. When defining a setting, be sure to specify the commands, if any, that must run when a window (or tab) opens with that particular setting. Next, open the Terminal windows (and tabs) that will go into the window group to make sure that the settings work properly. Once you're satisfied that the settings are correct for the window group's Terminal windows, make sure that only those windows that are to be members of the group are open. Then, select Window→Save Windows as Group. This selection will give you the opportunity to enter a name for the new window group and decide if the window group should open by default whenever the Terminal application starts. If you don't elect to start the window group by default, you can always make that choice later in Terminal's Startup preference pane. In the Window Group preference pane, you can delete window groups, export window groups as *.terminal* files, or import window groups.

Once you've established a window group, you can open it by selecting Window→Open Window Group→*Window_group_name.*

Customizing the Terminal on the Fly

You can customize the Terminal in shell scripts using escape sequences or AppleScript commands. *xterm* users may be familiar with the following command to set the *xterm* window's title:

```
echo '^[]0;My-Window-Title^G'
```

Mac OS X's Terminal accepts this sequence as well.

^[is the ASCII ESC character, and ^G is the ASCII BEL character. (The BEL character rings the Terminal bell, but in this context, it terminates an escape sequence.) The escape sequences described here are ANSI escape sequences. ANSI escape sequences are used to manipulate a Terminal window (such as by moving the cursor or setting the title).

To type the ^[characters on the command line in *bash* or *tcsh*, use the key sequence Control-V, Control-[(press Control-V and release, then press Control-[). To type ^G, use Control-V, Control-G. The *vim* editor supports the same key sequence, whereas Emacs uses Control-Q instead of Control-V.

You can capture the *bash* escape sequence in a function that you can include in your *.bash_profile* script:

```
function set_title ( )
{
    case $TERM in
        *term | xterm-color | rxvt | vt100 | gnome* )
            echo -n -e "\033]0;$*\007" ;;
        *)  ;;
    esac
}
```

Then you can change the title by issuing the following command:

$ set_title your fancy title here

You may want to package this as a shell script and make it available to everyone who uses your system, as shown in Example 1-4.

Example 1-4. Setting the Terminal title in a shell script

```
#!/bin/bash
#
# Script settitle
# Usage:  settitle title
#
if [ $# == 0 ]; then
  echo "Usage:  settitle title"
else
   echo -n -e "\033]0;$*\007"
fi
```

You can also use *osascript* to execute AppleScript commands that accomplish the same thing:

```
osascript -e \
   'tell app "Terminal" to set custom title of first window to
   "Hello, World"'
```

Exporting and Importing Terminal Settings

If you want to save your customizations, the procedure to follow depends on whether you are running Mac OS X 10.4 Tiger or 10.5 Leopard.

Saving Terminal settings in Mac OS X 10.4 Tiger

In pre-Leopard Mac OS X releases, you can launch a customized Terminal window from the command line by saving some prototypical Terminal settings to a *.term* file and then using the *open* command to launch the *.term* file. (For more information on *open*, see "The open Command," later in this chapter.) You can also launch a *.term* file by double-clicking it in the Finder. To create a *.term* file in Tiger, open a new Terminal window, then open the Terminal Inspector (File→Show Info or ⌘-I) and set the desired attributes, such as the window size, font, and text and background colors. Then save the Terminal session (File→Save or ⌘-S) to a *.term* file, such as *proto.term*. If you save this file to *~/Library/Application Support/Terminal*, you'll be able to launch a new Terminal window with the *proto.term* file's special attributes from the File→Library menu.

Alternatively, you can launch such a Terminal window from the command line by issuing a command like one of the following (depending on where you saved *proto.term*):

```
$ open ~/Library/Application\ Support/Terminal/proto.term
$ open ~/Documents/proto.term
```

The *.term* file is an XML property list (*plist*) that you can edit with a text editor such as *vim* (it can be invoked with *vi*, which is a symbolic link to *vim*) or with the Property List Editor application (*/Developer/Applications/Utilities*).* By default, opening the *.term* file creates a new Terminal window with the specified settings. You can configure the window so that it executes a command upon opening by adding an *execution string* to the *.term* file. When you launch the Terminal window, this string is echoed to standard output before it is executed. Example 1-5 shows an execution string that connects to a remote host via *ssh* and exits when you log out.

Example 1-5. An execution string to connect to a remote host

```
<key>ExecutionString</key>
<string>ssh xyzzy.oreilly.com; exit</string>
```

Saving Terminal settings in Mac OS X 10.5 Leopard

In Leopard, the closest thing to *.term* files are settings you create in the Terminal Preferences. Settings can be exported as (or imported from) *.terminal* files. Older *.term* files can also be imported as settings, so don't panic if you switched to Leopard from an earlier release of Mac OS X and don't want to lose all your *.term* files. We'll discuss how to import *.term* files later.

Terminal 2.0, which ships with Leopard, comes with several predefined settings. You can quickly see which predefined settings are available in the Terminal Inspector by opening a new Terminal window and then selecting Shell→Show Inspector from the menu bar or by pressing ⌘-I. You can also use the Inspector to change the setting of an open Terminal window or tab to another available predefined setting, as shown in Figure 1-3.

To create a new custom setting, select Terminal→Preferences from the menu bar (or press ⌘-,) and then select the Settings preference pane. On the left side of the Settings window, you'll see a listing of the predefined settings. The right portion of the Settings window shows the options associated with the currently selected setting.

You can define a new setting by clicking on the plus sign (+) at the bottom left of the Settings window and giving the new setting whatever name you want. In the example that follows, we've used "Proto." Once that's done, you can click the new setting (e.g., Proto) in the left side of the Settings window and set its attributes on the right.

 Each time you add a new setting, that new setting becomes your default.

---

* For more information on XML, see *Learning XML* by Erik T. Ray or *XML in a Nutshell* by Elliotte Rusty Harold and W. Scott Means (both from O'Reilly).

Figure 1-3. Changing a Terminal window setting with the Inspector

Settings are saved in the *~/Library/Preferences/com.apple.Terminal.plist* file. You'll be able to launch a new Terminal window with your new setting's special attributes from either the Shell→New Window menu or the Shell→New Tab menu.

You can also export your new setting as a *.terminal* file, which can be imported in another Leopard installation later. This is done as follows. In the Settings window, select the setting to be exported (e.g., Proto), then click on the gear icon (see Figure 1-4) at the bottom of the left part of the window and select Export to save the setting to a *.terminal* file, such as *Proto.terminal*. You can save the *.terminal* file to a convenient location, such as *~/Documents*. Like *.term* files in older Mac OS X versions, a *.terminal* file is an XML property list (*plist*), which you can edit.

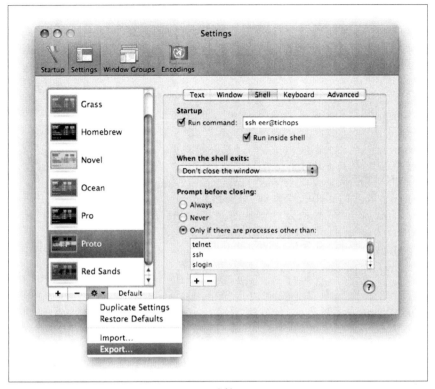

Figure 1-4. Exporting a setting as a .terminal file

 Although double-clicking a *.term* file in older Mac OS X versions opens a new Terminal window with the attributes defined in that file, double-clicking a *.terminal* (or *.term*) file in Leopard imports the settings it contains into Terminal's configuration. Every time you launch a given *.terminal* file, a new setting with the attributes defined in that *.terminal* file is created in Terminal's Preferences. The primary purpose of a *.terminal* file in Leopard is to save a setting that you can import to another Leopard installation. This means that *.terminal* files cannot be used to open new Terminal windows.

You can import a *.terminal* (or *.term*) file into the Terminal's list of settings without launching it by clicking on the gear icon at the bottom of the left part of the Settings window, selecting Import, and navigating to the desired *.terminal* file in the file browser that appears.

Working with File and Directory Names

Although Unix supports complex file and directory names containing spaces, Unix users have traditionally avoided using spaces in file and directory names. Instead, they may use capitalization or hyphens or underscores to imply spaces, as follows:

```
textFile.txt
text-file.txt
text_file.txt
```

However, most Mac users tend to insert spaces into file and directory names, and these names are often long and descriptive. Although this practice is okay if you're going to work in the graphical user interface (GUI) all the time, it creates a small hurdle to jump over when you're working on the command line. Unix shells will interpret a string containing embedded spaces as separate command-line arguments. A command such as the following, for example, would fail because the shell would interpret the string as separate arguments:

```
$ cd ~/Documents/My Shell Scripts
```

To get around this, you have two choices: escape the spaces, or quote the entire file or directory name.

 By default, files whose names begin with a dot are invisible in the Finder. You can make files named with a leading dot visible in the Finder by entering the command *defaults write com.apple.finder AppleShowAllFiles true* and then restarting the Finder with the command *killall Finder*.

To escape a space on the command line, simply insert a backslash (\) before the space. This also works with other special characters, such as parentheses. The following special characters have meaning to the shell and so must be escaped: * # ` " ' \ $ | & ? ; ~ ( ) < > ! ^. Here is an example of how to use a backslash to escape a space character in a file or directory name:

```
$ cd ~/Documents/My\ Shell\ Scripts
```

Alternatively, you can use quotation marks around the file or directory name that contains the space, as follows:

```
$ cd ~/Documents/"My Shell Scripts"
```

There is one other way to get around this problem, but it involves using the Finder in combination with the Terminal application. Let's look at an example. To launch Microsoft Word 2008 from the Terminal, you could enter the path as follows, using escape characters:

```
$ open -a /Applications/Microsoft\ Office\ 2008/Microsoft\ Word
```

Or you could enter the path using quotes:

```
$ open -a "/Applications/Microsoft Office 2008/Microsoft Word"
```

As you can see, neither method is very pretty, and both require you to know a lot of detail about the path. Now for the easy way:

1. Type the name of the command and any initial arguments it requires on the command line (in this case, *open -a*), followed by a space. Don't press Return yet!

2. Locate Microsoft Word in the Finder, and drag its icon to the Terminal window to insert the path after the space. When you do this, the spaces and any other special characters in the path will automatically be escaped with backslashes:

```
$ open -a /Applications/Microsoft\ Office\ 2008/Microsoft\ Word
```

3. Press Return to invoke the command and launch Word 2008.

You can also drag and drop URLs from a web browser. For example, to use *curl* to download files from the command line:

1. Open a new Terminal window and type *curl -O*, with a space after the *-O* switch.

2. Bring up your web browser and navigate to *http://www.oreilly.com*.

3. Drag the image at the top of the page to the Terminal window. You should now see the following in the Terminal window:

```
$ curl -O http://www.oreilly.com/graphics_new/header_main.gif
```

4. Press Return in the Terminal window to download *header_main.gif* to your computer.

Tab Completion

If you want to type a long pathname, you can cut down on the number of keystrokes required by using tab completion. For example, to enter the path */Library/StartupItems*, you can type */Li<Tab>*, which gives you */Library/*. (This works because */Library/* is the only folder at the root of the filesystem whose name begins with the letter "L.") Next, type *S<Tab>*. This time, because there is more than one folder under */Library/* that begins with the letter "S," instead of the path being completed automatically, you're given a choice of completions: *Screen Savers*, *Scripts*, *Security*, *Spotlight*, and *StartupItems*. Type as many letters as are necessary to narrow down your choice, followed by a Tab (in this case, *t<Tab>*). The full key sequence for */Library/StartupItems* would be */Li<Tab>St<Tab>*.

If you have multiple completions where a space is involved, you can type a literal space with \<Space>. For example, suppose you have two directories, *PROJECT FOLDER* and *PROJECT*. To get a completion for *PROJECT FOLDER*, you could use *PRO<Tab>\ <Space><Tab>*. The first *<Tab>* completes the word *PROJECT*, begun with the string "PRO". Adding the string "\ " at this point and pressing Tab again completes the folder name *PROJECT FOLDER*.

Changing Your Shell

Although other shells are available in Mac OS X, as we noted earlier, the default shell in Mac OS X releases beginning with Tiger is *bash*. (Early versions of Mac OS X shipped with *tcsh* as the default shell.) You can change the default shell for Terminal in its Preferences menu, but this does not affect the login shell used for remote or console logins. To change your default shell in a more pervasive manner, see "Modifying a user" in Chapter 5.

 If you install additional shells on the system, you'll need to add them to the */etc/shells* file to make Mac OS X aware that they are legitimate shells.

The Services Menu

The Mac OS X Services menu (Terminal→Services) exposes a collection of services that can work with the currently running application. In the case of the Terminal, the services operate on text that you have selected (the pasteboard). To use a service, select a region of text in the Terminal window and choose one of the following items from the Services menu:

ChineseTextConverter
: This service can be used to convert selected text to either simplified Chinese or traditional Chinese.

Disk Utility
: This service invokes Disk Utility to calculate either a CRC-32 or an MD5 image checksum of a disk whose path has been selected in the Terminal window.

Finder
: Once you have selected a filename in the Terminal window, the Finder Services menu allows you to open that file (Finder→Open), show its enclosing directory (Finder→Reveal), or show its information (Finder→Show Info).

Font Book
Not supported by the Terminal.

Grab
Not supported by the Terminal.

Import Image
Not supported by the Terminal.

Mail
The Mail→Send To service allows you to compose a new message to an email address, once you have selected that address in the Terminal window. You can also select a region of text and choose Mail→Send Selection to send a message containing the selected text.

Make New Sticky Note (Shift-⌘-Y)
This service creates a new Sticky (*/Applications/Stickies*) containing the selected text.

Open URL
This service opens the URL specified by the selected text in your default web browser.

Script Editor
This service gets the result of an AppleScript (after running the highlighted text as an AppleScript), makes a new AppleScript (in the Script Editor), or runs the selected text as an AppleScript without returning the result.

Search With Google (Shift-⌘-L)
This service searches for the selected text using *http://google.com* in your default web browser.

Send File To Bluetooth Device (Shift-⌘-B)
This service displays a dialog that lets you choose a file to send to a Bluetooth device.

Speech
This service begins speaking the selected text. (Use Speech→Stop Speaking to interrupt.)

Spotlight (Shift-⌘-F)
This service invokes Mac OS X's system-wide search technology, Spotlight, to search for the selected text. (Mac OS X provides command-line utilities for working with Spotlight. See Chapter 2.)

Summarize
This service condenses the selected text into a summary document. The summary service analyzes English text and makes it as concise as possible while retaining the original meaning.

TextEdit

The TextEdit service can open a filename, or open a new file containing the selected text.

When you use a service that requires a filename, you should select a fully qualified pathname, not just the filename, because the service does not know the shell's current working directory. (As far as the service is concerned, you are invoking it on a string of text.)

Third-party applications may install additional services of their own.

Bonjour

Bonjour (*http://developer.apple.com/networking/bonjour/index.html*), originally announced in 2002 as Rendezvous, is a networking technology that allows Bonjour-enabled devices on a local network to automatically discover each other. It is based on a standard called ZeroConf (*http://www.zeroconf .org*) and allows computers on a network to assign useful IP addresses among themselves, without the need for a DHCP server (or, as the ZeroConf working group puts it, "a man in a white lab coat"). Bonjour works with multicast DNS (mDNS) and DNS Service Discovery (DNS-SD) to allow your Mac to discover computers and services (such as SSH and web servers) on the local network.

Like many Mac OS X applications (e.g., iTunes), Terminal is Bonjour-enabled. For example, you can select Shell→New Remote Connection (or press Shift-⌘-K) to make an SSH connection to any other Mac OS X system on the local area network (LAN), provided it allows such connections. The other Macs on the LAN are identified by their computer names, as specified in their Sharing System Preferences panes.

If you have computers with other operating systems on your network, they may be able to take advantage of Bonjour, too. Apple makes a Bonjour for Windows available at *http://www.apple.com/support/downloads/bonjourfor windows.html*, and most current Linux distributions include the *avahi* package, which provides what you need to work with Bonjour services from Linux.

 You can learn more about Bonjour by reading Apple's Bonjour Overview Document, available here: *http://developer.apple .com/documentation/Cocoa/Conceptual/NetServices/NetServi ces.pdf*.

Alternative Terminal Applications

As noted earlier, other Aqua-native terminal applications are available; the freeware iTerm (*http://iterm.sourceforge.net*), developed by Fabian and Ujwal S. Sathyam, is a particularly attractive one. Although Mac OS X's Terminal is rich with useful features, iTerm offers some interesting features that make it worthy of consideration. We won't cover iTerm in great detail, but we will touch on a few of its more attractive aspects.

Before getting into what makes iTerm distinct, here are some similarities between iTerm and Terminal:

- iTerm and Terminal use the same Services menu.
- Both iTerm and Terminal support transparency, language encodings, and AppleScript, and both have contextual menus that can be accessed by Control-clicking (or right-clicking, if you have a two- or three-button mouse) in a window. iTerm has a slightly more extensive contextual menu than Terminal, though.
- Both iTerm and Terminal (beginning with Leopard) support tabs.
- Both iTerm and Terminal support Bonjour.

iTerm supports several language encodings, `xterm-color/vt100/xterm-new/xterm-256color/ansi/rxvt/linux` emulations, and many GUI features. Particularly interesting features of iTerm include support for multiple tabbed terminal sessions within each window, support for background images, profiles that allow you to open new iTerm sessions with preset terminal settings, and bookmarks for launching iTerm windows or tabs that automatically execute commands. The default value for `$TERM` is `xterm-color`, but this can be changed either on the fly, with a *bash* shell command such as *TERM=vt100*, or by selecting Bookmarks→Manage Profiles→Terminal Profiles and adjusting the Terminal Settings Type field.

iTerm's tabbed view is similar to Terminal's tabbed view, as shown in Figure 1-5.

Tabs in iTerm can be dragged to new windows, and one iTerm window can be dragged onto another to form a new tab. The effect of dragging and dropping windows and tabs in iTerm is no different from the same set of actions in Terminal. Additionally, the same *bash* (or *tcsh*) shell commands that can be used to customize the Terminal's title bar and tabs work just as well in iTerm, as shown in Figure 1-6.

iTerm's support for profiles and bookmarks is similar to Terminal's support for settings. Bookmarks are used to define iTerm sessions with preset terminal

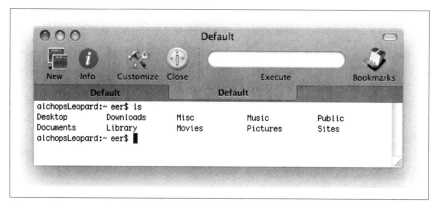

Figure 1-5. Using tabs with iTerm

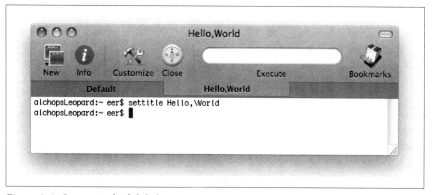

Figure 1-6. Customized tab labels in iTerm

settings. For example, you can define the color or typeface to use for text as well as a command to execute upon opening a new tab or window with a given bookmark. Aside from the command that a bookmark will execute, other attributes must be selected from predefined profiles. There are three types of profiles in iTerm: Keyboard, Terminal, and Display profiles. To define new profiles, select Bookmarks→Manage Profiles (or press Option-⌘-B) to access the Profiles window, shown in Figure 1-7. Click the Add button at the bottom left of the Profiles window to add a new profile in any of the three categories. After you've added a new profile, select it in the left subwindow of the Profiles window to reveal its options in the right subwindow, as shown in Figure 1-7.

While a profile determines certain attributes of an iTerm window (or tab), bookmarks are used to open windows and tabs with those attributes. A bookmark may also be defined to execute commands within a window or tab.

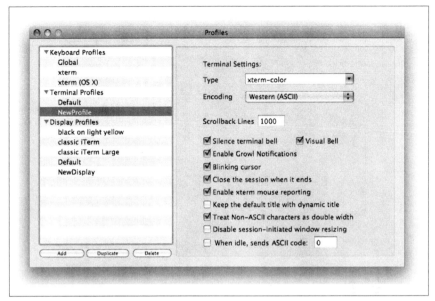

Figure 1-7. Adding a Terminal profile in iTerm

The default bookmarks are Default, which specifies the default login shell, and Bonjour, which includes *ssh* and *sftp* connections to SSH- and Bonjour-enabled computers on the LAN. To define a new bookmark, select Bookmarks→Manage Bookmarks (or press Shift-⌘-B). Then, click the plus sign in the bottom-left corner of the Bookmarks window to add a new bookmark. You'll need to specify the bookmark's name, and a command (which can be a login shell). You may also select predefined Terminal, Keyboard, and Display profiles as well as a shortcut key, as shown in Figure 1-8.

The bookmark's name is used when you open a session from the New icon in iTerm's toolbar. You can also create a bookmark group (similar to Terminal's window groups), by clicking on the icon with the red plus sign to add a folder in the bookmark listing and then, in the Bookmarks window, dragging and dropping bookmarks onto the new bookmark folder. Figure 1-9 shows a Bookmark folder with two bookmarks, in the Bookmark window.

Once you've defined a bookmark group, you can open any individual bookmark in the bookmark group by selecting Bookmarks→BookmarkGroupName→Individual Bookmark. If no iTerm window is open, the bookmark will open in a new iTerm window; otherwise, the bookmark will open in the frontmost iTerm window. If you'd like to open every member of the bookmark group at the same time, you can select Bookmarks→*BookmarkGroupName*→Open All. In this case, the set of bookmarks associated with the group will open as

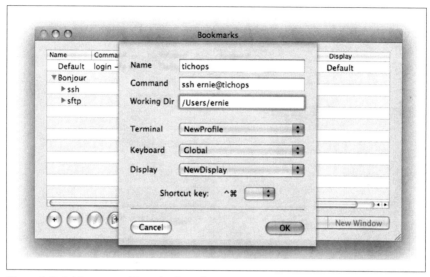

Figure 1-8. Adding a new iTerm bookmark

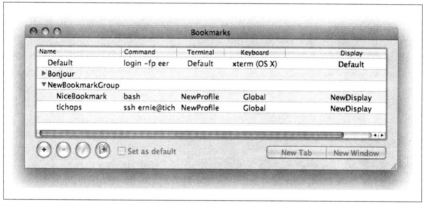

Figure 1-9. A bookmark group in iTerm

tabs within the same iTerm window. If at least one iTerm window is already open, the group will open as tabs in the frontmost window, adding to whatever tabs are already present in that window. The effect of an iTerm bookmark group is similar to that of a window group in Terminal, but Terminal window groups are not restricted to opening as tabs in the same window.

Though we've borrowed Terminal's "window group" terminology to describe iTerm's bookmark folders as "bookmark
groups," iTerm actually had the bookmark group capability
(along with tabs) several years before Terminal received a major overhaul for Leopard.

iTerm's contextual menu (the menu that appears when you right-click or
Control-click in a window) consists of the following items: New Tab (allows
you to choose a session from the bookmarks), Select (selects a tab from the
current window), Browser (opens the selected URL in your default web
browser), Mail (opens a compose mail window with the selected email address
as the recipient), Copy, Paste, Save, Select All, Clear Buffer, Info, and Close.

Although iTerm had some clear advantages over Terminal in pre-Leopard releases of Mac OS X (most notably bookmarks and tabs), that is no longer the
case at the time of this writing, considering the impressive array of features in
Leopard's Terminal application. The one feature that could tip the scale in
favor of iTerm is its support of background images in iTerm windows, assuming that this feature is of paramount importance to you. Oddly enough, Tiger's
version of the Terminal application supported background images, but it
lacked tabs and window groups. Overall, with the addition of useful features
such as tabs and window groups, Leopard's Terminal application makes the
search for an alternative much less appealing than it was in Tiger.

Terminator (*http://software.jessies.org/terminator/*) is a cross-
platform, Java-based, freeware alternative to Terminal.
Though it supports tabs, its feature set seems to come up short
when compared to Terminal and iTerm. On the other hand,
if having a cross-platform terminal emulator program is important to you, this one is worth a try.

The open Command

The *open* shell command lets you open Finder windows and launch Aqua
applications. To open a directory in the Finder, use *open* followed by the name
of the directory. For example, to open a Finder window containing the current
directory, enter the following command:

```
$ open .
```

To open your Public folder (*~/Public*) in a Finder window, use the following:

```
$ open ~/Public
```

To open the /*Applications* folder in a Finder window, use the following:

```
$ open /Applications
```

To open an application, you need only its name and the -*a* switch. For example, to open Xcode (/*Developer/Applications*), you would use the following:

```
$ open -a Xcode
```

To open multiple instances of a program, give the -*n* switch a whirl (but note that some applications, such as Firefox, may refuse to open a second instance):

```
$ open -n -a Terminal
```

 You are not required to enter the path for the application, only its name. The only time you are required to enter the path is if you have two different versions of an application with similar names on your system.

You can also use the -*a* option to open a file with something other than the application with which it's associated. For example, to open an XML file in Xcode instead of the default XML editor, the Property List Editor, enter this command:

```
$ open -a Xcode data.xml
```

To open multiple files, you can use wildcards:

```
$ open *.c
```

To force a file to be opened with TextEdit, use -*e*:

```
$ open -e *.c
```

The -*e* option directs the file to be opened in TextEdit; it cannot be used to open a file in another text editor, such as BBEdit, Smultron, or TextMate However, if you want to open a file using BBEdit, you can use the following:

```
$ open -a BBEdit filename
```

 Many popular text editors include their own command-line applications for editing documents from the command line: BBEdit uses *bbedit*, TextWrangler has *edit*, Smultron gives you *smultron* (after you choose Help→Install Command-Line Utility from within Smultron), and TextMate uses *mate*.

If you want to use TextEdit on a file that is owned by an administrator (or *root*), *sudo open -e* won't work. You'll need to specify the full path to the TextEdit executable, as in:

```
$ sudo /Applications/TextEdit.app/Contents/MacOS/TextEdit filename
```

If you find yourself doing this often, you might want to create an alias for the path to *TextEdit's* executable file. For example, you could enter the following into your *.bash_profile* file:

```
alias sudotext="sudo /Applications/TextEdit.app/Contents/MacOS/TextEdit "
```

Then, the next time you want to open a text file that would otherwise require use of the *sudo* command, you could just enter the following:

```
$ sudotext filename
```

When you enter that command, you'll be prompted for the admin password; once authenticated, the file you've specified will be opened in TextEdit, just as you hoped it would.

 In pre-Leopard Mac OS X releases, the *open-x11* command is used to open X11-based applications in Apple's X11 environment. In Leopard, you can simply launch the X11 application as you would any other Unix application, as in:

```
$ xeyes
```

You can learn more about X11 in Chapter 7.

While the *open* command can be used to open a specific directory in a Finder window from Terminal (for example, with *open /Applications*), you might conversely want to open a Terminal window with its working directory set to the directory in the current Finder window. A nifty little freeware application that makes this process easy is Thomas Wiesehöfer's OpenTerminal (*http://homepage.mac.com/thomasw/OpenTerminal/*). To install OpenTerminal, download it from the OpenTerminal website, unzip the downloaded file, then drag and drop the enclosed OpenTerminal application icon to a convenient location (e.g., */Applications/Utilities*). Then, open another Finder window and select View→Customize Toolbar. Finally, drag the OpenTerminal icon to the Finder toolbar, as shown in Figure 1-10.

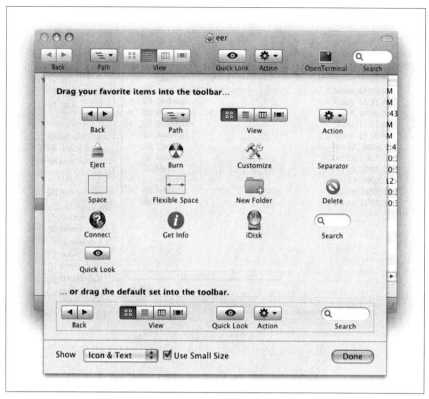

Figure 1-10. Installation of OpenTerminal in the Finder toolbar

Once OpenTerminal has been installed, you can click on its icon in the Finder toolbar to open a Terminal window with its working directory set to the directory in the current Finder window, as shown in Figure 1-11.

The first time you execute OpenTerminal you'll be presented with its Preferences window, in which you can configure OpenTerminal's various settings. If you want to change a setting in the Preferences later, you'll need to launch OpenTerminal by Option-clicking on its icon in the Finder toolbar.

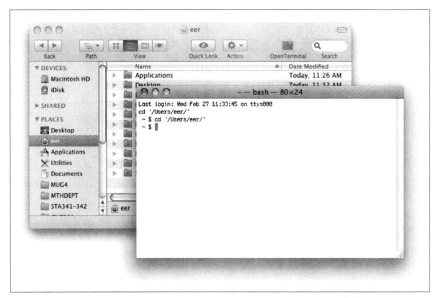

Figure 1-11. Using OpenTerminal

Finally, if you'd like to be able to open a Terminal window by Control/right-clicking on a folder in the Finder and selecting More→Open Terminal, you can add this optional contextual menu item by installing *OpenTerminalContext Menu.plugin*. To install the contextual menu item, drag and drop it into either */Library/Contextual Menu Items* (if you want to give this capability to all users) or *~/Library/Contextual Menu Items* (if you'd like to keep this capability to yourself).

## CHAPTER 2

Searching and Metadata

If a Unix geek needs to find something on her system, she'll probably use *locate* or *find*, depending on what she's looking for. Because *locate* is based on a static database that's regenerated only periodically (see "Periodic Jobs" in Chapter 4), it would be the best choice for things that don't change a lot (e.g., virtually anything in */usr*). It's also much faster because it has that database to consult. Trusty old *find*, slow as molasses, is what you want when you need more control over the search or when you're looking for something that *locate* doesn't know about, such as files that have been created recently.

Beginning with Tiger, though, Mac OS X has offered another search capability: Spotlight, which stores file metadata and sifts through it faster than a herd of sheep can clear a field. Spotlight comes in two forms: a GUI interface accessible from the menu bar, and a suite of command-line utilities. This chapter introduces you to Spotlight and shows you how to take advantage of all it has to offer.

Spotlight

Remember the relentless disk grinding you heard after you first installed the operating system? That was Spotlight creating its initial database. Spotlight is a repository of metadata for certain types of files. It gathers information about any file (or data record, such as an iCal event or video file) for which it has an *importer* (an operating system plug-in that extracts metadata from a file). To see all the importers on your system, look in */System/Library/Spotlight* and */Library/Spotlight*.

By default, Spotlight has importers for the following files and data:

- AppleWorks files
- Applications

- Archives
- Audio files
- Automator actions
- Bookmarks
- Chat transcripts
- Fonts
- iCal entries
- Images
- iPhoto pictures
- iWeb documents
- Keynote presentations
- Mail messages
- Microsoft Entourage data
- Microsoft Office documents
- MIDI files
- Numbers documents
- Pages documents
- PDFs
- PostScript files
- Quartz Composer compositions
- QuickTime movies
- RTF documents
- System preferences
- vCard files

To perform a Spotlight query, simply click the magnifying glass icon in the top-right section of the menu bar or press ⌘-Space. A Spotlight search field drops down, in which you enter a search term, as shown in Figure 2-1. You can also invoke Spotlight to search for files right in the Search field in the upper-right part of a Finder title bar. (This is shown later in Figure 2-3.)

If you position your mouse over an item in the list that comes up from a Spotlight query, a little pop-up window shows you the location of the item, as shown in Figure 2-2.

You can get a more detailed Spotlight search window by pressing Option-⌘-Space. This window, shown in Figure 2-3, lets you configure a number of aspects of your search, such as Kind (Any, Applications,

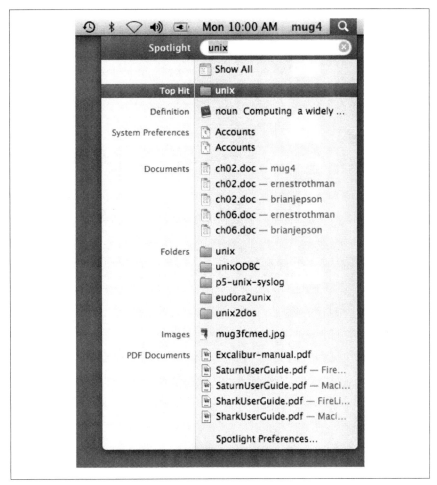

Figure 2-1. Using the Spotlight menu

Documents, Folders, Images, Movies, Music, PDF, Presentations, Text, and Other), Location, Date, Name, Contents, and Other. If you select Other, you'll be presented with a large array of search criteria choices.

Performing Spotlight Searches

Unix geeks might never use Spotlight if Mac OS X didn't include some command-line goodies for performing searches. You can perform a simple Spotlight search from the shell with the following syntax:

```
$ mdfind term
```

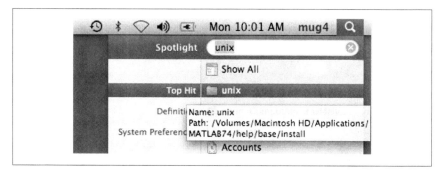

Figure 2-2. Spotlight menu item location

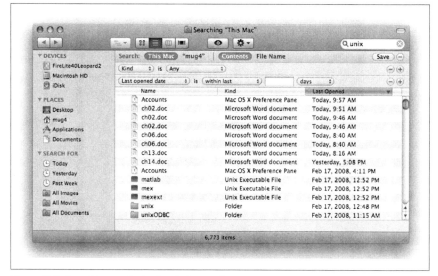

Figure 2-3. Searching with the Spotlight window

For example:

```
$ mdfind Newfoundland
/Users/eer/Sites/index.html
/Volumes/Macintosh HD/Applications/Microsoft Office 2008/Office/
timezones.xml
/Volumes/Macintosh HD/Applications/Microsoft Office 2008/Office/
Holidays
/Volumes/Macintosh HD/Developer/Documentation/DocSets/
com.apple.ADC_Reference_Library.DeveloperTools.docset/Contents/
Resources/Documents/documentation/Darwin/Reference/ManPages/man1/
tsort.1.html
/Volumes/Macintosh HD/Library/Dictionaries/
New Oxford American Dictionary.dictionary/Contents/Images/
Newfoundland (dog).png
```

```
/Volumes/Macintosh HD/usr/share/zoneinfo/Canada/Newfoundland
/Volumes/Macintosh HD/Library/Documentation/Acknowledgements.rtf
/Users/eer/Sites/JOEY/Joseph.html
/Users/eer/Sites/MaxBear/MaxBear.html
/Users/eer/Sites/Samson/Samson.html
/Applications/Microsoft Office 2008/Office/timezones.xml
/Applications/Microsoft Office 2008/Office/Holidays
/Developer/Documentation/DocSets/
com.apple.ADC_Reference_Library.DeveloperTools.docset/Contents/
Resources/Documents/documentation/Darwin/Reference/ManPages/man1/
tsort.1.html
/Library/Dictionaries/New Oxford American Dictionary.dictionary/
Contents/Images/Newfoundland (dog).png
/usr/share/zoneinfo/Canada/Newfoundland
/Library/Documentation/Acknowledgements.rtf
```

If you have a good idea of where you want to search, you can use the *-onlyin* option, as shown here:

```
$ mdfind -onlyin /Users/eer/Sites Newfoundland
/Users/eer/Sites/index.html
/Users/eer/Sites/JOEY/Joseph.html
/Users/eer/Sites/MaxBear/MaxBear.html
/Users/eer/Sites/Samson/Samson.html
```

Of course, you can also do the following:

```
$ mdfind Newfoundland | grep /Users/eer/Sites
/Users/eer/Sites/index.html
/Users/eer/Sites/JOEY/Joseph.html
/Users/eer/Sites/MaxBear/MaxBear.html
/Users/eer/Sites/Samson/Samson.html
```

You can use the *-live* option to update the results in real time as they change, and as quickly as Spotlight can index them.

Although you can find interesting results with simple keyword searches, you can refine your search by specifying any of the metadata attribute keys. You can find a comprehensive list of common metadata attribute keys and descriptions in the *MDItem.h* header file, located deep in the */System/Library/ Frameworks/CoreServices.framework/Versions/A/Frameworks/Meta data.framework/Versions/A/Headers/* directory.

For example, to find all the songs on your system authored by Jethro Tull (as indicated by the kMDItemAuthors key), you could use this search:

```
$ mdfind "kMDItemAuthors == 'Jethro Tull'"
/Users/.../iTunes Music/Jethro Tull/Songs From The Wood/Pibroch.mp3
/Users/.../iTunes Music/Jethro Tull/Songs From The Wood/Fire At Midnight.mp3
/Users/.../iTunes Music/Jethro Tull/Stand Up/A New Day Yesterday.m4a
[... and so forth ...]
```

You can perform more complex queries using regular expressions with *mdfind*, as well. For example, the following query uses the *and* (*&&*) operator to combine two search criteria (the author is "Jethro Tull" and the genre does not contain "Rock"):

```
$ mdfind "kMDItemAuthors == 'Jethro Tull' && \
  kMDItemMusicalGenre != '*Rock*'"
/Users/.../iTunes Music/Jethro Tull/A Little Light Music/15 Bouree.m4a
/Users/.../iTunes Music/Jethro Tull/A Little Light Music/
Locomotive Breath.m4a
/Users/.../iTunes Music/Jethro Tull/Stand Up/A New Day Yesterday.m4a
[... and so forth ...]
```

Including the wildcard characters (*) around *Rock* allow you to match genres such as "Prog Rock" and "Rock and Roll."

Inspecting a File's Attributes

Now that you've found some songs by Jethro Tull that aren't classified as Rock, how do you figure out what the deal is with those tunes? Are they easy listening? Something worse? The *mdls* utility lets you see all of the attributes for a given file:

```
$ cd ~/Music/iTunes/iTunes\ Music/Jethro\ Tull/A\ Little\ Light\ Music/
$ mdls "15 Bouree.m4a"
kMDItemAlbum                    = "A Little Light Music"
kMDItemAudioBitRate             = 255
kMDItemAudioChannelCount        = 2
kMDItemAudioTrackNumber         = 15
kMDItemAuthors                  = (
    "Jethro Tull"
)
kMDItemCodecs                   = (
    AAC
)
kMDItemContentCreationDate      = 2007-11-27 19:17:23 -0500
kMDItemContentModificationDate  = 2007-11-27 19:17:23 -0500
kMDItemContentType              = "public.mpeg-4-audio"
kMDItemContentTypeTree          = (
    "public.mpeg-4-audio",
    "public.audio",
    "public.audiovisual-content",
    "public.data",
    "public.item",
    "public.content"
)
kMDItemCopyright                = "® Digital Remaster (P) 2006 The
copyright in this sound recording is owned by The Ian Anderson
Group Of Companies Ltd under exclusive licence to Chrysalis
Records Ltd"
kMDItemDisplayName              = "15 Bouree.m4a"
kMDItemDurationSeconds          = 366.2016666666667
kMDItemFSContentChangeDate      = 2007-11-27 19:17:23 -0500
kMDItemFSCreationDate           = 2007-11-27 19:17:23 -0500
```

```
kMDItemFSCreatorCode         = "hook"
kMDItemFSFinderFlags         = 0
kMDItemFSHasCustomIcon       = 0
kMDItemFSInvisible           = 0
kMDItemFSIsExtensionHidden   = 0
kMDItemFSIsStationery        = 0
kMDItemFSLabel               = 0
kMDItemFSName                = "15 Bouree.m4a"
kMDItemFSNodeCount           = 0
kMDItemFSOwnerGroupID        = 502
kMDItemFSOwnerUserID         = 502
kMDItemFSSize                = 11969252
kMDItemFSTypeCode            = ""
kMDItemKind                  = "MPEG-4 Audio File"
kMDItemLastUsedDate          = 2007-11-27 19:17:23 -0500
kMDItemMediaTypes            = (
    Sound
)
kMDItemMusicalGenre          = "Pop"
kMDItemRecordingYear         = 2007
kMDItemStreamable            = 0
kMDItemTitle                 = "Bouree"
kMDItemTotalBitRate          = 255
kMDItemUsedDates             = (
    2007-11-27 00:00:00 -0500
)
```

This sampling gives you an idea of what sorts of search terms you can use with your *mdfind* queries—that's a lot of information, all stored in */.Spotlight-V100*! Note also that importers are free to define their own attributes.

Keep in mind an important distinction when speaking of metadata: the owner (in terms of filesystem permissions) of a file is not necessarily its author. For example, if you rip an MP3 file from a CD-ROM, you're the owner. However, iTunes consults the Gracenote database (formerly the CDDB, located at *http://www.gracenote.com*) and uses the information it finds there to determine the file's authors. On the other hand, if you create a Word document on your Mac, you'll not only be the owner of the file, but also its author.

Managing Spotlight

Spotlight is modestly configurable: you can use System Preferences→Spotlight to control the order in which results are presented, exclude certain file types, and specify directories that the indexing process can skip. You can do quite a bit from the shell prompt as well.

The *mdutil* command controls Spotlight settings on a volume-by-volume basis, and *mdimport* lets you work with the various importers installed on your system. For example, *mdutil* can turn indexing on or off for an entire volume with the -*i* option (it takes an argument of *on* or *off*):

```
$ sudo mdutil -i off "/Volumes/Macintosh HD/"
/Volumes/Macintosh HD:
        Indexing disabled for volume.
```

This setting is persistent across reboots. You can inspect a volume's setting with the -*s* option:

```
$ sudo mdutil -s "/Volumes/Macintosh HD/"
/Volumes/Macintosh HD/:
        Status: Indexing Disabled
```

You can use *mdimport* to list all the importers installed on your system and to debug or view statistics on the import process (see the *mdimport(1)* manpage for more details):

```
$ mdimport -L
2008-02-25 15:36:24.037 mdimport[467:10b] Paths: id(502) (
    "/System/Library/Spotlight/Audio.mdimporter",
    "/System/Library/Spotlight/Chat.mdimporter",
    "/Developer/Applications/Xcode.app/Contents/Library/Spotlight/
        SourceCode.mdimporter",
    "/Library/Spotlight/Microsoft Entourage.mdimporter",
    "/System/Library/Spotlight/QuickTime.mdimporter",
[... and so forth ...]
```

You can also use *mdimport* to list all the attributes supported by the importers on your system:

```
$ mdimport -A
'kMDItemAcquisitionMake'                'Device make'
    'Make of the device used to acquire this document'
'kMDItemAcquisitionModel'               'Device model'
    'Model of the device was used to acquire this document'
'kMDItemAlbum'          'Album'
    'Title for a collection of media, such as a record album'
'kMDItemAperture'                'Aperture'
    'Aperture setting of the camera when the picture was taken'
[... and so forth ...]
```

mdimport also has a number of features of interest to people developing their own metadata importers. For example, the -*X* option prints out an XML schema for the metadata on your system, and -*p* displays performance statistics for a run of *mdimport*.

It's possible that at some point you may need to rebuild your Spotlight database. Fortunately, that's quite easy to do. Select System Preferences→Spotlight, click the Privacy tab, and drag your hard drive icon from your Desktop to the list. Then select System Preferences→Quit System Preferences from the menu bar. Next, select System Preferences→Spotlight again, select your hard drive icon in the list on the Privacy tab, and press the minus button (–). Then quit System Preferences again, as described previously.

 Spotless (*http://www.fixamacsoftware.com/software/spot2/*) is a shareware utility to help manage Spotlight. You can use Spotless to enable or disable indexing on selected volumes.

Apple's Hiding Places for File Metadata

Apple's HFS+ filesystem has been stashing away metadata since its introduction in Mac OS X 8.1. *Resource forks* are invisible portions of files used for stashing additional or secondary information or metadata. The primary portion of the file—indeed, the only part of a file most Unix geeks are used to thinking about—is called the *data fork*. Before Mac OS X, files contained data forks containing the file's data and resource forks containing application resources. These are now contained in the application bundle itself, although resource forks are still used in a few odd places (such as text clippings, which you can create by dragging and dropping text selections to the Finder).

You can inspect a file's resource fork by appending */rsrc* to the filename. For example:

```
$ ls -l Sample.textClipping
-rw-r--r--@ 1 bjepson  bjepson  0 Apr  5 19:42 Sample.textClipping
$ ls -l Sample.textClipping/rsrc
-rw-r--r--  1 bjepson  bjepson  1350 Apr  5 19:42 Sample.textClipping/rsrc
```

The contents of a resource fork, even for something simple like a text clipping, are not necessarily human-readable, but there's usually something you can dig out:

```
$ file Sample.textClipping/rsrc
Sample.textClipping/rsrc: ms-windows icon resource
$ strings Sample.textClipping/rsrc
Apple's HFS  filesystem has been stashing away metadata since its
introduction in Mac OS X 8.1. Resource forks are invisible portions
of files used for stashing
```

Note that when you used *ls -l* to look at the *Sample.textClipping* file, it displayed the @ symbol just after the permissions, which indicates the file has extended attributes. You can use the @ option to get some information about these attributes:

```
$ ls -l@ Sample.textClipping
-rw-r--r--@ 1 bjepson  bjepson  0 Apr  5 19:42 Sample.textClipping
    com.apple.FinderInfo    32
    com.apple.ResourceFork  1350
```

Mac OS X also makes use of HFS+ metadata, which consists of extended attributes that are associated with files. For example, if you look at the root of your Mac's hard drive in the Finder, you'll see only a small subset of the directories (such as *Library*, *System*, *Applications*, and *Users*). But if you drop down into the Terminal, you'll find plenty more. The files that don't appear in the Finder have an attribute (V) that makes them invisible to it. The traditional hidden files in Unix—files whose names begin with a dot (.)—are also hidden from the Finder, even though they do not necessarily have the V attribute.

You can inspect a file's HFS+ metadata with *GetFileInfo* and set it with *SetFile*, both of which are located in */usr/bin* and are part of the Xcode package. Here's what *GetFileInfo* has to say about one of those invisible files (in this case, the Mac OS X kernel):

```
$ GetFileInfo /mach_kernel
file: "/mach_kernel"
type: ""
creator: ""
attributes: aVbstclinmedz
created: 03/05/2008 00:25:01
modified: 03/05/2008 00:25:01
```

An uppercase attribute is toggled on, and a lowercase attribute is toggled off. The *SetFile* manpage describes all these attributes. For example, to make the kernel visible in the Finder, you can use this command (you'll only need to use *sudo* for files that you don't own):

```
$ sudo SetFile -a v /mach_kernel
```

And to change it back (which we suggest you do), you can use this:

```
$ sudo SetFile -a V /mach_kernel
```

 You can also set a Finder option to show all hidden files; that is, those with the V attribute and those whose names begin with a dot (.). See the section "Working with File and Directory Names" in Chapter 1 for details.

Unix File System (UFS)

Although UFS doesn't natively support resource forks or HFS+ (Hierarchical File System) attributes, Mac OS X finds a place to stash that info for UFS files. If the file has either a resource fork or any attributes that depend on HFS+ semantics, this information goes into a separate file named *.filename*, where *filename* is the name of the original file (this is known as the *AppleDouble* format):

```
$ touch Foo
$ ls -al
total 4
drwxr-xr-x   2 bjepson  bjepson  1024 Feb 21 20:54 .
drwxr-xr-x   6 bjepson  bjepson  1024 Feb 21 20:53 ..
-rw-r--r--   1 bjepson  bjepson     0 Feb 21 20:54 Foo
$ SetFile -a S Foo
$ ls -al
total 6
drwxr-xr-x   2 bjepson  bjepson  1024 Feb 21 20:54 .
drwxr-xr-x   6 bjepson  bjepson  1024 Feb 21 20:53 ..
-rw-r--r--   1 bjepson  bjepson    82 Feb 21 20:54 ._Foo
-rw-r--r--   1 bjepson  bjepson     0 Feb 21 20:54 Foo
```

Preserving Metadata

In older versions of Mac OS X (before Tiger), you had to be very careful with what you did at the command line. If you used *cp*, *mv*, *rsync*, or any of the other command-line utilities that move files around, you could have lost part of your files and consequently wound up with files without applications associated with them. It was easy to miss this sort of mayhem, since this metadata isn't apparent until you go looking for it, and it wasn't always a disaster. For example, you could have copied a graphics file that kept its preview in its resource fork, and you probably wouldn't have missed it—after all, the next time you opened the image, the application most likely regenerated the preview. But with other files, such as text clippings and web locations (drag a URL from Safari to the Finder to create one of these), you would have lost everything, since all of these files' contents are contained in the resource fork. Here's how it would go on Mac OS X 10.3 and earlier, using a Safari web location as an example:

```
$ ls -l "Resource Fork Example.webloc"
-rw-r--r--   1 bjepson  bjepson  0 Feb 21 15:54 Resource Fork
Example.webloc
$ ls -l "Resource Fork Example.webloc/rsrc"
-rw-r--r--   1 bjepson  bjepson  624 Feb 21 15:54 Resource Fork
Example.webloc/rsrc
$ cp "Resource Fork Example.webloc" foo.webloc
$ ls -l foo.webloc
-rw-r--r--   1 bjepson  bjepson  0 Feb 26 23:18 foo.webloc
$ ls -l foo.webloc/rsrc
-rw-r--r--   1 bjepson  bjepson  0 Feb 26 23:18 foo.webloc/rsrc
```

If the file had any HFS+ metadata, you would lose that, too. Compare the results of running *GetFileInfo* on a Firefox web location before and after copying it:

```
$ GetFileInfo "Resource Fork Example.webloc"
file: "/Users/bjepson/Desktop/Resource Fork Example.webloc"
type: "ilht"
```

```
creator: "MACS"
attributes: avbstclinmEdz
created: 02/26/2005 23:18:33
modified: 02/26/2005 23:18:33
$ cp "Resource Fork Example.webloc" foo.webloc
$ GetFileInfo foo.webloc
file: "/Users/bjepson/Desktop/foo.webloc"
type: ""
creator: ""
attributes: avbstclinmedz
created: 02/26/2005 23:18:52
modified: 02/26/2005 23:18:52
```

You could get around the problem with the help of *ditto*, a powerful command-line utility used to copy directories while preserving resource forks. The *ditto* utility has been kept in current releases of Mac OS X, even though other copying utilities have evolved. (See the *ditto* manpage for more details.)

Mac OS X Tiger and later finally made this problem (mostly) go away by making all the *cp*, *mv*, and *rsync* command-line utilities aware of the resource forks and HFS+ attributes:

```
$ cp "Resource Fork Example.webloc" foo.webloc
$ ls -l foo.webloc/rsrc
-rw-r--r--  1 bjepson  bjepson  444 Apr  5 20:22 foo.webloc/rsrc
$ GetFileInfo foo.webloc
file: "/Users/bjepson/Desktop/foo.webloc"
type: "ilht"
creator: "MACS"
attributes: avbstclinmEdz
created: 04/05/2008 20:22:01
modified: 04/05/2008 20:22:01
```

 Recent versions of Firefox are smart enough to stash the URL in the file itself, so although Firefox *.webloc* files contain resource forks and metadata, they will work fine even if this information is lost:

```
$ cat foo.webloc
<?xml version="1.0" encoding="UTF-8"?>
<!DOCTYPE plist PUBLIC "-//Apple//DTD PLIST 1.0//EN"
    "http://www.apple.com/DTDs/PropertyList-1.0.dtd">
<plist version="1.0">
  <dict>
    <key>URL</key>
    <string>http://www.cnn.com/</string>
  </dict>
</plist>
```

If you copy or move the file to a non-Mac system such as a FAT-formatted memory card, AppleDouble comes in to save the day:

```
$ cp "Resource Fork Example.webloc" "/Volumes/NO NAME/"
$ ls -al "/Volumes/NO NAME/" | grep Res
-rwxrwxrwx  1 bjepson  bjepson    4434 Feb 27 09:45 ._Resource Fork
Example.webloc
-rwxrwxrwx  1 bjepson  bjepson       0 Feb 27 09:45 Resource Fork
Example.webloc
```

And if you *rm* a file on a volume that's using AppleDouble (including UFS as
well), it cleans up the file:

```
$ rm "/Volumes/NO NAME/Resource Fork Example.webloc"
remove /Volumes/NO NAME/Resource Fork Example.webloc? y
$ ls -al "/Volumes/NO NAME/" | grep Res
[... no results ...]
```

For the most part, Mac OS X has you covered when it comes to preserving
resource forks. There are a few gotchas that you need to watch out for, though.
For example, *sftp*, *ftp*, and *scp* won't preserve the resource fork for you.

Also, some tools, such as the Unison File Synchronizer (*http://www.cis.upenn
.edu/~bcpierce/unison/*), will try to create the resource forks on the Unix, Linux,
or Windows end of the transaction. While this sort of thing works smoothly
for the most part, it can occasionally trip you up. We'll talk about those issues
and many others in the next chapter.

## CHAPTER 3

Files and Filesystems

Apple's Mac OS Extended filesystem, HFS+, has a lot going for it. Although its case-insensitivity caused trouble back in the very early days of Mac OS X, it is rarely a problem these days. Its transparent support of the metadata that is so crucial to Mac OS X, coupled with its excellent support for journaling, make it the filesystem of choice for the operating system today. But even if your hard disks, iPods, and external drives are all happily formatted with HFS+, chances are you'll have to exchange files with something other than a Mac one of these days.

 Trouble? What kind of trouble? Here's an example: Library for WWW in Perl (LWP), a suite of Perl modules for interacting with web servers, also includes a number of command-line utilities. One of these is named HEAD. Once upon a time, installing LWP on Mac OS X with the default options led to the command-line utilities being dropped in /usr/bin. This resulted in /usr/bin/head being overwritten with HEAD. I was surprised by how many things rely on that useful little utility. Although such mishaps are still possible today, they are less likely. LWP no longer installs HEAD by default, but you should always pay careful attention to what you're installing, especially with older software.

Though it is not recommended for most users—even Unix geeks—you can format a filesystem as case-sensitive and journaled HFS+. You can even install Mac OS X on a case-sensitive journaled HFS+ partition, but you may run into trouble installing some third-party applications.

Mac OS X files are complicated constructs. Chapter 2 introduced you to the metadata that can lurk on the HFS+ filesystem and also discussed how that metadata is stored on other types of filesystems using the AppleDouble format.

With much more than the usual contents of files to worry about, it's very easy to drop bits of your files all over the place, especially on foreign filesystems. This chapter talks a bit more about these details, explains what you need to consider when you move files from HFS+ to other filesystems, and ends with a description of how files are laid out on a Mac.

Sharing Files with Other Operating Systems

If you're going to move files between your Mac and another operating system, there are some things you need to watch out for. As we discussed in Chapter 2, the AppleDouble format will sprinkle some files with odd names across the filesystem, such as ._filename files. You'll also find a few files created in the root, such as .Trashes (see Table 3-1, later in this chapter).

The most significant problem you'll run into is moving large files around; if you're not using a third-party utility, the only common filesystem that Mac OS X, Windows, and Linux can read and write is the ancient FAT32, which has a limit of 2 GB per file. However, if you don't have Windows in the mix, you can take advantage of Linux's support for Apple's HFS+ filesystem. Linux will mount journaled HFS+ filesystems in read-only mode; if you're willing to disable journaling, you can get read/write support. For example, if you have an external (such as USB) HFS+-formatted drive called *iPod* plugged into your Mac, you can turn off journaling with:

```
$ diskutil disableJournal /Volumes/iPod
```

Most Linux systems will automatically mount external drives when you plug them in. If this doesn't happen, you can mount an external drive manually; see the *mount(8)* manpage for more details.

If you need to get a variety of computers talking to each other and sharing files, there are several solutions you can use for exchanging files across the network:

Virtual SSH filesystems (Nautilus)
    If you've enabled SSH (System Preferences→Sharing→Remote Login), some versions of Linux will let you access your Mac's hard drive over SSH. For example, if you're using the default GNOME desktop on Ubuntu, you can click Places→Network, and your Mac will appear as an SSH server. Double-click the icon and provide your user ID and password, and your Mac's hard drive will appear in GNOME's Nautilus file manager. Note that this doesn't actually mount your Mac's hard drive on your Linux system, but instead lets you work with the SSH server through Nautilus and GTK+ applications. To actually mount directories from an SSH server, you'll need to use *sshfs*, described next.

FUSE and sshfs

Linux and some Unix systems are compatible with FUSE (Filesystem in Userspace), which allows users to mount filesystems without having to use *sudo* or add modules to their kernels. One of the filesystems supported by FUSE is *sshfs*. Most current Linux distributions have FUSE and *sshfs* in their package repositories, but they are not usually installed by default. If you can't find them, visit the FUSE website at *http://fuse.sourceforge .net* for installation instructions. Once you've installed FUSE and *sshfs*, you can mount an SSH server into your filesystem using the *sshfs* command shown here (by default, this mounts the user's home directory; you can specify another directory by replacing *example.net:* with something such as *example.net:/opt*):

```
$ mkdir ~/server
$ sshfs example.net: ~/server/
bjepson@example.net's password: ********
$ ls ~/server/Maildir/
cur  maildircache  new  tmp
```

You can then unmount the server with *fusermount -u mountpoint*:

```
$ fusermount -u ~/server
```

FUSE supports many other filesystems; check out its website for details. FUSE is also available for Mac OS X from Amit Singh's MacFUSE project. For downloads and more information, see *http://code.google.com/p/mac fuse/* and Chapter 8 of this book.

Network File System (NFS)

Starting with Leopard (10.5), Mac OS X makes it extremely easy to set up NFS exports from your Mac. NSF security was also enhanced in Leopard with support of Kerberos authentication. Using *sudo*, create the */etc/ex ports* file. In a text editor, add a line for each directory you want to export. See the *exports(5)* manpage for more information. For example, you could export your */usr/local* directory in read-only mode to any computer that can reach yours with this line:

```
/usr/local -ro
```

After you've edited the *exports* file, force the NFS server to reload it with the following command:

```
$ sudo nfsd update
```

Now you'll be able to mount the NFS shares from your Linux and Unix systems.

To access NFS servers from Mac OS X 10.5 (Leopard), use the */net* directory. By default, the only directories in */net* are */net/localhost* and */net/ broadcasthost*. To mount an NFS server, you can *cd* to */net/HOSTNAME* or */net/IP_ADDRESS*. The server will be mounted on demand (*bjepson-desktop.local* is an Ubuntu system with a single NFS export, */usr*):

```
$ ls /net/
broadcasthost localhost
$ cd /net/bjepson-desktop.local
$ ls
usr
```

You can see a list of NFS exports on a host with *showmount -e*:

```
$ showmount -e bjepson-desktop.local
Exports list on bjepson-desktop.local:
/usr/local                          192.168.254.7
```

Samba

Samba (*http://www.samba.org*) is a file and printer sharing solution that's compatible with the SMB/CIFS (Server Message Block/Common Internet Filesystem) protocol used by Windows. Although Samba has no native support for HFS+ metadata or resource forks, Mac OS X creates AppleDouble files (described in Chapter 2) on Samba shares as needed.

Netatalk

Netatalk (*http://netatalk.sourceforge.net*) is best known as a suite for introducing Unix servers to AppleTalk networks. However, it has a daemon, *afpd*, that can share files from a Linux or Unix system using the native Apple sharing protocol, AFP (Apple Filing Protocol). Early versions (and the versions that are bundled with many Linux distributions) supported only an earlier version of AFP, and were limited in the length of filenames. The most recent version of Netatalk can be made to work with Mac OS X, although it may require recompilation in order to support the password authentication scheme used by Leopard. For a great how-to on getting Netatalk to work with Leopard, see *http://www.blackmac.de/archives/58 -Make-Netatalk-talk-to-Leopard-Mac-OS-X-10.5.html*.

afpfs-ng

If you'd like to mount AFP filesystems from a Linux or Unix system running FUSE, first make sure you have File Sharing enabled on your Mac under System Preferences→Sharing. Then, head on over to *http://source forge.net/projects/afpfs-ng/* and download the *afpfs-ng* package. This is a FUSE module that lets users mount AFP filesystems. Once you've installed *afpfs-ng*, you can mount filesystems using an *afp://* URL with the *afpfs* command. For example:

```
$ afpfs afp://bjepson:PASSWORD@192.168.254.7/bjepson ~/server/
Mounting 192.168.254.7 from bjepson on /home/bjepson/server/
Mounting of volume bjepson of server BCJ succeeded.
```

As with *sshfs*, you can unmount the directory with *fusermount -u mountpoint*.

Unison

Unison (*http://www.cis.upenn.edu/~bcpierce/unison/*) is a powerful file synchronizer that lets you keep Windows, Mac OS X, Linux, and Unix files in sync. It does so by maintaining a replica on each side of the synchronization, comparing the state of the filesystem against the last-known replica, and making intelligent decisions about which files are the most recent. In cases where it can't figure something out (perhaps you've changed the file in both places), it prompts you to tell it what to do. It's like *rsync* in many ways; in particular, it is fast and works well over a network (like *rsync*, it can work over *ssh*). However, its support for two-way syncing is what really differentiates it from the alternatives.

Working with Bonjour

If you want to integrate Apple's Bonjour with your Linux or Unix systems, you'll need two packages: Avahi and *nss-mdns*. Avahi is included with most current Linux distributions, and it supports service discovery on the local network. It is compatible with Apple's Bonjour, so you can configure Avahi to advertise network shares, among other things. For more information about Avahi, see *http://www.avahi.org*. The other package, *nss-mdns*, is a plug-in for the GNU C Library's Name Server Switch that lets you resolve hostnames ending in *.local* (the same scheme used by Bonjour). See *http://0pointer.de/lennart/projects/nss-mdns/* for more information. Avahi and *nss-mdns* work together to provide a Bonjour-compatible networking scheme that lets your Unix or Linux systems work with Mac OS X systems on your network. Avahi and *nss-mdns* are installed on most Linux distributions by default and should be available in your distribution's package repositories.

By default, Netatalk's AFP shares are not advertised over Bonjour. If your Linux system is running Avahi (most are), you can advertise AFP shares over Bonjour by creating a file called */etc/avahi/services/afp.service* with the following contents:

```
<?xml version="1.0" standalone='no'?><!--*-nxml-*-->
<!DOCTYPE service-group SYSTEM "avahi-service.dtd">
<service-group>
  <name replace-wildcards="yes">%h</name>
  <service>
    <type>_afpovertcp._tcp</type>
    <port>548</port>
  </service>
</service-group>
```

Once you've done this, AFP shares from your Unix or Linux host will be advertised via Bonjour and consequently will be easily accessible from Mac clients. You'll see these shares in the Shared section of the Finder sidebar. You can also create service files for SSH (type: _ssh._tcp, port: 22), Samba (type: _smb._tcp, port: 139), and NFS (type: nfs._tcp, port: 2049). However, neither of these will show up in the Finder. You can locate SSH servers over Bonjour by selecting Shell→New Remote Connection from within the Terminal. You can enumerate NFS exports over Bonjour by typing *showmount -A -e* in the Terminal.

Creating and Burning Disk Images

You can create a disk image from the Terminal using *hdiutil*. For example, you can create an image of *~/Documents/COURSES* with this command:

```
$ hdiutil create -srcdir ~/Documents/COURSES \
  ~/Desktop/COURSESBAK.dmg
```

Once this command has completed, enter the following command to burn the disk image to disc (you'll be prompted to insert a disc):

```
$ hdiutil burn ~/Desktop/COURSESBAK.dmg
Please insert a disc:
```

You can also create a disk image with a fixed size, copy files to it, and burn it:

```
$ hdiutil create -size 400m ~/Desktop/COURSESBAK.dmg \
  -fs HFS+ -volname COURSES
$ open ~/Desktop/COURSESBAK.dmg
$ cp -R ~/Documents/COURSES/ /Volumes/COURSES/
$ umount /Volumes/COURSES/
$ hdiutil burn ~/Desktop/COURSESBAK.dmg
```

Troubleshooting

If you use multiple solutions in combination, you may run into trouble if they disagree about what's going on under the hood of their AppleDouble implementations. For example, suppose you have a single Internet location (*.webloc*) file in the *~/Desktop* directory on your Mac:

```
$ cd ~/Desktop/
$ ls -l
total 8
-rw-r--r--@  1 bjepson  bjepson         0 May 16 11:44 Safari.webloc
```

Next, suppose you copy the file to a Linux server that you have mounted as a Samba share. After you copy the file, you'll see the same kind of AppleDouble file format that's used by Mac OS X. All is well with the world:

```
$ mount
/dev/disk0s2 on / (hfs, NFS exported, local, journaled)
```

```
devfs on /dev (devfs, local)
fdesc on /dev (fdesc, union)
map -hosts on /net (autofs, automounted)
map auto_home on /home (autofs, automounted)
//bjepson@bjepson-desktop/bjepson on /Volumes/bjepson (smbfs, nodev,
nosuid, mounted by bjepson)
$ cp Safari.webloc /Volumes/bjepson/Desktop/
$ ls -al /Volumes/bjepson/Desktop/
total 74
drwxr-xr-x  2 bjepson  bjepson  16384 May 16 11:54 .
drwx------  0 bjepson  bjepson  16384 May 15 21:44 ..
-rwx------  1 bjepson  bjepson   4495 May 16 11:52 ._Safari.webloc
-rwx------@ 1 bjepson  bjepson      0 May 16 11:52 Safari.webloc
```

Now, suppose this directory on the Linux server is also shared using Netatalk's *afpd*. Things will get weird if you create another Internet location file on the Mac and then use the Finder to drag and drop that file across to the AFP share on the Linux box.

Log into your Linux system over SSH (or open a shell window on it directly) and look at what's going on under the hood. Instead of creating a file that adheres to the AppleDouble format used by Apple, Netatalk creates an .*AppleDouble* directory that contains the metadata that HFS+ would normally store transparently. Here's what you've got on the Linux side now:

```
$ ls -al
total 20
drwxr-xr-x  3 bjepson bjepson 4096 2008-05-16 11:59 .
drwxr-xr-x 39 bjepson bjepson 4096 2008-05-16 11:59 ..
drwxr-xr-x  2 bjepson bjepson 4096 2008-05-16 11:59 .AppleDouble
-rw-r--r--  1 bjepson bjepson    0 2008-05-16 11:59 Hackszine.com.webloc
-rwx------  1 bjepson bjepson 4495 2008-05-16 11:52 ._Safari.webloc
-rwx------  1 bjepson bjepson    0 2008-05-16 11:52 Safari.webloc
$ ls -al .AppleDouble/
total 12
drwxr-xr-x 2 bjepson bjepson 4096 2008-05-16 11:59 .
drwxr-xr-x 3 bjepson bjepson 4096 2008-05-16 11:59 ..
-rw-rw-rw- 1 bjepson bjepson 1326 2008-05-16 11:59 Hackszine.com.webloc
```

We suggest that you use only one point of entry (either Samba *or* Netatalk, but not both) for a given directory, but if you need to have it both ways, a workaround is to add options:ro,noadouble to the filesystem's entry in *AppleVolumes.default* on the Linux server. For example, on Ubuntu, you'd change the home directory line in */etc/netatalk/AppleVolumes.default* to read:

```
~/     "Home Directory"      options:ro,noadouble
```

This makes the AFP share read-only and disables the creation of .*AppleDouble* (except when a resource fork is created, which won't happen because you're accessing it read-only). This solution gives you quick and dirty access to the files on the Linux server via AFP when you need it, but forces you to update them through only Samba.

Files and Directories

Mac OS X's filesystem contains traces of Unix, NeXTSTEP, and Mac OS 9. If you type *ls -a* / on your Mac (e.g., using the Terminal or a remote *ssh* connection), you'll see some familiar things, such as */etc* and */var*. However, you'll also notice some unfamiliar directories, such as */Desktop DB*, */Library*, and */Documents*. The tables in the rest of this chapter list and describe some of the files and directories you may encounter.

The Root Directory

Table 3-1 describes the files and directories (the latter are indicated with a trailing slash) that you may find in your root directory (*/*). Classic files that may appear in this directory are listed in Table 3-2, and the remaining tables in this chapter describe the contents of significant subdirectories.

Table 3-1. Mac OS X's root directory

File or directory	Description
/.DS_Store	Contains Finder settings, such as the icon location and window size. This file will appear in any directory that you've viewed with the Finder.
/.Spotlight-V100/	Contains metadata used by Spotlight. For more information, see Chapter 2.
/.Trashes/	Contains files that have been dragged to the Trash. On a boot volume, such files are stored in ~/.Trash. On a nonboot volume, these files are in /.Trashes/uid/.
/.com.apple.timemachine.supported	Indicates that a drive could be used by Time Machine as a backup target.
/.fseventsd/	Used by the FSEvents API, which provides notifications about changed files.
/.hotfiles.btree	A B-Tree index for providing fast access to frequently used files.
/Applications/	Holds all your Mac OS X applications. Its *Utilities* subdirectory includes lots of useful things, such as the Terminal, the Console, and the Activity Monitor.
/bin/	Contains essential system binaries.
/Desktop DB	Along with */Desktop DF*, contains housekeeping information used by the Finder.
/Desktop DF	See */Desktop DB*.
/dev/	Contains files that represent various devices. See Table 3-4.
/Developer/	Contains Apple's Xcode tools and documentation. Available only if you have installed the Xcode tools.

File or directory	Description
/etc/	Contains system configuration files. See Table 3-3. This directory is a symbolic link to /private/etc.
/home/	Used by the automounter for NFS-mounted home directories.
/Installer Log File	May be left by some third-party application installers.
/Library/	Contains support files for locally installed applications, among other things. See Table 3-7.
/lost+found/	Stores orphaned files discovered by fsck. You'll only find this on UFS volumes.
/mach_kernel	Contains the Darwin kernel.
/mach_kernel.ctfsys	Contains an alternate copy of the kernel, used by dtrace(1).
/net/	Used by the automounter for NFS-mounted directories.
/Network/	Contains network-mounted Application, Library, and Users directories, as well as a Servers directory that contains directories mounted by the auto mount daemon.
/opt/	Contains the MacPorts installation (see Chapter 13).
/private/	Contains the tmp, var, etc, and cores directories.
/sbin/	Contains executables for system administration and configuration.
/sw/	Contains the Fink installation (see Chapter 12).
/System/	Contains a subdirectory, Library, that holds support files for the system and system applications, among other things. See Table 3-6.
/tmp/	Holds temporary files. This directory is a symbolic link to /private/tmp.
/User Guides And Information/	An alias to /Library/Documentation/User Guides and Information; contains hardware-specific documentation and information about Mac OS X.
/Users/	Contains home directories for the users on the system. The root user's home directory is /var/root (actually /private/var/root).
/usr/	Contains BSD Unix applications and support files.
/var/	Contains frequently modified files, such as log files. This directory is a symbolic link to /private/var.
/Volumes/	Contains all visible mounted filesystems, including removable media and mounted disk images.

Although neither Intel-based Macs nor Mac OS X Leopard supports Mac OS 9 (Classic), you may find the files and directories listed in Table 3-2 in the root directory of older Macs, or installations that have been upgraded.

Table 3-2. Classic files in the root directory

File or directory	Description
/Applications (Mac OS 9)/	Contains all of your OS 9 applications, if you have Mac OS X and Mac OS 9 (Classic) installed.

File or directory	Description
/Desktop Folder/	The Mac OS 9 desktop folder used by Classic.
/Documents/	The Mac OS 9 documents folder used by Classic.
/Shared Items/	Gives OS 9 multiuser systems a place where users can store files for other users to access.
/System Folder/	The Mac OS 9 system folder.
/Temporary Items/	Contains temporary files used by Mac OS 9.
/TheFindByContentFolder/	Created by Sherlock 2.
/TheVolumeSettingsFolder/	Keeps track of shared volume details, such as open windows and desktop printers.
/Trash/	Used by Mac OS 9 to store deleted files until the Trash is emptied.
/VM Storage	The Mac OS 9 virtual memory file.

The /etc Directory

The *etc* directory contains configuration files for Unix applications and services. Table 3-3 lists the contents of the *etc* directory.

Table 3-3. The /etc directory

File or directory	Description
6to4.conf	Configuration file for encapsulating IPv6 within IPv4. See *ip6config(8)*.
AFP.conf	Contains the AFP Reconnect Server key, which is used to authenticate clients that attempt to reconnect. (This file is created by Mac OS X when it is needed.)
afpovertcp.cfg	Causes Mac OS X to use TCP/IP as the default transport protocol for the Apple File Protocol (AFP). Use this file to configure the defaults for AFP over TCP/IP.
aliases	Mail aliases file. Symbolic link to */etc/postfix/aliases*.
aliases.db	Mail aliases *db* file created when you run *newaliases*.
amavisd.conf	Configuration file for *amavisd(8)*, an interface between mail servers and content scanners (such as virus or spam filters).
apache2/	Contains configuration files for the Apache web server.
appletalk.cfg	AppleTalk configuration file for routing or multihoming. See the *appletalk.cfg(5)* manpage.
asl.conf	Configuration file for the *syslogd(8) asl_action* module, which can take actions when certain messages appear in the system log. See *asl.conf(5)*.
authorization	Controls how applications, such as installers, can temporarily obtain *root* privileges.
auto_home	Configuration file used for NFS-automounted home directories.
auto_master	Configuration file for automounting NFS servers.
autofs.conf	Configuration file for the automounter.

File or directory	Description
bashrc	Global configuration file for *bash*, the Bourne-again shell.
csh.cshrc	Global *csh* configuration file, processed when the shell starts up. If you have a *.cshrc* or *.tcshrc* file in your home directory, *tcsh* will execute its contents as well.
csh.login	Global *csh* login file, processed when a login shell starts up. If you have a *.login* file in your home directory, *tcsh* will execute its contents as well.
csh.logout	Global *csh* logout file, processed when a user logs out of a login shell.
cups/	Contains configuration files for the Common Unix Printing System (CUPS).
defaults/	Contains default configuration files for applications and utilities.
dnsextd.conf	Configuration file for *dnsext(8)*, a daemon that provides certain extensions to BIND.
dumpdates	Dump date records created by *dump(5)*, which is run by */etc/daily*.
efax.rc	Configuration file for *fax(1)*.
find.codes	Undocumented.
fstab	Configuration file for network shares that should be mounted at boot. Edit with *sudo vifs* and use *sudo automount -cv* to have changes take effect without rebooting.
fstab.hd	Undocumented.
ftpusers	List of users who are prohibited from using FTP.
gdb.conf	Global *gdb* configuration file.
gettytab	Terminal configuration database.
group	Group permissions file. See Chapter 5.
hostconfig	System configuration file that controls many of the startup items described in Chapter 4.
hosts	Host database; a mapping of IP addresses to hostnames. You can use this as a supplement to other directory services, such as DNS. Mac OS X 10.1 and earlier consulted this file only in single-user mode, but as of Mac OS X 10.2 (Jaguar), this file is used at other times. For more information, see Chapter 5.
hosts.equiv	List of trusted remote hosts and host/user pairs. This is used by *rsh* and is inherently insecure. You should instead use *ssh*, which is a secure alternative. See *ssh-keygen(1)* for details on generating key pairs that can be used to set up a trust relationship with remote users.
irbrc	Configuration file for *irb(1)*, the Interactive Ruby Interpreter.
kcpassword	Stores an encrypted version of a user's password for autologin.
kern_loader.conf	Mach's kernel server loader configuration file. Empty in the current version of Mac OS X.
krb5.keytab	The Kerberos V5 keytab. Use *ktutil(8)* to manipulate this file.

File or directory	Description
localtime	Symbolic link to your system's time zone (e.g., */usr/share/zoneinfo/US/Eastern*).
locate.rc	Configuration for *updatedb(8)*.
mach_init.d/	Mach bootstrap daemons. See Chapter 4.
mach_init_per_login_session.d/	Per-session Mach bootstrap daemons. See Chapter 4.
mach_init_per_user.d/	Per-user Mach bootstrap daemons. See Chapter 4.
mail.rc	Global configuration file for */usr/bin/mail*.
man.conf	Configuration file for *man(1)*.
manpaths	Default paths to search for manpages.
manpaths.d/	Contains files that hold additional manpage search paths.
master.passwd	Shadow *passwd* file, consulted only in single-user mode. During normal system operation, Open Directory manages user information (see Chapter 5).
memberd.conf	Configuration file for the group membership resolution daemon, *memberd(8)*.
moduli	System-wide prime numbers used for cryptographic applications such as *ssh*.
named.conf	Configuration file for *named*, the DNS daemon. For more details, see *named(8)*.
nanorc	Configuration file for the *nano* text editor.
networks	Network name database.
newsyslog.conf	Configuration file for *newsyslog(8)*.
notify.conf	Configuration file for the Notification Center.
ntp.conf	Specifies the Network Time Protocol (NTP) servers used to update the system time.
openldap/	Contains configuration files for OpenLDAP, an implementation of the Lightweight Directory Access Protocol.
pam.d/	Contains configuration files for Pluggable Authentication Modules (PAM).
passwd	Password file. For more information, see Chapter 5.
paths	Contains a list of default paths for building the PATH environment variable.
paths.d/	Contains files that hold additional search paths.
periodic/	Contains configuration files for the *periodic* utility, which runs *cron* jobs on a regular basis.
php.ini.default	Default PHP initialization file.
podcastproducer/	Contains support files for Podcast Producer. See *podcast(1)* for more information.
postfix/	Contains *postfix* configuration files.
ppp/	Contains configuration files for the Point-to-Point Protocol (PPP).
profile	Global profile for the Bourne-again shell, *bash*.

File or directory	Description
protocols	Network protocol database.
racoon/	Contains configuration files for *racoon*, the IKE key management daemon.
rc.common	Common settings for startup scripts.
rc.netboot	Startup script for booting from the network using NetBoot.
resolv.conf	DNS resolver configuration. Symlink to */var/run/resolv.conf*.
rmtab	Remote NFS mount table.
rpc	RPC number-to-name mappings. Mac OS X 10.1 and earlier consulted this file only in single-user mode, but newer versions of Mac OS X use this file at other times.
rtadvd.conf	Configuration file for the router advertisement daemon. For more details, see *rtadvd(8)*.
services	Internet service name database. Mac OS X 10.1 and earlier consulted this file only in single-user mode, but newer versions of Mac OS X use this file at other times. For more information, see Chapter 5.
shells	List of shells.
smb.conf	Samba configuration file.
smb.conf.template	Template configuration file for Samba.
snmp/	Contains configuration files for *snmpd(8)*.
ssh_config	Global configuration file for OpenSSH client programs.
ssh_host_dsa_key	Private DSA host key for OpenSSH. This file, and the other *ssh_host_* * files, are created the first time you start Remote Login in the Sharing System Preferences pane.
ssh_host_dsa_key.pub	Public DSA host key for OpenSSH.
ssh_host_key	Private host key for OpenSSH when using SSH 1 compatibility.
ssh_host_key.pub	Public host key for OpenSSH when using SSH 1 compatibility.
ssh_host_rsa_key	Private RSA host key for OpenSSH.
ssh_host_rsa_key.pub	Public RSA host key for OpenSSH.
sshd_config	Configuration file for the OpenSSH *sshd* daemon.
sudoers	Configuration file for the *sudo* command. Make sure you use the *visudo* command only to edit this file.
syslog.conf	*syslogd* configuration file.
ttys	Terminal initialization file.
xgrid/	Configuration files for Xgrid.
xtab	Lists current NFS exports.
zprofile	Global profile for the Z shell, *zsh(1)*.

The /dev Directory

The /dev directory contains files that represent devices attached to the system, including physical devices such as serial ports and pseudodevices such as a random number generator. Table 3-4 lists the contents of the /dev directory.

Table 3-4. The /dev directory

File or directory	Description
ath0	Device representing the AirPort adapter.
autofs	Used by autofsd(8).
autofs_control	Used by autofsd(8).
autofs_nowait	Used by autofsd(8).
bpf[0–3]	Berkeley Packet Filter devices. See bpf(4).
console	The system console. This is owned by whoever is currently logged in. If you write to it, the output ends up in /var/tmp/console.log, which you can view with the Console application (/Applications/Utilities).
cu.*	Modem devices for compatibility with the Unix cu (call up) utility.
disk[0-n]	Disk device.
disk[0-n]s[0-n]	Disk partition. For example, /dev/disk0s1 is the first partition of /dev/disk0.
dtrace	Device used by dtrace(1).
dtracehelper	Device used by dtrace(1).
fbt	Device used by dtrace(1).
fd/	Devices that correspond to file descriptors. See the fd manpage for more details.
fsevents	Undocumented.
klog	Device used by syslogd to read kernel messages.
lockstat	Used to gather kernel lock data for dtrace(1).
machtrace	Device used by dtrace(1).
nsmb0	Device file used for smbfs.
null	Bit bucket. You can redirect anything here, and it disappears.
pmCPU	CPU power management device.
profile	Undocumented
ptmx	Device used to manage pseudoterminals.
ptyp[0-f]	Master ends of the first 16 pseudoterminals.
pty[q-w][0-f]	Master ends of the remaining pseudoterminals.
random	Source of pseudorandom data. See random(4).
rdisk[0-n]	Raw disk device.
rdisk[0-n]s[0-n]	Raw disk partition.

File or directory	Description
sdt	Undocumented.
stderr	Symbolic link to /dev/fd/2.
stdin	Symbolic link to /dev/fd/0.
stdout	Symbolic link to /dev/fd/1.
systrace	Used by sandbox(7).
tty	Standard output stream of the current Terminal or remote login session.
tty.*	Various modem and serial devices.
ttyp[0-f]	Slave ends of the first 16 pseudo-ttys.
tty[q-w][0-f]	Slave ends of the remaining pseudo-ttys.
urandom	Source of pseudorandom data, not guaranteed to be strong. See random(4).
vn[0–3]	Pseudo disk devices.
zero	Infinite supply of null characters. Often used with dd to create a file made up of null characters.

The /var Directory

The /var directory (really a symlink to /private/var) contains transient and volatile files, such as PID files (which tell you the process ID of a currently running daemon), log files, and many others. Table 3-5 lists the contents of the /var directory.

Table 3-5. The /var directory

File or directory	Description
agentx/	Used by snmpd(8) to support the AgentX protocol.
amavis/	Contains support files for amavisd(8).
at/	Contains information about jobs scheduled with the at command.
audit/	Undocumented.
backups/	Contains backups of the NetInfo database.
db/	Includes a grab bag of configuration and data files, including the locate database, the NetInfo database, and network interface information.
empty/	Used as an unwritable chroot(8) environment.
folders/	Caches used by various applications.
launchd/	Contains launchd's working files.
log/	Contains a variety of log files, including syslog, mail, and web server logs.
mail/	Contains inboxes for local users' email.
msgs/	Holds system-wide messages that were delivered using msgs -s.
named/	Includes various files used for local DNS services.

File or directory	Description
Netboot/	Contains various files used for NetBoot.
root/	Serves as the *root* user's home directory.
run/	Holds PID files for running processes. Also contains working files used by programs such as *sudo*.
rwho/	Contains information used by the *rwho* command.
samba/	Contains Samba support files.
spool/	Serves as a spool directory for mail, printer queues, and other queued resources.
tmp/	Serves as a temporary file directory.
virusmails/	Quarantine location used by *amavisd(8)*.
vm/	Contains your swap files.
xgrid/	Holds working files used by Xgrid.
yp/	Contains files used by Network Information System (NIS).

The /System/Library Directory

Table 3-6 lists the directories (and one file) stored under the */System/Library* directory. You should not modify the contents of these directories or add new files to them. Instead, use their counterparts in the */Library* folder. For example, to install a new font, drag it into */Library/Fonts*, not */System/Library/Fonts*.

Table 3-6. The /System/Library directory

File or directory	Description
Automator/	Contains Automator actions and supporting files.
BridgeSupport/	Holds XML files that contain API symbols for frameworks and libraries that don't support runtime introspection.
Caches/	Contains caches used by various parts of the operating system.
CFMSupport/	Holds shared libraries used by Carbon applications.
ColorPickers/	Stores localized resources for Mac OS X color pickers.
Colors/	Contains the names and values of colors used in color picker controls.
ColorSync/	Contains ColorSync profiles.
Components/	Contains application building blocks (components), such as AppleScript and color pickers. Components are not applications themselves and are generally shared between applications.
Compositions/	Contains the Quartz Composer compositions that ship with Mac OS X.
Contextual Menu Items/	Contains plug-ins for the Finder's contextual menu (accessed via Control- or right-clicking).
CoreServices/	Contains system applications, such as *SystemStarter*, *BootX*, the Finder, and the login window.

File or directory	Description
DirectoryServices/	Holds support files for Directory Services (see Chapter 5).
Displays/	Contains ColorSync information for external monitors.
DTDs/	Contains document type definitions for XML documents used by the system, such as property lists.
Extensions/	Holds Darwin kernel extensions.
Extensions.mkext	Contains the kernel extension cache, which is created at boot by */etc/rc*.
Filesystems/	Contains drivers and utilities for various filesystems (MS-DOS, AppleShare, UFS, etc.).
Filters/	Contains Quartz filters that are used in the Print dialog's ColorSync section.
Find/	Stores support files for Sherlock's content indexing.
Fonts/	Contains core Mac OS X fonts.
Frameworks/	Holds a collection of reusable application frameworks, including shared libraries, headers, and documentation.
Graphics/	Holds Quartz Composer patches and plug-ins.
Image Capture/	Contains device support files for the Image Capture application.
Input Methods/	Stores input methods for various languages.
Java/	Contains Java *.class* and *.jar* files.
KerberosPlugins/	Stores Kerberos plug-ins.
Keyboard Layouts/	Contains bundles that support internationalized keyboard layouts.
Keychains/	Contains system-wide keychain files.
LaunchAgents/	Contains configuration files for *launchd* items that are started at login (see Chapter 4).
LaunchDaemons/	Contains configuration files for *launchd* items that are run even when no user is logged in (see Chapter 4).
LoginPlugins/	Contains helper applications that are launched as you log in.
Modem Scripts/	Contains modem configuration scripts.
MonitorPanels/	Stores panels used by System Preferences→Displays.
OpenSSL/	Holds OpenSSL configuration and support files.
Perl/	Holds Perl Libraries.
PodcastProducer/	Contains support files for Podcast Producer.
PreferencePanes/	Contains all the preference panes for the Preferences application.
Printers/	Contains printer support files.
PrivateFrameworks/	Holds private frameworks meant to support Mac OS X. These frameworks are not meant for programmers' use.
QuickLook/	Contains system-supplied QuickLook generators.
QuickTime/	Holds QuickTime support files.
QuickTimeJava/	Stores support files for the QuickTime/Java bridge.

File or directory	Description
Screen Savers/	Contains screensavers that you can select from System Preferences→Desktop & Screen Saver.
ScreenReader/	Contains Braille drivers for the screen reader.
ScriptingAdditions/	Holds AppleScript plug-ins and libraries.
ScriptingDefinitions/	Contains a scripting definition file that is common to all applications. Scripting definition files represent information about the scriptability of applications.
Security/	Stores support files for various authentication methods.
Services/	Contains services that are made available through the Services menu.
Sounds/	Contains sounds that are available in System Preferences→Sound.
Speech/	Holds speech recognition and generation support files.
Spotlight/	Contains metadata importers for Spotlight (see Chapter 2).
StartupItems/	Contains startup scripts, as described in Chapter 4.
SyncServices/	Contains iSync conduits.
SystemConfiguration/	Contains plug-ins used to monitor various system activities (for Apple use only).
SystemProfiler/	Contains support files for System Profiler.
Tcl/	Holds Tcl libraries.
TextEncodings/	Contains localized text encodings.
User Template/	Holds localized skeleton files for user directories. See "Creating a user's home directory" in Chapter 5.
UserEventPlugins/	Undocumented.
WidgetResources/	Contains support files for Dashboard.

The /Library Directory

Table 3-7 lists the contents of the *Library* directory. The *Library* directory contains counterparts to many directories found in *System/Library* (Table 3-6). You can use the */Library* counterparts for system-wide customization. If you find a directory of the same name in your home *Library* directory (*~/Library*), you can use that for user-level customization. For example, you can install fonts for a particular user by moving them into *~/Library/Fonts*.

Table 3-7 lists only the directories found in */Library* that are not also found in */System/Library* (with the exception of *Java* and *Perl*, which bear additional discussion).

Table 3-7. The /Library directory

File or directory	Description
Address Book Plug-Ins/	Contains plug-ins for the Address Book application.
Application Support/	Contains support files for locally installed applications.
Audio/	Contains audio plug-ins and sounds.
Automator/	Stores Automator actions.
ColorSync/	Contains user-installed ColorSync profiles and scripts.
Components/	Holds QuickTime components.
Desktop Pictures/	Contains desktop pictures used by System Preferences→Desktop & Screen Saver.
Developer/	Contains various development support files.
Dictionaries/	Contains various dictionaries.
Documentation/	Provides documentation for locally installed applications.
Graphics/	Undocumented.
Internet Plug-Ins/	Contains locally installed browser plug-ins.
iTunes/	Contains iTunes plug-ins.
Java/	Contains locally installed Java classes (you can drop *.jar* files into */Library/Java/Extensions*), as well as a suitable directory to use as your $JAVA_HOME (*/Library/Java/Home*).
Logs/	Holds logs for services such as Apple File Services, the Crash Reporter, and Directory Services.
Mail/	Holds support files for *Mail.app*.
PDF Services/	Contains various PDF workflows.
Perl/	Contains locally installed Perl modules (MakeMaker's INSTALLSITELIB).
Preferences/	Holds global preferences.
Python/	Contains locally installed Python modules.
Receipts/	Holds the receipts left in the form of *.pkg* directories after you install applications with the Mac OS X installer. The *.pkg* directory contains a bill of materials file (*.bom*), which you can read with the *lsbom* command. Bills of materials for core Mac OS X packages are contained in *Receipts/boms/*.
Ruby/	Contains Gems and other support files for Ruby.
Scripts/	Contains a variety of AppleScripts installed with Mac OS X.
User Pictures/	Contains user pictures that are used in the login panel.
WebServer/	Contains the Apache CGI and document root directories.
Widgets/	Contains Dashboard widgets.

## CHAPTER 4

Startup

The most striking difference between Mac OS X and other flavors of Unix is in how Mac OS X handles the boot process. Gone are the */etc/inittab* and */etc/init.d* from traditional Unix systems. In their place is a BSD-like startup sequence sandwiched between a Mach* foundation and the Aqua user interface.

This chapter describes Mac OS X Leopard's startup sequence, beginning with the boot loader and progressing to full multiuser mode, at which time the system is ready to accept logins from normal users. The chapter also covers custom startup items, network interface configuration, and Mac OS X's default system maintenance jobs.

Booting Mac OS X

When the computer is powered up, the firmware—Open Firmware on PowerPC Macs and Extensible Firmware Interface on Intel Macs—is in complete control. After the firmware initializes the hardware, it hands off control to the boot loader, *BootX* (Power PC) or *boot.efi* (Intel), which bootstraps the kernel. After a trip into Mach, the control bubbles up into the Berkeley Software Distribution (BSD) subsystem, and from there into the Aqua user interface.

By default, Mac OS X boots graphically. If you'd like to see console messages as you boot, hold down ⌘-V (the "V" stands for "verbose") as you start the computer. If you'd like to always boot in verbose mode, you can specify a flag in the boot arguments that are stored in your system's firmware. First, use the command *nvram boot-args* to make sure there aren't any flags already set (if

---

* Mach is a microkernel operating system developed at Carnegie Mellon University. The Mac OS X kernel, *xnu*, is a hybrid of Mach and BSD.

there are, and you didn't set them, you probably should not change this setting). Set your boot arguments to *-v* with this command:

```
$ sudo nvram boot-args="-v"
```

The next time you boot your Mac, it will boot in verbose mode. To turn off
this setting, use this command:

```
$ sudo nvram boot-args=
```

To boot in single-user mode, hold down ⌘-S as you start the computer. In
single-user mode your filesystem is mounted as read-only, which limits what
you can do. Although you can enable write access to your filesystem via the
mount –uw / command, this is not usually recommended. Single-user mode
should generally be used only to repair a system that has been damaged. Unlike
with other Unix systems, we do not suggest that you use single-user mode to
perform *fsck* repairs manually. Instead, restart your Mac and boot from the
Mac OS X install disc (insert the disc and hold down the C key as your Mac
starts up), and then run the Disk Utility (Installer→Open Disk Utility) to repair
a problem disk volume.

The Boot Loader

The *BootX* and *boot.efi* boot loaders are located in */System/Library/CoreServi
ces*. They draw the Apple logo on the screen and proceed to set up the kernel
environment. The boot loader first looks for an up-to-date version of the kernel
that's been prelinked to all required kernel extensions (drivers, also known as
kexts). If it doesn't find one, the boot loader loads all the kernel extensions
that are cached in the *mkext cache*. If this cache does not exist, the boot loader
loads only those extensions in */System/Library/Extensions* that have the
OSBundleRequired key in their *ExtensionName.kext/Info.plist* files. Example 4-1
is an excerpt from the */System/Library/Extensions/System.kext/Info.plist* file.

Example 4-1. A portion of a kernel extension's Info.plist file

```
<?xml version="1.0" encoding="UTF-8"?>
<!DOCTYPE plist PUBLIC "-//Apple Computer//DTD PLIST 1.0//EN"
        "http://www.apple.com/DTDs/PropertyList-1.0.dtd">
<plist version="1.0">
  <dict>
    <key>CFBundleDevelopmentRegion</key>
    <string>English</string>
    <!-- multiple keys and strings omitted -->
  </dict>
</plist>
```

After the required drivers are loaded, the boot loader hands off control to the
kernel (*/mach_kernel*).

Initialization

The kernel first initializes all the data structures needed to support Mach and BSD. Next, the kernel initializes the I/O Kit, which connects the kernel with the set of extensions that correspond to the machine's hardware configuration. The kernel then finds and mounts the root filesystem. Finally, it launches the first process on the system, *launchd*, which is responsible for bootstrapping the system as well as launching daemons on behalf of the system or users.

 Mac OS X Panther (10.3) and earlier does things differently. The first process the kernel loaded was *mach_init*, which started Mach message handling. *mach_init* then launched the BSD *init* process. In keeping with Unix conventions, *init* was process ID (PID) 1, even though it was started second. *mach_init* was given PID 2, and its parent PID was set to 1 (*init*'s PID). Beginning with Mac OS X Tiger (10.4), *launchd* replaces both of these processes.

By default, *launchd* starts up *SystemStarter*, which is used to start programs that aren't launched on demand: SystemStarter looks in the */System/Library/StartupItems* and then the */Library/StartupItems* directories to find items to start (see the "SystemStarter" section later in this chapter). Although Mac OS X no longer uses any */etc/rc** scripts to start the system, SystemStarter will run any commands in an */etc/rc.local* file and an */etc/rc.shutdown.local* file at system startup and shutdown, respectively.

After that, *launchd* starts *loginwindow*, which authenticates users and sets up their user sessions. From this point on, all remaining services are launched on demand through *launchd*.

In previous versions of Mac OS X, the */etc/hostconfig* file was used to enable or disable services such as file sharing and the web server. As of Mac OS X 10.5, settings such as **AFPSERVER** are present but apparently unused, and at the top of the file is a comment reading, "This file is going away." The type of preferences previously found in *hostconfig* is now contained within the *launchd .plist* files themselves. For example, when you turn off Apple Filing Protocol (AFP) sharing in System Preferences, the following is added to the *com.apple.AppleFileServer.plist* (located in */System/Library/LaunchDaemons*) file:

```
<key>Disabled</key>
<true/>
```

When you turn AFP back on, Mac OS X removes the `Disabled` entry.

---

launchd

Mac OS X Tiger introduced the latest and greatest startup scheme, *launchd*. It has launch-on-demand capabilities and also supports on-demand launching via Mach ports (as does the *mach_init.d* scheme). *launchd* additionally offers the ability to launch on demand based on filesystem and Unix domain socket events.

launchd manages two types of services: launch daemons (services that can run even when no user is logged in, such as *sshd*) and launch agents (services that run on behalf of a logged-in user; for example, when you launch an X11-based application). Launch daemons cannot connect to the window server and thus cannot display a GUI. Launch agents, however, can connect to the window server and can present a GUI. Further, since a launch agent runs on behalf of a user, the agent can access files in that user's home directory. For example, the OpenSSH server is managed as a launch daemon (see *ssh.plist* in */System/Library/LaunchDaemons*); Spotlight's menu and results window are managed as a launch agent (see *com.apple.Spotlight.plist* in */System/Library/Launch Agents*).

The property list (*.plist*) files for system-installed launch daemons are located in */System/Library/LaunchDaemons*. Locally installed daemons (including ones you create yourself) must be installed into */Library/LaunchDaemons*. Similarly, system-installed launch agents go into */System/Library/Launch Agents* and locally installed ones go into */Library/LaunchAgents*. You can install user-specific launch agents in *~/Library/LaunchAgents*.

 For an example of a launch daemon property list, see "Launching with launchd," later in this chapter.

You can control launch daemons with the *launchctl* utility. To enable a daemon that's disabled (that is, one with a `Disabled` key in its property list file), use *launchctl load -w* followed by the path to the property list. For example, the following command would enable the telnet server (the daemon itself is executed as defined in the *telnet.plist* file):

```
$ sudo launchctl load -w /System/Library/LaunchDaemons/telnet.plist
```

You can stop and disable this daemon with *unload -w*:

```
$ sudo launchctl unload -w /System/Library/LaunchDaemons/telnet.plist
```

For more information, see the *launchctl* manpage and Apple Technical Note 2083, "Daemons and Agents" (*http://developer.apple.com/technotes/tn2005/*

tn2083.html), which has an in-depth explanation of *launchd* and other facilities for managing background processes.

 Peter Borg's Lingon (*http://lingon.sourceforge.net*) is an open source graphical tool for creating and editing *launchd* configuration files.

SystemStarter

SystemStarter examines */System/Library/StartupItems* and */Library/StartupItems* for applications that should be started at boot time. */Library/StartupItems* contains items for locally installed applications. */System/Library/StartupItems* contains items for the system. You should not modify these or add your own items here.

Because many of SystemStarter's responsibilities are now handled by *launchd*, the number of startup items has dramatically decreased since Mac OS X 10.3. However, some third-party applications continue to add startup items here rather than using the preferred *launchd* facility.

Mach Bootstrap Services

Mac OS X Panther introduced *Mach bootstrap services*, which are services that a process can launch using Mach messaging (a messaging facility supported by the Mac OS X kernel). Services can be loaded at two points: at system startup and at user login, which includes local and remote (such as SSH) logins. System startup scripts go into one of the */etc/mach_init*.d* directories. Bootstrap service daemons are identified to the system by using the `ServiceName` key in their *.plist* files. The operating system can load a bootstrap service on demand if the `OnDemand` option is set to `true` (this is the default); it will either launch the service or wake it if it is sleeping (when a bootstrap service goes unused for a period of time, it can sleep).

As of Mac OS X 10.5, few services are started in this fashion, most of the operating system has moved over to *launchd*.

Creating Programs that Run Automatically

You have two choices for automatically starting applications: you can start them when a user logs in, or start them when the system boots up. On most Unix systems, startup applications reside in either the */etc/rc.local* script or the */etc/init.d* directory. Under Mac OS 9, you could add a startup item by putting its alias in *System Folder/Startup Items*. Mac OS X has a different approach, described in the following sections.

Login Preferences

To start an application each time you log in, use the Login Items tab of the System Preferences Accounts panel. This is a good choice for user applications, such as Stickies or an instant messenger program. These preferences are saved in *~/Library/Preferences/loginwindow.plist*. There is also a global (or system-wide) counterpart to this file, located at */Library/Preferences/loginwindow.plist*. Some third-party applications will stash startup items in the global file, so check there if you can't otherwise track down the source of a mysterious startup item.

The global *loginwindow.plist* file is owned by *root*. To edit it, change its permissions using the Finder (Control-click or right-click, select Get Info, and click the lock to authenticate) or the command line. Then, double-click it to edit it in the Property List Editor, save it, and change the permissions back to their original values.

SystemStarter

If you compile and install a daemon, you'll probably want it to start at boot time. In most cases, you can start a daemon using *launchd*. But in some cases, you may want to use the (now deprecated) approach used in Mac OS X 10.3 and earlier: SystemStarter, introduced in the "Initialization" section of this chapter. This is because some of the Unix programs that you are likely to find in the wild (or write yourself) do things the old-school Unix way, which will annoy *launchd*. For example, the *launchd.plist(5)* manpage specifically warns against using *launchd* with applications that call *daemon* (a Unix utility that spawns a program that runs without a user) or act like it (by spawning a subprogram and exiting, for example).

What's more, *launchd* would prefer that you don't do any of the following:

- Set up the user ID or group ID.
- Set up the working directory.
- Invoke *chroot(2)* or *setsid(2)*.
- Close "stray" file descriptors.
- Change *stdio(3)* to */dev/null*.
- Set up resource limits with *setrusage(2)*.

- Set up priorities with *setpriority(2)*.
- Ignore the *SIGTERM* signal.

 Although launch daemons do not have a facility for invoking an explicit shutdown script, they will be killed by *launchd* when you shut down/reboot the system or explicitly stop them. Many applications, including database servers such as MySQL, know what to do when they are killed; in the case of MySQL, it shuts down cleanly, logging that fact to the system log with the message "Normal shutdown."

If you are setting up a daemon that cannot abide by the *launchd* restrictions, or one that need its hand held by a shutdown script, you should create a startup item, as described in this section. Otherwise, you should use *launchd* (see the upcoming section "Launching with launchd").

It's possible to modify many Unix daemons to behave themselves under *launchd*. If you peruse the Darwin source code at *http://www.opensource.apple .com/darwinsource/*, you'll find *launchd*-specific patches for many of the Unix daemons, such as OpenSSH and *cron*. For example, Apple's source code for *cron.c* contains this little snippet to make everything *launchd*-safe:

```
#ifdef __APPLE__
/* Don't daemonize when run by launchd */
  if (getppid() != 1 && daemon(1, 0) == -1) {
#else
  if (daemon(1, 0) == -1) {
#endif
```

As time goes on, you'll probably find that popular open source packages will incorporate Apple's patches into their official code releases.

Consider the MySQL database server. To start it up, you use a program called *mysqld_safe*, which in turn starts the MySQL database server. However, to shut it down, you issue the command *mysqladmin shutdown*. If you use *launchd* to manage starting up and shutting down MySQL, it will kill the MySQL server in a less-than-graceful manner (fortunately, MySQL knows how to handle this, but some other systems may not be as flexible). If, on the other hand, you use a startup item, you can define how the process gets shut down.

A startup item is controlled by three things: a folder (such as */Library/StartupItems/MyItem*), a shell script with the same name as the directory (such as *MyItem*), and a property list named *StartupParameters.plist*. The shell script and the property list must appear at the top level of the startup item's folder. You can also create a *Resources* directory to hold localized resources, but this is not mandatory.

To set up a MySQL startup item, create the directory */Library/StartupItems/ MySQL* as *root*. Then, create two files in that directory: the startup script *MySQL* and the property list *StartupParameters.plist*. The *MySQL* file must be an executable because it is a shell script:

```
$ sudo mkdir /Library/StartupItems/MySQL
$ sudo touch /Library/StartupItems/MySQL/MySQL
$ sudo touch /Library/StartupItems/MySQL/StartupParameters.plist
$ sudo chmod +x /Library/StartupItems/MySQL/MySQL
```

After you put the right information into these two files (as directed in the following sections), MySQL will be launched at each boot. Use your favorite text-only editor to edit these files and put the information into them. Because the files are owned by *root*, you will have to authenticate to use them. Smultron and TextMate are two editors that will allow you to authenticate in order to edit *root*'s files; if you prefer to use *vi* from the Terminal, you can run it under *sudo*, as in *sudo vi /Library/StartupItems/MySQL/MySQL*.

The startup script

The startup script should be a shell script with StartService(), StopService(), and RestartService() functions. The contents of */Library/StartupItems/MySQL/MySQL* are shown in Example 4-2. The function call at the bottom of the script invokes the RunService() function from */etc/rc.common* (this is a file that is part of Mac OS X), which in turn invokes StartService(), StopService(), or RestartService(), depending on whether the script was invoked with an argument of start, stop, or restart.

Example 4-2. A MySQL startup script

```
#!/bin/sh

# Source common setup, including hostconfig.
#
. /etc/rc.common

StartService()
{
  # Don't start unless MySQL is enabled in /etc/hostconfig
  if [ "${MYSQL:=-NO-}" = "-YES-" ]; then
    ConsoleMessage "Starting MySQL"
    /usr/local/mysql/bin/mysqld_safe --user=mysql --skip-networking &
  fi
}

StopService()
{
  ConsoleMessage "Stopping MySQL"
  # If you've set a root password within mysql, you may
  # need to add --password=password on the next line.
```

```
    /usr/local/mysql/bin/mysqladmin shutdown
}

RestartService()
{
  # Don't restart unless MySQL is enabled in /etc/hostconfig
  if [ "${MYSQL:=-NO-}" = "-YES-" ]; then
    ConsoleMessage "Restarting MySQL"
    StopService
    StartService
  else
    StopService
  fi
}

RunService "$1"
```

Because it consults the settings of the $MYSQL environment variable, the startup script won't do anything unless you've enabled MySQL in the */etc/hostconfig* file. To do this, edit */etc/hostconfig* in a text editor, and add this line:

```
    MYSQL=-YES-
```

 Mac OS X does not recognize any special connections between *hostconfig* entries and startup scripts. Instead, the startup script sources the */etc/rc.common* file, which in turn sources *hostconfig*. The directives in *hostconfig* are merely environment variables, and the startup script checks the values of the variables that control its behavior (in this case, $MYSQL).

The property list

The property list (*StartupParameters.plist*) contains attributes that describe the item and determine its place in the startup sequence. It can be in XML or NeXT format. The NeXT format uses NeXTSTEP-style property lists, as shown in Example 4-3.

Example 4-3. The MySQL startup parameters as a NeXT property list

```
{
  Description = "MySQL";
  Provides = ("MySQL");
  Requires = ("Network");
  OrderPreference = "Late";
}
```

The XML format adheres to the *PropertyList.dtd* Document Type Definition (DTD). You can use your favorite text editor or the Property List Editor (*/Developer/Applications/Utilities*) to create your own XML property list, as shown in Example 4-4.

Example 4-4. The MySQL startup parameters as an XML property list

```
<?xml version="1.0" encoding="UTF-8"?>
<!DOCTYPE plist
        SYSTEM "file://localhost/System/Library/DTDs/PropertyList.dtd">
<plist version="0.9">
  <dict>
    <key>Description</key>
    <string>MySQL</string>
    <key>Provides</key>
    <array>
      <string>MySQL</string>
    </array>
    <key>Requires</key>
    <array>
      <string>Network</string>
    </array>
    <key>OrderPreference</key>
    <string>Late</string>
  </dict>
</plist>
```

The following list describes the various keys you can use in a startup parameters property list:

Description
> This is a phrase that describes the item.

Provides
> This is an array of services that the item provides (e.g., Apache provides "Web Server"). These services should be globally unique. In the event that SystemStarter finds two items that provide the same service, it starts the first one it finds.

Requires
> This is an array of services on which the item depends. It should correspond to another item's Provides attribute. If a required service cannot be started, the system won't start the item.

Uses
> This is similar to Requires, but it is a weaker association. If SystemStarter can find a matching service, it will start it. If it can't, the dependent item will still start.

OrderPreference
> The Requires and Uses attributes imply a particular order, in that dependent items will be started after the services on which they depend. You can specify First, Early, None (the default), Late, or Last here. SystemStarter does its best to satisfy this preference, but dependency orders prevail.

You can now manually start, restart, and stop MySQL by invoking System-Starter from the command line:

```
$ sudo SystemStarter start MySQL
$ sudo SystemStarter restart MySQL
$ sudo SystemStarter stop MySQL
```

Launching with launchd

Creating a *launchd* startup item (a launch agent or launch daemon) is more declarative than procedural. Instead of writing scripts that directly control your daemon, you create an XML *.plist* file with as much information as you can possibly provide; this tells Mac OS X how it should handle starting the server.

You can use a launch daemon to start up MySQL, in fact. You lose the ability to specify that *mysqladmin shutdown* be run when you are terminating MySQL, but MySQL can shut down gracefully even when *launchd* kills it outright. Here's a modified version of the MySQL startup script that ships with the Mac OS X Leopard server. Save it in */Library/LaunchDaemons/org.mysql.mysqld.plist*:

```
<?xml version="1.0" encoding="UTF-8"?>
<!DOCTYPE plist PUBLIC "-//Apple//DTD PLIST 1.0//EN"
          "http://www.apple.com/DTDs/PropertyList-1.0.dtd">
<plist version="1.0">
  <dict>
    <key>Label</key>
    <string>org.mysql.mysqld</string>
    <key>OnDemand</key>
    <false/>
    <key>ProgramArguments</key>
    <array>
      <string>/usr/local/mysql/bin/mysqld</string>
      <string>--user=mysql</string>
      <string>--skip-networking</string>
    </array>
    <key>ServiceIPC</key>
    <false/>
  </dict>
</plist>
```

The first key/string pair defines the label that identifies this daemon (*org.mysql.mysqld*). This can be used with some *launchctl(1)* commands. The second pair (OnDemand: false) indicates that *mysqld* is not an on-demand daemon: it should be started as soon as possible and kept running until it is un-loaded (either explicitly or at system shutdown). The ProgramArguments key simply specifies the command line used to launch the program, and ServiceIPC: false indicates that *mysqld* is unable to communicate with *launchd* using interprocess communication. After you create this file, you can load it and enable it with this command:

```
$ sudo launchctl load -w /Library/LaunchDaemons/org.mysql.mysqld.plist
```

Since this is not an OnDemand daemon, it's started immediately. To unload it (and shut it down), use:

```
$ sudo launchctl unload -w /Library/LaunchDaemons/org.mysql.mysqld.plist
```

> Note that we launch *mysqld* here, rather than starting MySQL with *mysqld_safe*, as we did with the startup item. This is because upon shutdown, *launchd* will try to kill the program it started; however, it won't be able to kill *mysqld_safe*, because it stays around until *mysqld* dies. In other words, *mysqladmin shutdown* knows exactly what to kill, but *launchd* doesn't.

For more information on launching with *launchd*, see the *launchd.plist(5)* manpage.

Periodic Jobs

Like other flavors of Unix, Mac OS X supports *cron* to schedule tasks for periodic execution. Each user's *cron* jobs are controlled by configuration files that you can edit with *crontab -e*. (To list the contents of the file, use *crontab -l*.) Beginning with Mac OS X Tiger, the global *crontab* (*/etc/crontab*) has been replaced with three launch daemons. The original *crontab* looked like this:

```
15 3 * * *      root    periodic daily
30 4 * * 6      root    periodic weekly
30 5 1 * *      root    periodic monthly
```

But now, each line has been replaced by a file in */System/Library/LaunchDae mons* (*com.apple.periodic-daily.plist*, *com.apple.periodic-weekly.plist*, and *com.apple.periodic-monthly.plist*) that uses the StartCalendar key to specify when it is to be run. For example, here is the *com.apple.periodic-daily.plist* file:

```
<?xml version="1.0" encoding="UTF-8"?>
<!DOCTYPE plist PUBLIC "-//Apple Computer//DTD PLIST 1.0//EN"
        "http://www.apple.com/DTDs/PropertyList-1.0.dtd">
<plist version="1.0">
  <dict>
    <key>Label</key>
    <string>com.apple.periodic-daily</string>
    <key>ProgramArguments</key>
    <array>
      <string>/usr/sbin/periodic</string>
      <string>daily</string>
    </array>
```

```
<key>LowPriorityIO</key>
<true/>
<key>Nice</key>
<integer>1</integer>
<key>StartCalendarInterval</key>
<dict>
  <key>Hour</key>
  <integer>3</integer>
  <key>Minute</key>
  <integer>15</integer>
</dict>
  </dict>
</plist>
```

These *.plists* launch the periodic jobs in the wee hours of the morning, but *launchd* does not skip jobs even if your computer is shut off: the next time the computer wakes up or boots up, the missed jobs will be run.

These three launch daemons run the scripts contained in subdirectories of the */etc/periodic* directory: */etc/periodic/daily*, */etc/periodic/weekly*, and */etc/periodic/monthly*. Each of these directories contains one or more scripts:

```
/etc/periodic/daily/100.clean-logs
/etc/periodic/daily/110.clean-tmps
/etc/periodic/daily/130.clean-msgs
/etc/periodic/daily/430.status-rwho
/etc/periodic/daily/500.daily
/etc/periodic/monthly/200.accounting
/etc/periodic/monthly/500.monthly
/etc/periodic/monthly/999.local
/etc/periodic/weekly/310.locate
/etc/periodic/weekly/320.whatis
/etc/periodic/weekly/999.local
```

You should not modify these files, because they may be replaced by future system updates. Instead, create an */etc/daily.local*, */etc/weekly.local*, or */etc/monthly.local* file to hold your site-specific *cron* jobs. The *cron* jobs are simply shell scripts that contain commands to be run as *root*. The local *cron* jobs are invoked at the end of the *500.daily*, *999.weekly*, and *999.monthly* scripts found in the */etc/periodic* subdirectory. Within a directory, the files with lower numbers in their names execute before scripts with higher numbers.

## CHAPTER 5

Directory Services

A *directory service* manages information about users and resources such as printers and servers. It can manage this information for anything from a single machine to an entire corporate network. The Directory Services architecture in Mac OS X is called *Open Directory*. Open Directory includes flat files (such as */etc/hosts*), LDAPv3, other services available through third-party plug-ins, and even its own XML-based data store.

This chapter describes how to perform common configuration tasks, such as adding a user or host on a standalone Mac. If your system administrator has configured your Macintosh to consult an external directory server, some of these instructions may not work. If that's the case, you should ask your system administrator to make the changes you need.

Understanding Directory Services

Coming from Unix or Linux, you're probably used to modifying files such as */etc/passwd* and */etc/group* to add and edit users and groups. On Mac OS X, however, if you need to do something simple such as adding a user, you can't just add the new user to */etc/passwd* and be done with it. Instead, you'll need to work with Mac OS X's Directory Services.

In Mac OS X 10.1.*x* and earlier, the system was configured to consult the NetInfo database for all directory information. To make changes to the directory, you had to use the NetInfo Manager (or NetInfo's command-line utilities).

As of Mac OS X 10.2 (Jaguar), NetInfo functions started to become more of a legacy protocol and were reduced to handling the local directory database for machines that did not participate in a network-wide directory, such as Active Directory or OpenLDAP. NetInfo was still present in Mac OS X 10.3 and 10.4, but it has been eliminated in 10.5. By default, Mac OS X is now configured to

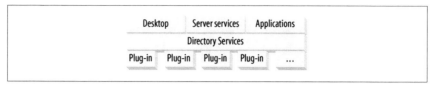

Desktop	Server services	Applications
Directory Services		
Plug-in	Plug-in	Plug-in	Plug-in	...

Figure 5-1. The Directory Services architecture

consult a collection of XML property list files that contain directory data and are stored in */var/db/dslocal*.

To work with Mac OS X's Directory Services from within Unix scripts and applications, you must first understand the overall architecture, which is known as Open Directory. Directory Services is the part of Mac OS X (and the open source Darwin operating system) that implements this architecture. Figure 5-1 shows the relationship of Directory Services to the rest of the operating system. The server processes, the user's Desktop, and applications act as clients to Directory Services, which delegates requests to specific directory service plug-ins (see the next section for descriptions of these plug-ins).

Configuring Directory Services

To configure Directory Services, use the Directory Utility application (*/Applications/Utilities*), shown in Figure 5-2. You can enable or disable various directory service plug-ins, or change their configuration.

Directory Utility supports the following plug-ins (click the Services icon at the top of the Directory Utility window to see them; you'll need to click the lock icon at the bottom of the window and provide your password to make changes):

Active Directory
> This plug-in enables Mac OS X to consult an Active Directory domain on a server running Windows 2000 or Windows 2003.

BSD Flat File and NIS
> This plug-in handles the Network Information Service (NIS) and the flat files located in the */etc* directory, such as *hosts* and *passwd*. Although this option is on by default, */etc/passwd* and */etc/group* are not consulted by default. To enable them, double-click on the "BSD Flat File and NIS" entry (or highlight it and click the pencil/edit button), check the box next to "Use User and Group records in BSD local mode" in the resulting dialog box, and click OK (you can also set NIS options in this dialog box).

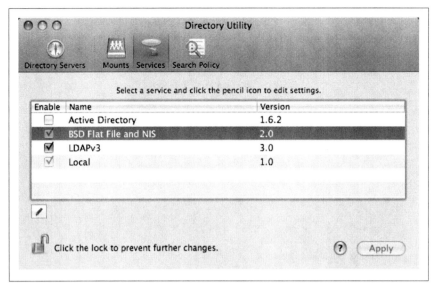

Figure 5-2. The Directory Utility application shows the available plug-ins

LDAPv3
> This plug-in supports the same version of LDAP used by Microsoft's Active Directory and Novell Directory Services (NDS). In addition to the client components, Mac OS X includes *slapd*, a standalone LDAP daemon from the OpenLDAP (*http://www.openldap.org*) project.

Local
> This plug-in supports the local Directory Services database that is stored in */var/db/dslocal* as a collection of XML property list files.

All of the plug-ins on the Services tab except for Active Directory are enabled by default.

Click the Search Policy icon to see where Directory Services looks for user authentication and contact information. If you go to the Authentication tab (Figure 5-3), you'll see that its Search pop up is set to Automatic by default. You can set the Search pop up to any of the following:

Automatic
> This is the default option, which searches the local directory and (if enabled as described in the previous section) BSD flat files.

Local directory
> This option searches only the local directory.

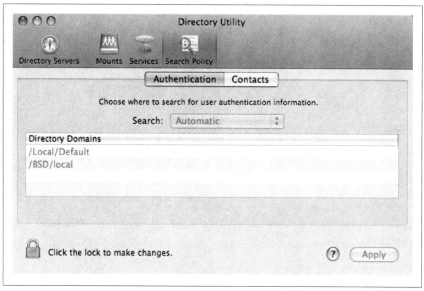

Figure 5-3. The Directory Utility Authentication options

Custom path

   This option allows you to modify the defaults and to add directory domains.

The Contact tab is set up identically to the Authentication tab and is used by programs that search Directory Services for contact information (office locations, phone numbers, full names, etc.), such as the Directory application in */Applications/Utilities* or *Address Book.app*.

Managing Directory Services Data

Mac OS X 10.5 (Leopard) has made it easier to add and edit Directory Services data, especially users and groups. Previous versions of Mac OS X did not offer many options for creating and editing groups and users, but in Leopard you can use System Preferences→Accounts to work with this data. To add a user or group in System Preferences, click the lock icon to authenticate yourself, and then press the + button. The drop-down menu labeled "New" lets you create a user or group. You can edit the advanced options of a user who is not currently logged in by Control/right-clicking on the user's name in the list of users and choosing Advanced Options. There, you can set the user ID, group ID, short name, shell, home directory, Universally Unique Identifier (UUID), and aliases.

If you want to do things the traditional Unix way, Mac OS X includes *chsh*, *chfn*, and *chpass* in version 10.3 and beyond.

You can also manipulate Directory Services data from the command line. Table 5-1 lists the available Directory Services utilities. For more information, see the manpage for each.

Table 5-1. Directory Services tools

Tool	Description
dirt(1)	Testing tool for Directory Services.
dscacheutil(1)	Utility for working with the Directory Services cache. Replaces many of the functions handled by *lookupd* in previous versions of Mac OS X.
dscl(1)	Command-line interface to Directory Services.
dsconfigad(8)	Configuration tool for the Active Directory plug-in.
dsconfigldap(1)	Configuration tool for the LDAPv3 plug-in.
dseditgroup(8)	Tool for working with group records.
dsenableroot(8)	Utility to disable or enable the *root* account.
dsexport(1)	Exports data from Directory Services.
dsimport(1)	Imports data into Directory Services.
dsmemberutil(1)	Utility for working with Directory Services' membership APIs.
dsperfmonitor(1)	Tool for monitoring the performance of Directory Services plug-ins.

Managing Users and Passwords from the Terminal

The Directory Services equivalent of the *passwd* file resides under the */Users* portion of the directory. Although Mac OS X includes */etc/passwd* and */etc/master.passwd* files, they are consulted only while the system is in single-user mode, or if the system has been reconfigured to use BSD Flat Files (see "Configuring Directory Services," earlier in this chapter).

You can list all users with the *dscacheutil* utility:

```
$ dscacheutil -q user
name: _amavisd
password: *
uid: 83
gid: 83
dir: /var/virusmails
shell: /usr/bin/false
gecos: AMaViS Daemon
```

```
name: _appowner
password: *
uid: 87
gid: 87
dir: /var/empty
shell: /usr/bin/false
gecos: Application Owner

name: _appserver
password: *
uid: 79
gid: 79
dir: /var/empty
shell: /usr/bin/false
gecos: Application Server
[...]
```

Creating a user

To create a user with *dscl*, you'll need to create an entry under */Users* and set the *uid*, *gid*, *shell*, *realname*, and *home* properties.

The following commands will create a new user, *rothman*:

```
$ sudo dscl . create /Users/rothman uid 701
$ sudo dscl . create /Users/rothman gid 701
$ sudo dscl . create /Users/rothman shell /bin/bash
$ sudo dscl . create /Users/rothman home /Users/rothman
$ sudo dscl . create /Users/rothman realname "Ernest Rothman"
$ sudo dscl . create /Groups/rothman gid 701
$ sudo dscl . create /Groups/rothman passwd \*
$ sudo passwd rothman
Changing password for rothman.
New password: ********
Retype new password: ********
```

After you create the user, you should create his home directory, as shown next.

Creating a user's home directory

One thing that *dscl* can't do for you is create the user's home directory. Mac OS X keeps a skeleton directory under the */System/Library/User Template* directory. If you look in this directory, you'll see localized versions of a user's home directory. To copy the localized English version of the home directory, use a command like this:

```
$ sudo cp -R "/System/Library/User Template/English.lproj" /Users/rothman
```

Then, use *chown* to recursively set the ownership of the home directory and all its contents (make sure you set the group to a group of which the user is a member):

```
$ sudo chown -R rothman:rothman /Users/rothman
```

This change makes the new user the owner of his home directory and all its contents.

Granting administrative privileges

To give someone administrative privileges, add that user to the *admin* group (*/Groups/admin*). This gives the user the ability to use *sudo* and to run applications (such as software installers) that require administrative privileges, such as:

```
$ sudo dscl . merge /Groups/admin users rothman
```

Modifying a user

You can change a user's properties by using the *create* command (even if the property already exists). For example, to change *rothman*'s shell to *zsh*, use:

```
$ sudo dscl . create /Users/rothman shell /bin/zsh
```

Deleting a user

To delete a user, use *dscl*'s *delete* command. Since *delete* recursively deletes everything under the specified directory, use this command with caution:

```
$ sudo dscl . delete /Users/rothman
```

If you want to also delete the user's home directory, you'll have to do it manually.

 Be sure to delete the group you created for the user as well ("rothman" in this example), as shown in the next section.

Managing Groups

Directory Services stores information about groups in the */Groups* directory. You can explore it with the *dscl* utility (the "." specifies the local directory):

```
$ dscl .
Entering interactive mode... (type "help" for commands)
 > cd /Groups/
/Groups > ls
_amavisd
_appowner
_appserveradm
_appserverusr
[...]
```

You can also use *dscacheutil* with the argument *-q group*, which displays all the groups:

```
$ dscacheutil -q group
name: _amavisd
password: *
gid: 83

name: _appowner
password: *
gid: 87

name: _appserveradm
password: *
gid: 81

name: _appserverusr
password: *
gid: 79
[...]
```

Creating a group

To create a group with *dscl*, you'll need to create a directory under */Groups* and set the *gid* and *passwd* properties. An asterisk (*) specifies no password; be sure to quote it so that the shell does not attempt to expand it. The following commands create a group named *writers* as GID 5005 with no password and no members:

```
$ sudo dscl . create /Groups/writers gid 5005
$ sudo dscl . create /Groups/writers passwd '*'
```

Adding users to a group

You can add users to a group by appending values to the *users* property with *dscl*'s *merge* command at the command line (or by using the *merge* command interactively; start *dscl* in interactive mode with *sudo dscl .*):

```
$ sudo dscl . merge /Groups/writers users bjepson rothman
```

If the *users* property does not exist, *dscl* creates it. If the users are already part of the group, they are not added to the list (contrast this with the *-append* command, which can result in the same user being added more than once if the command is invoked multiple times).

Deleting a group

To delete a group, use *dscl*'s *delete* command. Be careful with this command, since it deletes everything in and below the specified NetInfo directory:

```
$ sudo dscl . delete /Groups/writers
```

Managing Hostnames and IP Addresses

Mac OS X consults both the *letc/hosts* file and the */machines* portion of the local directory. For example, the following entry in *letc/hosts* would map the hostname *xyzzy* to 192.168.0.1:

```
192.168.0.1   xyzzy
```

Creating a host

To add a new host, create an entry under */Hosts* and specify an IP address. This example adds the host *xyzzy*:

```
$ sudo dscl . -create /Hosts/xyzzy ip_address 192.168.254.7
```

If you add an entry that already exists, it will be overwritten.

The local directory takes precedence over the *letc/hosts* file, so if you enter the same hostname with different IP addresses in both places, Mac OS X uses the one in the local directory. (In this case, it would map host *xyzzy* to 192.168.254.7, overriding the value of 192.168.0.1 set in *letc/hosts*.)

Flat Files and Their Directory Services Counterparts

Directory Services manages information for several flat files in earlier releases of Mac OS X, including *letc/printcap*, *letc/mail/aliases*, *letc/protocols*, and *letc/services*.

Although you can edit these flat files directly as you would on any other Unix system, you can also use Directory Services to manage this information. Table 5-2 lists each flat file, the corresponding portion of the directory, and important properties associated with each entry. Properties marked with "(list)" can take multiple values using the *dscl merge* command (for an example, see "Adding users to a group," earlier in this chapter). The "Flat files or local database?" column in Table 5-2 indicates whether Directory Services consults the flat file, the local database, or both. Recall that you can use Directory Utility to modify the way information is looked up on your Macintosh.

Table 5-2. Flat files and their NetInfo counterparts

Flat file	NetInfo directory	Important properties	Flat files or local database?
/etc/fstab	/Mounts	name, dir, type, opts (list), passno, freq	Local database
/etc/group	/Groups	name, passwd, gid, users (list)	Local database
/etc/hosts	/Hosts	ip_address, name (list)	Both; entries in the local directory take precedence

Flat file	NetInfo directory	Important properties	Flat files or local database?
/etc/mail/aliases	/Aliases	name, members (list)	Flat files
/etc/networks	/Networks	name (list), address	Flat files
/etc/passwd, /etc/master.passwd	/Users	name, passwd, uid, gid, realname, home, shell	Local database
/etc/printcap	/Printers	name, and various printcap properties (see the printcap(5) manpage)	Flat files
/etc/protocols	/Protocols	name (list), number	Flat files
/etc/rpc	/Rpcs	name (list), number	Flat files
/etc/services	/Services	name (list), port, protocol (list)	Flat files

Programming with Directory Services

As a programmer, you frequently need to deal with directory information, whether you realize it or not. Your application uses Directory Services each time it looks up a host entry or authenticates a password. The Open Directory architecture unifies what used to be a collection of assorted flat files in /etc.

Working with Passwords

One traditional route to user and password information is through the getpw* family of functions. In the interest of thwarting dictionary attacks against password files, many operating systems have stopped returning encrypted passwords through those APIs. Many Unix and Linux systems simply return an x when you invoke a function like getpwnam(). However, those systems can return an encrypted password through functions like getspnam(), which consult shadow password entries and can generally be invoked by the root user only. Example 5-1 shows the typical usage of such an API, where the user enters her plain-text password, and the program encrypts it and then compares it against the encrypted password stored in the system.

Example 5-1. Using getpwnam() to retrieve an encrypted password

```
/*
 * getpw* no longer returns an encrypted password.
 *
 * Compile with: gcc checkpass.c -o checkpass
 * Run with: ./checkpass
 */
```

```
#include <pwd.h>
#include <stdio.h>
#include <stdlib.h>

int main(int argc, char *argv[])
{
  const char *user = NULL;
  struct passwd *pwd;

  /* Set the username if it was supplied on the command
   * line. Bail out if we don't end up with a username.
   */
  if (argc == 2)
    user = argv[1];
  if(!user)
  {
    fprintf(stderr, "Usage: checkpass <username>\n");
    exit(1);
  }

  /* Fetch the password entry. */
  if (pwd = getpwnam(user))
  {
    char *password = (char *) getpass("Enter your password: ");

    /* Encrypt the password using the encrypted password as salt.
     * See crypt(3) for complete details.
     */
    char *crypted  = (char *) crypt(password, pwd->pw_passwd);

    /* Are the two encrypted passwords identical? */
    if (strcmp(pwd->pw_passwd, crypted) == 0)
      printf("Success.\n");
    else
    {
      printf("Bad password: %s != %s\n", pwd->pw_passwd, crypted);
      return 1;
    }
  }
  else
  {
    fprintf(stderr, "Could not find password for %s.\n", user);
    return 1;
  }
  return 0;

}
```

Beginning with Mac OS X 10.3 (Panther), your code no longer has a chance to look at an encrypted password. There are no functions such as getspnam(), and if you invoke a function like getpwnam(), you'll get one or more asterisks as the result. For example:

```
$ gcc checkpass.c -o checkpass
$ ./checkpass bjepson
Enter your password:
Bad password: ******** != **yRnqib5QSRI
```

 There are some circumstances where you can obtain an encrypted password, but this is not the default behavior of Mac
OS X. See the *getpwent(3)* manpage for complete details.

Instead of retrieving and comparing encrypted passwords, you should go
through the Linux-PAM (Pluggable Authentication Modules for Linux) APIs.
Since Linux-PAM is included with (or available for) many flavors of Unix, you
can use it to write portable code. Example 5-2 shows a simple program that
uses Linux-PAM to prompt a user for his password.

Example 5-2. Using Linux-PAM to authenticate a user

```
/*
 * Use Linux-PAM to check passwords.
 *
 * Compile with: gcc pam_example.c -o pam_example -lpam
 * Run with: ./pam_example <username>
 */
#include <stdio.h>
#include <pam/pam_appl.h>
#include <pam/pam_misc.h>

int main(int argc, char *argv[])
{

  int retval;
  static struct pam_conv pam_conv;
  pam_conv.conv = misc_conv;
  pam_handle_t *pamh = NULL;
  const char *user = NULL;

  /* Set the username if it was supplied on the command
   * line. Bail out if we don't end up with a username.
   */
  if (argc == 2)
    user = argv[1];
  if(!user)
  {
    fprintf(stderr, "Usage: pam_example <username>\n");
    exit(1);
  }

  /* Initialize Linux-PAM. */
  retval = pam_start("pam_example", user, &pam_conv, &pamh);
  if (retval != PAM_SUCCESS)
```

```
{
  fprintf(stderr, "Could not start pam: %s\n",
      pam_strerror(pamh, retval));
  exit(1);
}

/* Try to authenticate the user. This could cause Linux-PAM
 * to prompt the user for a password.
 */
retval = pam_authenticate(pamh, 0);
if (retval == PAM_SUCCESS)
  printf("Success.\n");
else
  fprintf(stderr, "Failure: %s\n", pam_strerror(pamh, retval));

/* Shut down Linux-PAM. Return with an error if
 * something goes wrong.
 */
return pam_end(pamh, retval) == PAM_SUCCESS ? 0 : 1;
}
```

For this to work, you must create a file called *pam_example* in */etc/pam.d* with the following contents (the filename must match the first argument to pam_start(), which is shown in bold in Example 5-2):

```
auth        required   pam_securityserver.so
account     required   pam_permit.so
password    required   pam_deny.so
```

Be careful when making any changes in the */etc/pam.d* directory. If you change one of the files that is consulted for system login, you may lock yourself out of the system. For more information on Linux-PAM, see the *pam(8)* manpage.

Once you've compiled this program and created the *pam_example* file in */etc/pam.d*, you can test it:

```
$ gcc pam_example.c -o pam_example -lpam
$ ./pam_example bjepson
Password: ********
Success.
```

## CHAPTER 6

Printing

Mac OS X offers a rich and flexible set of tools for administering and using a wide variety of printers. Common Unix tools—such as *lpr*, *lpq*, and *lprm*—are here as well, along with a few new ones just for Mac OS X.

This chapter starts with a basic discussion of how to use the AddPrinter utility, a GUI tool for configuring local and network printers. Then we'll move on to discuss the Mac OS X implementation of the Unix printing tools. In particular, we will discuss the Common Unix Printing System (CUPS).

AddPrinter

If you're using a popular USB printer under Mac OS X, it is likely that all you'll need to do is connect it to the USB port and choose the printer in the Print dialog when you want to print a document. However, there are some circumstances where it's not so simple:

- Your USB printer might not automatically show up as an available printer in the Print dialog.
- You might want to share your printer with other computers on your LAN.
- You might want to use a network printer such as one listed in Open Directory, an AppleTalk printer, or a printer for which all you have is an IP address.

In Leopard, the utility for setting up a new printer is called AddPrinter. (In pre-Leopard releases of Mac OS X, it was called the Printer Setup Utility and was located in the */Applications/Utilities* folder.) In most cases, AddPrinter is launched to add a new printer in Mac OS X in one of two indirect ways:

Using System Preferences
Open System Preferences, choose Print & Fax, click the + sign, and click Add when the AddPrinter utility appears. To share your printers with

other computers, open System Preferences, choose Print & Fax→Sharing, select the printers you want to share, and click "Share these printers with other computers."

Adding a printer automatically

Attempting to print a document from virtually any application for the first time (before any printers are defined) will display the printer selection dialog shown in Figure 6-1, informing you that there is no installed printer and providing an Add Printer option in the drop-down list. Selecting the Add Printer option opens the Printer Browser, shown in Figure 6-2.

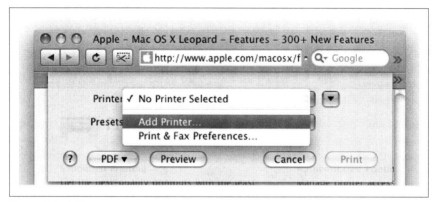

Figure 6-1. Adding a printer

You can also launch AddPrinter directly, either by double-clicking it in the Finder in the */System/Library/CoreServices* folder or from the Terminal with the command:

```
$ open -a AddPrinter
```

Whichever way you end up launching AddPrinter, once launched, it automatically searches for printers that are directly connected (usually via USB) and for Bonjour-enabled printers on your network. If either a Bonjour-enabled printer or a locally attached printer is found, you can easily add this printer, and you'll be ready to use it immediately. If you have a USB printer connected directly to your Mac, it will most likely show up as your default printer automatically. Other options in the AddPrinter window include:

Fax

Set up a fax machine, connected either via a modem or via Bluetooth

IP

Add an IP printer connected to your network

Windows printer

Add a printer shared by a Windows system on your network

Figure 6-2. AddPrinter's Printer Browser

Bluetooth
> Add a printer that's available via Bluetooth

AppleTalk
> Add a network printer using an AppleTalk connection

More Printers
> Set up third-party printer types that are installed on your system

However you add a printer, Mac OS X tries to identify the printer type and attempts to select a PostScript Printer Description (PPD) file automatically. (Although the first P in PPD stands for PostScript, CUPS has extended the PPD file format to include non-PostScript printers.)

The PPD file provides the operating system with specific information about your printer, including available fonts, paper sizes, installable options, and other features. The printer's driver uses the PPD file. If an appropriate PPD file for your printer is not included with Mac OS X, one may be available from the printer's manufacturer or on the CD that came with the printer. If Mac OS X does not find it automatically, you can try to find it in the list.

Adding an IP Printer

If you have a printer on your network that is not Bonjour-enabled, you'll need to have some information about it on hand, including:

- The printer's IP address or hostname
- The manufacturer and model of the printer
- Any installed options (such as a duplexer)

 If you don't know the exact model of the printer, you may still be able to set it up, albeit with reduced functionality. For example, if all you know is that you've got some kind of HP DeskJet, you can configure the printer as a generic DeskJet by selecting ESP→HP New DeskJet Series CUPS from the Printer Model options when you add the printer. However, specifying the exact model may cause Mac OS X to enable a fuller set of printing features, including options such as duplex printing (a generic version of the driver generally includes only the minimum set of features needed to print to a broad range of models).

To set up an IP printer, click the IP Printer icon in the Printer Browser window and select the protocol, as shown in Figure 6-3.

You need to select a protocol from the following choices:

- Internet Printing Protocol – IPP
- Line Printer Daemon – LPD
- HP Jetdirect – Socket

For example, suppose you have a Konica Minolta Magicolor 2450 on your LAN and that its IP address is 192.168.0.77. In this case, you would select "Line Printer Daemon – LPD" as the Protocol, enter 192.168.0.77 as the Address, specify a Queue name if required (otherwise it is called "default") and a Name and Location for the printer, and select Konica Minolta Magicolor in the Print Using box, if that model is available. In this case, the model could not be found in this dialog box, as shown in Figure 6-4.

If you cannot find your printer in the "Print Using" list, you should make sure that you've updated your Mac OS X installation via Software Update (either from the menu bar or through System Preferences→Software Update). Apple provides drivers for most of the popular printers, and you may find that yours has been added. (If your driver has not been installed with Mac OS X, the most likely explanations are that your printer is either a very old model or a very

Figure 6-3. Selecting the LPD protocol in the AddPrinter utility's Printer Browser

new model.) If your Mac OS X installation is up-to-date and your printer model's driver is still not installed, you can check the printer manufacturer's website to determine if the appropriate printer driver is available for Mac OS X. If not, in most cases you should still be able to use the printer by selecting "Generic Postscript Printer" in the "Print Using" list. In the case of the Konica Minolta Magicolor 2450 printer, a driver was available on the manufacturer's website. Once the driver is installed, the printer should turn up in the "Print Using" list, as shown in Figure 6-5.

After clicking the Add button, you will be prompted to enter printer-specific information such as printer installable options, as shown in Figure 6-6.

Once you've added a printer, the printer will show up in the Print & Fax preference pane, as shown in Figure 6-7.

Setting up an LPD printer in this manner allows you not only to print documents by selecting Print from the File menus of GUI-based applications, but also to manipulate the print queue from the Terminal using the CUPS *lp*, *lpq*,

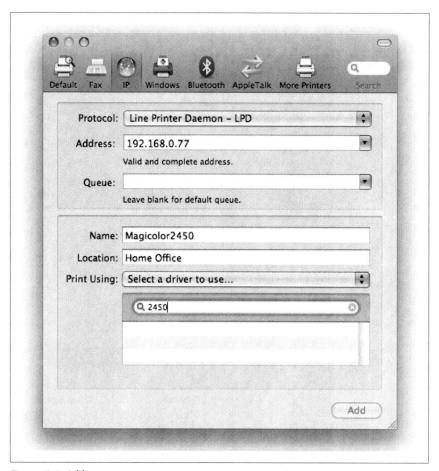

Figure 6-4. Adding a printer

lprm, *lpstat*, and *cancel* shell commands. (See "Printing-Related Shell Commands," later in this chapter, for a more complete listing of command-line utilities.)

Creating a Desktop Icon for a Printer

You can use the Print & Fax preference pane to place an icon for your printer on the Desktop. (You can actually place the icon in any folder in which you have write permission, but we'll assume you're using the Desktop.) Using your mouse, drag your printer's icon from the left subwindow of the Print & Fax preference pane to the Desktop. Two printer icons will be created by this action: one will be an application in *~/Library/Printers*, while the other (the one

Figure 6-5. Finding your printer's driver

on the Desktop) will be an alias to the printer icon application in *~/Library/ Printers*. You can just leave this icon on your Desktop, or you can place it in the left section of the Dock with the application icons, or in the lower section of the Finder's Places sidebar. In each case, you'll be able to print a document by dragging its icon to the printer's icon.

 Double-clicking a Desktop printer icon opens a window that shows you the status of the printer and any items in the print queue. This comes in handy for times when you need to quickly cancel a print job or start/stop the print queue to service a printer.

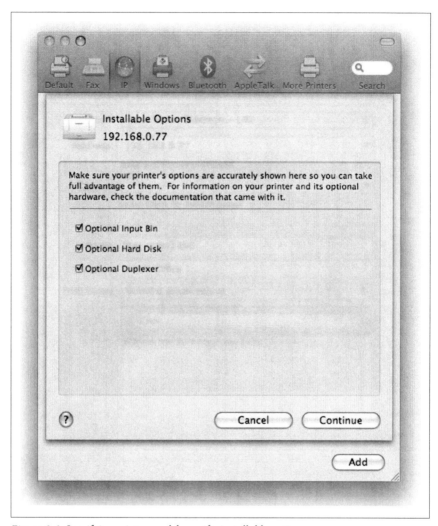

Figure 6-6. Specifying printer model-specific installable options

Modifying a Printer's Settings

Once your printer has been added, you can change some of its settings (location, printer model, and any installable options) by selecting System Preferences→Print & Fax→Options & Supplies. Before clicking the Options & Supplies tab, make sure that you've selected the correct printer in the left subwindow of the Print & Fax preference pane, in case more than one printer has been added to your installation. Alternatively, if you've created a printer icon on your Desktop, you can open the Options & Supplies window by

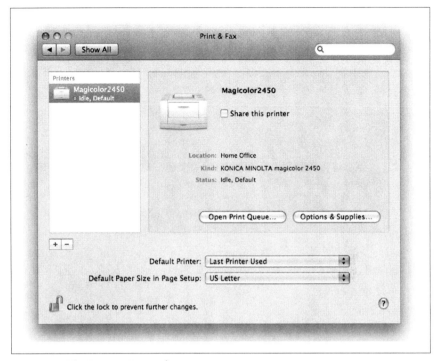

Figure 6-7. The Print & Fax preference pane

double-clicking the icon and then clicking on Info in the printer window's title bar. Under Options & Supplies, you can also check on the supply levels of the toner in your printer.

You can change the driver by selecting System Preferences→Print & Fax→Open Print Queue, clicking the Info tab, and then clicking on the Driver tab.

Monitoring Printer Status and Troubleshooting

If you select System Preferences→Print & Fax→Open Print Queue, you'll be able to check on the status of the print queue, as shown in Figure 6-8.

From the Printer option in the menu bar, you can select from the following options:

- Make Default
- Supply Levels
- Print Test Page
- Network Diagnostics

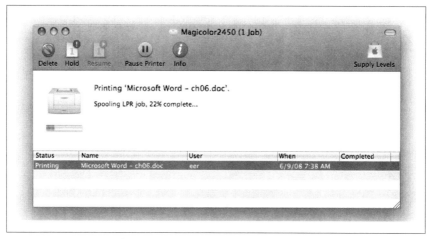

Figure 6-8. Monitoring the print queue

- Log & History
- Pause Printer
- Show Printer List

Printer Sharing

Printers with network adapters are not necessarily the only printers available on your LAN. You can share a printer that's connected to your computer with other computers. For example, you can share your USB (or network) printer with all the computers on your LAN in the Print & Fax preference pane. To do so, highlight the printer that you'd like to share and select "Share this printer."

 You may need to click the lock in the lower-left corner to authenticate yourself as an administrative user before you make changes to the system preferences.

The Sharing preference pane will reflect this change, as shown in Figure 6-9.

If you've activated the firewall, enabling Printer Sharing in the Sharing preference pane opens up incoming ports 631 (Internet Printing Protocol) and 515 (*lpd*) for printing. Selecting System Preferences→Security→Firewall will also reveal that Printer Sharing has been enabled, as shown in Figure 6-10.

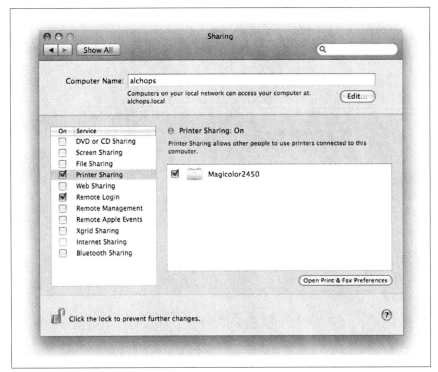

Figure 6-9. Sharing preferences

 To verify which ports are open in the firewall, you can launch the Network Utility in */Applications/Utilities* and perform a port scan on *localhost*.

Once you've shared your printer, other Macs on your subnet should automatically see it in their Print dialog boxes. Users on your local network but not on your subnet will be able to connect to the printer using the IP address or hostname of your Mac.

In addition to sharing your printer with Mac users, you can share it with Linux, Unix, and Windows users. If a Unix or Linux computer is on the same subnet as the computer sharing its printer and has CUPS installed, it will see the shared printer. If not, you will need to provide the IP address of the computer sharing the printer (see "Printing from Remote Systems," later in this chapter).

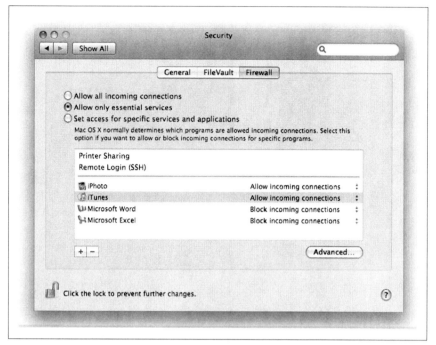

Figure 6-10. Printer sharing revealed in the Security preference pane

It is also easy to print from your Mac to a printer that is shared by a Windows computer. If your computer is on the same subnet as the Windows machine, click the Windows icon at the top of the Printer Browser window and select the workgroup and then the computer, and you should see the printer listed. Highlight the printer and click Add. Subsequently, this printer will be available in your Print dialogs.

After you've activated Printer Sharing, you may want to add some information about the physical location of the printer. As noted earlier, you can do this on the Options & Supplies tab of the Print & Fax preference pane: select System Preferences→Print & Fax→Options & Supplies→General and enter your printer's information in the Location field. For example, if the marketing group is sharing a printer, you might type "Marketing" in the Location field.

If you have trouble getting a printer to work correctly, check out the Printer Setup Repair shareware utility (*http://www.fix amac.net/software/index.html*). Though at the time of this writing a version for Leopard is not available, the developer's website reports that the Leopard version is "coming soon." This utility has been available for Mac OS X since 10.1 and seems to be popular (as judged from its ratings on *http://www .versiontracker.com* and *http://www.macupdate.com*).

The Common Unix Printing System (CUPS)

The Common Unix Printing System, a core component of Mac OS X, is free, open source software that provides a portable and extensible printing system for the Unix-based Internet Printing Protocol (IPP/1.1).

Extensive documentation and source code is available for CUPS online (*http://www.cups.org*). As noted in the online documentation, the goal of CUPS is "to provide a complete, modern printing system for Unix that can be used to support new printers, devices, and protocols while providing compatibility with existing Unix applications."

CUPS provides System V- and Berkeley-compatible command-line interfaces and a web-based interface to extensive documentation and status monitoring and printer administration tools. You can access the web-based administration interface by pointing your web browser to port 631 on the your local machine (*http://127.0.0.1:631* or *http://localhost:631*). (To access CUPS from a remote machine, enable Printer Sharing [System Preferences→Sharing], and use your machine's IP address instead of 127.0.0.1.) The main page of the web-based administrative interface is shown in Figure 6-11.

The CUPS web interface provides some functionality not available directly through the System Preferences and AddPrinter GUIs. For example, you can use the web interface to configure CUPS to use Kerberos authentication, move print jobs, allow/deny specified users access to selected printers, and manage classes. The CUPS web interface also provides extensive documentation on its use (*http://localhost:631/help/*).

Printing from Remote Systems

CUPS is available on a wide variety of Unix-based systems and makes both the administration and use of shared printers easy. For example, a shared USB printer connected to your Mac is immediately visible to a Solaris-based SUN

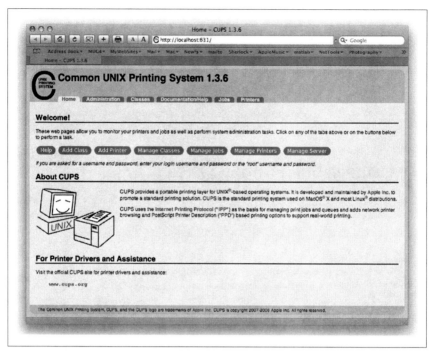

Figure 6-11. CUPS's web-based interface

workstation running CUPS, provided the Solaris machine is on the same subnet (if not, remote users can connect to the printer by supplying your Mac's IP address or hostname).

GNOME and KDE, the most popular desktop environments for Linux, have utilities that make it easy to connect to a printer you've shared from your Mac. Before you proceed, you should find out the queue name of your printer, as described in the following steps:

1. Select System Preferences→Print & Fax.

2. Select your printer and click the Options & Supplies button. (The General tab will be selected by default.)

3. Figure 6-12 shows the settings for an HP LaserJet P1505 connected to the USB port. The queue name for this printer is "HP_LaserJet_P1505."

GNOME

To connect to your Mac's printer from GNOME:

1. Launch the GNOME printer configuration tool. This may appear in a menu (on Ubuntu Linux, select System→Administration→Printing), or

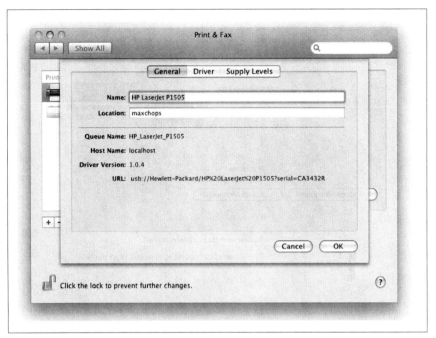

Figure 6-12. Inspecting the properties of an HP LaserJet P1505

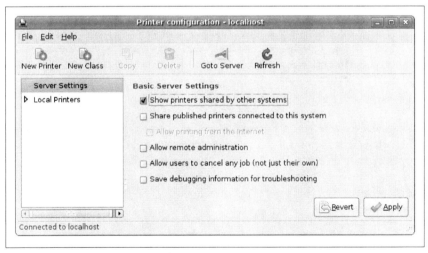

Figure 6-13. GNOME printer configuration

you can run the command *system-config-printer*. The Printer configuration tool appears as shown in Figure 6-13.

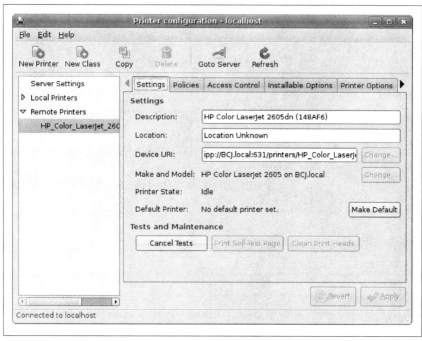

Figure 6-14. Examining a remote printer under GNOME

2. Select "Show printers shared by other systems" and click Apply.

3. Quit the Printer configuration tool and relaunch it. The shared printers on your network should now appear under a Remote Printers heading, as shown in Figure 6-14. Note that GNOME has automatically detected the correct printer driver.

KDE

To connect to your Mac's printer using KDE, launch the KDE Control Panel (in OpenSUSE, for example, click the Start menu and select Configure Desktop) and choose Peripherals→Printers. You may find that your printer is already detected. Depending on whether your Linux system can resolve your Mac's hostname properly, this printer may work as-is.

 Right-click on the printer, select Printer IPP Report, and browse the results. If you see "Unknown host" and/or "Unable to lookup host" in the printer-state-message attribute, it probably won't work out of the box.

If the printer is not detected automatically, you can follow these steps to add it manually:

1. Click Add→Add Printer/Class.

2. The Add Printer Wizard appears. Click Next to start the wizard.

3. The Backend Selection screen will appear. Choose Remote CUPS Server (IPP/HTTP) and click Next.

4. The next screen asks for user identification. Leave this set to the default (Anonymous) and click Next.

5. Specify your Mac's IP address and CUPS port (normally 631), as shown in Figure 6-15. Click Next.

6. You'll see a list of shared printers on your Mac, as shown in Figure 6-16. Choose one, and click Next.

7. The next screen asks you to select the printer manufacturer and model. Click Next when you're done.

8. The Driver Selection screen appears. This displays all the detected drivers for your printer. Choose the correct one, and click Next.

9. At this point, you're prompted to test the printer. When we tried this, it didn't work, but it wasn't a showstopper. If it doesn't work for you, click Next anyway and keep on moving through the wizard.

10. There are a few more screens: Banner Selection, Printer Quota Settings, and Users Access Settings. Leave the defaults and click Next for each one.

11. The next screen asks for the printer name, location, and description. Specify something that you think is useful, and then click Next.

12. The final screen shows you a summary of the selected settings. Review them, clicking Back if necessary to change anything, and click Finish when you are ready.

13. After the printer is installed, you can right-click on it in the Printing Manager and select Test Printer to send it a test page.

Manual printer configuration (Linux and Unix)

You can also configure a CUPS client manually. To add your Mac OS X printer as the default printer, edit /etc/cups/printers.conf on the Linux (or other Unix) machine, and add the following entry, replacing OfficeJet-D135, 192.168.254.150, and officejet_d_series with the appropriate values:

```
<DefaultPrinter OfficeJet-D135>
Info OfficeJet-D135
DeviceURI http://192.168.254.150:631/printers/officejet_d_series
State Idle
```

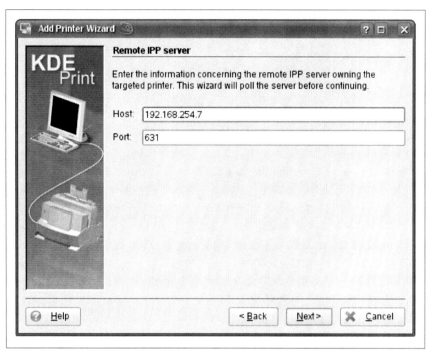

Figure 6-15. Setting the host and port

```
Accepting Yes
JobSheets none none
QuotaPeriod 0
PageLimit 0
KLimit 0
</Printer>
```

If you don't want the printer to be the default printer, change `DefaultPrinter` to `Printer`. After you've added the entry, stop and restart CUPS on the Linux (or other Unix) machine to load the new printer configuration.

Printing from Linux

After you get your Mac's printer to appear in the list of available printers, you don't need to do any further configuration. To print from an application such as Firefox, simply select the Print option from the application's main menu. Your Mac's printer will appear by name, as shown in Figure 6-17.

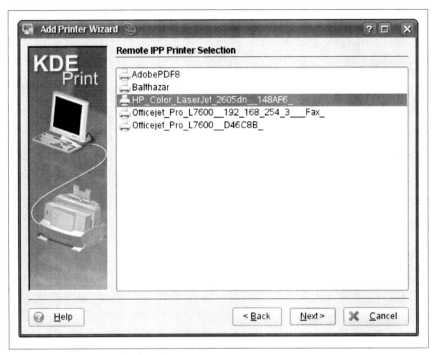

Figure 6-16. Choosing the shared printer on your Mac

Printing-Related Shell Commands

As noted earlier, Mac OS X provides the printing-related command-line utilities that most Unix users will find familiar: *lp, lpr, lpq, lprm,* and *lpstat.* Table 6-1 provides a more extensive list of printing-related commands available in Mac OS X. For more detailed descriptions of each utility listed in Table 6-1, see the appropriate manpage.

Table 6-1. Printing-related command-line utilities

Command	Description
cups-calibrate	Used to calibrate color output of printers
cups-config	Used to obtain the CUPS API, compiler, directory, and link information
cups-genppdconfig.5.1	Interface to generate Gutenprint PPD files, used by CUPS
cups-genppdupdate.5.1	Updates Gutenprint PPD files
cupsaddsmb	Exports printers to Samba for Windows clients
cupsctl	Used to set or obtain configuration values in the */private/etc/cupsd.conf* file
cupsdisable/cupsenable	Used to stop/start printers and classes

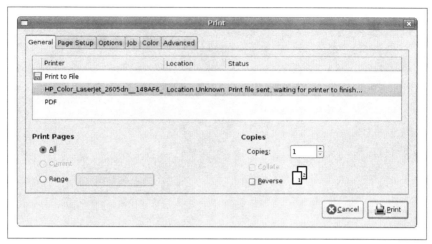

Figure 6-17. Printing to your Macintosh's shared printer from Ubuntu Linux

Command	Description
cupsfilter	Used as a frontend to CUPS filters to convert files to various formats (the default format is PDF)
cupstestdsc	Tests the conformance of PostScript files to the Adobe PostScript Language Structuring Conventions Specification V. 3.0
cupstestppd	Tests the conformance of PostScript files to the Adobe PostScript Description file format V. 4.3
lp	Used to submit and alter print jobs
lpadmin	Configures CUPS printer and class queues
lpq	Used to display the printer queue
lpr	Used to send a file to a printer
lprm	Used to remove (or cancel) a print job
lpstat	Displays the CUPS status of jobs, classes, and printers

Open Source Printer Drivers

A couple of open source projects offer printer drivers for many printer models. One of these, Gutenprint, is included with recent versions of Mac OS X. The other, HPIJS, is available as a separate download.

Gutenprint

Gutenprint (*http://gimp-print.sourceforge.net*), formerly known as Gimp-Print, is a package of printer drivers that is bundled with Mac OS X. The Gutenprint drivers support printers from Epson, Canon, Lexmark, HP, and other manufacturers. In many cases, drivers for these printers are not available from the printer manufacturers themselves. Even if drivers are available, the Gutenprint drivers are often of better quality than those offered by the manufacturers.

 If you are using a version of Mac OS X prior to 10.3 (Panther), you'll need to download the drivers from the Gutenprint website (*http://gimp-print.sourceforge.net/MacOSX.php3*).

The HP InkJet Server (HPIJS) Project

The Hewlett-Packard InkJet Server (HPIJS) Project is a collection of drivers from Hewlett-Packard that has been released as open source software. Although HPIJS was originally released for Linux, it has been ported to Mac OS X (*http://www.linux-foundation.org/en/OpenPrinting/MacOSX/hpijs*). HPIJS supports over 600 Hewlett-Packard printer models.

If you find both a Gutenprint driver and an HPIJS driver for your printer, we suggest that you try both and compare the quality.

CHAPTER 7

The X Window System and VNC

Although the X in "Mac OS X" is not the same X as in "the X Window System," you can get them to play nicely together.

Most Unix systems use the X Window System as their default GUI. (We'll refer to the X Window System as *X11* instead of *X*, to avoid confusion with Mac OS X.) X11 includes development tools and libraries for creating graphical applications for Unix-based systems. Mac OS X does not use X11 as its GUI; it relies instead on the Quartz Compositor, which manages all onscreen activity, including the windowing environment. However, Apple's own implementation of X11 for Mac OS X, based on the X.Org Foundation's open source X11 (*http://www.x.org*), is bundled with Mac OS X. (In Mac OS X 10.4 Tiger, X11 was not installed by default, although it was available as an optional installation on the Mac OS X install media.) Apple also provides an X11 software development kit (the X11 SDK) that is installed along with the Xcode tools (it is a component of the Unix Development Support package, which is selected by default during the Xcode installation).

This chapter highlights some of the key features of Apple's X11 distribution and explains how to use X11 in both the rootless and full-screen modes. You'll also learn how to connect to other X Window systems using Virtual Network Computing (VNC), as well as how to remotely control the Mac OS X desktop from remote X11 systems.

About Apple's X11

As noted earlier, Apple's X11 distribution is based on the open source X.Org Foundation codebase, X11R7.x. (Pre-Leopard Mac OS X releases based their X11 implementations on the open source XFree86 codebase.) Apple's X11 package has been optimized for Mac OS X and offers the following features:

- The X11R7.2 window server
- Support for the RandR (Resize and Rotate) extension
- Strong integration with the Mac OS X environment
- A Quartz window manager that provides Aqua window decorations, the ability to minimize windows to the Dock, and pasteboard integration
- The ability to use other window managers
- Compatibility with Exposé
- Compatibility with Spaces
- *launchd* integration
- Support for rootless and full-screen modes
- A customizable Application menu, which allows you to add applications for easy launching and to map keyboard shortcuts
- A customizable Dock menu, which allows you to add applications for easy launching, to map keyboard shortcuts, and to list all open windows
- Finder integration, which supports autodetection of X11 binaries and double-clicking to launch X11 binaries, starting the X server if it is not already running
- Preference settings for the system color map, key equivalents, system alerts, keyboard mappings, and multibutton mouse emulation
- Hardware acceleration support for OpenGL (GLX) and Direct CG (AIPI)

At the time of this writing, however, Apple's X11 package is somewhat buggy; some features, such as full-screen mode, simply do not work at all. The best way to stay ahead of the shortcomings is to use Apple's bleeding-edge version, which is available for free download at *http://trac.macosforge.org/projects/xquartz/*.

MacOSXHints maintains an excellent FAQ on X11 and Leopard at *http://forums.macosxhints.com/showthread.php?t=80171*.

Installing X11

Apple's X11 for Mac OS X is installed by default in Mac OS X 10.5 Leopard (if you so desire, you can customize your installation and deselect it). It's also available in Tiger but is not selected by default, so Tiger users will need to perform a customized installation of Mac OS X or install the package from the original installation discs.

Once you've installed X11, you'll find an application named X11 in the */Applications/Utilities* folder. If you're going to build X11-based applications, you'll also need to install the Xcode tools; this installation includes the *X11SDK* package by default. To install the Xcode tools, insert the Mac OS X Install DVD, open the *Optional Installs* folder, then open the *Xcode Tools* folder. Find *XcodeTools.mpkg* and double-click it to begin the installation process.

If you opted out of installing the X11 SDK when you installed the Xcode tools, you can install it now by inserting the Mac OS X Install DVD, opening the *Xcode Tools* folder, then opening the *Packages* folder. There, you will find the *X11SDK.pkg* installer. Double-click it to begin the installation of *X11SDK*. Instructions for building X11 applications are included in Chapter 10; this chapter focuses on using X11.

 Though double-clicking the X11 application in the */Applications/Utilities* folder starts X11 and opens an *xterm* window, it is generally unnecessary to do that to start X11-based applications. X11 is launched automatically whenever is it's needed, thanks to its *launchd* support.

Running X11

To launch the X server, just start any X11-based application. For example, you can just enter the command *xterm &* in a Terminal window; an *xterm* window (which looks similar to a Mac OS X Terminal window) will open, sporting Aqua-like buttons for closing, minimizing, and maximizing the window. X11 windows minimize to the Dock, just like other Aqua windows. Figure 7-1 shows a Terminal window and an *xterm* window side-by-side.

 Avoid setting the DISPLAY environment variable; it's set automatically by *launchd*, even before you launch any X11-based applications.

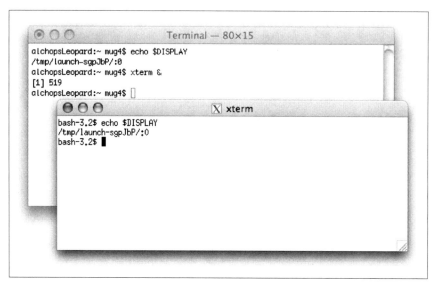

Figure 7-1. A Terminal window and an xterm window sporting the Aqua look

If you're using the default configuration, you'll notice three obvious differences from a Terminal window. In particular:

- The *xterm* window has a title bar that reads simply "xterm."
- The *xterm* window does not have vertical or horizontal scrollbars.
- The *xterm* window does not support tabs.

A less obvious difference between a Terminal window and an X11 *xterm* window is that Control-clicking in an *xterm* window does not invoke the same contextual menu that it does in a Terminal window. Control-clicking, Control-Option-clicking, and Control-⌘-clicking in an *xterm* window instead invokes the *xterm*-specific contextual menus shown in Figures 7-2, 7-3, and 7-4. (If you have a one-button mouse, you'll need to enable "Emulate three button mouse" under X11→Preferences→Input for this to work.)

Mac OS X emulates right-mouse-button clicks with Control-clicks. In X11, you can configure key combinations that simulate clicking the buttons on two- and three-button mice.

With "Emulate three button mouse" enabled, Option-clicking simulates clicking the middle mouse button, and ⌘-clicking simulates clicking the right mouse button. You can use X11→Preferences to enable or disable this option, but you cannot change which key combinations are used (although you can use *xmodmap* as you would under any other X11 system to remap pointer buttons).

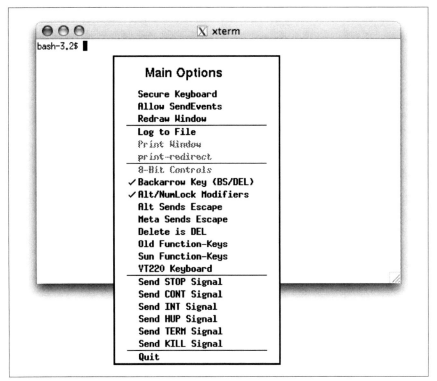

Figure 7-2. Control-clicking (or Control-left-clicking) in an xterm window

If you have a three-button mouse, Control-clicking with the right mouse button does the same thing as Control-⌘-clicking, Control-clicking with the middle button does the same thing as Control-Option-clicking, and Control-clicking with the left button does the same as Control-clicking with a single-button mouse.

You can use MacPorts or Fink to install an *xterm* replacement such as *rxvt* or *eterm*. See Chapter 12 for more information on Fink and Chapter 13 for more information on MacPorts.

Customizing X11

You can customize a number of things in X11. For example, you can customize your *xterm* window, set X11 application preferences, customize the X11 application and Dock menus, and specify which window manager to use.

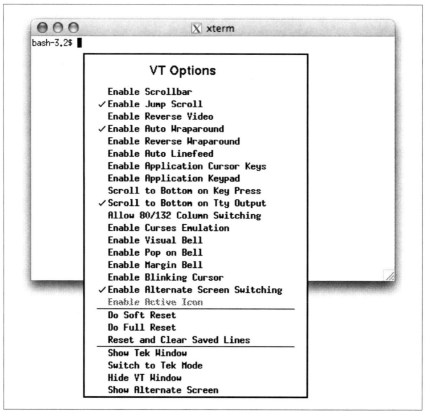

Figure 7-3. Control-Option-clicking (or Control-middle-clicking) in an xterm window

Dot-Files, Desktops, and Window Managers

To customize X11, you can create an *.xinitrc* script in your home directory. A sample *.xinitrc* script is provided in */usr/X11/lib/X11/xinit/xinitrc*.

Using the script as a starting point, you can specify which X11-based applications to start when X11 is launched, including which window manager you'd like to use as your default. The default window manager for X11 is Quartz (*quartz-wm*). The tab window manager (*twm*) is also bundled with X11, but many other window managers are available, along with additional desktop environments (DTEs), through Fink and MacPorts (see Chapters 12 and 13, respectively). If you're going to use your own *.xinitrc* file and want to use the Quartz window manager, make sure you start it by putting this command in the file:

```
exec quartz-wm
```

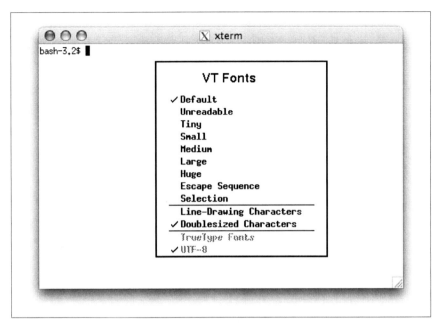

Figure 7-4. Control-⌘-clicking (or Control-right-clicking) in an xterm window

Once you've installed X11, you'll probably want to install additional X11 applications and window managers, and perhaps other DTEs. (Even if you are using Apple's window manager, you can still run most binaries from a different DTE, such as GNOME or KDE, without using that DTE as your desktop.) One of the easiest ways to install additional window managers is to use MacPorts. Table 7-1 lists some of the window managers and desktops offered by MacPorts. If you'd prefer, you can just as easily install additional window managers with Fink.

Table 7-1. Window managers available for MacPorts

Window manager/desktop	MacPorts package name
aewm	*aewm*
AfterStep	*afterstep*
awesome	*awesome*
Blackbox	*blackbox*
Enlightenment	*enlightenment*
evilwm	*evilwm*
fluxbox	*fluxbox*
FVWM	*fvwm, fvwm2*

Window manager/desktop	MacPorts package name
GNOME	gnome
IceWM	icewm
Ion	ion3
KDE	kde
Metacity	metacity
MWM	openmotif
Openbox	openbox
Oroborus	oroborus
ratpoison	ratpoison
Sawfish	sawfish
vtwm	vtwm
Window Maker	windowmaker
Window Manager Improved	wmii
Xfce	xfce

Fink has entire sections devoted to GNOME and KDE (*http://pdb.finkproject .org/pdb/*), where you will find extensive sets of libraries, utilities, and plugins. Also included in the GNOME section are GTK+, *glib*, and Glade. Installing GNOME and KDE may be especially useful if you want to develop software for these desktops.

Fink installs everything in its */sw* directory, and MacPorts installs everything in */opt/local*. If you've installed Fink or MacPorts according to its instructions, the installation location is automatically added to your command path. Otherwise, you may need to specify the full path in your *.xinitrc*.

You can customize the *xterm* window in Apple's X11 in the same way you would customize *xterm* on any other system running X11. You can, for example, set resources in an *.Xdefaults* file in your home directory or use escape sequences to set the title bar text (see "Customizing the Terminal on the Fly" in Chapter 1).

X11 Preferences, Applications Menu, and Dock Menu

You can also customize your X11 environment by setting X11's preferences via the X11→Preferences window (⌘-,) and adding programs to its Application menu. X11's Preferences are organized into three categories: Input, Output, and Security.

Input

The following options are used for controlling how X11 interacts with input devices:

Emulate three-button mouse
> Determines whether Option-clicking and ⌘-clicking mimic clicking the middle and right buttons on a three-button mouse.

Follow system keyboard layout
> Allows input menu changes to overwrite the current X11 keymap.

Enable keyboard shortcuts under X11
> Enables menu bar key equivalents, which may interfere with X11 applications that use the Meta modifier. This option is checked by default.

Output

The following options are used for configuring X11's look and feel:

Colors
> This pop-up menu offers the following options:
> - From Display
> - 256 Colors
> - Thousands
> - Millions
>
> By default, the Colors pop up is set to "From Display." If you change this setting to something else, you will need to relaunch X11 for the change to take effect.

Full-screen mode
> This option controls whether X11 runs in rootless (the default) or full-screen mode. See the sidebar "Full-Screen X11" for details on these modes.

Full-Screen X11

X11 can be run in two modes, *full screen* or *rootless* (the default). Both of these modes run side-by-side with Aqua, although full-screen mode hides the Finder and Mac OS X's desktop. (To hide X11 and return to the Finder, press Option-⌘-A.)

In rootless mode, X11 applications appear in their own windows on your Mac OS X desktop. In full-screen mode, X11 takes over the entire screen. This mode is suitable for running an X11 desktop environment such as GNOME, KDE, or Xfce. If you want to run X11 in full-screen mode, you'll

---

have to enable this option in X11's Preferences by selecting the "Full-screen mode" checkbox on the Output tab. (At the time of this writing, however, full-screen mode doesn't work in Leopard.)

Use system alert sounds

Determines whether X11's beeps use the system alert sound, as specified in the Sound Effects preference pane (System Preferences→Sound→Sound Effects). If this option is left unchecked, X11 windows use the standard Unix system beep to sound an alert.

Security

The following options are used for configuring X11's security:

Authenticate connections

When this option is checked (the default), Xauthority access-control keys are created when X11 is launched.

Allow connections from network clients

When this option is checked (the default), connections from remote applications are allowed. If it's unchecked, such connections are not allowed. (If this option is checked, be sure to also enable "Authenticate connections" to ensure security.)

Customizing X11's Applications menu

X11's Applications menu can be used to quickly launch X11 applications, so you don't have to enter their command paths. You can add other X11 applications to this menu and assign them keyboard shortcuts by selecting Applications→Customize to bring up the X11 Application Menu dialog window, shown in Figure 7-5.

You can also open the X11 Application Menu window by Control-clicking X11's Dock icon while X11 is running and selecting Applications→Customize from the contextual menu. When you Control-click on X11's Dock icon, you'll see that the applications shown in Figure 7-5 are listed there as well. X11's contextual menu allows you to quickly launch other X11 applications and to switch between windows of currently running X11 applications.

X11-Based Applications and Libraries

You can use MacPorts (or Fink) to install many X11-based applications, such as the GNU Image Manipulation Program (GIMP), *xfig/transfig*, ImageMagick, *nedit*, and many others. Since MacPorts understands dependencies, installing some of these applications will cause MacPorts to first install

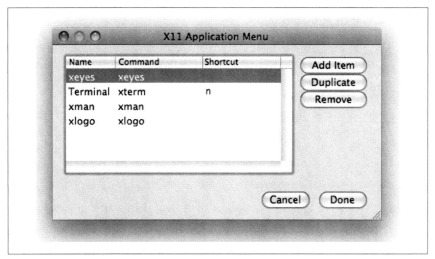

Figure 7-5. X11 Application Menu customization window

several other packages. For example, since the text editor *nedit* depends on Motif libraries, MacPorts will first install *openmotif*. (This also gives you the Motif window manager, *mwm*.) Similarly, when you install GIMP via Mac-Ports, you will also install the packages for many GNOME libraries, GTK+, and *glib*. Fink can be used in a similar manner.

You can also use Fink or MacPorts to install libraries directly. For example, the following command can be used to install the X11-based Qt libraries with Fink:

```
$ sudo fink install qt
```

An Aqua version of Qt for Mac OS X is available from Trolltech (*http://www .trolltech.com*). You can use MacPorts to install it with the following command:

```
$ sudo port install qt4-mac
```

However, Qt applications won't automatically use the library. Instead, you'll need to recompile and link the applications against the Aqua version of Qt, which may not always be a trivial task.

KDE and GNOME are both available for Mac OS X. MacPorts and Fink generally stay close to the most recent releases of GNOME. At the time of this writing, KDE3 has been ported and a port of KDE4 is, according to the "KDE on Mac OS X" website, close to reaching a stable stage. To keep abreast of developments pertaining to KDE on Mac OS X, see *http://techbase.kde.org/ index.php?title=Projects/KDE_on_Mac_OS_X* and *http://www.racoonfink .com/archives/cat_kde.html*.

X11 and the Rest of Mac OS X

X11-based applications rely on a different graphics system from Mac OS X, and even when running X11 in rootless mode, you would not necessarily expect to see GUI interactions run smoothly between these two graphics systems. But actually, there are several such interactions that run very well.

As one example, it is possible to open X11-based applications from the Terminal application. If you're running a pre-Leopard release of Mac OS X, you can use the *open* command to launch an X11-based application from the Terminal as follows:

```
$ open-x11 /usr/X11/bin/xeyes
```

Beginning with Leopard, it's even easier than that, thanks to the *launchd* support in Leopard's X11:

```
$ /usr/X11/bin/xeyes &
```

In Leopard, the X11 application is started automatically, whenever it's needed.

You can also copy and paste between X11 and Mac OS X applications. For example, to copy from an *xterm* window, select some text with your mouse and use the standard Macintosh keyboard shortcut to copy, ⌘-C. This places the selected text onto the clipboard. To paste the contents of the clipboard into a Mac OS X application (such as the Terminal), simply press ⌘-V.

To copy from a Mac OS X application, again highlight some text and press ⌘-C. You can paste the copied text into an *xterm* window by pressing the middle button of a three-button mouse or, if you've enabled the "Emulate three button mouse" option in X11's Preferences, by Option-clicking in the X11 application.

TKAqua

Though Tcl/Tk is included with Mac OS X, an Aqua-fied version of the scripting language, TKAqua, is available from *http://tcltkaqua.sourceforge.net*. Included in that distribution is a double-clickable Wish Shell, which is an application bundle.

Connecting to Other X Window Systems

You can connect from Mac OS X to other X Window systems using *ssh* with X11 forwarding. If you use OpenSSH (which is included with Mac OS X), you must use the -*X* (or -*Y*) option to request X11 forwarding. When used with the *ssh* command, the -2 option specifies the SSH version 2 protocol, as opposed to the older version 1 protocol. For example:

```
$ ssh -2 -X remotemachine -l username
```

This command can be entered either in an *xterm* window or in the Terminal. Beginning with Leopard, X11 does not have to be running when you enter this command. When the connection is made, X11 will be launched automatically. If you enter in the remote X11-based shell a command that launches an X11-based graphical application, that application will run on your Mac's Desktop. For example, suppose that in a Mac OS X Terminal window, you log into a Sun workstation running Solaris via SSH (as described earlier), and then in the Solaris shell running in the Terminal, you enter this command:

```
$ xclock &
```

This command will display the *xclock* application right on your Mac OS X Desktop. In pre-Leopard releases of Mac OS X, you had to launch the X11 application prior to making the X11 forwarding-enabled SSH connection.

It is also possible to create a double-clickable application that connects to a remote machine via SSH 2, with X11 forwarding enabled. You can use the following script for this purpose:

```
#!/bin/sh
/usr/X11/bin/xterm -e ssh -2 -X remotemachine -l username
```

If you've installed the commercial version of SSH from *http://www.ssh.com*, the equivalent of the preceding script is as follows:

```
#!/bin/sh
/usr/X11/bin/xterm -e ssh2 remotemachine -l username
```

 The X11 forwarding flag is +x with the commercial SSH, but it is enabled by default, so you do not need to include it in the command.

Using Apple's X11, you can add an item to the Applications menu to accomplish the same task. You can do this in at least two ways: for example, you can add the shell script to the X11 Applications menu, or you can add the *ssh* command itself to the menu. If you're going to add the script to the menu, start by saving the script to whatever you'd like to call the application. For instance, if you wanted to connect to a remote machine named *mrchops* with a username of *eer*, you might name the application *sshmrchops.sh* and save it as *~/bin/sshmrchops.sh*. Once you've saved the script, select Applications→Customize in X11 and click the Add button, as shown in Figure 7-6.

Figure 7-6 also shows the *sshmrchops.sh* script added under the name *sshmrchops.sh*, while the *ssh* command itself was added under the name *sshmrchops*. That's it! Now you're ready to launch the connection to the re-

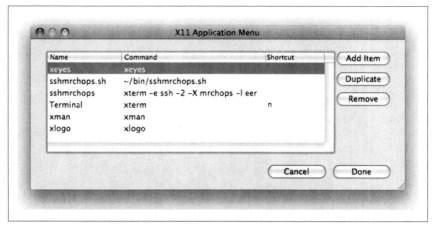

Figure 7-6. Adding items to the X11 Applications menu

mote machine via the menu bar and the Dock. Once you've connected to a machine running X11, you can start X11-based applications on the remote machine and display them on your Mac OS X machine.

You can also do the reverse (*ssh* to your Mac and run X11 applications on the Mac, but display them on the local machine), but first be sure to edit */etc/ sshd_config* and change this line:

```
#X11Forwarding no
```

to this:

```
X11Forwarding yes
```

 You'll also need to stop and restart Remote Login using System Preferences→Sharing for this change to take effect.

OSX2X

These days, it's fairly common to find a Mac sitting next to a Linux or Unix system running an X11-based desktop. In such situations, it would be convenient to be able to use only one keyboard and mouse to control all of your Mac OS X and X11-based desktops, saving valuable desktop space. Enter Michael Dales's free BSD-licensed application *osx2x* (*http://homepage.mac.com/ mdales/osx2x/*).

To use this handy little application, log into your Linux/Unix box running an X11 server, and enter this command:

```
$ xhost + mymachost
```

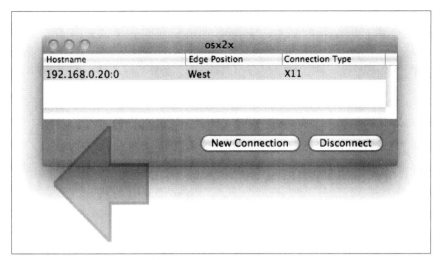

Figure 7-7. Controlling a neighboring X11 desktop with osx2x

Then, double-click the *osx2x* application to launch it, and when the main window appears, click New Connection. In the drop-down window that opens, supply the hostname or IP address of the Unix box running the X11 desktop in the Hostname field, followed by either :0 or :0.0 (without any spaces), as in *myhost*:0.0. Next, select the Edge Position (East, West, North, or South) and the Connection Type. This will generally be X11, but if you are connecting your Mac to a machine running a VNC server, as described in the next section (for example, another Mac), select VNC as the Connection Type rather than X11 and enter the VNC server password. You can switch back and forth between the Mac and the remote machine with ⌘-T, or you can enable edge detection and choose the position of your X11 system relative to your Mac. For example, if your Mac is to the right of your destination X11 machine, select West, as illustrated in Figure 7-7.

In addition to using one keyboard and mouse to control up to four systems, you can use *osx2x* to copy text from an X11 clipboard using ⌘-C and paste on the Mac OS X side using ⌘-V.

Virtual Network Computing (VNC)

One of the attractive features of Mac OS X is the ease with which you can integrate a Mac OS X system into a Unix environment consisting of multiple Unix workstations with X11-based GUIs. In the previous section, for example, we explained how to log into a remote Unix machine, launch an X11 application, and display the application on your Mac. The reverse process is also possible: you can log into a remote Mac OS X machine from another computer, launch an application on the remote Mac OS X machine, and have the application display on your local machine. The local machine, meanwhile, can be running the X Window System, Microsoft Windows, or any another platform supported by VNC.

VNC consists of two components:

- A VNC server, which must be installed on the remote machine
- A VNC viewer, which is used on the local machine to view and control applications running on the remote machine

The VNC connection is made through a TCP/IP connection.

In addition to being on different machines, the VNC server and viewer may be installed on different operating systems. This allows you, for example, to connect from Solaris to Mac OS X. In other words, using VNC you can launch and run both X11 and Aqua applications on Mac OS X but view and control them from your Solaris box.

Standard X11 Unix versions of VNC, which may be installed on Mac OS X via MacPorts or Fink, translate X11 calls into the VNC protocol. All you need on the client machine is a VNC viewer. Two attractive Mac-friendly alternatives to the strictly X11-based VNC server are the freeware *Vine Server* (*http://www .redstonesoftware.com/products/vine_server/*) and Apple's *AppleVNCServer*, which is bundled with Mac OS X. Mac OS X 10.5+ also comes bundled with a VNC viewer, *Screen Sharing*, which is located in */System/Library/CoreServi ces*. You can drag the Screen Sharing icon to the Dock for easy access.

Vine Server may be an attractive alternative to AppleVNC-Server for many users because it supports multiple VNC servers running on a single computer, each on a different port (making it possible for multiple users to connect to a single Mac at the same time). In such a scenario, fast user switching must be enabled, and each user must be logged in. To see more details, select Help→Vine Server from the application's menu bar and navigate to the Multiple Desktop Servers section described in Chapter 1.

Rather than interacting with your display, the standard Unix version of the VNC server intercepts and translates the X11 network protocol. (In fact, the Unix version of the server is based on the X.Org source code.) Applications that run under the Unix server are not displayed on the server's screen (unless you set the DISPLAY environment variable to :0.0, in which case the applications will be displayed only on the remote server, not on your VNC client).

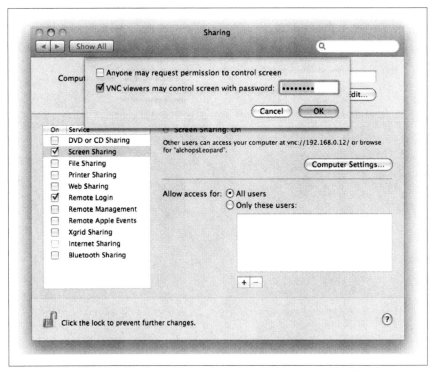

Figure 7-8. Allowing VNC control of your Mac in the Sharing System Preferences pane

Instead, the applications are displayed on an invisible X11 server that relays its virtual display to the VNC viewer on the client machine.

Vine Server and AppleVNCServer work in a similar manner, except they support the Mac OS X Aqua desktop instead of X11. With either Vine or AppleVNCServer running on your Mac OS X system, you can use a VNC client on another system—for example, a Unix system—to display and control your Mac OS X Aqua desktop. You can even tunnel these VNC connections (both X11 and Aqua) through SSH.

Launching VNC

If you want to share your Mac OS X desktop with another system, start the AppleVNCServer VNC server on your Mac by enabling Screen Sharing (select System Preferences→Sharing and select Screen Sharing). Then, while Screen Sharing is selected, click the Computer Settings button to set a password for VNC viewers to control the screen of your Mac, as shown in Figure 7-8. (More information on configuring these settings can be found in Chapter 15.)

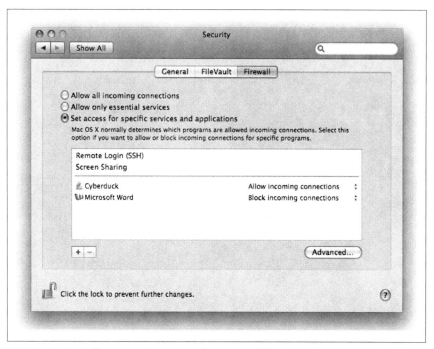

Figure 7-9. Firewall setting in System Preferences to allow (VNC) screen sharing

The AppleVNCServer will listen for incoming connections on port 5900, and the firewall will be adjusted automatically to allow the screen sharing, as shown in Figure 7-9.

You can also run a VNC server that allows users to log into an X11-based desktop. If you have installed another VNC server (for example, TightVNC, described in the next section) on your Mac OS X system via MacPorts—or on any Unix system, for that matter—you can start the VNC server by issuing the following command:

```
$ vncserver
```

If you don't have physical access to the system on which you want to run the VNC server, you can log into it remotely and then enter this command before logging out:

```
$ nohup vncserver
```

vncserver starts the VNC server, and *nohup* makes sure that it continues to run after you log out.

In either case, the first time you start *vncserver*, you'll need to supply a password, which you'll need anyway when connecting from a remote machine. (This password can be changed using the command *vncpasswd*.) You can run several servers; each server is identified by its hostname with a *:number* appended. For example, if you start the VNC server twice on a machine named *abbott*, the first server will be identified as *abbott:1* and the second as *abbott: 2*. You'll need to supply the numerical identifier when you connect from a client machine.

By default the VNC server runs *twm*, so when you connect, you will see an X11 desktop instead of Mac OS X's desktop. You can specify a different window manager in *~/.vnc/xstartup*. To terminate the VNC server, use the following command syntax:

```
$ vncserver -kill :display
```

For example, to terminate *abbott:1*, you would issue the following command while logged into *abbott* as the user who started the VNC server:

```
$ vncserver -kill :1
```

 If you're going to run an alternative VNC server, such as TightVNC, you should either disable the built-in Mac OS X AppleVNCServer or run the alternative server using a port number other than 5900.

VNC and SSH

In general, VNC passwords and network traffic are sent over the wire as plain text. However, you can use SSH with VNC to encrypt this traffic.

There is a derivative of VNC called TightVNC (*http://www.tightvnc.com*) that is optimized for bandwidth conservation. (If you've installed MacPorts, you can install TightVNC with the command *sudo port install tightvnc*.) Although TightVNC also offers encryption of passwords, in the TightVNC website's FAQ, the developers recommend tunneling your VNC connection through SSH for better security.

 If you use AppleVNCServer on a remote Mac running Leopard, and Screen Sharing on a local Mac also running Leopard, you can select to encrypt all data in the Screen Sharing VNC viewer by selecting Preferences→Encrypt all Network Data, or you can elect to "encrypt password and keystrokes only." These options work only when you use AppleVNCServer and Screen Sharing, with Leopard on both sides of the communication. If you use Apple's commercial Apple Remote Desktop (ARD) 3 (*http://www.apple.com/remotedesktop/*), the encryption of all data can be enabled even if you connect to a VNC server on Solaris or Linux, provided that the VNC server side is running *sshd*.

To illustrate how to tunnel your VNC connection through SSH, let's consider an example using a computer running Linux named *briansLinux* at IP 192.168.254.9 and a PowerBook named *alchops* running Mac OS X Leopard. In the following example, the VNC server is running on the Linux machine and the Screen Sharing VNC viewer is running on the Mac OS X machine. To display and control the remote Linux GNOME desktop on your local Mac OS X system, do the following:

1. Log into the Linux machine, *briansLinux*, via SSH if you need to log in remotely.

2. On *briansLinux*, enter the following command to start the VNC server on *display :1*:

   ```
   $ nohup vncserver :1
   ```

3. In your *~/.vnc* directory, edit the *xstartup* file so *gnome-session* starts when you connect to the VNC server with a VNC viewer. In particular, your *xstartup* file should look like this:

   ```
   #!/bin/sh
   xrdb $HOME/.Xresources
   xterm  -geometry 80x24+10+10 -ls -title "$VNCDESKTOP Desktop" &
   exec /usr/bin/gnome-session
   ```

4. Log out from the Linux box, *briansLinux*.

5. From a Terminal (or *xterm*) window on your Mac OS X machine, log into *briansLinux* via *ssh*:

   ```
   $ ssh -L 5902:127.0.0.1:5901 192.168.254.9
   ```

   You could add the *-N* option to the preceding command, if you just want to establish an SSH tunnel to *briansLinux* without opening a login shell window. Any references to *display :2* on your Mac will connect to the Linux machine's *display :1* through an SSH tunnel (*display :1* uses port 5901; *display :2* uses 5902). You may need to add the *-l* option to this command if your username on the Linux machine is different from the one you're using on your Mac OS X machine. For example, say your username on *briansLinux* is *brian*, but on *alchops* it's *eer*. In this case, you would need to issue the following command instead of the preceding one:

   ```
   $ ssh -L 5902:127.0.0.1:5901 192.168.254.9 -l brian
   ```

   Additionally, you may need to open ports through any firewalls you have running on the Linux machine. Open ports 5900–5904 for VNC and port 22 for *ssh*.

6. On your Mac, you can either start X11 or run *vncviewer* from the command line:

   ```
   $ vncviewer localhost:2
   ```

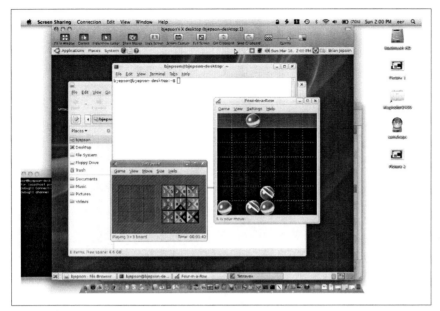

Figure 7-10. Screen Sharing VNC viewer displaying a remote Linux machine's GNOME desktop

You can also run an Aqua VNC client such as Leopard's built-in Screen Sharing, JollysFastVNC (*http://www.jinx.de/JollysFastVNC.html*), or Chicken of the VNC (*http://sourceforge.net/projects/cotvnc/*). For example, to run Screen Sharing, click on a Finder window to make it the frontmost window, select Go→Connect to Server, enter *vnc://localhost:5902* in the Server Address field in the "Connect to Server" window that appears, and then enter the VNC server password when prompted for it. Alternatively, you can enter *vnc://localhost:5902* as the URL in your web browser. Figure 7-10 shows a Screen Sharing VNC connection to a Linux GNOME desktop.

Connecting to the Mac OS X VNC Server

Before you connect to a Mac OS X machine via VNC, you'll need to make sure that it's running a VNC sever. As noted earlier, you have at least three options for VNC servers on Mac OS X: the built-in AppleVNCServer, Vine Server, and an X11-based VNC server.

X11-based VNC servers

Establishing an SSH-tunneled VNC connection from the Aqua desktop on a Mac to another Mac's X11 desktop is no different from connecting a Mac to

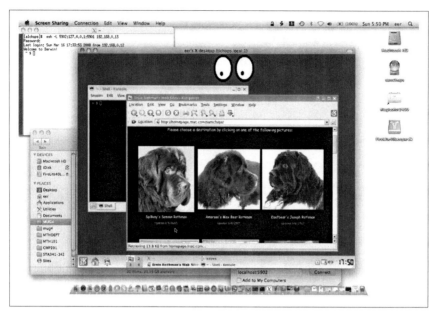

Figure 7-11. Screen Sharing VNC viewer displaying a remote Mac's KDE desktop

any other X11 desktop. Figure 7-11 shows a Screen Sharing client on Leopard displaying a full-screen X11-based KDE desktop running on a remote Mac OS X machine through a VNC connection, which was tunneled through SSH. The remote Mac is running TightVNC's server and the X11-based KDE window manager, both installed with MacPorts.

Aqua-based VNC servers

The easiest way to run an Aqua-based VNC server in Mac OS X is to enable the built-in AppleVNCServer via System Preferences, as noted earlier. If you're running Leopard both on your local and remote Macs, thanks to Bonjour (Apple's implementation of Zeroconf/Rendezvous) the remote Mac will show up in the Shared section of the Finder sidebar, as shown in Figure 7-12. (In fact, any computers on the network that broadcast their open VNC connectivity via Zeroconf will show up there.)

To connect to the remote Mac OS X machine, simply select it from the Shared list in the Finder sidebar, then click the Share Screen button in the upper-right part of the Finder window to launch the Screen Sharing VNC viewer on your local Mac. The VNC session will be fully encrypted if you've selected "Encrypt all data" in the Screen Sharing Preferences pane.

If, on the other hand, you prefer to use one of the other Mac OS X VNC viewers —for example, JollysFastVNC or Chicken of the VNC—you'll need to tunnel

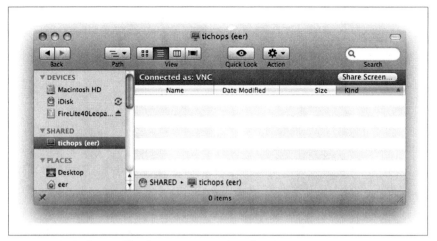

Figure 7-12. Finder window showing Bonjour-broadcast Mac running a VNC server

the connection through SSH to establish a secure VNC connection. The SSH tunneling works with the Screen Sharing application, too. Additional Mac OS X viewers can be found on Version Tracker or MacUpdate (*http://www.ver siontracker.com/macosx/* or *http://www.macupdate.com*) by searching for "VNC," while VNC and TightVNC provide viewers for Unix systems. Each VNC viewer can be used to display and control the Mac OS X client machines, and can do so through SSH tunnels.

To illustrate this process, let's do the reverse of what we did in our last example; let's make an SSH-secured connection from a Solaris machine to a Mac OS X machine running the VNC server. Let's assume that the name of the Solaris machine is *mrchops* and the Mac OS X machine has a hostname of *alchops*:

1. On *alchops*, start the built-in AppleVNCServer (which, as noted earlier, listens for VNC connections on port 5900).

2. On the Solaris machine, *mrchops*, enter:

   ```
   $ ssh -L 5902:localhost:5900 alchops
   ```

3. Then, in another *xterm* window on *mrchops*, enter:

   ```
   $ vncviewer -depth 24 -truecolor localhost:2
   ```

You can control the Mac OS X desktop from the SUN Solaris machine, but the image quality of the Mac OS X desktop may be poor unless you invoke the *vncviewer* with the options *-depth 24 -truecolor*. The resulting VNC connection is shown in Figure 7-13.

Vine Server, also known as *OSXvnc-server*, is an alternative Aqua-based VNC server freely provided by Redstone Software. To install Vine Server, download

Figure 7-13. Mac OS X desktop displayed and controlled on a Solaris GNOME desktop

the *Vine.dmg* file from the Redstone Software website (*http://www.redstone software.com/products/vine_server/*), locate and double-click the downloa-ded *.dmg* file in the Finder to mount the disk image, and drag the Vine Server icon to a convenient location, such as the */Applications* folder. (The disk image also contains a commercial VNC viewer, Vine Viewer, which you do not have to install for Vine Server to work.)

To launch Vine Server, double-click its icon in the Finder. When you launch it for the first time, you'll be prompted to configure the Firewall to either allow or deny Vine Server permission to accept incoming connections. If you click the Allow button, the firewall will be adjusted to allow such incoming con-nections both for the GUI VNC Vine Server and the command-line *OSXvnc-server*. If you click the Deny button, the firewall will be adjusted to deny incoming connections to those VNC server applications. Either way, you can change the firewall setting later, either by selecting System Preferen-ces→Security in the Apple menu bar and clicking on the Firewall tab, or by selecting Help→Configure Firewall in Vine Server's menu bar, which opens the Security System Preferences pane, and then clicking on the Firewall tab. You can select the port that Vine Server uses to listen for VNC connections by

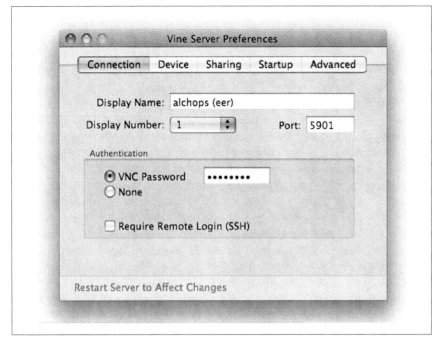

Figure 7-14. Vine Server connection preferences

selecting Vine Server→Preferences in the menu bar and clicking on the Connection tab. This is also where you can set the VNC password, as shown in Figure 7-14.

The command-line capability of Vine Server can be quite useful. For example, suppose you want to establish a VNC connection to a remote Mac on which no VNC server is running. In that case, you can log into the remote Mac via SSH (assuming Remote Login has been enabled on the remote Mac) and start the VNC server at the command line. For a list of command-line options, enter this command:

```
$ /Applications/Vine\ Server.app/Contents/MacOS/OSXvnc-server -help
```

Vine Server has several configuration options in its Preferences window. If you click the Device tab, you can select "Allow machine to sleep," "Allow display dimming," "Allow screen saver to start," and "Swap Mouse Buttons 2 and 3." You can also configure various keyboard settings on this tab.

On the Sharing preference pane, you can select "Disable remote control of keyboard and mouse," "Disable rich clipboard support (Vine Viewer Only)," "Advertise server via Bonjour," "Always allow multiple VNC connections," "Let viewers request exclusive access," and "Allow only one VNC connection at a time" (with the option to keep the existing viewer if a new viewer tries to connect).

In Vine Server's Startup preference pane, you can enable the options "Start server when Vine Server application is launched," "Stop server on a fast user switch," and "Restart server if it stops unexpectedly." Clicking the System Server button in Vine Server's Startup preference pane opens the System Server window, in which you can configure *OSXvnc-server* to start automatically when the machine boots. To do that, click the Start System Server button and authenticate yourself as an administrative user. In the System Server window, you can also set various connection preferences, such as the display name and number and the VNC password for the VNC server that will run automatically when the system boots. Configuring *OSXvnc-server* to start automatically when the system boots places *com.redstonesoftware.VineServer.plist* in */Library/LaunchAgents*. Subsequently, the *OSXvnc-server* application will start automatically when you boot up your Mac. If you decide later to disable this option, launch Vine Server, open its Startup preference pane, and click the System Server button; then, when the System Server window appears, click the Stop System Server button. After you authenticate yourself as an administrative user, the *com.redstonesoftware.VineServer.plist* item in */Library/LaunchAgents* will be deleted and *OSXvnc-server* will no longer start automatically when the system boots.

Finally, you can enter various command-line arguments and select the remote framebuffer (RFB) protocol in Vine Server's Advanced preference pane.

 You can run both Vine Server and AppleVNCServer on the same system, but since AppleVNCServer listens for clients on port 5900, you should avoid using this port for Vine Server. This rule applies for any alternate VNC server you might choose to run on your Mac.

VNC clients and servers are available for Windows machines, so Windows clients can connect to Mac OS X and other Unix VNC servers, and Mac OS X clients can connect to and control Windows VNC servers. Such VNC connections can also be tunneled through SSH (see *http://www.realvnc.com*). As an alternative to VNC, you can use Microsoft's free Remote Desktop Client (RDC, available at *http://www.microsoft.com/mac/downloads.mspx*) to remotely control a Windows desktop from a Mac OS X machine. An open source X11-based remote desktop client for Windows named *rdesktop* (*http://www .rdesktop.org*) is also available and can be installed with Fink or MacPorts.

Screen Sharing with iChat

We conclude this chapter by noting that, beginning with Leopard, Apple's instant messaging client (iChat) supports screen sharing via VNC connections. When you select in your iChat buddy list a buddy who has enabled Screen Sharing, you can click on the Screen Sharing icon at the bottom of the iChat buddy list window (shown in Figure 7-15) to either share your screen with that buddy or request to share that buddy's screen.

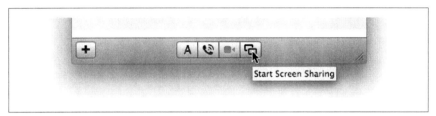

Figure 7-15. The Start Screen Sharing icon in iChat

Alternatively, you may select either of those screen-sharing options from iChat's menu bar, under Buddies. When you start Screen Sharing with a particular buddy via iChat, an audio chat is automatically initiated with that buddy.

Restarting VNC Connections

In case your VNC connection gets locked up while you're connecting to your Mac from a remote computer, you can set things up so that your VNC server will restart automatically. Just log into an administrator account remotely via *ssh*, and enter the following command:

```
$ sudo \
/System/Library/CoreServices/RemoteManagement/ARDAgent.app/Contents/\
Resources/kickstart -restart -agent
```

See Chapter 15 for more details on Screen Sharing and Mac OS X's built-in VNC capabilities.

## CHAPTER 8

Third-Party Tools and Applications

Although Mac OS X ships with an impressive number of applications—including Mail, Safari, the Address Book, iCal, iSync, Automator, and the Xcode tools, just to name a few—many third-party freeware and shareware applications are available to further enrich the Mac OS X experience. This chapter provides an overview of a few applications that we feel will appeal to Unix aficionados.

Frontends for SSH and SFTP

OpenSSH is a free version of the SSH suite of network connectivity tools that provides encrypted replacements for *telnet*, *ftp*, *rlogin*, *rcp*, and more. As noted earlier in the book, OpenSSH is bundled with Mac OS X. The SSH tools are fully functional from the command line, but several GUIs are available to make SSH-based file transfers easier. One such frontend that may be familiar to some Unix/Linux users is Brian Masney's GTK+/*glib*-based *gftp* (*http://www.gftp .org*). If you're a *gftp* fan, you can install it on Mac OS X using MacPorts. (Despite its name, *gftp* supports SFTP, a secure file transfer protocol that piggybacks on top of SSH.)

A cross-platform GUI SFTP application that will be familiar to most Microsoft Windows users is Filezilla (*http://www.filezilla-project.org*). Though it was designed for Windows, Filezilla has been ported to Linux and Mac OS X. Its capabilities are similar to those of some of the other GUIs we'll look at here, such as Cyberduck and Fugu.

The GUI SFTP application that will be most familiar to old-time Mac users is Fetch (*http://www.fetchsoftworks.com*). Fetch is also similar in capabilities to the other applications discussed here. Though it is shareware, it's free for educational users.

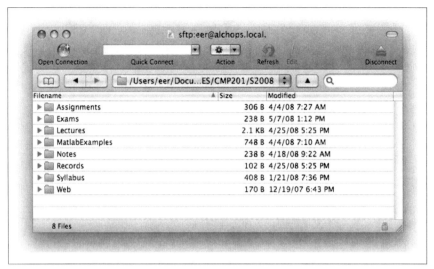

Figure 8-1. An sftp connection via Cyberduck

Cyberduck

Cyberduck, shown in Figure 8-1, is graphical user interface to *ftp* and *sftp*. It's available from *http://cyberduck.ch*.

Cyberduck has many useful features, including (but not limited to) support for all of the following:

- FTP and SFTP
- Dragging and dropping files on its interface to upload/download files
- Showing/hiding hidden files (i.e., files whose names begin with .)
- Directory upload
- Permissions, owner, and group modification
- Directory histories
- Moving, creating, and deleting remote files
- Keychain
- Bookmarks list for frequently visited hosts
- Bonjour

Fugu

Fugu (*http://rsug.itd.umich.edu/software/fugu/*) is a graphical interface to OpenSSH, developed and provided as freeware by the University of Michigan's

---

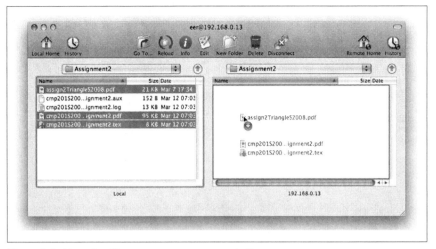

Figure 8-2. Dragging files to a remote computer in Fugu

Research Systems Unix Group. Fugu is shown in Figure 8-2. It has many useful features, including:

- Support for SFTP and SCP
- Support for SSH command-line options
- Ability to create SSH tunnels
- Ability to drag and drop files to upload/download
- External editor support
- Image previews
- Permissions, owner, and group modification
- Keychain support
- Bonjour support

SSH Agent

SSH Agent (*http://www.phil.uu.nl/~xges/ssh/*) is a GUI frontend to OpenSSH utilities provided with Mac OS X. You can use it to, among other things, start *ssh-agents*, generate identities, add identities to agents, and establish secure tunnels. Figure 8-3 illustrates using SSH Agent to set up an SSH tunnel in order to make a secure connection to a VNC server.

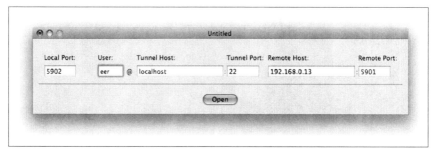

Figure 8-3. Setting up an SSH tunnel to a VNC server with SSH Agent

Starting with Mac OS X Leopard, Apple has integrated the OpenSSH *ssh-agent* into the operating system. If you have created an SSH key on the local machine using *ssh-keygen* and have configured your account on a remote server to use your public key, Mac OS X will allow you to use that key. The first time you attempt to connect to a host using public key authentication, you'll see a Mac OS X keychain access dialog asking for permission to use the key. Because your permission lasts across your entire login, you don't need to set up an *ssh-agent* process to manage this key.

For more information on *ssh-agent(1)*, see the manpage. To see how Mac OS X handles launching *ssh-agent* for you, check out the launch agent in */System/Library/LaunchAgents/ org.openbsd.ssh-agent.plist*. See Chapter 4 for more information on launch agents and launch daemons.

Mounting SSH Servers As Network Volumes

Linux users may be familiar with the versatile FUSE (*http://fuse.sourceforge .net*) mechanism for implementing filesystems in user space, which we introduced in Chapter 3. Google's MacFUSE (*http://code.google.com/p/macfuse/*) brings FUSE to Mac OS X 10.4 and above. Filesystems that are known to work with MacFUSE include *sshfs*, *ntfs-3g*, *ftpfs*, *wdfs* (WebDAV), *cryptofs*, *encfs*, *bindfs*, *unionfs*, and *beaglefs*. MacFUSE includes an Objective-C framework (*/Library/Frameworks/MacFUSE.framework*) for filesystem development. We won't discuss filesystem development here, but we will discuss how to install MacFUSE and the *sshfs* filesystem, as well as how to use MacFUSE/*sshfs*.

The easiest way to install MacFUSE is to download the appropriate disk image (*.dmg*) file containing the MacFUSE Core package installer file from *http://code .google.com/p/macfuse/*. At the time of this writing, two versions are available: one for Mac OS X 10.4 and the other for Mac OS X 10.5. Once you've downloaded the *.dmg* file, double-click it to mount the disk image. Then, double-click the *.pkg* installer file that's revealed to install MacFUSE. If you decide to uninstall MacFUSE, you can run the included uninstall script. Use this command on Mac OS X 10.4:

```
$ sudo /System/Library/Filesystems/fusefs.fs/Support/\
uninstall-macfuse-core.sh
```

or this command on Mac OS X 10.5:

```
$ sudo /Library/Filesystems/fusefs.fs/Support/uninstall-macfuse-core.sh
```

Alternatively, you can install MacFUSE from source via MacPorts (see Chapter 13 for information on MacPorts).

After you've installed MacFUSE, you can install *sshfs* by downloading it from the MacFUSE website, mounting the downloaded disk image, and dragging the *sshfs.app* application to */Applications* in the Finder. (Alternatively, as with MacFUSE itself, you can install *sshfs* from source via MacPorts. You'll need to install *sshfs* first to get the command-line tool, and then you'll be able to install *sshfs-gui* to get the double-clickable *sshfs.app* application.)

The *sshfs.app* application available from the MacFUSE website also includes a command-line *sshfs* tool, *sshfs-static* (and *sshfs-static-10.5*). If you've installed *sshfs.app* in */Applications*, the command-line *sshfs* utility *will have the absolute pathname /Applications/sshfs.app/Contents/Resources/sshfs-static-10.5.*

You'll be able to run it by double-clicking its icon in the Finder, selecting File→Connect to SSH Server in the menu bar (or pressing ⌘-O), and entering the server name and your remote username in the dialog window that pops up. If the connection goes through, you'll be prompted for your remote password on the remote SSH server. Once the password is authenticated, you'll be able to open a Finder window showing the contents of the remote SSH server by selecting Go→Go to Folder in the Finder menu bar and entering the mount point of the *sshfs* filesystem (for example, */Volumes/192.168.0.12*). The remote filesystem will also show up in the output of a *df* command, as shown in Figure 8-4.

You can unmount the *sshfs* filesystem via the *umount* command. For example:

```
$ umount /Volumes/192.168.0.12
```

Assuming that you've either installed *sshfs* with MacPorts or installed it manually and adjusted your $PATH accordingly, the following sequence of commands illustrates how to mount a remote SSH server called *alchops.local* on a user-defined mount point ~*/alchops*:

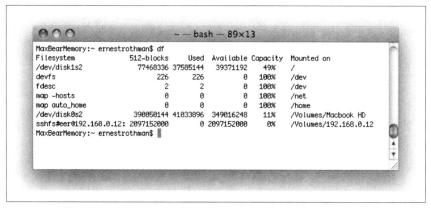

Figure 8-4. df command output revealing mounted sshfs filesystem

Figure 8-5. A remote SSH filesystem on the Desktop

```
$ cd
$ mkdir alchops
$ sshfs eer@alchops.local: alchops
```

After executing those commands, the *df* command reveals the *sshfs* filesystem mounted on *~/alchops* and the *sshfs* filesystem appears on the Desktop, as shown in Figure 8-5.

You can unmount the *sshfs* filesystem either via the usual *umount* command or by Control/right-clicking the SSH filesystem icon on the Desktop and selecting Eject in the contextual menu.

TeX

TeX was developed by computer scientist Donald Knuth as a special programming language used to typeset mathematical and scientific publications. LaTeX, developed by Leslie Lamport and subsequently further developed by Frank Mittelbach (among others), is essentially a rather large set of macros built on top of TeX.

The TeX Users Group (TUG) website, *http://www.tug.org*, contains an enormous amount of information on TeX-related projects and resources. The most comprehensive, and perhaps most popular, cross-platform distribution of TeX is TeX Live (*http://www.tug.org/texlive*). MacTeX (*http://www.tug.org/mac tex/*), an easy-to-install TeX system for Mac OS X, is based on TeX Live. In addition to installing a comprehensive TeX system, MacTeX also installs several Mac-specific TeX-related tools.

 The MacTeX website (*http://www.esm.psu.edu/mac-tex/*), maintained by Gary L. Gray and Joseph C. Slater, is devoted to tracking TeX developments for the Mac platform. This site is a must-visit if you're interested in using TeX on Mac OS X.

You can install TeX Live via MacPorts, but at the time of this writing Fink provides only teTeX (*http://www.tug.org/tetex*), a TeX distribution for Unix-compatible systems that is no longer being actively developed (it has been superseded by TeX Live). For more on Fink and MacPorts see Chapter 12 and Chapter 13, respectively.

In this section, we'll discuss how to install MacTeX and then briefly describe TeXShop, a graphical frontend to LaTeX. (TeXShop is actually more than a frontend; it provides a unified LaTeX environment, complete with editors and other tools.) We'll round out this section with an interesting TeX-related application, LaTeXiT, which allows you to easily use your LaTeX installation to add mathematical typesetting capabilities to applications such as Mail, iChat, and Keynote.

Installing MacTeX

To install MacTeX, first download the disk image containing the MacTeX package installer from *http://mirror.ctan.org/systems/mac/mactex/MacTeX .dmg*. Double-click the *.dmg* file to mount the virtual disk, and then double-click the *MacTeX-2007.mpkg* file in the virtual disk to install MacTeX. The installer installs the full version of TeX Live, including various TeX-related command-line utilities in */usr/local/texlive* and Ghostscript, ImageMagick, and PNG Library in appropriate subdirectories of */usr/local*. The MacTeX installer also installs several Mac-specific utilities in */Applications/TeX*, including TeX-Shop (*http://www.uoregon.edu/~koch/texshop/*), BibDesk (*http://bibdesk.sour ceforge.net*), Excalibur (*http://excalibur.sourceforge.net*), and LaTeXiT (*http:// ktd.club.fr/programmation/latexit_en.php*). You may want to visit the websites of those utilities to ensure that you have the most up-to-date versions.

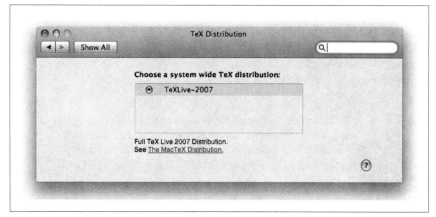

Figure 8-6. TeX Distribution System Preferences pane

The MacTeX installer installs Gerben Wierda's i-Installer in */Applications/Utilities*. According to the MacTeX website, the i-Installer utility cannot be used to update your MacTeX installation, but it can be used to maintain and update Ghostscript, ImageMagick, and Font Utilities, which the MacTeX installer installs from Gerben Wierda's TeX distribution. At the time of this writing, when you run the i-Installer utility, a pop-up message warning that i-Installer is "not supported" appears. The advice on the TeXShop website is to ignore that warning; it means only that you should not expect email support and that i-Installer comes with no guarantees.

The MacTeX installer also installs a new System Preferences pane, shown in Figure 8-6, in which you can select your preferred TeX engine if you have more than one TeX distribution installed on your system. This is useful, for example, if you install a new version of MacTeX (which, in 2008, will show up in the preference pane as TeXLive-2008) but want to revert to the older version. You can select your preferred distribution from those available in the preference pane.

The MacTeX installer additionally installs various configuration files in */Library/TeX*; adds a symbolic link, */usr/texbin*, to */Library/TeX/Distributions*; and adds */usr/texbin* and */Library/TeX/Distributions/.DefaultTeX/Contents/Man* to the `PATH` and `MANPATH` environment variables, respectively. Local system modifications—for example, addition of new LaTeX packages (i.e., **.sty* files)—can be made to */usr/local/texlive/texmf-local*. Changes can also be made on a per-user basis by modifying *~/Library/texmf* in accordance with TeX conventions. If you subsequently upgrade your LaTeX installation with i-Installer, these local modifications are not affected. The MacTeX search order for files is:

1. *~/Library/texmf*
2. */usr/local/texlive/texmf-local*
3. */Library/TeX/Root/texmf*

If you need to change the paper size of your TeX documents, you can do so with the *texconfig-sys* command (see its manpage for details).

Once the installation and configuration of MacTeX is complete, you can run *latex* (or *pdflatex*) from the command line. However, even the most hardcore command-line fanatics may find the available Aqua-based interfaces enticing.

TeXShop

As noted earlier, TeXShop is installed automatically in */Applications/TeX* when you install MacTeX. If a newer version of TeXShop becomes available, you can easily replace the one that was installed by MacTeX: just download the *TeXShop.dmg* file from the TeXShop website (*http://darkwing.uoregon.edu/~koch/texshop/texshop.html*), mount the disk image by double-clicking on it, and then drag the TeXShop application to your */Applications/TeX* folder to replace the older version.

TeXShop includes a specialized editor with syntax highlighting, LaTeX macros accessible from a toolbar menu, and a previewer. The LaTeX macros can be used to insert LaTeX code into your documents.

By default, TeXShop uses *pdftex* and *pdflatex* (part of the standard MacTeX distribution) to produce output in PDF instead of the more traditionally used Device Independent (DVI) format. Figure 8-7 shows TeXShop's previewer.

Among its many useful features, TeXShop supports AppleScript and is highly configurable. For example, you can configure the LaTeX Panel, autocompletion, the keyboard menu shortcuts, and the Macro menu. These user-level configurations are written to *.plist* files stored in *~/Library/TeXShop*: *completion.plist*, *autocompletion.plist*, *KeyEquivalents.plist*, and *Macros.plist*. If you add your own templates to the *~/Library/TeXShop/Templates* folder, they'll show up in the TeXShop editor's Templates drop-down menu. Figure 8-8 shows TeXShop's Macro Editor, which can be opened from the Macros toolbar (Macros→Open Macro Editor).

Select Window→LaTeX Panel to open the LaTeX Panel, shown in Figure 8-9.

Similarly, to open the Matrix Panel, shown in Figure 8-10, select Window→Matrix Panel.

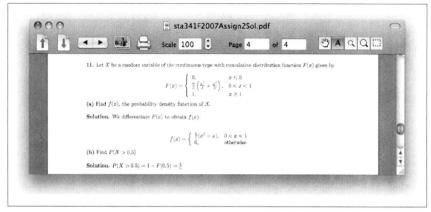

Figure 8-7. TeXShop's built-in previewer

The LaTeX and Matrix Panels make it simple to insert LaTeX code, so you won't have to embark on an Internet search for how to code various things in LaTeX. They can also save you quite a bit of typing.

TeXShop (together with the MacTeX-installed TeX Live distribution) provides a highly customizable, complete, and unified TeX environment that is nicely integrated for Mac OS X.

An open source X11-based WYSIWYM (What You See Is What You Mean) document processor, LyX (*http://www.lyx.org*), uses your TeX system as a rendering engine and runs on most Unix/Linux systems, Windows OS/2, and Mac OS X. There are essentially two versions of LyX: one built on *xforms* and another on *Qt*. Thanks to Qt/Mac (*http://trolltech.com/developer/downloads/qt/mac/*), an Aqua-native port of LyX named LyX/Mac (*http://wiki.lyx.org/Mac/*) is available as a self-installing binary. To run LyX/Mac, however, you must first install a TeX distribution such as MacTeX.

Two alternatives to TeXShop that are worth considering are iTeXMac (*http://itexmac.sourceforge.net*) and the cross-platform Texmaker (*http://www.xm1math.net/texmaker/*). Both of these applications are free and have capabilities similar to TeXShop's.

LaTeXiT

Though you can use LaTeX to generate complete documents, you can also use it just to generate equations within other documents. For example, suppose you need to use Microsoft Word (or OpenOffice.org) to create a document, but you don't get along with the equation editor that comes bundled with the

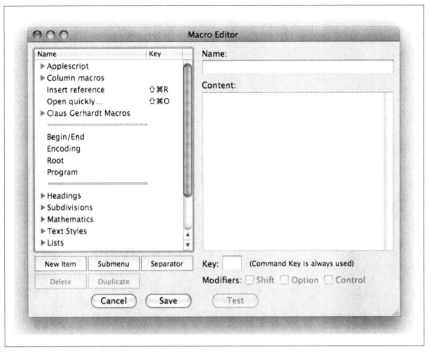

Figure 8-8. TeXShop's Macro Editor

product. If you're comfortable with LaTeX, you'll be happy to know about LaTeXiT, which works by creating small image files of equations from user-supplied LaTeX code. Once created, the image files can simply be dragged and dropped onto the appropriate locations in the given Office document. For example, to create an image file for inclusion in a Word document, you can enter the LaTeX code in the lower part of LaTeXiT window, click on the appropriate button (Eqnarray, Display, Inline, or Text), and then drag the resulting image from the top part of the LaTeXiT window to the appropriate location in the Word document.

As noted earlier, LaTeXiT is installed automatically with MacTeX, but you can install it easily enough manually by downloading the *LaTeXiT_1.15.0.dmg* file, double-clicking it in the Finder, and dragging and dropping the *LaTeXiT* application file into your */Applications/TeX* folder. LaTeXiT uses your existing LaTeX installation, so you may need to configure LaTeXiT's LaTeX search path by selecting LaTeXiT→Preferences→Composition and entering the correct path to *pdflatex*. If you've installed MacTeX, it is unlikely that you will have to change the default path selections.

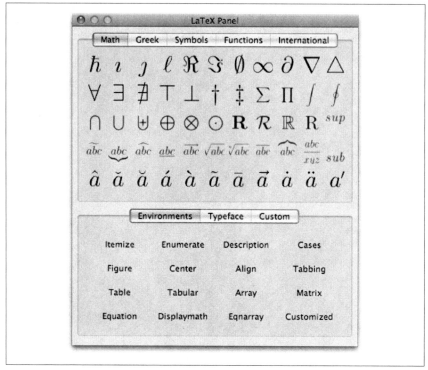

Figure 8-9. TeXShop's LaTeX Panel

To illustrate how LaTeXiT works, observe that this equation:

$$e^x = \sum_{k=0}^{\infty} \frac{x^k}{k!}$$

was created with LaTeXiT by clicking on the Inline button, as shown in Figure 8-11.

The following equation, on the other hand, was generated with the Display option:

$$e^x = \sum_{k=0}^{\infty} \frac{x^k}{k!}$$

Though the default image format is PDF, you can alternatively use LaTeXiT to produce PDFs with outlined fonts, as well as EPS, TIFF, PNG, and JPEG images. You can set several preferences in LaTeXiT, including the font size, text color, and background color of the typeset equations. LaTeXiT also comes

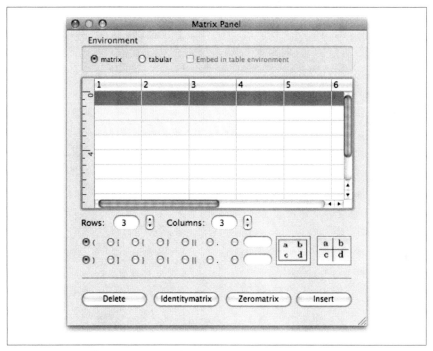

Figure 8-10. TeXShop's Matrix Panel

with several palettes, which can save you a Google search or a trip to your bookshelf for your LaTeX manual. Figure 8-12 shows the LaTeX palette.

One useful feature of Mac OS X is its Services menu and the many options programmers offer there. For example, Apple's Mail application allows you to select text in an email message and then select Mail→Services→Speech→Start Speaking Text to activate Mac OS X's speech synthesis component, which jumps into action and speaks the selected text back to you. LaTeXiT provides a Services menu selection to typeset LaTeX strings within other applications. To use LaTeXiT Services to typeset LaTeX within an application, highlight a LaTeX string in the application window and select from the application menu bar Services→LaTeXiT→Typeset LaTeX Maths. When it typesets the LaTeX code, LaTeXiT replaces it with an image file. Figure 8-13 shows an iChat message with an equation rendered by LaTeXiT.

At the time of this writing, the LaTeXiT Service works with the TextEdit application but does not work with Mac OS X Mail. Nevertheless, even if the LaTeXiT Service menu bar option does not work with a given application, you can still drag and drop the small image file produced in the LaTeXiT main window into the other application document.

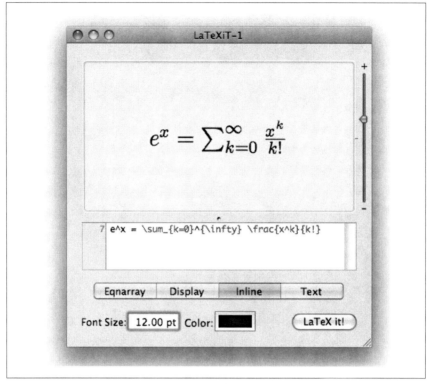

Figure 8-11. Generating mathematical image files with LaTeXiT

R with an Aqua GUI

The open source statistical computing package R is similar to Bell Laboratories's S statistical package. R runs on a variety of platforms, including most X11-based systems and Windows. Although an X11-based version of R can be installed with Fink or MacPorts, another port of R that supports both X11 and Quartz on Mac OS X, *R.app*, has been developed by Stefano M. Iacus and others associated with the R-Core/R-Foundation. A binary distribution of R for Mac OS X, among other systems, is distributed through the Comprehensive R Network (CRAN; *http://cran.r-project.org*).

The installer places an application named R in your */Applications* folder. It also places *R*, a symbolic link to */Library/Frameworks/R.framework/Resources/bin/R*, in */usr/bin*. Double-clicking the R icon opens an Aqua-based console window in which you can enter R commands, as shown in Figure 8-14.

Figure 8-15 shows an R graphics window containing a histogram.

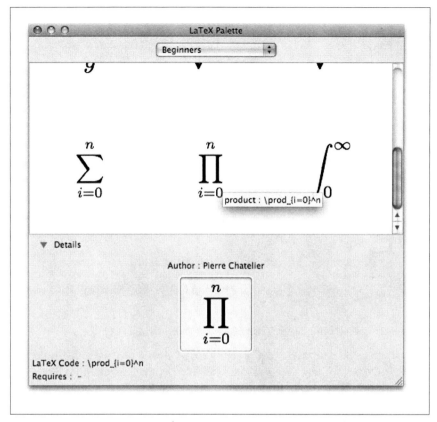

Figure 8-12. LaTeXiT's LaTeX palette

One of the features of R unique to its Mac OS X port is that it is AppleScript-able. Example 8-1 shows an AppleScript that instructs R to store some values in a variable x and display a histogram corresponding to those values.

Example 8-1. AppleScript to interact with R

```
try
    tell application "R"
    activate
        with timeout of 1000 seconds
            cmd "x = c(77, 79, 90, 69, 75, 73, 71, 69, 84)"
            cmd "hist(x)"
            cmd "hist(x,probability=TRUE)"
            cmd "rug(jitter(x))"
        end timeout
    end tell
end try
```

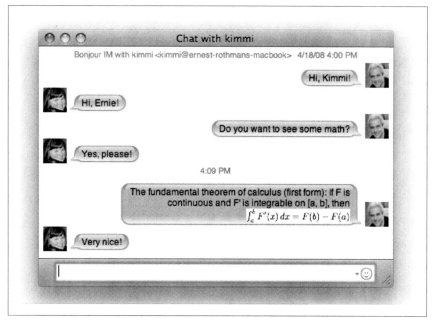

Figure 8-13. An iChat message with an equation rendered by LaTeXiT

You can use X11 graphics with R from the R console or from a Terminal (or *xterm*) window. To use X11 graphics from the R console, you must first enter X11() in the R console to start the X11 window server and open an X11-graphics device window. You can switch back to a Quartz-based graphics device by entering quartz() in the R console. If, on the other hand, you start R from a Terminal window, X11 will be the default graphics device, and thanks to Mac OS X's *launchd* support, an X11 graphics device window will open automatically when you enter a graphics command in R. Figure 8-16 shows the same histogram shown in Figure 8-15, but this time it's displayed in an X11 window.

This example was tested with Release R-2.7.0, which is the latest release available at the time of this writing. Be sure to consult the CRAN website for up-to-date information.

Open Source Replacements for Microsoft Office

OpenOffice.org (*http://www.openoffice.org*) is well known as a powerful and free alternative to the Microsoft Office productivity suite. OpenOffice.org in-

```
                          R Console

R version 2.7.0 (2008-04-22)
Copyright (C) 2008 The R Foundation for Statistical Computing
ISBN 3-900051-07-0

R is free software and comes with ABSOLUTELY NO WARRANTY.
You are welcome to redistribute it under certain conditions.
Type 'license()' or 'licence()' for distribution details.

  Natural language support but running in an English locale

R is a collaborative project with many contributors.
Type 'contributors()' for more information and
'citation()' on how to cite R or R packages in publications.

Type 'demo()' for some demos, 'help()' for on-line help, or
'help.start()' for an HTML browser interface to help.
Type 'q()' to quit R.

> x=scan()
1: 63.0 76.9 77.1 89.7 95.0 92.5 99.0 53.0 86.5 65.0 84.0 74.0 75.0 100.0
15: 77.0 83.0 83.0 99.0 87.0 91.0 72.0
22:
Read 21 items
> hist(x)
> hist(x,probability=TRUE)
> rug(jitter(x))
>
```

Figure 8-14. R's Aqua-based console

cludes the word processor Writer, the spreadsheet Calc, the presentation tool
Impress, and the drawing tool Draw. OpenOffice.org also includes a set of
database tools and a mathematical equation editor. Aside from providing a
powerful set of productivity tools, OpenOffice.org can import and export to
Microsoft Office documents, including those in *.docx* (Office 2007) format.

 Though WYSIWYG (What You See Is What You Get) applications like those in the Microsoft Office and OpenOffice.org
suites provide equation editors for including mathematical
equations in documents, they fall short of the capabilities of
the typesetting language and associated macros provided by
TeX distributions.

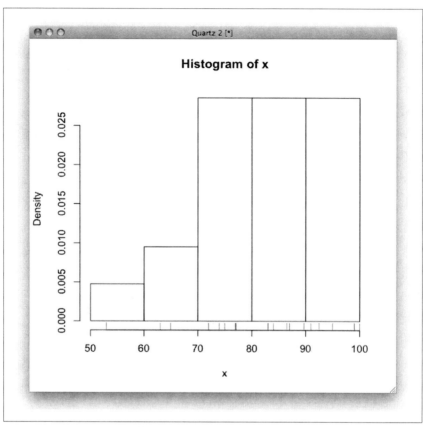

Figure 8-15. R's Quartz graphics window

At the time of this writing, OpenOffice.org provides a binary for the X11-based Mac OS X port of OpenOffice.org 2.4 at *http://download.openoffice.org/index .html*, while a binary for a beta release of the Aqua-based port of the upcoming OpenOffice.org 3.0 is available at *http://porting.openoffice.org/mac/download/ aqua.html*. The X11-based port is based on the latest official point-release of OpenOffice.org, and it looks the same on Mac OS X as it does on other X11-based platforms.

Additionally, the NeoOffice group (*http://www.neooffice.org*) provides a Carbon- and Java-based Mac OS X version of OpenOffice.org called NeoOffice. Though NeoOffice is usually based on a slightly older OpenOffice.org codebase (at the time of this writing, Release 2.2.x versus Release 2.4), it has better integration with Mac OS X and runs natively on the Mac as a Java application. Among other things, NeoOffice uses Mac OS X fonts, native printer drivers, and Mac OS X's menu bar, unlike the X11 version of OpenOffice.org.

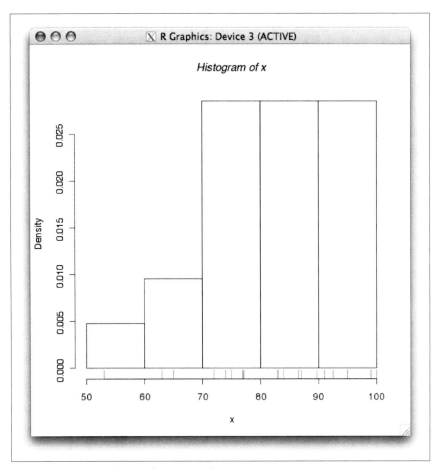

Figure 8-16. R's graphics window, X11 style

If you have the space on your hard drive, you can install both the X11-based OpenOffice.org and NeoOffice on the same system, but our experience has been better with NeoOffice. Figure 8-17 shows a Calc spreadsheet document in NeoOffice.

Video

Mac OS X ships with QuickTime Player, an application that supports several video formats, including MPEG and MPEG4. You can extend the variety of formats supported by QuickTime by downloading and installing the collection of video codecs from the Perian project (*http://www.perian.org*). Perian is a

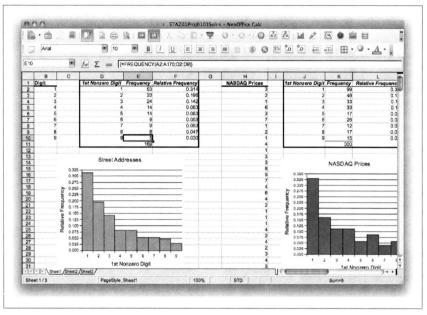

Figure 8-17. A NeoOffice Calc document

plug-in for QuickTime that supports over two dozen video formats, including DivX and Xvid.

Since QuickTime is unavailable for Unix- and Linux-based systems (other than Mac OS X), most Unix and Linux users are familiar with X11-based open source alternatives. In Mac OS X, you can install any of several X11-based open source applications for viewing video formats by using the MacPorts package manager (see Chapter 13). These applications will run under Apple's X11 environment. Also, some open source video applications have been ported to Mac OS X using Aqua, rather than relying on X11.

Open Source Video Players

MPlayer (*http://www.mplayerhq.hu*), an audio/video player popular among Linux/Unix users, can be installed to run on Mac OS X. This application is one of the many packages that the MacPorts project has ported to Mac OS X; it's also available as MPlayer OS X, a Mac OS X binary distribution with an Aqua GUI, at the MPlayer website.

Once you've downloaded and mounted the disk image, drag the MPlayer OS X application to your */Applications* folder, and then unmount and trash the

Figure 8-18. MPlayer OS X

disk image if you don't plan to install it anywhere else. That completes the installation.

To play videos with MPlayer OS X (shown in Figure 8-18), you can drag and drop a video file onto the MPlayer OS X icon in the Finder, or select a video from the MPlayer OS X menu bar by using File→Open.

Another popular open source, cross-platform multimedia player that has been ported to Mac OS X and sports an Aqua-native GUI is VLC (shown in Figure 8-19). VLC is distributed by the VideoLAN project (*http://www.videolan .org*) and supports a wide variety of video and audio formats. To play a video using VLC, either select File→Open from the menu bar or drag and drop the video file onto the VLC icon in the Finder.

These alternatives (MPlayer and VLC) support some formats that Apple's QuickTime Player does not. If you find that QuickTime does not support a particular file, you may want to try it with VLC or MPlayer OS X.

Figure 8-19. VLC

Image Editing

The GNU Image Manipulation Program, or GIMP (*http://www.gimp.org*), is one of the best-known open source image manipulation programs. You can get GIMP for Mac OS X from MacPorts (see Chapter 13), and you can use it to create drawings, touch up photographs, convert images, and do much more.

You can even use GIMP as iPhoto's default image editor. To do this, you first need to install *Gimp.app*, an application frontend for the X11 version of GIMP. You can either download it from *http://gimp-app.sourceforge.net/* or install it using MacPorts.

Next, go to iPhoto's Preferences window (iPhoto→Preferences or ⌘-,) and follow these steps:

1. In the Click section under General, select "in application" from the "Edit photo" drop-down menu. If you have already chosen an application (such as Adobe Photoshop), click that "in application name" (e.g., "in Adobe

Figure 8-20. Using GIMP as iPhoto's default editor

Photoshop CS2"), and you'll be prompted to select an application. If not, just click the Select button.

2. Navigate to the */Applications* folder and choose *Gimp* as the application.

3. Close the Preferences window (⌘-W).

You'll be able to use GIMP as your image-editing tool immediately by double-clicking on an image file. If you later return to iPhoto's Preferences and set the "Edit photo" option back to one of the options that opens images for editing in iPhoto, you'll still be able to use GIMP for that purpose by right-clicking or Control-clicking an image and selecting "edit in external editor" from the contextual menu. Figure 8-20 shows an iPhoto image being edited in GIMP.

A modified version of GIMP, CinePaint (*http://cinepaint.sourceforge.net*), was designed to meet the needs of film professionals. (It has been used in the *Harry Potter* movies, *Scooby Doo*, and other films.) CinePaint was originally known as Film GIMP, and an earlier version was available through Fink at the time of this writing. Check out the CinePaint website for the latest version.

3D Modeling

Blender (*http://www.blender.org*) is a popular cross-platform, open source, integrated 3D graphics package for modeling, animation, rendering, post-

Figure 8-21. Blender running on Mac OS X

production, real-time interactive 3D modeling, and game creation and play-back. A complete list of features can be found on Blender's website. In addition to source code, binaries are available for a variety of platforms, including Mac OS X.

To install Blender on Mac OS X, download the appropriate disk image from Blender's site and, after it has mounted, copy Blender to your /Applications folder. To run Blender, double-click its icon.

As you can see in Figure 8-21, the look and feel of Blender on Mac OS X is different from that of most standard Aqua applications. The reason is that OpenGL is used to draw Blender's interface.

Since Blender makes extensive use of OpenGL, you'll find that drawing images in large windows can be slow if your Mac's graphics card does not have suffi-cient memory or horsepower. In this case, you can switch to fewer screen colors in System Preferences→Displays, then click on the Display button and choose the Thousands option as the number of colors to display onscreen.

Although Blender is designed for use with a three-button mouse, the standard single-button Apple mouse can also be used in combination with various keystrokes:

• The left button of a three-button mouse is used to activate screen menus and buttons in the GUI, to resize subwindows, and to set the 3D cursor.

The same effect can be achieved with the single button of a standard one-button Apple mouse.

- The middle button of a three-button mouse is used to move, rotate, and zoom the 3D views. To access this functionality with a one-button mouse, simultaneously press the Shift-Control-Option keys and click the mouse button.

- The right button of a three-button mouse is used to select 3D objects. The right-mouse-button effect can be achieved by ⌘-clicking.

There are more Mac OS X-specific details to be aware of when using Blender. For example, on other platforms, the F12 key is used to render an image in Blender; however, on Mac OS X, you must press either Control-F12 or Option-F12 to render an image. This is because the F12 key is used on a Mac to activate the Dashboard.

CHAPTER 9

Dual-Boot and Beyond

With the arrival of Intel-based Macs came the ability to easily run multiple operating systems. PowerPC-based Macs had this ability to a limited extent, but the switch to widely supported Intel hardware gave Mac users access to more operating systems that they could install on their Macs. Not only that, but the performance of virtual machines on Macs suddenly increased by orders of magnitude, because users were no longer dependent on software that emulated an Intel CPU on a PowerPC: they could take advantage of the ability to virtualize key components of the underlying hardware. You have a couple of choices for running multiple operating systems on the Mac:

Running on the bare metal
> If you want to run an alternative operating system on your Mac, many choices are available. Linux and NetBSD will run on just about any kind of Mac, all the way back to the 68k-based Macintoshes, and Intel-based Macs can run nearly any operating system that can run on a stock Intel-based PC. However, if you want to be able to boot into another operating system on your Mac, you'll need to repartition your drive. We'll talk about this in the "Linux on Mac Hardware" section later in this chapter; much of what you read in that section will apply to other operating systems as well.

Running on Mac OS X
> When it comes to running Windows, Linux, or other operating systems under Mac OS X, you have several options. VMware Fusion and Parallels Desktop are two of the best known, but there are also two open source applications that can serve your needs very well: Sun's VirtualBox and Fabrice Bellard's QEMU (which also can run on PowerPC Macs, as described in the next paragraph).

> Even for older PowerPC Macs, a good selection of emulators run on Mac OS X. With Microsoft's Virtual PC (no longer available for sale, but you may be able to find a used copy), you can run x86-based operating systems.

Amit Singh's legendary "Many Systems on a PowerBook" article (*http://www.kernelthread.com/mac/vpc/*) documents dozens of operating systems that run under Virtual PC. In addition to Virtual PC, there are two open source x86 emulators of note: Bochs, a portable (but very slow) x86 emulator; and QEMU, a highly tuned x86 emulator that comes close to Virtual PC in speed. We'll discuss Virtual PC and QEMU in the "Emulators on Mac OS X" section later in this chapter.

Of course, all of these operating systems wouldn't be very useful if they didn't talk to the outside world. Whether you're running an alternative operating system on the bare hardware or under an emulator, getting the network up and running can sometimes be tricky. We'll cover the essential configuration steps in detail later in this chapter.

Virtualization Versus Emulation

There are two classes of products that let you run one operating system within another. An *emulator* (such as Virtual PC, Bochs, or DOSBox) translates every CPU instruction that a program needs to execute, turning it into the equivalent instruction or instructions used by the target CPU. A *virtualizer* (such as VMware Fusion, Parallels, or VirtualBox) does something very different: it lets the program run directly on the CPU without translation. (QEMU can run either as an emulator or a virtualizer.)

As a result, virtualizers such as Parallels and VMware can run Intel-based operating systems very fast, but unlike QEMU and the other emulators, they can't run Intel-based operating systems on PowerPC CPUs. Apple's Rosetta technology is an emulator that goes the other way: it emulates a PowerPC CPU on an Intel CPU.

Even virtualizers rely in part on emulation, using a large disk image that contains the virtualized operating system's files to emulate a hard disk.

Why Bother?

All this discussion of how to run another operating system on your Mac raises the question of why you'd even do it in the first place. Here are a few reasons:

Portability
> First and foremost, dual-booting and virtualization give you portability. Wherever you travel with your Mac, why not bring a dozen Linux distributions and flavors of Windows around with you? It's easier than carrying several computers.

Software testing

There are a lot of flavors of Linux, so if you're developing an application that has to run on Linux, you'll need to do extensive testing. You *could* set up a multiboot configuration with all the flavors of Linux, but working with virtual machines is much easier and requires less time spent juggling partition configurations. With virtualizers, you can even run all these systems at once (albeit incurring something of a performance hit).

Further, with virtualizers and emulators you can suspend an operating system and resume it later, so if you have some testing to do, you can get in and out quickly.

Browser testing

Nothing beats virtual machines for browser testing. You can develop your web application (or site) on your Mac and, in very little time, fire up several emulated operating systems and test it in a wide array of browsers on Windows, Linux, and Mac OS X.

> If browser testing is all you need, check out Browser Pool at *http://www.browserpool.de*. You can get inexpensive (or free, if you don't mind waiting in line) access to browsers on Linux, Mac OS X, and Windows operating systems for testing your websites.

Freeze and thaw

When you set up an operating system with an emulator, the system's hard disk is just a file on your Mac's filesystem. If you keep this to around 4 GB, you can burn a snapshot of the operating system to a DVD for a very quick restore. This is ideal in testing scenarios where you frequently need to test your software on a clean install or standardized software configuration.

Running Windows applications

There are plenty of applications that either don't run on the Mac at all (this is often a problem with games and specialized apps) or don't run exactly the way you'd like them to. For example, although recent versions of Microsoft Office for Macintosh have made great improvements in compatibility, we ran into some problems ourselves during the creation of this book: some documents that were edited in Microsoft Office 2008 for the Mac crashed Microsoft Office 2003 for Windows. So, if you need to run a certain Windows application, you may need to dual boot or run Windows under emulation.

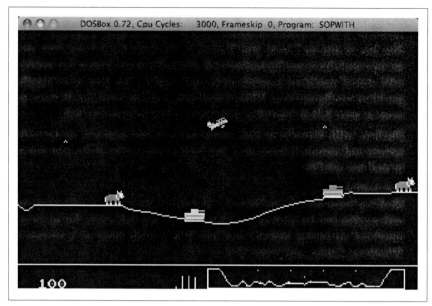

Figure 9-1. A little Sopwith, anyone?

Fun

Got an old MS-DOS game you want to play on your Mac? Nothing beats an emulator for running these old games (see Figure 9-1), except maybe an old Tandy home computer. Furthermore, there's plenty to be said for running an old operating system just for the fun of it.

 Your best bet for MS-DOS emulation is DOSBox (*http:// www.dosbox.com*), which has one feature that sets it apart from other emulators: it lets you mount parts of the host filesystem as DOS drives. So, you can download that old MS-DOS game, unzip it into *~/Games*, and mount *~/Games* as your *D:* drive in DOSBox. Figure 9-1 shows a real classic running under DOSBox.

Linux on Mac Hardware

In theory, nearly any operating system that can run on a modern Intel-based personal computer can also be made to run on a Macintosh: simply boot your Mac from the boot disc, run the installer, and you're done. If you're only interested in running one operating system on your Mac, that's pretty much all you have to do (at first, anyhow; later in this section we'll get into the details of configuring hardware support). But if you want to keep Mac OS X on your computer and dual-boot between Mac OS X and some other operating system, you'll need to do some prep work.

Partitioning for Linux

If you can plan ahead, partitioning for Linux is a piece of cake. That is, if you are installing Mac OS X from scratch, you may as well partition your drive beforehand (to do this, launch Disk Utility during installation) and leave some space for Linux.

If you aren't installing Mac OS X from scratch, you can take advantage of *diskutil(8)*'s ability to resize volumes. Before you do this, you should use Carbon Copy Cloner (*http://www.bombich.com/software/ccc.html*) or Super-Duper! (*http://www.shirt-pocket.com/SuperDuper/*) to make a bootable backup of your Mac's hard drive (although you can restore from a Time Machine backup, it's quicker and easier to work with a bootable clone of your hard drive).

 If you don't want to repartition, you can install Linux on a separate drive. Given that storage is cheap, it shouldn't be hard for you to put a second drive in your Mac, assuming you're running a Mac Pro. 13" MacBook users can also swap drives easily, which is another way you can switch between Linux and Mac OS X without having to modify your partitions. See *http://manuals.info.apple.com/en/MacBook _13inch_HardDrive_DIY.pdf* for a guide to installing a new drive in the MacBook. It takes only a few minutes to swap drives on the MacBook.

To resize your Mac OS X partition and set aside some space for a Linux install, first check the current partition system with *diskutil list*:

```
$ diskutil list
/dev/disk0
   #:                       TYPE NAME              SIZE        IDENTIFIER
   0:      GUID_partition_scheme               *186.3 Gi    disk0
   1:                        EFI               200.0 Mi    disk0s1
   2:          Apple_HFS Macbook HD            186.0 Gi    disk0s2
```

You'll notice that three items are listed for disk0. The first represents the partitioning scheme of the entire disk (GUID partitioning, the default and preferred partitioning scheme for Mac OS X). The second, disk0s1, is the Extensible Firmware Interface (EFI), which is included to comply with the EFI specification. The third, disk0s2, is the main Mac OS X partition; when you resize the disk, this is the partition you need to resize.

The first step is to determine how much space you have to play with. Use *diskutil resizeVolume partition limits* to figure this out:

```
$ diskutil resizeVolume disk0s2 limits
For device disk0s2 Macbook HD:
     Current size:   199705673728 bytes
     Minimum size:   11756769280 bytes
     Maximum size:   199705673728 bytes
```

Next, do the math on the partition sizes. In this example, we'll shrink disk0s2 to 80 GB (85,899,345,920 bytes) and set aside everything else for Linux (maximum size − new size = everything else). Use B to specify bytes when you resize the volume:

```
$ diskutil resizeVolume disk0s2 85899345920B MS-DOS Untitled 113806327808B
Started resizing on disk disk0s2 Macbook HD
Verifying
Resizing Volume
Adjusting Partitions
Formatting new partitions
Formatting disk0s3 as MS-DOS (FAT) with name Untitled
[ + 0%..10%..20%..30%..40%..50%..60%..70%..80%..90%..100% ]
Finished resizing on disk disk0
/dev/disk0
   #:                     TYPE NAME             SIZE        IDENTIFIER
   0:      GUID_partition_scheme               *186.3 Gi    disk0
   1:                      EFI                  200.0 Mi     disk0s1
   2:              Apple_HFS Macbook HD          79.9 Gi     disk0s2
   3:      Microsoft Basic Data UNTITLED       106.1 Gi     disk0s3
```

When you're done resizing, you'll have an MS-DOS-formatted (also known as FAT32) partition that you can delete once the Linux installer is up and running, as described in the next section.

Installation and Configuration

You've got some free space to play around with now, so installing Linux is mostly straightforward. Here's how you'd install Ubuntu 8.04 on a Mac after setting up the partitions:

1. Install rEFIt (*http://refit.sourceforge.net*). rEFIt is a boot loader for Macintoshes that will let you choose between Linux and Mac OS X at each boot.

2. Shut down the Mac and power it up while you hold down the Alt/Option key. When the boot menu appears, insert the Ubuntu installation CD (using the Live CD installer on the desktop edition of Ubuntu).

3. Oddly enough, the Ubuntu installation CD will appear as a CD called "Windows." Select this CD and click the arrow to boot from it.

4. After the Ubuntu desktop appears, double-click on the installer icon. Make your way through the following installer screens, accepting the defaults or changing them as needed:

   a. Welcome

   b. Where Are You?

   c. Keyboard Layout

5. When you come to the Prepare Disk Space screen, choose Manual and click Forward. The Prepare Partitions screen will appear.

6. On the Prepare Partitions screen, highlight the FAT32 partition (this is the MS-DOS partition you created earlier) as shown in Figure 9-2, and click Delete Partition. Be sure to leave the first and second partitions (sda1 and sda2 in this example) untouched, or you will lose your data.

7. Next, highlight the free space you just liberated and create two partitions: a swap partition equal to your amount of RAM at the end of the free space, and an *ext3* partition at the beginning of the free space. Be sure to specify / as the mount point for the *ext3* partition. Figure 9-3 shows the configuration.

8. Click Forward and proceed through the rest of the Ubuntu installation. You'll be prompted to supply a username and specify the name of the computer, and then you'll be given a chance to review the settings. Don't click Install just yet.

9. Click the Advanced button and specify */dev/sda* (or whichever disk you created the Linux partition on) as the location of the boot loader. Click OK.

10. Click Install.

After installation is complete, reboot as directed by the installer. The rEFIt menu will appear, letting you choose between Mac OS X and Ubuntu. Don't choose either just yet; instead, start the Partition Tool and accept its recommendation to sync the partition tables. After it's finished, shut down your Mac, restart, and choose Mac OS X or Ubuntu.

Depending on the model and vintage of your Mac, some things may work right out of the box, but you may have to install updated versions of some drivers and software packages. As cruel fate would have it, AirPort networking is one piece of hardware that often needs updated drivers, so things will go most smoothly if you can arrange for a wired network connection over Ethernet during your initial configuration. If you can't arrange for this, you can use another computer to download files and transfer them to your Mac using a USB memory device.

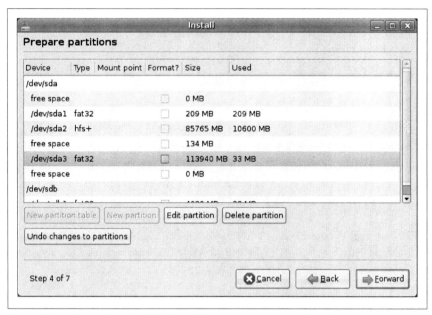

Figure 9-2. Deleting the FAT32 (MS-DOS) partition you created earlier

The best way to get help configuring your Mac with a particular Linux distribution is to visit the wiki, forums, or support pages for that distribution. For example, the Ubuntu community documentation (*https://help.ubuntu.com/community/*) includes guides for specific Mac models such as the MacBook (*https://help.ubuntu.com/community/MacBook/*).

Linux on Older Macs

Linux will also run on Apple hardware based on the Motorola 68020 (and higher), as well as PowerPC-based Macs.

 You can learn how to get Linux running on that old Centris you're using as a doorstop at the Linux/mac68k Project website (*http://www.linux-m68k.org*), or the Debian on Motorola 680x0 pages (*http://www.debian.org/ports/m68k/*).

There are several distributions of Linux you can choose for your PowerPC Macintosh. Speaking of an old Centris, if you want to see something really wild, how about a 25 MHz Centris running Linux running PearPC running Mac OS X Panther? See all the gory details at *http://www.appletalk.com.au/articles/68kpanther/*.

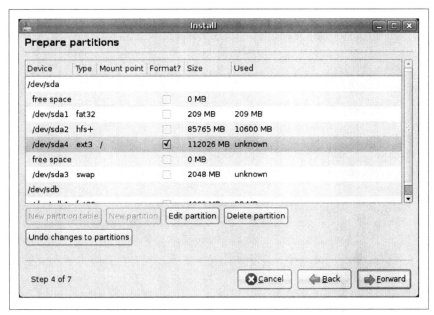

Figure 9-3. Partition settings

If you're going to run Linux on your pre-Intel Mac, you'll need to know which distribution will work with your hardware. This list should give you an idea of what's available for your Linux hacking needs:

Fedora
Fedora (*http://fedoraproject.org*) is widely used on a large variety of platforms and forms the basis of several other Linux distributions, including Red Hat Enterprise Linux, the One Laptop per Child XO (*http://www.laptop.org*), and Yellow Dog Linux. Fedora is actively developed and brings with it a large number of up-to-date packages. Fedora will run on PowerPC-based Macs, but you may need to tweak some configuration files. For example, on some old Macs you may need to modify the */etc/xorg.conf* file or borrow the */etc/xorg.conf* automatically generated by an installation of Yellow Dog Linux to get the X server to start.

Yellow Dog Linux
Based on Red Hat's Fedora Core, Yellow Dog Linux (*http://www.yellowdoglinux.com*) is one of the most popular Mac-based Linux distributions; it runs on Macintoshes based on the G3 (with built-in USB), G4, and G5. If your Mac can run Mac OS X, it will probably run YDL.

Gentoo Linux

> Gentoo Linux (*http://www.gentoo.org*) is a hacker's dream. Although you can install it using prebuilt binaries, the preferred method is to bootstrap a minimal system and compile the bulk of it by source. Gentoo will run on the PowerPC chipset, as well as pre-G3, G3, G4, and G5 Macs.

Debian GNU/Linux

> Debian (*http://www.debian.org/ports/powerpc/*) runs on a lot of different hardware, including PowerPC (from pre-G3 all the way up to G5) Macs. Debian is known for its wide selection of packages, hacker-friendly configuration, and bleeding-edge releases that are hard to resist even when you know better.

Ubuntu

> If you like Debian, there's a very good chance that you'll adore Ubuntu (*https://wiki.ubuntu.com/PowerPCDownloads/*). This Debian-based distro is an excellent desktop Linux, but it's not dumbed-down. Ubuntu detects and configures your oddball hardware and launches X11 with a very pretty face, but it still lets you take control.

Although Linux is generally compatible with PowerPC-based Macintosh hardware, there are a few areas that you'll need to watch out for: hardware on newer Macs, AirPort Extreme, Bluetooth, and power management. For more details, check the documentation for the Linux distribution you've chosen. For example, Ubuntu maintains a PowerPC FAQ at *https://wiki.ubuntu.com/Power PCFAQ/*.

Linux installs a boot loader (such as Yaboot, available at *http://yaboot.ozlabs .org*), which is used to boot the Linux distribution, much in the same way Mac OS X boots with help from BootX (see Chapter 4). If the boot loader is installed on the Linux partition, you'll see it only if your Linux partition remains selected as your Startup Disk. If you switch the Startup Disk settings (System Preferences→Startup Disk), you can easily boot into Linux by holding down the Option key when you boot your Mac. Choose the disk with the Linux penguin (Tux) logo to boot into Linux.

Mac-on-Linux

Mac-on-Linux (*http://mac-on-linux.sourceforge.net*) is a hardware virtualizer that provides a virtual machine environment that is Mac-compatible enough for you to run Linux, Mac OS (7.5.2 through 9.2.2), and Mac OS X (10.1 through 10.3.3 as of this writing). Mac-on-Linux emulates the bits that it needs to, but when the operating system running in the virtual machine accesses the hardware of the virtual environment, Mac-on-Linux virtualizes the call and passes it right on down to the real hardware.

Emulators on Mac OS X

Emulation has been a hot area for the past few years. It's emerged as a way to defeat obsolescence, by letting you run software for obsolete computers. Have a favorite Atari 800 game but your old Atari won't boot? You can download the emulator, point it at the disk image containing that old game, and start playing. Repeat as necessary for Apple II, Commodore 64, Atari VCS, and more.

Copyrights and Vintage Games

If your favorite old games aren't shareware or in the public domain, you may need to poke around various corners of the world, including yard sales, thrift stores, eBay, or your own attic, to find copies of them.

There are a several sites with information about vintage games and computer emulators for the Mac, including:

- *http://emulation.victoly.com*
- *http://www.zophar.net/mac/mac.phtml*
- *http://www.macemu.com*
- *http://www.emaculation.com*
- *http://www.bannister.org/software*

Given the speeds of today's Macs, it's not surprising that you can easily emulate a 1 MHz computer from the old days. What's fantastic is how you can emulate most current x86 operating systems at near-full speed on the most recent Intel Macs.

Getting a Linux Installation Disk Image

Once you've picked which virtualization or emulation package you want, you can set up a virtual machine using either a Linux installation disk or an ISO disk image. For example, to install Ubuntu (used in the following examples), visit *http://www.ubuntu.com/getubuntu/download/* and download the desktop edition for a "Standard personal computer." For Ubuntu Linux 8.04, this will leave you with a file called *ubuntu-8.04-desktop-i386.iso*. There's no need to burn this file to a CD; simply keep it around for when you start the installation.

Do This After Installing Ubuntu

After you install Ubuntu in a virtual machine, you'll want to run a couple of commands to prepare for installing any software, such as VMware's Tools, that needs to compile kernel modules.

Open a terminal (Application→Accessories→Terminal), then type the following commands to upgrade Ubuntu and install the C compiler (this will require a working network connection and a virtualized network connection, which most virtualizers and emulators enable by default):

```
$ sudo apt-get update
$ sudo apt-get dist-upgrade
$ sudo apt-get install build-essential
```

Other Linux operating systems will have similar procedures.

Parallels

Parallels is a recent entry into the virtualization market. After Microsoft decided not to release an Intel version of Virtual PC, Parallels filled the gap with Parallels Desktop for Mac.

To get started with Parallels, buy a copy of the package from an online vendor or a retail store, install it, and set up a Linux operating system. You can also download a trial version of Parallels from *http://www.parallels.com/en/prod ucts/desktop/*.

Here's how to set up Ubuntu Linux on Parallels Desktop:

1. Click New or choose File→New. The OS Installation Assistant appears.
2. Select Typical and click Next.
3. Set the OS Type to Linux and the OS Version to Ubuntu Linux, then click Next.
4. Give the virtual machine a name, and click More Options if you want to choose a specific location. Be sure to put it on a disk where you have plenty of free space. Click Next.
5. Pick your performance options. You can choose to make the virtual machine faster or to make Mac OS X faster.
6. Now you're prompted to insert the Ubuntu disk. Choose the Ubuntu ISO that you downloaded (as instructed in the preceding section). Click Finish.

To install Parallels Tools, select Actions→Install Parallels Tools from the Parallels menu. Follow the instructions provided to get the tools running.

VMware Fusion

VMware Fusion was one of the first virtualization products to appear on the market. It gained popularity as a way to run Linux on Windows, Windows on Linux, and various other interesting combinations.

Shortly after Parallels appeared on the market, VMware introduced the Macintosh version of its software. It matches Parallels well on a feature-by-feature basis and has better support for Linux guest operating systems (in particular, VMware lets you copy and paste between Mac OS X and Linux guest operating systems, whereas as of this writing, Parallels does not).

To get started with VMware Fusion, buy a copy of it from an online vendor or a retail store, install it, and set up a Linux operating system. You can also download a trial version of VMware from *http://www.vmware.com/mac*.

Here's how to set up Ubuntu Linux 8 under VMware Fusion:

1. Choose File→New. The New Virtual Machine Assistant appears.

2. Click Continue. On the next screen, choose Linux as your operating system, specify Ubuntu, and click Continue.

3. Now you'll be asked to choose a location for the virtual machine. Pick a disk with plenty of free space, and click Continue.

4. Choose the size of your virtual hard disk; 8 GB is a good size for Ubuntu. If you are storing this virtual machine on a hard drive that's formatted with the FAT32 filesystem, click "Advanced disk options" and choose "Split disk into 2GB files."

5. On the next screen, click "Use operating system installation disk image file," select None→Other, and choose the Ubuntu ISO that you downloaded (see "Getting a Linux Installation Disk Image," earlier in this chapter). Click Finish to boot Ubuntu and install it as you would on a normal computer.

After you've installed Ubuntu, log into it and set up the VMware Tools to get faster graphics, a more responsive mouse, and copy/paste integration:

1. Choose Virtual Machine→Install VMware Tools from the VMware menu (not the menu inside the virtual machine). A window appears on your desktop with two files: a *tar.gz* file and an RPM. These contain the VMware tools that you need to install.

2. Double-click the *tar.gz* file and click the Extract button in the window that appears. Extract the file to somewhere in your home directory.

3. Select Application→Accessories→Terminal inside Ubuntu to launch a Linux terminal.

4. Next, change directories to wherever you extracted the VMware tools and run the installer:

```
$ cd vmware-tools-distrib
$ sudo ./vmware-install.pl
```

When it's finished, you may want to reboot the virtual machine to verify that all the settings have taken effect.

Virtual PC

Microsoft's Virtual PC has been letting Mac users run Windows and DOS on their Macs for years. You can also run dozens of other operating systems, including Linux, Darwin, and Net/Free/OpenBSD (some are easier to install than others). Virtual PC does not run on Intel Macs.

Virtual PC 7 is no longer available for sale, although you may be able to find used copies on eBay, Amazon, and other locations.

Once you've got Virtual PC up and running, you can install an operating system. You can install from an ISO image, a CD-ROM, or a DVD. For example, here's how to install Ubuntu Linux from an ISO image:

1. Select File→New. You'll be prompted to select a setup method.

2. Select Install Your Own Operating System, and then click Begin.

3. You're prompted to choose an operating system and hard disk format. One of the choices that you'll notice is missing is the size of the drive. Virtual PC defaults to a 15 GB drive, but it doesn't use up all the space at once. Instead, the size of the drive grows as you add files to it. Select Linux for the operating system and Unformatted for the hard disk format, and click Continue.

4. Now you need to choose a filename and a location for the virtual machine.

 The file that gets created is actually a bundle, so if you locate it in the Finder, Control/right-click on it and select Show Package Contents from the contextual menu, you'll see all sorts of files, including configuration data, the hard disk image, and any saved states.

5. Next, Virtual PC prompts you to start the PC. Click Start PC to begin. When the Virtual PC starts up, the first thing you'll see is an annoying help document and an error message in the virtual machine.

6. You now need to "capture" the CD-ROM and reboot the virtual machine. Select Drives→Capture CD Image and choose the CD-ROM ISO image

you obtained (see "Getting a Linux Installation Disk Image" earlier in this chapter). If you want to capture a CD-ROM that's sitting in your optical drive, you can select Drives→Capture Disk.

After you've captured the drive, select PC→Reset to reboot the PC. You'll be launched into the installer for Ubuntu.

VirtualBox

VirtualBox is a virtualization application that was purchased by Sun Microsystems and released as open source software. Two versions are available: the VirtualBox Open Source Edition, which is available as source code, and the binary release, which includes some components that are not open source. After you install VirtualBox, you can install an operating system from a disk image, DVD, or CD-ROM. Here's how you'd install Ubuntu Linux from an ISO disk image:

1. Click New in the VirtualBox main window. The Create New Virtual Machine Wizard appears. Click Next.

2. Give the installation a name, such as Ubuntu 8.04, and specify the OS type as Ubuntu. Click Next.

3. Specify the amount of memory you want to give the virtual machine. 256 MB is a reasonable minimum. Click Next.

4. Now you're prompted to specify the hard disk image. Click New, and the Create New Virtual Disk Wizard appears. Click Next, then:

   a. Choose the disk type (dynamically expanding or fixed-size) and click Next.

   b. Specify the filename and size, then click Next.

   c. Click Finish to return to the Create New Virtual Machine Wizard.

5. The wizard automatically selects the disk you specified. Click Next.

6. Review your choices, then click Finish.

Now you'll see a summary of your virtual machine in the main window, as shown in Figure 9-4. Click CD/DVD-ROM, and then click Mount CD/DVD Drive. Specify ISO Image File and choose the Ubuntu install image you downloaded earlier (see "Getting a Linux Installation Disk Image"). Click OK, then click Start to launch the virtual machine and boot from the installation disk.

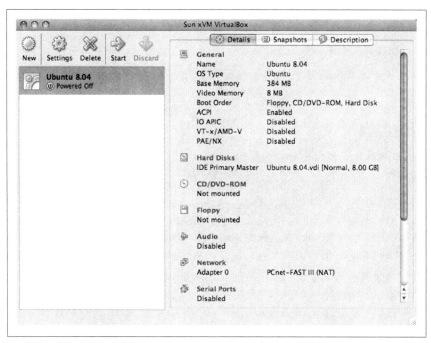

Figure 9-4. Find the CD/DVD-ROM options and set them here

QEMU

QEMU (*http://www.bellard.org/qemu/*) is a state-of-the-art open source emulator and virtualizer. Like Bochs (*http://bochs.sourceforge.net*), QEMU can
emulate an x86 CPU. However, QEMU is significantly faster than Bochs and
can also emulate a number of other CPUs, including SPARC and PowerPC. Q
(*http://www.kju-app.org*) is a Mac OS X version of QEMU that comes with a
nice user interface for working with virtual machines.

To get started with QEMU, download the latest version of Q, or download
the source code to QEMU. The easiest way to get up and running is to download and install a prebuilt virtual machine image for QEMU from the Free
Operating Systems Zoo (*http://www.oszoo.org/wiki/index.php/Main_Page*).
However, you can also start with an installation image, as described in the
instructions for the other software described in this section.

Here's how to get up and running with a prebuilt virtual machine image for
Ubuntu 7.10:

1. Unzip the Ubuntu image from Free OS Zoo. You'll end up with a file such
   as *ubuntu_gutsy_7.10_x86.img*.
2. Start up Q. The Q Control window appears.

3. Press the + button at the top, name the virtual machine "Ubuntu," and select Q Standard Guest as the operating system. Click Create PC. A window appears that lets you set several options in four categories: General, Hardware, Network, and Advanced.

4. Click Hardware, and then click the pop-up menu next to Hard Disk. Select Choose Diskimage and navigate to where you extracted the Ubuntu image. Select this image and click Open.

5. Set any other options as you'd like, and click Create PC. The Ubuntu virtual machine appears in the list on the Q Control. Double-click it to run it.

## PART II

Building Applications

Although Apple's C compiler is based on the GNU Compiler Collection (GCC), there are important differences between compiling and linking on Mac OS X and on other platforms. This part of the book describes these differences.

Chapters in this part of the book include:

## CHAPTER 10

Compiling Source Code

The Xcode tools that ship with Mac OS X provide a development environment for building applications using Cocoa, Carbon, Java, and even AppleScript. (For details about obtaining these tools, see the "Xcode Tools" section in the Preface.) The Xcode tools include utilities that should be familiar to any Unix developer who works with command-line compilers. They also include all sorts of other goodies, including an advanced Integrated Development Environment (IDE), but coverage of those tools is beyond the scope and intent of this book.

To learn more about the Xcode tools, go to *http://developer .apple.com/referencelibrary/DeveloperTools/index.html.*

A variety of compilers can be used with Mac OS X. The C compiler that comes with Xcode is based on the Free Software Foundation's (FSF's) GNU Compiler Collection, or GCC. Apple's modifications to GCC include an Objective-C compiler, as well as various modifications to deal with the Darwin operating system. The development environment in Mac OS X includes:

AppleScript
> This is an English-like language used to script events in applications and in the operating system. AppleScript is installed as part of the Mac OS X operating system and does not require Xcode. To write AppleScripts, use the Script Editor (*/Applications/AppleScript*).

AppleScript Studio
> This is a high-level development environment based on AppleScript that allows you to build GUI applications by hooking AppleScript into the Cocoa framework. If you plan to build AppleScript Studio applications, you will need to use the Xcode IDE instead of the Script Editor.

Compiler tools

These include the Mac OS X Mach-O GNU-based assemblers, Mach-O static link editor, Mach-O dynamic link editor, and Mach-O object file tools (such as *nm*, *otool*, and *otool64*).

Compilers

These compilers are based on GCC and provide support for C, C++, Objective-C, Objective-C++, Objective-C 2.0, and assembly. Apple's enhancements to GCC for Leopard include support for the Intel x86 and G5 (also known as the PowerPC 970) processors, as well as the ability to generate optimized code to run on Intel x86, G5, and G4 systems. Though 64-bit support in Tiger is limited to the Unix level, Leopard adds 64-bit support to the Mac OS X application level.

Dashcode

Located in */Developer/Applications*, Dashcode is an IDE for developing JavaScript-based widgets such as those used in Dashboard.

Debugger

The Apple debugger is based on GNU's *gdb*. In Leopard, DTrace is also available.

Documentation

Extensive documentation for Xcode, found in */Developer/Documentation/DocSets*, can be viewed with Xcode's document viewer. These documents are also available online from the Apple Developer Connection (ADC) website, *http://developer.apple.com*.

 You can access the documentation for GCC after you've installed Xcode by running the Xcode application in */Developer/Applications* and selecting Help→Documentation from the menu bar.

Header Doc 8

This is a set of command-line tools for including structured comments in source code and header files, which are later used to create HTML and XML output. A set of manpage-generation tools is also included. Header Doc's two main Perl scripts are *headerdoc2html* and *gatherheaderdoc*. Kyle Hammond's Cocoa frontend to Header Doc is available at *http://www.cpinternet.com/~snowmint/CocoaProgramming.html*. See Developer Tools Reference Library→Tools→Darwin→HeaderDoc User Guide in the Xcode document viewer for details.

Instruments

Located in */Developer/Applications*, Instruments is a timeline-based GUI performance visualization tool for Cocoa and Carbon applications built on top of the open source DTrace utility.

Interface Builder

Located in */Developer/Applications*, Interface Builder is a GUI editor for Cocoa and Carbon applications.

Miscellaneous tools

These include traditional development tools, such as *make* (both GNU *make*, which is the default, and BSD *make*) and GNU *libtool*, graphical and command-line performance tools, Xcode for WebObjects, parsing tools (such as *lex*, *flex*, *yacc*, and *bison*), standard Unix source code management tools (such as *CVS* and *RCS*), and an extensive set of Java development tools. There's also a frontend to GCC, *distcc*, which uses Bonjour to distribute builds of C, C++, Objective-C, or Objective-C++ code across computers on a network.

Xcode

Located in */Developer/Applications*, Xcode is an IDE for Mac OS X that supports Cocoa and Carbon programming with C, C++, Objective-C, and Java.

We won't address the complete Mac OS X development suite in this chapter. Instead, we'll focus on the command-line development tools and how they differ from the implementations of such tools on other Unix platforms.

Java programmers will find that the Mac OS X command-line Java tools behave as they do under Unix and Linux. Another resource for Java developers is Will Iverson's *Mac OS X for Java Geeks* (O'Reilly).

Perl programmers coming from previous Macintosh systems will find that Mac OS X does not use MacPerl (*http://www.macperl.com*), but instead uses the standard Unix build of the core Perl distribution (*http://www.perl.org*). For additional information on using Perl under Mac OS X, see Chapter 17.

Compiler Differences

GCC is supported on a wide range of platforms, and it is the default compiler on Mac OS X. There are, however, some important differences between the version of GCC that ships with Mac OS X and compilers found on other Unix systems.

One difference that experienced GCC users may notice, particularly if they have extensive experience with mathematical and scientific programming, is that the Xcode Tools do not include FORTRAN. However, MacPorts (*http://www.macports.org*) includes *g95*, the GNU FORTRAN 95 compiler that is based on GCC. (For information on using MacPorts, see Chapter 13.) Additionally, the open source FORTRAN 95 Gfortran project is available for Mac OS X. Though not provided with the GCC distribution included with Leopard, the *gfortran* compiler is part of GCC. (See *http://gcc.gnu.org/wiki/HomePage* for details.)

Mac OS X's C compiler contains a number of Mac-specific features that have not been folded into the main GCC distribution. (It is up to the Free Software Foundation [FSF] to accept and merge Apple's patches.) For information on how Apple's compiler differs from the GNU version, see the *README.Apple* file in the *gcc4* subdirectory of the Darwin CVS archive.

As of this writing, Apple's *cc* compiler is based on GCC 4.0.1. Though not installed with Xcode by default, GCC 3.3 is available as part of the optional installation of Mac OS X 10.3.9 Support (you would install Mac OS X 10.3.9 Support only if you wanted to build applications for the target Mac OS X 10.3.9 PPC systems). By default, invoking *cc* or *gcc* invokes GCC 4.0; both */usr/bin/cc* and */usr/bin/gcc* are symbolic links to */usr/bin/gcc-4.0*.

The Mac OS X Compiler Release Notes (*/Developer/ADC Reference Library/Documentation/releasenotes*) should be consulted for details on the most currently known problems, issues, and features.

Perhaps the most important improvement in GCC 4.0.x is the incorporation of Tree Single Static Assignment (SSA) optimization rather than Register Transfer Language (RTL), used in older versions of GCC. SSA was available in some earlier versions, but it was experimental and had to be switched on by the special compiler flag *-fssa*. The incorporation of Tree SSA has enabled optimizations in the following areas:

- Scalar replacement of aggregates
- Constant propagation
- Value range propagation
- Partial redundancy elimination

- Load and store motion
- Strength reduction
- Dead store elimination
- Dead and unreachable code elimination
- Auto-vectorization to take advantage of the Velocity Engine
- Loop interchange
- Tail recursion by accumulation

See *http://gcc.gnu.org/projects/tree-ssa/* for more details on Tree SSA.

Additional improvements in GCC 4.0.x include a more efficient C++ parser and a dynamic C++ standard library, *libstdc++* (in pre-Tiger releases of Mac OS X you could only statically link *libstdc++*). Support has also been added for 128-bit long double floating-point types and 64-bit computing.

Compiling Unix Source Code

Many of the differences between Mac OS X and other versions of Unix become apparent when you try to build Unix-based software on Mac OS X. Most open source Unix software uses GNU *autoconf* or a similar facility, which generates a *configure* script that performs a number of tests of the system—especially of the installed Xcode tools—and finishes by constructing one or more makefiles. After the *configure* script has done its job, you run the *make* command to first compile and then, if all goes well, install the resulting binaries.

 Most tarballs include a *configure* script, so you do not need to generate it yourself. However, if you retrieve *autoconf*-managed source code from a CVS archive, you may have to run *autoconf.sh* manually to generate the *configure* file.

In most cases, it's pretty easy to compile a Unix application on Mac OS X, provided the required dependencies are present. After unpacking the tarball and changing to the top-level source code directory, just issue the following three commands to compile the application:

```
$ ./configure
$ make
$ make install
```

Mac OS X web browsers are configured to unpack compressed archives. If you click on a link to a tarball, you may find that it gets downloaded to your Desktop and extracted there. If you'd prefer to manage the download and extraction process yourself, Control-click (or right-click) on the link so you can specify a download location.

The following sections deal with issues involved in successfully performing these steps. Determining how to improvise within that three-step procedure reveals some of the differences between Mac OS X and other Unix systems.

The First Line of Defense

Most Unix software applications and libraries are built from a set of files called *source code*. To distribute software, it is common in the Unix world to package source code in the form of a *tarball*, which is a single compressed file usually in the form of *foo.tar.gz* or *foo.tar.bz2*. (Tarballs are discussed in more detail in Chapter 14.) Most tarballs include the following files in the top-level directory:

README
> This document is an introduction to the application and source code. It often contains copyright information, notes about bug fixes or improvements made to different versions, and pointers to websites, FAQs, and mailing lists.

INSTALL
> This document contains step-by-step installation instructions.

PORT or PORTING
> If present, one of these documents will include tips for porting the application to another Unix platform.

These files contain useful information that may help you get the application running on Mac OS X.

Host Type

One of the first difficulties you may encounter when running a *configure* script is that the script aborts with an error message stating that the host system cannot be determined.

Strictly speaking, the *host type* refers to the system on which the software will run, and the *build type* refers to the system on which the software is built. It is possible to build software on one system to run on another system, but doing so requires a cross-compiler, and dealing with cross-compiler issues is beyond the scope of this chapter. Thus, for our discussion, the host type and the build (and target) types will be the same: `i386-apple-darwinVERSION`, where the *VERSION* denotes the particular version of Darwin. (A *configure* script detects Mac OS X by the host/build type named *Darwin*, since Darwin is the actual operating system underlying Mac OS X. This can be verified by issuing the *uname -v* command, which tells you that you're running a Darwin kernel, the kernel version, and when it was last built.)

Many *configure* scripts are designed to determine the host system, since the resulting makefiles differ depending on the type of system for which the software is built. The *configure* script is designed to be used with two files related to the host type, usually residing in the same directory as the *configure* script. These files are *config.guess*, which is used to help guess the host type, and *config.sub*, which is used to validate the host type and to put it into a canonical form (e.g., *CPUTYPE-MANUFACTURER-OS*, as in `i386-apple-darwin9.2.0` or `powerpc-apple-darwin9.2.2`).

Although Mac OS X and Darwin have been around for a while now, you may still run across source code distributions that contain older *config.** files that don't work with Mac OS X. You can find out whether these files support Darwin by running the *./configure* script: if the script complains about an unknown host type, you know that you have a set of *config.** files that don't support Darwin.

To remedy that problem, you can replace the *config.guess* and *config.sub* files with the Apple-supplied, like-named versions residing in */usr/share/auto make-1.10*. These replacement files originate from the FSF and include the code necessary to configure a source tree for Mac OS X. To copy these files into the source directory, which contains the *configure* script, simply issue the following commands from within the source directory:

```
$ cp /usr/share/automake-1.10/config.sub .
$ cp /usr/share/automake-1.10/config.guess .
```

Macros

You can use a number of predefined macros to detect Apple systems and Mac OS X in particular. For example, `__APPLE__` is a macro that is defined on every Apple *gcc*-based Mac OS X system, and `__MACH__` is one of several macros specific to Mac OS X. Table 10-1 lists the predefined macros available on Mac OS X. To determine all of the predefined macros enabled on your system, run the command *cpp -dM < /dev/null*.

Table 10-1. Mac OS X C macros

Macro	Defined
__OBJC__	When the compiler is compiling Objective-C .m files or Objective-C++ .M files. (To override the file extension, use -ObjC or -ObjC++.)
__ASSEMBLER__	When the compiler is compiling .s files.
__NATURAL_ALIGNMENT__	When compiling for systems that use natural alignment, such as *powerpc*.
__STRICT_BSD__	If, and only if, the -bsd flag is specified as an argument to the compiler.
__MACH__	When compiling for systems that support Mach system calls.
__APPLE__	When compiling for any Apple system. Defined on Mac OS X systems running Apple's variant of the GNU C compiler and third-party compilers.
__APPLE_CC__	When compiling for any Apple system. Integer value that corresponds to the (Apple) version of the compiler.
__MMX__	When Intel PentiumMMX instruction set support has been enabled with the -maltivec flag.
__VEC__	When AltiVec support has been enabled with the -mmx flag.
__APPLE_VEC__	When AltiVec support has been enabled with the -mpim-altivec flag.
__LP64__	On 64-bit systems such as the G5 and Intel x86 CPUs. This macro can be used to conditionally compile 64-bit code.

Do not rely on the presence of the __APPLE__ macro to determine which compiler features or libraries are supported. Instead, we suggest using a package such as GNU *autoconf* to tell you which features the target operating system supports. This approach makes it more likely that your applications will compile out of the box (or with minimal effort) on operating systems to which you don't have access.

Supported Languages

When using the *cc* command, which supports more than one language, the language is determined either by the filename suffix or by explicitly specifying the language using the -x option. Table 10-2 lists some of the more commonly used filename suffixes and -x arguments supported by Apple's version of GCC.

Table 10-2. File suffixes recognized by cc

File suffix	Language	-x argument
.c	C source code to be preprocessed and compiled	c
.C, .cc, .cxx, .cpp	C++ source code to be preprocessed and compiled	c++
.h	C header that should be neither compiled nor linked	c-header

File suffix	Language	-x argument
.i	C source code that should be compiled but not preprocessed	cpp-output
.ii	Objective-C++ or C++ source code that should be compiled but not preprocessed	c++-cpp-output
.m	Objective-C source code	objective-c
.M, .mm	Mixed Objective-C++ and Objective-C source code	objective-c++
.s	Assembler source code that should be assembled but not preprocessed	Assembler
.S	Assembler source code to be preprocessed and assembled	assembler-with-cpp

Although (by default) the HFS+ filesystem is case-insensitive, the *cc* compile driver distinguishes between uppercase and lowercase in command-line arguments. For example, *cc foo.C* invokes *cc*'s C++ compiler because the file extension is an uppercase C, which denotes a C++ source file. (To *cc*, it's just a command-line argument.) So, even though HFS+ will find the same file whether you type *cc foo.c* or *cc foo.C*, what you enter on the command line makes all the difference in the world, particularly to *cc*.

Preprocessing

When you invoke *cc* without options, it initiates a sequence of four basic operations, or stages: preprocessing, compilation, assembly, and linking. In a multifile program, the first three stages are performed on each individual source code file, creating an object code file for each source code file. The final linking stage combines all the object codes that were created by the first three stages, along with the user-specified object code that may have been compiled earlier, into a single executable image file.

Frameworks

In Mac OS X, a framework is a type of bundle that is named with a *.framework* extension. Before discussing frameworks, let's first briefly explore the notion of a bundle. A bundle is an important software packaging model in Mac OS X consisting of a directory that stores resources related to a given software package, or resources used by many software packages. Bundles, for example, can contain image files, headers, shared libraries, and executables. In addition to frameworks, at least two other types of bundles are used in Mac OS X: applications (named with the *.app* extension) and loadable bundles, including plug-ins (which are usually named with the *.bundle* extension). Here's a comparison of the three types:

- An *application bundle* contains everything an application needs to run: executables, images, etc. You can actually see these contents in the Finder if you Control/right-click on an application's icon and select Show Package Contents.

- A *framework bundle* contains a dynamic shared library along with its resources, including header files, images, and documentation.

- A *loadable bundle* contains executables and associated resources, which are loaded into running applications; these include plug-ins and kernel extensions.

The top-level folder for application and loadable bundles is named *Contents* and contains the entire bundle. Take, for example, Safari. If you Control/right-click on the Safari application in the Finder and select Show Package Contents, the *Contents* folder will be revealed in the Finder. To see what's in the *Contents* folder, press ⌘-3 to switch the Finder to column view, and then press the C key on your keyboard (this highlights the *Contents* folder). You will see the typical contents of an application bundle, including:

- The required XML property list file, *Info.plist*, which contains information about the bundle's configuration

- A folder named *MacOS*, which contains the executable

- A folder named *Resources*, which contains, among other resources, image files

- Files named *CodeResources*, *version.plist*, and *PkgInfo*

Applications can also contain application-specific frameworks, which are not used by any other application or plug-in.

Framework structure

Frameworks are critical in Mac OS X. Cocoa, the toolkit for user interface development, consists of the Foundation and Application Kit (or AppKit) frameworks for Objective-C and Java. Frameworks use a *versioned* bundle structure, which allows multiple versions of the same information (for example, framework code and header files). Frameworks are structured in one of the following ways:

- Symbolic links are used to point to the latest version. This allows for multiple versions of the framework to be present.

- In the Framework bundle structure, the top-level folder is named *Resources*. The actual *Resources* folder need not be located at the top level of the bundle; it may be located deeper inside of the bundle. In this case, a symbolic link pointing to the *Resources* folder is located at the top level.

In either case, an *Info.plist* file describing the framework's configuration must be included in the *Resources* folder. (Chapter 11 discusses how to create frameworks and loadable bundles. This chapter only describes how to use the frameworks.)

Before discussing how to use frameworks, let's look at the different kinds of frameworks. A *private framework* is one that resides in a directory named *PrivateFrameworks* and whose implementation details are not exposed. Specifically, private frameworks reside in one of the following locations:

- *~/Library/PrivateFrameworks*
- */Library/PrivateFrameworks*
- */System/Library/PrivateFrameworks*

An *application-specific framework* can be placed within the given application's package. For example, consider the private framework *iTunesAccess.frame work*, which is located in */System/Library/PrivateFrameworks*. This private framework consists of a directory named *iTunesAccess.framework/*, which, aside from symbolic links and subdirectories, contains the iTunesAccess executable and files named *Info.plist* and *version.plist*. No implementation details are revealed.

A *public framework*, on the other hand, is one whose API can be ascertained, for example, by viewing its header files. Public frameworks reside in appropriate directories named *Frameworks/*. For example, the OpenGL framework resides in */System/Library/Frameworks*. This public framework consists of the directory */System/Library/Frameworks/OpenGL.framework*, which contains (among other things) a subdirectory named *Headers*. Implementation details can be ascertained by examining the header files.

Precisely where a public framework resides depends on its purpose. When you build an application, you can program the path of the framework. Later, when the application is run, the dynamic link editor looks for the framework in the path that was programmed into the application. If the framework is not found there, the following locations are searched in the order shown here:

~/Library/Frameworks
> This is the location for frameworks used by an individual user.

/Library/Frameworks
> Third-party applications that are intended for use by all users on a system should have their frameworks installed in this directory.

/Network/Library/Frameworks
> Third-party applications that are intended for use by all users across a local area network (LAN) should have their frameworks installed in this directory.

/System/Library/Frameworks

This is the location for frameworks provided by Apple (e.g., the AppKit) whose shared libraries are to be used by all applications on the system.

There are three types of frameworks in */System/Library/Frameworks*:

Simple public frameworks

Apple defines a *simple framework* as one that is neither a subframework nor an umbrella framework and has placed in this category only those frameworks that have been used in older versions of Mac OS X. One such example is AppKit, which is located in */System/Library/Frameworks/App Kit.framework* and can be examined in the Finder.

Subframeworks

A subframework is public but has a restriction in that you cannot link directly against it: subframeworks reside in umbrella frameworks, and to use a subframework you must link against the umbrella framework in which it resides. A subframework's API is exposed, however, through its header files.

Umbrella frameworks

An umbrella framework can contain other umbrella frameworks and subframeworks. The exact composition of an umbrella's subframeworks is an implementation detail that is subject to change over time, but the developer need not be concerned with such changes since it is only necessary to link against the umbrella framework and include the umbrella framework's header file. One advantage of this approach is that not only can definitions be moved from the header file of one framework to that of another, but, in the case of umbrella frameworks, the definition of a function can even be moved to another framework if that framework is included in the umbrella framework.

To better understand the difference between simple and umbrella frameworks, compare the composition of the simple framework */System/Library/Frame works/AppKit.framework* with the umbrella framework */System/Library/ Frameworks/CoreServices.framework*. The umbrella framework contains several other frameworks: namely, *AE*, *CarbonCore*, *CFNetwork*, *DictionaryServices*, *LaunchServices*, *Metadata*, *OSServices*, and *SearchKit*. The simple framework does not contain any other subframeworks, and neither is it a subframework contained within an umbrella framework.

Including a framework in your application

When including application-specific frameworks, you must let the preprocessor know where to search for framework header files. You can do this with the -*F* option, which is also accepted by the linker (this is similar to the -*I* option, which lets you specify directories to search for *.h* files). A command of this form:

```
$ cc -F directoryname myprog.c
```

instructs the preprocessor to search the directory *directoryname* for framework header files. The search begins in *directoryname* and then, if necessary, continues in the standard framework directories in the order listed earlier. For example, this command:

```
$ cc -F dir1 -F dir2 -no-cpp-precomp myprog.c
```

results in the linker first searching *dir1*, followed by *dir2*, followed by the standard framework directories (*/Local/Library/Frameworks* and */System/Library/Frameworks*).

To include a framework object header, use `#include` in the following format:

```
#include <framework/filename.h>
```

Here, `framework` is the name of the framework without the extension, and `filename.h` is the source for the header file. If your code is in Objective-C, the `#import` preprocessor directive may be used in place of `#include`. The only difference beyond that is that `#import` makes sure the same file is not included more than once.

The *-F* flag is needed only when building application-specific frameworks, but the *-framework* flag is always needed to link against a framework. Specifically, inclusion of this flag results in a search for the specified framework named when linking. Example 10-1 shows "Hello, World" in Objective-C. Notice that it includes the AppKit framework.

Example 10-1. Saying hello from Objective-C

```
#include <Appkit/AppKit.h>

int main(int argc, const char *argv[])
{
  NSLog(@"Hello, World\n");
  return 0;
}
```

Save Example 10-1 as *hello.m*. To compile it, use *-framework* to pass in the framework name:

```
$ cc -framework AppKit -o hello hello.m
```

The *-framework* flag is accepted only by the linker and is used to name a framework.

Compiler Flags

The *gcc* manpage provides an extensive list of compiler flags. In particular, it describes many flags specific to the PowerPC, Intel x86, and Darwin processors. Table 10-3 describes a few common GCC compiler flags that are specific to Mac OS X. These flags should be used when porting Unix-based software to Mac OS X. We've also included a few flags that enable various Tree-SSA-based optimizations. These are the flags that begin with *-ftree*. Compiler flags of particular interest in Mac OS X are related to the peculiarities of building shared code—for example, the compiler flag *-dynamiclib* is used to build Mach-O dynamic library (*.dylib*) files. For more details, see Chapter 11.

Table 10-3. Selected Mac OS X GCC compiler flags

Flag	Effect
-no-cpp-precomp	Turns off the Mac OS X preprocessor in favor of the GNU preprocessor.
-ObjC, -ObjC++	Specifies *objective-c* and *objective-c++*, respectively. Also passes the *-ObjC* flag to *ld*.
-faltivec	Enables AltiVec language extension (PowerPC only). Provided for compatibility with earlier versions of GCC.
-maltivec	Enables AltiVec language extension (PowerPC only).
-mpim-altivec	Enables AltiVec language extension as defined in the Motorola AltiVec Technology Programming Interface Manual, or PIM (PowerPC only). This option is similar in effect to *-maltivec*, but there are some differences. For example, *-mpim-altivec* disables inlining of functions containing AltiVec instructions as well as inline vectorization of *memset* and *memcopy*.
-mabi-altivec	Adds AltiVec ABI extensions to the current ABI (PowerPC only).
-mnoabi-altivec	Disables AltiVec ABI extensions for the current ABI (PowerPC only).
-mnopim-altivec	Disables the effect of *-mpim-altivec* (PowerPC only).
-mno-altivec-long-deprecated	Disables the warning about the deprecated *long* keyword in AltiVec data types (PowerPC only).
-mnoaltivec	Disables AltiVec language extension (PowerPC only).
-arch ppc970 -arch pp64	Compiles for the PowerPC 970 (a.k.a. G5) processor, and assembles only 64-bit instructions.
-arch x86_64	Compiles for the x86 processor, and assembles only 64-bit instructions.
-m64	Assembles only 64-bit instructions.
-m32	Assembles only 32-bit instructions.
-arch i386	Compiles for the i386 processor, and assembles only 32-bit instructions.
-mcpu=970 -mcpu=G5	Enables the use of G5-specific instructions (PowerPC only).
-force_cpusubtype_ALL	Forces a runtime check to determine which CPU is present and allows code to run on the G4 or G5, regardless of which CPU was used to compile the

Flag	Effect
	code. Exercise caution if you use this compiler flag and G5-specific features at the same time.
-mpowerpc64	When used in combination with -mcpu=970, -mtune=970, and -force_cpusubtype_ALL, enables the G5's support for native 64-bit long-long.
-mpowerpc-gpopt	Uses the hardware-based floating-point square function on the G5. (Use with -mcpu=970, -mtune=970, and -mpowerpc64.)
-ftree-pre	Enables partial redundancy elimination on trees.
-ftree-fre	Enables full redundancy elimination on trees.
-ftree-ccp	Enables sparse conditional constant propagation on trees.
-ftree-ch	Enables loop header copying on trees. This is enabled by default with -O, but not with -Os.
-ftree-dce -ftree-dominator-opts	Enables dead code elimination on trees.
-ftree-elim-checks	Eliminates checks based on scalar evolution information.
-ftree-loop-optimize	Enables loop optimization on trees.
-ftree-loop-linear	Enables linear loop transformations on trees to improve cache performance and allow additional loop optimizations.
-ftree-lim	Enables loop invariant motion on trees.
-ftree-sra	Enables scalar replacements of aggregates.
-ftree-copyrename	Enables copy renaming on trees.
-ftree-ter	Enables temporary expression replacement during SSA to normal phase.
-ftree-lrs	Enables live range splitting during SSA to normal phase.
-ftree-vectorize	Enables loop vectorization on trees. This enables -fstrict-aliasing, by default.
-fstrict-aliasing	Applies the strictest aliasing rules.
-fasm-blocks	Allows blocks and functions of assembly code in C or C+ source code.
-fconstant-cfstrings	Enables automatic creation of a Core Foundation-type constant. (See the gcc manpage for details.)
-fpascal-strings	Allows the use of Pascal-style strings.
-fweak-coalesced	Causes the linker to ignore weakly coalesced definitions in favor of one ordinary definition.
-findirect-virtual-calls	Uses the vtable to call virtual functions, rather than making direct calls.
-fapple-kext	Makes kernel extensions loadable by Darwin kernels. Use in combination with -fno-exceptions and -static.
-fcoalesce-templates	Coalesces instantiated templates.
-fobjc-exceptions	Supports structured exception handling in Objective-C. (See the gcc manpage for more details.)
-fzero-link	Instructs dyld to load the object file at runtime.

Flag	Effect
-Wpragma-once	Causes a warning about #pragma use only once, if necessary.
-Wextra-tokens	Causes a warning if preprocessor directives end with extra tokens.
-Wnewline-eof	Causes a warning if a file ends without a newline character.
-Wno-altivec-long-deprecated	Disables warnings about the keyword "long" being used in an AltiVec data type declaration.
-Wmost	Same effect as *-Wall -Wno-parentheses* (that is, suppress warnings if parentheses are omitted in certain contexts).
-Wno-long-double	Disables warnings about the long-double type being used.
-fast	Optimizes for G5 by default, or for PPC7450 if used in conjunction with the flag *-mcpu=7450*. To build shared libraries with *-fast*, include the *-fPIC* flag.
-static	Inhibits linking with shared libraries, provided that all of your libraries have also been compiled with *-static*.
-shared	Not supported on Mac OS X.
-dynamiclibs	Used to build Mach-O dylibs (see Chapter 11).
-mdynamic-no-pic	Ensures that compiled code will not itself be relocatable, but will have external references that are relocatable.
-mlong-branch	Ensures that calls that use a 32-bit destination address are compiled.
-all_load	Ensures that all members of static archive libraries will be loaded. (See the *ld* manpage for more information.)
-arch_errors_fatal	Causes files that have the wrong architecture to result in fatal errors.
-bind_at_load	Binds all undefined references when the file is loaded.
-bundle	Results in Mach-O bundle format. (See the *ld* manpage for more information.)
-bundle_loader executable	Specifies the *executable* that will load the output file being linked. (See the *ld* manpage for more information.)
-fnon-lvalue-assign	Allows casts and conditionals to be used as lvalues. Although this is on by default in Apple's GCC 4.0, a deprecation warning will be issued whenever an lvalue cast or lvalue conditional is encountered, as such lvalues will not be allowed in future versions of Apple's GCC.
-fno-non-lvalue-assign	Disallows lvalue casts and lvalue conditionals.
-msoft-float	Enables software floating-point emulation rather than using the floating-point register set. This emulation is not performed on Mac OS X, because the required libraries are not included. On Mac OS X this flag prevents floating-point registers from copying data from one memory location to another.
-mmacosx-version-min= version	Sets the earliest version of Mac OS X on which the resulting executable will run.

Flag	Effect
-Os	Optimizes for size and enables -O2 optimizations for speed. On PowerPC, this disables string instructions. To enable string instructions, use -mstring.
-Oz	Optimizes for code size without consideration for speed.

Architectural Issues

There are a few architectural issues to be aware of when developing software on or porting software to Mac OS X. In particular, the most common issues developers run into have to do with vectorization, pointer size, endianness, inline assembly code, and multiple *architectures*.

Universal Binaries for Multiple Architectures

At the time of this writing, Mac OS X is supported on two families of CPUs, each supporting two architectures: for the PowerPC family you can create binaries for *ppc* and *ppc64* architectures, whereas the Intel x86 supports i386 and x86_64 architectures. Fortunately, Apple has introduced something called a *universal binary*, which is a binary that contains object code for multiple architectures.

You can create a four-way universal binary that will run on each of the four architectures just mentioned with the use of *-arch* flags:

```
$ gcc -o hello -arch i386 -arch x86_64 -arch ppc -arch ppc64 hello.c
$ file hello
hello: Mach-O universal binary with 4 architectures
hello (for architecture ppc7400):   Mach-O executable ppc
hello (for architecture i386):  Mach-O executable i386
hello (for architecture ppc64): Mach-O 64-bit executable ppc64
hello (for architecture x86_64):   Mach-O 64-bit executable x86_64
```

You can then run the resulting executable *hello* on any of the four architectures. If you run it on a 64-bit-capable CPU—for example, a PowerPC G5 or an Intel Core 2 duo—the code will run in 64-bit mode. On the other hand, if you run it on a 32-bit-only system—for example, a G4-based system—*hello* will run in 32-bit mode.

Though universal binaries have the flexibility to run on multiple architectures, their file sizes are greater than those of their single-architecture counterparts. For example, the file size of the *hello* binary is 53,576 bytes when created as a four-way universal binary; 28,972 bytes when created as a two-way (*ppc* and i386) universal binary; 8,508 bytes when created as a single-architecture *ppc* binary; and 12,588 bytes when created as a single-architecture i386 binary.

AltiVec

The Velocity Engine, Apple's name for the Motorola 128-bit AltiVec vector processor that allows up to 16 operations in a single clock cycle, is supported on both G4 and G5 processors by the Mac OS X GCC implementation. The Velocity Engine executes operations concurrently with existing integer and floating-point units, which can result in significant performance gains, especially for highly parallel operations. The compiler flag *-maltivec* can be specified to compile code engineered to use the AltiVec instruction set. Inclusion of this command-line option to *cc* defines the preprocessor symbol __VEC__. (See Table 10-3 earlier in this chapter for more AltiVec-related compiler flags.)

64-Bit Computing

On a 32-bit system, such as Mac OS X running on the PowerPC G4 or Intel Core duo, C pointers are 32 bits (4 bytes). On a 64-bit system, such as Mac OS X running on the G5, Quad-Core Intel Xeon, or Intel Core 2 duo, they are 64 bits (8 bytes), provided they are compiled with the *-m64* compiler flag. As long as your code does not rely on any assumptions about pointer size, it should be 64-bit clean. For example, on a 32-bit system the following program prints "4", and on a 64-bit system it prints "8":

```
#include <stdio.h>
int main()
{
  printf("%d\n", sizeof(void *));
  return 0;
}
```

Some 64-bit operating systems, such as Solaris 8 on Ultra hardware (sun4u) and Mac OS X Leopard on Intel Core 2 duo hardware, have a 64-bit kernel space but support both 32- and 64-bit-mode applications, depending on how they are compiled. On G5, Quad-Core Intel Xeon, and Intel Core 2 duo systems, the pointer size is 64 bits, and other data types are mapped onto the 64-bit data type. For example, single-precision floats, which are 32-bit, are converted to double-precision floats when they are loaded into registers. In the registers, single-precision instructions operate on these single-precision floats stored as doubles, performing the required operations on the data. The results, however, are rounded to single-precision 32-bit values. Apple has provided technical documentation containing information and advice on optimizing code to take advantage of the 64-bit architectures that run Mac OS X Leopard. The 64-Bit Transition Guide can be found at *http://developer.apple.com/docu mentation/Darwin/Conceptual/64bitPorting/64bitPorting.pdf*.

Additional information can be found at *http://developer.apple .com/hardware/*. These documents describe in detail the issues involved in tuning code for the G5. We note only a few issues here.

Mac OS X Leopard running on G5 and Intel x86 Core 2 hardware allows applications to access a 64-bit address space. Since both Tiger and Leopard support 64-bit arithmetic instructions even if your code is compiled in 32-bit mode, your code will not necessarily run more efficiently when compiled in 64-bit mode. It should be noted that even on a G4 system, 32-bit applications have a 128-bit long-double data type and a 64-bit long-long data type.

Whether or not you should compile your code in 64-bit mode depends on how important performance is to your application, as well as whether or not 64-bit mode will improve it. The 64-Bit Transition Guide referenced earlier has detailed guidelines on the circumstances that warrant 64-bit binaries. Here, we'll just mention that you'll likely see some performance improvement when you transition your 32-bit application to 64-bit on Intel-based Macs. The main reason is that 64-bit applications on x86_64 architecture use more CPU registers, resulting in faster memory traffic relative to 32-bit compiled versions of the same code. Nevertheless, there are some potential performance inhibitors in 64-bit mode, both on G5 and 64-bit Intel systems. A thorough discussion of the potential benefits and pitfalls of 64-bit computing is beyond the scope of this book. Ultimately, you'll need to benchmark your code to determine if there's a benefit to running a 64-bit version.

To compile 64-bit code using GCC, you can simply use the *-m64* compilation flag, but the resulting executable will run only in 64-bit mode on the host architecture. For example, if you compile using *-m64* on a G5 system, the resulting binary will run on the *ppc64* architecture only. To allow your code to run in 64-bit mode on 64-bit-capable systems and 32-bit mode on 32-bit-only systems, use the *-arch* compiler flags. The *-arch ppc* compiler flag together with *-arch ppc64* produces a "fat" binary: that is, one that can be run on either 32-bit or 64-bit PowerPC systems. Similarly, the *-arch i386* compiler flag together with *-arch x86_64* produces a fat binary that can be run on either 32-bit or 64-bit Intel systems. When a fat binary is run on a 64-bit system, it runs as a 64-bit executable. On the other hand, when the same fat binary is run on a 32-bit system, it runs as a 32-bit executable. Specifying the *-arch ppc* or *-arch i386* compiler flag alone produces a 32-bit executable; since this is the default, it is unnecessary to specify these flags alone. To create a universal binary that will run in 64-bit mode on 64-bit-capable systems and 32-bit mode on non-64-bit systems, use the combination *-arch x86_64 -arch ppc64 -arch i386 -arch ppc*.

The *-Wconversion* compiler flag may also be useful when converting 32-bit code to 64-bit code. The __LP64__, __ppc__, __i386__, and __x86_64__ macros can be used to conditionally compile 64-bit code. At the time of this writing, you can build 64-bit applications in C, and C++ can be compiled in 64-bit mode.

Following is a list of things to bear in mind when engaging in 64-bit computing on Mac OS X:

- Mac OS X follows the LP64 64-bit data model, also used by Sun and SGI: ints are 32-bit, whereas longs, long-longs, and pointers are 64-bit.
- In 64-bit code, ints cannot hold pointers.
- Use of a cast between a 64-bit type and a 32-bit type can destroy data.
- In Tiger, only non-GUI applications can be compiled as 64-bit. You can, however, use a 32-bit GUI to launch and control a 64-bit application. In Leopard, you can compile both GUI and non-GUI applications as 64-bit.
- Compiling an application as 64-bit produces a 64-bit version of the Mach-O binary format, used in Mac OS X. You can determine if a program was compiled as 64-bit, 32-bit, or flat using the *file* command.
- 64-bit applications may use only 64-bit frameworks, and 32-bit applications may use only 32-bit frameworks.

Endianness

CPU architectures are designed to treat the bytes of words in memory as being arranged in big- or little-endian order: big-endian ordering has the most significant byte in the lowest address, whereas little-endian ordering has the most significant byte at the highest byte address.

In general, Intel architectures are little-endian, whereas most Unix/RISC machines, including PowerPC-based Macs, are big-endian.

 The PowerPC is actually *bi-endian*, meaning that it can run as either big- or little-endian. In practice, bi-endian CPUs run exclusively as big- or little-endian.

Inline Assembly

As far as inline assembly code is concerned, if you have any, it will have to be rewritten. Heaven help you if you have to port a whole Just-in-Time (JIT) compiler! For information on the assembler and PowerPC machine languages, see the Mac OS X Assembler Guide (*http://developer.apple.com/documenta tion/DeveloperTools/Reference/Assembler/Assembler.pdf*).

X11-Based Applications and Libraries

Fink and MacPorts (covered in Chapters 12 and 13, respectively) can be used to install many X11-based applications, such as the GNU Image Manipulation Program (GIMP), *xfig/transfig*, ImageMagick, *nedit*, and more. Since Fink understands dependencies, installing some of these applications causes Fink to first install several other packages. For example, since the text editor *nedit* depends on Motif libraries, Fink will first install *lesstif*. (This also gives you the Motif window manager, *mwm*.) Similarly, when you install GIMP via Fink, you will also install the packages for GNOME, GTK+, and *glib*.

You can also use Fink to install libraries directly. For example, this command installs the X11-based Qt libraries:

```
$ fink install qt
```

MacPorts can be used in a similar manner.

Building X11-Based Applications and Libraries

If you cannot find binaries for X11-based applications, or you simply prefer to build the applications yourself, many tools are available to help you do so. When you install the Xcode tools, make sure you install the optional *X11SDK*, which contains development tools and header files for building X11-based applications. If you didn't install *X11SDK* when you first installed Xcode, you can still install it from the *Xcode Tools* folder on the Mac OS X Install DVD.

The process of building software usually begins with generating one or more makefiles customized to your system. For X11 applications, there are two popular methods for generating makefiles:

- One method is to use a *configure* script, as described earlier in this chapter.
- The other popular method involves using the *xmkmf* script, which is a frontend to the *imake* utility. *xmkmf* invokes *imake*, which creates the makefile for you. To do this, *imake* looks for a template file called *Imake file*.

With *imake*-driven source releases, you'll find *Imakefile* in the top-level source directory after you download and unpack a source tarball. After reading the *README* or *INSTALL* files, examine the *Imakefile* to see if you need to change anything. The next step is usually to issue this command:

```
$ xmkmf -a
```

When invoked with the -a option, *xmkmf* reads *imake*-related files in */usr/X11R6/lib/X11/config* and performs the following tasks recursively, beginning in the top-level directory and then continuing in the subdirectories, if there are any:

```
$ make Makefiles
$ make includes
$ make depend
```

The next steps are usually *make, make test* (or *make check*), and *make install*.

To illustrate this method of building software, consider the following example in which we download and build an X11-based game:

1. Download the source tarball:

    ```
    $ ftp ftp://ftp.x.org/contrib/games/xtic1.12.tar.gz
    ```

2. Unpack the source tarball:

    ```
    $ gnutar xvfz xtic1.12.tar.gz
    ```

3. Change to the top-level directory:

    ```
    $ cd xtic1.12/
    ```

4. Generate the makefile:

    ```
    $ xmkmf -a
    ```

5. Build everything (some X11 apps use *make World*):

    ```
    $ make
    ```

6. Have fun:

    ```
    $ ./src/xtic
    ```

AquaTerm

The X Window System is useful to Unix developers and users, since many Unix-based software packages depend on X11 libraries. An interesting project that sometimes eliminates the need for the X Window System is the BSD-licensed *AquaTerm* application, developed by Per Persson (*http://aquaterm.sourceforge.net*). AquaTerm is a Cocoa application that can display vector graphics in an X11-like fashion. It does not replace X11, but it is useful for applications that generate plots and graphs.

The output graphics formats that AquaTerm supports are PDF and EPS. Applications communicate with AquaTerm through an adapter that acts as an intermediary between your old application's API and AquaTerm's API.

At the time of this writing, AquaTerm has adapters for *gnuplot* and *PGPLOT*, as well as example adapters in C, FORTRAN, and Objective-C. For example, assuming that you have installed both X11SDK and AquaTerm, you can build *gnuplot* (*http://www.gnuplot.info*) so that graphics can be displayed in either an AquaTerm window or under X11.

See AquaTerm's website for extensive documentation, including the latest program developments, examples, mailing lists, and other helpful resources.

## CHAPTER 11

Libraries, Headers, and Frameworks

In the previous chapter, we gave an overview of the development tools that ship with Mac OS X and emphasized the compilation phase of building executable code. In this chapter, we'll discuss the linking phase of building Unix-based software under Mac OS X: in particular, header files and libraries.

Header Files

There are two types of header files in Mac OS X:

Ordinary header files
    These header files are inserted into source code by a preprocessor prior to compilation. Ordinary header files have an *.h* extension.

Precompiled header files
    These header files have an *.h.gch* extension.

Header files serve four functions:

- They contain C declarations.
- They contain macro definitions.
- They provide for conditional compilation.
- They provide line control when combining multiple source files into a single file that is subsequently compiled.

Unix developers will find the ordinary header files familiar, since they follow the BSD convention. The C preprocessor directive #include includes a header file in a C source file. There are essentially three forms of this syntax:

```
#include <headername.h>
```
This form is used when the header file is located in the directory */usr/include*.

```
#include <directory/headername.h>
```
This form is used when the header file is located in the directory */usr/include/directory*, where *directory* is a subdirectory of */usr/include*.

```
#include "headername.h"
```
This form is used when the header file is located in a user or nonstandard directory. The file should be either in the same directory as the source file you are compiling or in a directory specified by *cc*'s *-Idirectory* switch.

You can also use #include followed by a macro, provided that when expanded the macro is in one of the aforementioned forms.

As noted in the previous chapter, frameworks are common in Mac OS X when you step outside of the BSD portions of the operating system. To include a framework header file in Objective-C code, use the following format:

```
#import <frameworkname/headerfilename.h>
```

where *frameworkname* is the name of the framework without the extension and *headerfilename* is the name of the header file. For example, the include/import declaration for a Cocoa application would look like this:

```
#import <Cocoa/Cocoa.h>
```

Note that you must use #include rather than #import when including a framework in Carbon code.

When preprocessing header files or any preprocessor directives, the following three actions are always taken:

- Any comment is replaced by a single space.
- Any backslash line continuation escape symbol is removed, and the line following it is joined with the current line. For example:

```
#def\
ine \
NMAX 2000
```

  is processed as:

```
#define NMAX 2000
```

- Any predefined macro name is replaced with its expression. In Mac OS X, there are standard ANSI C predefined macros as well as several predefined macros specific to Mac OS X. For example, __APPLE_CC__ is replaced by an integer that represents the compiler's version number.

Keep the following rules in mind:

- The preprocessor does not recognize comments or macros placed between the < and > symbols in an `#include` directive.

- Comments placed within string constants are regarded as part of those string constants and are not recognized as C comments.

- If ANSI trigraph preprocessing is enabled with *cc -trigraphs*, you must not use a backslash continuation escape symbol within a trigraph sequence, or the trigraph will not be interpreted correctly. ANSI trigraphs are three-character sequences that represent characters that may not be available on older terminals. For example, ??< translates to {. ANSI trigraphs are a rare occurrence these days.

Precompiled Header Files

Mac OS X's Xcode tools support and provide extensive documentation on building and using precompiled header files. This section highlights a few of the issues that may be of interest to Unix developers new to Mac OS X when it comes to working with precompiled headers.

Precompiled header files are binary files that have been generated from ordinary C header files and preprocessed and parsed using *cc*. When such a precompiled header is created, both macros and declarations present in the corresponding ordinary header file are sorted, resulting in a faster compile time and a reduced symbol table size, and consequently faster lookup. Precompiled header files are given an *.h.gch* extension and are produced from ordinary header files that end with an *.h* extension. There is no risk that a precompiled header file will get out of sync with the *.h* file, because the compiler checks the timestamp of the actual header file.

When using precompiled header files, you should not refer to the *.h.gch* version of the name, but rather to the *.h* version in the `#include` directive. If a precompiled version of the header file is available, it is used automatically; otherwise, the real header file (*.h*) is used. So, to include *foo.h.gch*, specify *foo.h*. The fact that *cc* is using a precompiled header is totally hidden from you.

You can create precompiled header files by using either the *cc -precomp* or *cc -x c-header -c* compile driver flags. For example, the following command illustrates this process in its simplest, context-independent form:

```
$ cc -precomp header.h
```

The following command has the same effect:

```
$ cc -x c-header -c header.h
```

In either case, the resulting precompiled header is named *header.h.gch*. If there is context dependence (for example, some conditional compilation), the *-Dsymbol* flag is used. In this case, the command to build a precompiled header file (with the *FOO* symbol defined) is:

```
$ cc -precomp -DFOO header.h -o header.h.gch
```

The *-x* switch supplies the language (see "Supported Languages" in Chapter 10):

```
$ gcc -x c c-header header.h
```

Then, you can compile *main.c* as usual:

```
$ gcc -o main main.c
```

Example 11-1 shows *header.h*, and Example 11-2 shows *main.c*.

Example 11-1. The header .h file

```
/* header.h: a trivial header file. */

#define x 100
```

Example 11-2. The main .c application

```
/* main.c: a simple program that includes header.h. */

#include "header.h"
#include <stdio.h>

int main()
{
  printf("%d\n", x);
  return 0;
}
```

Here are a few issues to keep in mind when you use a precompiled header file:

- You can include only one precompiled header file in any given compilation.
- Although you can place preprocessor directives before it, no C tokens can be placed before the #include of the precompiled header. For example, if you switch the positions of the two #include directives in Example 11-2, the compiler will ignore the precompiled header (*header.h.gch*).
- The language of the precompiled header must match the language of the source in which it is included.
- The version of *gcc* that produced the precompiled header and the version of *gcc* being used in the compilation in which the precompiled header is being included must be the same. So, for example, you can't include a

procompiled header that was produced by GCC 3.3 in code being compiled with GCC 4.0.1.

For more details on building and using precompiled header files, read the documentation available at *http://developer.apple.com/documentation/Develo perTools/gcc-4.0.1/gcc/Precompiled-Headers.html*.

 Persistent Front End (PFE) precompilation (needed for C++ and Objective-C++ in pre-Tiger versions of Mac OS X) and *cpp-precomp* are not supported in Tiger or later releases of Mac OS X.

malloc.h

malloc.h is a header file associated with memory allocation. Software designed for older Unix systems may expect to find this header file in */usr/include*; however, *malloc.h* is not present in this directory. The set of `malloc()` function prototypes is actually found in *stdlib.h*, so for portability, your programs should include *stdlib.h* instead of *malloc.h*. (This is the norm; systems that require *malloc.h* are the rare exception these days.) GNU *autoconf* will detect systems that require *malloc.h* and define the `HAVE_MALLOC_H` macro. If you do not use GNU *autoconf*, you will need to detect this case on your own and set the macro accordingly. You can handle such cases with this code:

```
#include <stdlib.h>
#ifdef HAVE_MALLOC_H
#include <malloc.h>
#endif
```

For a list of libraries that come with Mac OS X, see the "Interesting and Important Libraries" section later in this chapter.

poll.h

In pre-Tiger versions of Mac OS X (a BSD platform), one issue when porting software from a System V platform was the lack of the `poll()` system call function, which provides a mechanism for I/O multiplexing. Mac OS X 10.3 (Panther) provided this function through emulation, making use of its BSD analog, `select()`. Beginning with Mac OS X 10.4 (Tiger), `poll()` has been provided as a native function. The associated header file, */usr/include/poll.h*, is included with Mac OS X 10.3 and higher.

wchar.h and iconv.h

Another issue in porting Unix software to pre-Panther versions of Mac OS X was the relatively weak support for wide (i.e., more than 8 bits) character data types (e.g., Unicode). Releases of Mac OS X beginning with Panther provide better support for wide character data types by including the GNU *libiconv*, which provides the `iconv()` function to convert between various text encodings. Additionally, the *wchar_t* type is supported in Mac OS X 10.3 and higher. The header files *iconv.h* and *wchar.h* are also included. Alternatively, you can use the APIs available in the Core Foundation String Services, which are described in *CFString.h*.

dlfcn.h

The *dlfcn.h* header file, associated with `dl` functions such as `dlopen()`, is included with Mac OS X 10.4 and higher. The `dl` functions themselves are actually included in *libSystem*.

alloc.h

alloc.h is another header file associated with memory allocation. Although this header file is not included with Mac OS X, its functionality is provided by *stdlib.h*. If your code makes a specific request to include *alloc.h*, you have several choices. One option is to remove the `#include <alloc.h>` statement in your source code. This may be cumbersome, however, if your `#include` statement appears in many files. Another alternative is to create your own version of *alloc.h*. A sample *alloc.h* is provided in the ADC's Technical Note TN2071 (*http://developer.apple.com/technotes/tn2002/tn2071.html*).

lcyrpt.h and values.h

Although *lcrypt.h* is not included with Mac OS X, its functionality is provided by *unistd.h*, in which various symbolic constants are defined. Similarly, *values.h*—another header file found on many Unix systems—is not included with Mac OS X. Its functionality, however, is provided by *limits.h*, which specifies parameters such as the largest and smallest integers, largest and smallest unsigned integers, largest and smallest floating-point numbers, and so on.

The System Library: libSystem

In Darwin, much is built into the system library, */usr/lib/libSystem.dylib*. In particular, the following libraries are included in *libSystem*:

libc
> The standard C library. This library contains the functions used by C programmers on all platforms.

libinfo
> The Directory Services library.

libkvm
> The kernel virtual memory library. (Present as a symbolic link in Mac OS X 10.4, but not in 10.5.)

libm
> The math library, which contains arithmetic functions.

libpoll
> The poll library.

libpthread
> The POSIX threads library, which allows multiple tasks to run concurrently within a single program.

librpcsvc
> The RPC services library.

librproc
> The *libproc* library, used to obtain process information.

libdbm
> Database routines.

libdl
> The dynamic loader library.

Symbolic links are provided as placeholders for these libraries. For example, *libm.dylib* and *libpthread.dylib* are symbolic links in */usr/lib* that point to *libSystem.dylib*. Thus, while it won't do any harm, supplying flags such as *-lm* and *-lpthread* to the linker is technically unnecessary. (The *-lm* option links to the math library, whereas *-lpthread* links to the POSIX threads library; since *libSystem* provides these functions, you don't need to use these options.) That said, you should still include these flags to ensure your application is portable to other systems.

In Mac OS X 10.1 and earlier versions, the *curses* screen library (a set of functions for controlling a terminal display) was part of *libSystem.dylib*. In Mac OS X 10.2 and higher, the *ncurses* library (*/usr/lib/libncurses.5.4.dylib*) is used in place of *curses*. However, you may still encounter source code releases that look for *curses* in *libSystem.dylib*, which results in linking errors. You can work around this problem by adding *-lcurses* to the linker arguments. This is portable to earlier versions of Mac OS X as well, since */usr/lib/libcurses.dylib* is a symlink to *libncurses* in versions 10.2 through 10.5 and to *libSystem* in earlier versions.

Interestingly enough, in Max OS X 10.4 and earlier, there is no symbolic link for *libutil*, whose functionality is also provided by *libSystem*. In Mac OS 10.5 *libutil* is a symbolic link to *libutil1.0* and has evidently been moved out of *libSystem* in Leopard. (*libutil* is a library that provides functions related to login, logout, terminal assignment, and logging.) So, if a link fails because of *-lutil*, try taking it out to see if that solves the problem.

---

libstdc++

In Apple's implementation of GCC prior to GCC 4.0, *libstdc++* was included only as a static library (*libstdc++.a*). In contrast, only the dynamic version of this library, (*libstdc++.dyld*), is included in Mac OS X 10.3.9 and higher. As a consequence, any C++ application compiled with GCC 4.0.x won't run on releases of Mac OS X earlier than 10.3.9.

Shared Libraries Versus Loadable Modules

The Executable and Linking Format (ELF), developed by the Unix System Laboratories, is common in the Unix world. On ELF systems, no distinction is made between shared libraries and loadable modules; shared code can be used as a library for dynamic loading. ELF is the default binary format on Linux, Solaris 2.*x*, and SVR4. Since these systems cover a large share of the Unix base, most Unix developers have experience on ELF systems. Thus, it may come as a surprise to experienced Unix developers that shared libraries and loadable modules are not the same on Mac OS X. This is because Mac OS X uses a different binary format: the Mach object format, known as Mach-O.

Mach-O was initially designed as a replacement for the standard BSD *a.out* format to contain statically linked executables, but dynamically linked code capability was subsequently added. Mach-O is more flexible than the older BSD *a.out* format. Mach-O shared libraries have the file type `MH_DYLIB` and

---

the *.dylib* (dynamic library) suffix and can be linked to with static linker flags. So, if you have a shared library named *libcool.dylib*, you can link to this library by specifying the *-lcool* flag. Although shared libraries cannot be loaded dynamically as modules, they can be loaded through the *dyld* API (see the manpage for *dyld*, the dynamic link editor). It is important to point out that in releases of Mac OS X prior to Leopard, shared libraries cannot be unloaded. In Leopard, shared libraries can be unloaded using `dlopen()` and `dlclose()`.

Loadable modules, called *bundles* in Mac OS X, have the file type `MH_BUNDLE`. To maintain consistency across platforms, most Unix-based software ports usually produce bundles with a *.so* extension. Although Apple recommends giving bundles a *.bundle* extension, it isn't mandatory.

You need to use special flags with *cc* when compiling a shared library or a bundle on Darwin. One difference between Darwin and many other Unix systems is that no *position-independent code* (PIC) flag is needed, because it is the default for Darwin. Also, since the linker does not allow common symbols, the compiler flag *-fno-common* is required for both shared libraries and bundles. (A common symbol is one that is defined multiple times. You should instead define a symbol once and use C's *extern* keyword to declare it in places where it is needed.)

Loading a Bundle

You cannot link directly against a bundle. Instead, bundles must be dynamically loaded and unloaded by the *dyld* APIs. */usr/lib/libdl.dylib* is provided as a symbolic link to *libSystem.dylib*.

In Panther, `dlopen()`, `dlclose()`, `dlsym()`, `dlerror()` functions were provided as interfaces to the dynamic linker using the native *dyld*, `NSModule()`, and `NSObjectFileImage()` functions. This made porting common Unix source code relatively painless.

In Tiger and Leopard, the `dlopen()`, `dlclose()`, `dlsym()`, and `dlerror()` functions are natively part of *dyld*, providing both improved performance and better standards compliance.

To build a shared library, use *cc*'s *-dynamiclib* option. Use the *-bundle* option to build a loadable module or bundle.

Building a Shared Library

Suppose you want to create a shared library containing one or more C functions, such as the one shown in Example 11-3.

Example 11-3. A simple C program

```
/*
 * answer.c: The answer to life, the universe, and everything.
 */
int get_answer()
{
  return 42;
}
```

If you compile the program containing the function into a shared library, you can test it with the program shown in Example 11-4.

Example 11-4. Compiling answer.c into a shared library

```
/*
 * deep_thought.c: Obtain the answer to life, the universe,
 * and everything, and act startled when you actually hear it.
 */
#include <stdio.h>
int main()
{
  int the_answer;
  the_answer = get_answer();
  printf("The answer is... %d\n", the_answer);

  fprintf(stderr, "%d??!!\n", the_answer);
  return 0;
}
```

The makefile shown in Example 11-5 compiles and links the library and then compiles, links, and executes the test program.

Example 11-5. Sample makefile for creating and testing a shared library

```
# Makefile: Create and test a shared library.
#
# Usage: make test
#
CC = cc
LD = cc
CFLAGS = -O -fno-common
OBJS = answer.o

all: deep_thought

# Create the shared library.
#
answer.o: answer.c
    $(CC) $(CFLAGS) -c answer.c

libanswer.dylib: answer.o
    $(LD) -dynamiclib  -install_name  libanswer.dylib \
    -o libanswer.dylib answer.o
```

```
# Test the shared library with the deep_thought program.
#
deep_thought.o: deep_thought.c
    $(CC) $(CFLAGS) -c deep_thought.c

deep_thought: deep_thought.o libanswer.dylib
    $(LD) -o deep_thought deep_thought.o -L. -lanswer

test: all
    ./deep_thought

clean:
    rm -f *.o core deep_thought libanswer.dylib
```

This makefile makes use of the *ld* flag *-install_name*, which is the Mach-O analog of *-soname*, used for building shared libraries on ELF systems. The *-install_name* flag is used to specify where the executable linked against it should look for the library. The *-install_name* in the makefile shown in Example 11-5 specifies that the *deep_thought* executable is to look for the library *libanswer.dylib* in the same directory as the executable itself. The command *otool* can be used to verify this:

```
$ otool -L deep_thought
deep_thought:
    libanswer.dylib (compatibility version 0.0.0, current version 0.0.0)
    /usr/lib/libgcc_s.1.dylib (compatibility version 1.0.0, current version
    1.0.0)
    /usr/lib/libSystem.B.dylib (compatibility version 1.0.0, current version
    111.0.0)
```

In Tiger, the *-install_name* flag is often used with *@execution_path* to specify the relative pathname of the library (i.e., the pathname of the library relative to the executable). For example, suppose we change the makefile in Example 11-5 by adding an install target:

```
install: libanswer.dylib
    cp libanswer.dylib ../lib/.
```

and then add *install* to the *all* target's dependency list and change the *libanswer* target to the following:

```
libanswer.dylib: answer.o
    $(LD) -dynamiclib -install_name  @execution_path/../lib/\
    libanswer.dylib -o libanswer.dylib answer.o
```

Then the *deep_thought* executable built using this makefile looks for the *libanswer.dylib* in *../lib*. The output from *otool* shows this change:

```
$ otool -L deep_thought
deep_thought:
    @execution_path/../lib/libanswer.dylib (compatibility version 0.0.0,
    current version 0.0.0)
```

```
/usr/lib/libgcc_s.1.dylib (compatibility version 1.0.0, current
version 1.0.0)
/usr/lib/libSystem.B.dylib (compatibility version 1.0.0, current
version 111.0.0)
```

This is often done in Tiger when building a private framework associated with
an application, since private frameworks are located within the application's
contents. Things are a bit different in Leopard.

In Leopard, the first step is to create a dynamic library with a *.dylib* extension with an *-install_name* that begins with *@rpath*. The second step is to use
the linker flag *-rpath* to specify a list of directories that should be searched at
runtime. The directory pathnames can be absolute or relative. Relative pathnames are relative to the executable and begin with *@loader_path*. The
makefile shown in Example 11-6 compiles and links the library and then compiles, links, and executes the test program.

Example 11-6. Sample makefile for creating and testing a shared library

```
# Makefile: Create and test a shared library.
#
# Usage: make test
#
CC = cc
LD = cc
CFLAGS = -O -fno-common

all: install deep_thought

# Create the shared library.
#
answer.o: answer.c
    $(CC) $(CFLAGS) -c answer.c

libanswer.dylib: answer.o
    $(LD) -dynamiclib -o libanswer.dylib answer.o \
    -install_name @rpath/libanswer.dylib

# Test the shared library with the deep_thought program.
#
deep_thought.o: deep_thought.c
    $(CC) $(CFLAGS) -c deep_thought.c

deep_thought: deep_thought.o libanswer.dylib
    $(LD) -o deep_thought deep_thought.o ../lib/libanswer.dylib \
    -Wl,-rpath -Wl,@loader_path/../lib

test: all
    ./deep_thought

install: libanswer.dylib
    cp libanswer.dylib ../lib/.
```

```
clean:
    rm -f *.o core deep_thought libanswer.dylib ../lib/libanswer.dylib
```

Dynamically Loading Libraries

You can turn *answer.o* into a bundle, which can be dynamically loaded using the following command:

```
$ cc -bundle -o libanswer.bundle answer.o
```

You don't need to specify the bundle at link time; instead, use the *dyld* functions NSCreateObjectFileImageFromFile() and NSLinkModule() to load the library. Then, you can use NSLookupSymbolInModule() and NSAddressOfSymbol() to access the symbols that the library exports. Example 11-7 loads *libanswer.bundle* and invokes the get_answer() function. It is similar to Example 11-4, but many lines (shown in bold) have been added.

Example 11-7. Dynamically loading a bundle and invoking a function

```
/*
 * deep_thought_dyld.c: Obtain the answer to life, the universe,
 * and everything, and act startled when you actually hear it.
 */
#include <stdio.h>
#import <mach-o/dyld.h>

int main()
{
  int the_answer;
  int rc;                 // Success or failure result value
  NSObjectFileImage img;  // Represents the bundle's object file
  NSModule handle;        // Handle to the loaded bundle
  NSSymbol sym;           // Represents a symbol in the bundle

  int (*get_answer) (void);  // Function pointer for get_answer

  /* Get an object file for the bundle. */
  rc = NSCreateObjectFileImageFromFile("libanswer.bundle", &img);
  if (rc != NSObjectFileImageSuccess) {
    fprintf(stderr, "Could not load libanswer.bundle.\n");
    exit(-1);   }

  /* Get a handle for the bundle. */
  handle = NSLinkModule(img, "libanswer.bundle", FALSE);

  /* Look up the get_answer function. */
  sym = NSLookupSymbolInModule(handle, "_get_answer");
  if (sym == NULL)
  {
    fprintf(stderr, "Could not find symbol: _get_answer.\n");
    exit(-2);
```

```
    }

    /* Get the address of the function. */
    get_answer = NSAddressOfSymbol(sym);

    /* Invoke the function and display the answer. */
    the_answer = get_answer();
    printf("The answer is... %d\n", the_answer);

    fprintf(stderr, "%d!\n", the_answer);
    return 0;
}
```

For more information on these functions, see the *NSObjectFileImage*, *NSModule*, and *NSSymbol* manpages. To compile the code in Example 11-7, use the following command:

```
$ cc -O -fno-common -o deep_thought_dyld deep_thought_dyld.c
```

Two-Level Namespaces

In Mac OS X 10.0, the dynamic linker merged symbols into a single (flat) namespace. So, if you linked against two different libraries that both defined the same function, the dynamic linker complained because the same symbol was defined in both places. This approach prevented collisions that were known at compile time. However, a lack of conflict at compile time does not guarantee that a future version of the library won't introduce a conflict.

Suppose you linked your application against version 1 of *libfoo* and version 1 of *libbar*. At the time you compiled your application, *libfoo* defined a function called logerror(), and *libbar* did not. But when version 2 of *libbar* came out, it included a function called logerror() too. Since the conflict was not known at compile time, your application doesn't expect *libbar* to contain this function. If your application happens to load *libbar* before *libfoo*, it will call *libbar*'s logerror() method, which is not what you want.

To deal with this problem, Mac OS X 10.1 introduced *two-level namespaces*, which the compiler uses by default. (No changes to two-level namespaces have been introduced in Mac OS X Releases 10.2 through 10.5.) With this feature, you can link against Version 1 of *libfoo* and *libbar*, and the linker will create an application that knows logerror() lives in *libfoo*. So, even if a future version of *libbar* includes a logerror() function, your application will know which logerror() it should use.

If you want to build an application using a flat namespace, use the *-flat_namespace* linker flag. See the *ld* manpage for more details.

Library Versions

Library version numbering is one area where Mac OS X differs from other Unix variants. In particular, the dynamic linker, *dyld*, checks both major and minor version numbers. Also, the manner in which library names carry the version numbers is different. On ELF systems, shared libraries are named with an extension similar to the following:

```
libname.so.major_version_no.minor_version_no
```

Typically, a symbolic link is created in the library named *libname.so*, which points to the most current version of the library. For example, on an ELF system such as Solaris, *libMagick.so.10.0.7* is the name of an actual library. If this is the latest installed version of the library, you can find symbolic links that point to this library in the same directory. These symbolic links are typically created during the installation process.

In this example, both *libMagick.so* and *libMagick.so.10* are symbolic links that point to *libMagick.so.10.0.7*. Older versions of the library, such as *libMagick.so.10.0.3*, may also be present, but the symbolic links will always point to the latest version because they are updated whenever a newer version is installed. This works because when you create a shared library, you need to specify the name of the library to be used when a program calls the library at runtime.

 In general, you should keep older versions of libraries around, just in case an application depends on them. If you are certain there are no dependencies, you can safely remove an older version.

On Mac OS X, the *libMagick* library is named *libMagick.10.0.7.dylib*, and the symbolic links *libMagick.dylib* and *libMagick.10.dylib* point to it. Older versions, such as *libMagick.10.0.3.dylib*, may also be found in the same directory. One difference that is immediately apparent on Mac OS X systems is that the version numbers are placed between the library name and the *.dylib* extension, rather than at the end of the filename as on other Unix systems (e.g., *libMagick.so.10.0.7*).

Another difference on Darwin is that the absolute pathname is specified when the library is installed. Thus, *ldconfig* is not used in Darwin, since paths to linked dynamic shared libraries are included in the executables. On an ELF system, you typically use *ldconfig* or set the LD_LIBRARY_PATH variable. In Darwin, you use DYLD_LIBRARY_PATH instead of LD_LIBRARY_PATH (see the *dyld* manpage for more details).

You can link against a particular version of a library by including the appropriate option for *cc*, such as *-lMagick.10.0.7*. Minor version checking is another way that the Mach-O format differs from ELF. To illustrate this, let's revisit Example 11-4 from earlier in this chapter.

Suppose that the library shown in Example 11-4 is continually improved: minor bugs are fixed, minor expanded capabilities are added, and (in time) major new features are introduced. In each of these cases, you'll need to rename the library to reflect the latest version. Assume that the last version of the library is named *libanswer.1.2.5.dylib*. The major version number is *1*, the minor revision is 2, and the bug-fix (i.e., fully compatible) revision number is 5. Example 11-8 illustrates how to update this library to release *libanswer.1.2.6.dylib*, which is fully compatible with Release 1.2.5 but contains some bug fixes.

In the makefile shown earlier in Example 11-5, replace the following lines:

```
libanswer.dylib: answer.o
    $(LD) -dynamiclib -install_name libanswer.dylib \
    -o libanswer.dylib answer.o
```

with the code shown in Example 11-8.

Example 11-8. Versioning the answer library

```
libanswer.dylib: answer.o
    $(LD) -dynamiclib -install_name libanswer.1.dylib \
        -compatibility_version 1.2 -current_version 1.2.6 \
        -o libanswer.1.2.6.dylib answer.o
    rm -f libanswer.1.dylib  libanswer.1.2.dylib libanswer.dylib
    ln -s libanswer.1.2.6.dylib libanswer.1.2.dylib
    ln -s libanswer.1.2.6.dylib libanswer.1.dylib
    ln -s libanswer.1.2.6.dylib libanswer.dylib
```

Symbolic links are established to point to the actual library: one link reflects the major revision, one reflects the minor revision, and one simply reflects the name of the library.

The compatibility version number checks that the library used by an executable is compatible with the library that was linked when the executable was created.

Creating and Linking Static Libraries

The creation of static libraries in Mac OS X is much the same as in other Unix variants, with one exception: after installing the libraries in their destination directories, you must use *ranlib* to recatalog the newly installed archive libraries (i.e., the *lib*.a* files).

Another issue involving static libraries on Mac OS X is the order in which things are listed when libraries are linked. The Darwin link editor loads object files and libraries in the exact order given in the *cc* command. For example, suppose you've created a static archive library named *libmtr.a*. Consider the following attempt to link to this library:

```
$ cc -L. -lmtr -o testlibmtr testlibmtr.o
/usr/bin/ld: Undefined symbols:
_cot
_csc
_sec
```

To avoid this problem, you would need to rewrite the command as follows:

```
$ cc -o testlibmtr testlibmtr.o -L. -lmtr
```

The key idea here is that the linker resolves symbols from left to right. In the first case, the library is placed first. When it is examined, no undefined symbols are encountered, so the library is ignored (there's nothing to be done with it). The object code from your program is then processed, but any references to functions in the library that was just ignored are unresolved, so the link fails. In contrast, the second attempt is successful because the object files are placed before the library. For the link editor to realize that it needs to look for undefined symbols (which are defined in the library), it must encounter the object files before the static library.

Creating Frameworks

In Chapter 10, we briefly discussed frameworks and how to use them. In this section, we'll show you how to create frameworks.

A shared library can be packaged, along with its associated resources, as a framework. To create a framework you must build and install a shared library in a framework directory. As an example, let's package the *libanswer.dylib* shared library as a versioned framework, using the name *ans*. That is, the framework will be a directory named *ans.framework*, which will contain the shared library file named *ans*. Three basic steps are required to build a versioned framework:

1. Create the framework directory hierarchy. If this is the first version of the framework on the system, the bottom-level directory will be A. This is where the shared library will be installed:

   ```
   $ mkdir -p ans.framework/Versions/A
   ```

   If you subsequently install a later version of the shared library, you will install it in directory B at the same level of the directory hierarchy as A.

2. Build the shared library in the framework *Versions* directory:

```
$ cc -dynamiclib -o ans.framework/Versions/A/ans answer.o
```

3. Create symbolic links:

```
$ ln -s ans.framework/Versions/A  ans.framework/Versions/Current
$ ln -s ans.framework/Versions/A/ans  ans.framework/ans
```

For the first installation of the shared library (i.e., in *A*), *Current* should point to *A*, as shown here. When a later version of the library is subsequently installed in *B*, you'll need to change the *Current* symbolic link to point to *B*; however, the older version in *A* can stay on the system in case some application needs that version. Since the symbolic link *ans.framework/ans* also points the most recent version of the shared library, it will also need to be updated when the framework is updated.

Performance Tools and Debugging Tools

The developer tools that ship with Mac OS X include an impressive array of debugging and tuning tools. These tools are extensively documented at the websites *http://developer.apple.com/performance/* and *http://developer.apple.com/documentation/MacOSX/Conceptual/OSX_Technology_Overview/Tools/chapter_952_section_2.html*. Those sites include more complete list of tools and offer examples to demonstrate their use. The following short list is intended to give you an idea of what is available:

Activity Monitor
> A GUI application, located in */Applications/Utilities*, that displays information on memory and CPU usage for running processes. This application is similar to the command-line utility *top*, which is also included with Tiger and later.

atos
> Converts to and from symbol names and the numeric addresses of symbols in running programs.

BigTop
> A GUI application, similar to both *top* and *vm_stat*, that displays information on memory, CPU, network, and disk usage for running processes.

c2ph
> Displays information on C structures in object files.

DTrace
> An open source command-line monitoring utility, developed by Sun Microsystems.

fs_usage
Displays information on filesystem activity.

gdb
The GNU debugger.

gprof
Profiles execution of programs by reporting information such as execution times and the number of calls for individual functions.

heap
Analyzes memory usage.

Instruments
A timeline-based performance visualization application to monitor CPU usage, disk I/O, memory usage, garbage collection, and events (Mac OS X 10.5 only). Instruments is built on top of the open source DTrace utility.

kdump
Displays kernel race data (no longer available in Mac OS X 10.5).

leaks
Lists the addresses and sizes of unreferenced *malloc* buffers.

MallocDebug
Analyzes memory usage.

malloc_history
Lists the *malloc* allocation history of a given process.

nm
Displays a symbol table for object files.

ObjectAlloc
Analyzes memory allocation and deallocation. (Replaced by Instruments template *ObjectAlloc.tracetemplate* in Mac OS X 10.5.)

OpenGL Profiler
Profiles OpenGL-based applications.

OpenGL Shader Builder
A debugger for OpenGL-based applications.

otool
A command-line utility used to display information associated with object files or libraries. Earlier, we used it with the -*L* option, which displays the names and version numbers of the shared libraries used by the given object file. For more details, see the *otool* manpage.

pagestuff
Displays information about the logical pages of a Mach-O executable file.

Pixie
A magnifying-glass tool for checking graphics.

pstruct

Same as *c2ph*.

QuartzDebug

A debugging tool related to the Quartz graphics system.

sample

A command-line tool used to profile a process over a time interval.

Sampler

Performs a statistical analysis of where an application spends its time by providing information such as how often allocation routines, system calls, or other functions are called. (Replaced by Instruments template *Sampler.tracetemplate* in Mac OS X 10.5.)

sc_usage

Displays information on system calls and page faults.

Shark

Provides instruction-level profiling of the execution time of a program, using statistical sampling. Advice on optimization is also provided. (A command-line version, */usr/bin/shark*, is also provided.)

Spin Control

Monitors programs that become unresponsive and cause the spinning cursor.

Thread Viewer

Profiles individual threads in multithreaded applications.

top

Reports dynamically updated statistics on memory and CPU usage for running processes.

vmmap

Displays a virtual memory map in a process, including the attributes of memory regions such as starting addresses, sizes, and permissions.

CHUD Tools

In addition to the tools listed in the previous section, a set of performance and optimization tools bundled as the Computer Hardware Understanding Development Tools (CHUD Tools) package is available as an optional installation with Xcode. You can also download the latest version from *http://devel oper.apple.com/tools/download/*.

CHUD tools are used to configure and display the performance monitor counters provided on Apple systems. These performance monitors record events such as cache misses, page faults, and other performance issues. The list pro-

---

vides information on a few of the tools provided with the CHUD collection (for more details, see *http://developer.apple.com/referencelibrary/Developer Tools/idxPerformance-date.html*):

acid
> A command-line tool used to analyze traces provided by *amber*.

amber
> A command-line tool for instruction-level traces of execution threads.

PMC Index
> Monitors performance counter events.

Reggie SE
> Analyzes and modifies CPU and PCI configuration registers.

Saturn
> Provides exact (as opposed to statistical) profiling at the function level. For example, Saturn reports how many times a given function is called. Results are represented in graphical format.

SpindownHD
> Monitors power state of hard drives.

simg4
> A command-line tool that simulates the G4 (7400/7410) processor. You can use this cycle-accurate simulator to run through a trace file generated by *amber*.

simg4_plus
> A command-line tool that simulates the G4 (7450) processor. You can use this cycle-accurate simulator to run through a trace file generated by *amber*.

simg5
> A command-line tool that simulates the G5 processor. You can use this cycle-accurate simulator to run through a trace file generated by *amber*.

A CHUD framework (*/System/Library/PrivateFrameworks/CHUD.frame work*) that enables you to write your own performance tools (among other things) is also provided.

Interesting and Important Libraries

Table 11-1 lists some significant libraries included with Mac OS X, and Table 11-2 lists some significant libraries that do not come with Mac OS X but that may be available through Fink (see Chapter 12) or MacPorts (see Chapter 13). You can get a more complete list of the libraries included with Mac OS X by listing the contents of the */usr/lib* and */usr/X11/lib* directories:

```
$ ls -l /usr/lib /usr/X11/lib
```

Table 11-1. Important Mac OS X libraries

Library	Description	Headers
libalias	Packet aliasing library for masquerading and network address translation (NAT)	Not included in Mac OS X; see the network_cmds module in the Darwin CVS archive
libatlas	Automatically tuned linear algebra library (this is a symbolic link to lib BLAS in the Accelerate framework)	Not included in Mac OS X
libdtrace_dyld	DTrace library	dtrace.h
libBSDPClient	BSDP client library	Not included in Mac OS X
libBSDPServer	BSDP server library	Not included in Mac OS X
libl.a	lex runtime library	Not applicable; lexical analyzers that you generate with lex have all the necessary definitions
libMallocDebug	Library for the MallocDebug utility (/Developer/Applications)	Not applicable; you don't need to do anything special with your code to use this utility
libSaturn	Library for the Saturn utility (/Developer/Applications)	Saturn.h
libamber	Library for the amber utility	amber.h
libbsm	Basic security library	/usr/include/bsm/libbsm.h
libedit	Replacement for readline library (libreadline is provided as a symbolic link to libedit)	histedit.h
libxslt	XSLT C library, based on the libxml2 XML C parser developed for the GNOME project	/usr/include/libxslt/xslt.h
libexslt	Provides extensions to XSLT functions	/usr/include/libexslt/exslt.h
libfl.a	Font library	Not included in Mac OS X
libform	Forms library	form.h
libncurses (libcurses is available for backward compatibility)	ncurses (new curses) screen library, a set of functions for controlling a terminal's display screen	/usr/include/ncurses.h (curses.h is available for backward compatibility)
libicucore	International Components for Unicode library	Not included in Mac OS X
libiodbc, libiodbcinst	Intrinsic Open Database Connectivity library	iodbcext.h, iodbcinst.h, iodbcunix.h
libipsec	IPsec library	/usr/include/netinet6/ipsec.h
liblber	lber library	lber.h

Library	Description	Headers
libltdl	GNU *ltdl*, a system-independent *dlopen* wrapper for GNU *libtool*	*ltdl.h*
libmenu	Menus library	*menu.h*
libmx	Math library with support for long double and complex APIs	*math.h*
libobjc	Library for the GNU Objective-C compiler	*/usr/include/objc/**
libpcap	Packet-capture library	*/usr/include/pcap**
libneon	HTTP/WebDAV client library with a C API (installed with Leopard, but not Tiger)	Not included in Mac OS X
libmpi	Message-passing interface library	*mpi.h*
libssl and *libcrypto*	Open source toolkit implementing the Secure Sockets Layer (SSL) versions 2 and 3 and Transport Layer Security (TLS) version 1 protocols and a full-strength, general-purpose cryptography library	*/usr/include/openssl/**
libsvn*	Subversion-related libraries	*/usr/include/subversion-1**
liby.a	*yacc* runtime library	Not applicable; parsers that you generate with *yacc* have all the necessary definitions
libz	General-purpose data-compression library (*Zlib*)	*zlib.h*
libbz2	File-compression library (*bzip2*)	*bzlib.h*
libxar	Extensible Archive format library	*xar.h*
libpoll	System V *poll(2)* poll library (symbolic link to *libSystem.dylib*)	*poll.h*
libiconv	Character set conversion library	*iconv.h*
libcharset	Character set determination library	*libcharset.h*
libcups	Common Unix Printing System (CUPS) library	*/usr/include/cups**
libcurl	Library for *curl*, a command-line tool for file transfer	*/usr/include/curl/**
libgutenprint	Library for Gutenprint (formerly known as Gimp-Print)	Not available
libpam	Interface library for the Pluggable Authentication Modules (PAM)	*/usr/include/pam/**
libpanel	Panel stack extension for *curses*	*panel.h*

Library	Description	Headers
libxml2	XML parsing library, version 2	*/usr/include/libxml2/**
libruby	Library for the interpreted object-oriented scripting language Ruby	*/usr/lib/ruby/1.8/universal-darwin9.0 /**
libtcl	Tcl scripting language library	*tcl.h*
libtk	Library for Tk, the graphical companion to Tcl	*tk.h*
libwrap	Library for TCP wrappers, which monitors and filters incoming requests for TCP-based services	*tcpd.h*
freetype2	TrueType font rendering library, version 2	*/usr/X11/include/freetype2/**
libexpat	C library for parsing XML (installed with Leopard but not Tiger)	*expat.h*
libdbm	Database management library	*ndbm.h*

Table 11-2. Libraries not included with Mac OS X

MacPorts or Fink package	Description	Home page
aalib	ASCII art library	*http://aa-project.sourceforge.net/aalib/*
db3	Berkeley DB embedded database library, version 3	*http://www.sleepycat.com*
db4	Berkeley DB embedded database library, version 4	*http://www.sleepycat.com*
fnlib	Font rendering library for X11	*http://www.enlightenment.org*
gc	General-purpose garbage collection library	*http://www.hpl.hp.com/personal/Hans_ Boehm/gc/*
gd2	Graphics generation library	*http://www.boutell.com/gd/*
gdal	Translator library for raster geospatial data formats	*http://www.remotesensing.org/gdal/*
gdbm	GNU *dbm* library	*http://www.gnu.org*
giflib	GIF image format handling library, LZW-enabled version	*http://prtr-13.ucsc.edu/~badger/software/libungif/*
glib	Low-level library that supports GTK+ and GNOME	*http://www.gtk.org*
gmp	GNU multiple-precision arithmetic library	*http://www.swox.com/gmp/*
gnome-libs	GNOME libraries	*http://www.gnome.org*
gtk	Library for GTK+, the GIMP widget toolkit used by GNOME	*http://www.gtk.org*

MacPorts or Fink package	Description	Home page
hermes	Optimized pixel format conversion library	http://www.canlib.org/hermes/
imlib2	General image handling library	http://www.enlightenment.org/pages/imlib2.html
libdnet	Networking library	http://libdnet.sourceforge.net
libdv	Software decoder for DV-format video	http://www.sourceforge.net/projects/libdv/
libfame	Fast-assembly MPEG encoding library	http://fame.sourceforge.net
libghttp	HTTP client library	http://www.gnome.org
libjpeg	JPEG image format handling library	http://www.ijg.org
libmpeg2	GIMP MPEG library	http://libmpeg2.sourceforge.net
libmusicbrainz	Client library for the MusicBrainz CD Index	http://www.musicbrainz.org
libnasl	Nessus Attack Scripting Language library	http://www.nessus.org
libnessus	Library package for Nessus without SSL support	http://www.nessus.org
libole2	Library for the OLE2 compound file format	http://www.gnome.org
libproplist	Routines for string list handling	http://www.windowmaker.org
libshout	Library for streaming to icecast	http://developer.icecast.org/libshout/
libsigc++	Callback system for widget libraries	http://developer.icecast.org/libshout/
libstroke	Stroke translation library (translates mouse strokes to program commands)	http://www.etla.net/libstroke/
libtiff	TIFF image format library	http://www.libtiff.org
libungif	GIF image format handling library (LZW-free version)	http://prtr-13.ucsc.edu/~badger/software/libungif/index.shtml
libwww	General-purpose Web API written in C for Unix and Windows	http://www.w3c.org/Library/Distribution.html
libxml	XML parsing library	http://www.gnome.org
libxml++	C++ interface to the libxml2 XML parsing library	http://sourceforge.net/projects/libxmlplusplus/
jakarta-log4j	Library that helps the programmer output log statements to a variety of output targets	http://jakarta.apache.org/log4j/
lzo 1 & 2	Real-time data compression library	http://www.oberhumer.com/opensource/lzo/
netpbm	Graphics manipulation programs and libraries	http://netpbm.sourceforge.net

MacPorts or Fink package	Description	Home page
pcre	Perl Compatible Regular Expressions library	http://www.pcre.org
pdflib	Library for generating PDFs	http://www.pdflib.com/products/pdflib-family/pdflib/
pil	Python Imaging Library; adds image-processing capabilities to Python	http://www.pythonware/products/pil/
pilot-link	Palm libraries	http://www.pilot-link.org
popt	Library for parsing command-line options	http://www.gnu.org/directory/popt.html
pth	Portable library that provides scheduling	http://www.gnu.org/software/pth/pth.html
readline	Terminal input library (provided in Leopard as a symbolic link to libedit)	http://cnswww.cns.cwru.edu/~chet/readline/rltop.html
slang	Embeddable extension language and console I/O library	http://space.mit.edu/~davis/slang/

The list of available libraries is ever-growing, thanks to an influx of open source ports from FreeBSD and Linux. One of the best ways to keep on top of the latest ports is to install Fink or MacPorts (see Chapters 12 and 13, respectively), either of which will let you either install precompiled versions of libraries and applications or install them from source.

Numerical Libraries

Mac OS X ships with an impressive array of resources used for numerical computing. It supports 64-bit computing on both PowerPC G5 and Intel-based systems, including 64-bit pointers for passing large arrays and the optimized and extended mathematical libraries *libm* and *libmx*. It also ships with the Accelerate framework, located at */System/Library/Frameworks/Accelerate.framework*, which includes many numerical libraries that have been optimized for high-performance computing, as well as several subframeworks. The Accelerate framework's libraries have been optimized to take advantage of the PowerPC as well as Intel-based CPUs. If you are interested in optimizing your code for Mac OS X, good places to start are the websites *http://developer.apple.com/hardwaredrivers/ve/sse.html* and *http://developer.apple.com/documentation/Performance/Conceptual/Accelerate_sse_migration/Accelerate_sse_migration.pdf*.

You will find the following in the Accelerate framework:

vecLib

A subframework of the Accelerate framework that includes BLAS (cblas and vBLAS), LAPACK, vBasicOps, vBigNum, vDSP, vecLib, vectorOps, vForce, and vfp. It is located at */System/Library/Frameworks/vecLib.frame work*.

BLAS

A complete and optimized set (levels 1, 2, and 3) of the basic linear algebra subprograms. (See *http://www.netlib.org/blas/faq.html*.)

LAPACK

A linear algebra package written on top of the BLAS library. (See *http:// www.netlib.org/lapack/index.html*.) LAPACK is designed to run efficiently, having most of the actual computations performed by optimized BLAS routines.

vDSP

A collection of digital signal processing functions. (See *http://developer .apple.com/hardware/ve/downloads/vDSP.sit.hqx*.)

vBasicOps

A set of basic arithmetic operations.

(See */System/Library/Frameworks/vecLib.framework/Versions/Current/ Headers/vBasicOps.h*.)

vBigNum

A set of basic arithmetic operations for manipulating large (128-bit) integers.

(See */System/Library/Frameworks/vecLib.framework/Versions/Current/ Headers/vBigNum.h*.)

vectorOps

A set of BLAS vector and matrix functions, optimized for AltiVec.

(See */System/Library/Frameworks/vecLib.framework/Versions/Current/ Headers/vectorOps.h*.)

vForce

A set of highly optimized elementary functions on many operands.

(See */System/Library/Frameworks/vecLib.framework/Versions/Current/ Headers/vForce.h*.)

vfp

A set of MathLib-style numerical functions, optimized for AltiVec.

(See */System/Library/Frameworks/vecLib.framework/Versions/Current/ Headers/vfp.h*.)

vImage

A subframework of the Accelerate framework that contains a set of highly optimized image-processing filters.

(See */System/Library/Frameworks/vImage.framework/Versions/Current/ Headers/vImage.h*.)

To compile code using a subframework of Accelerate, you must include the header file with the following line of code:

```
#include <Accelerate/Accelerate.h>
```

For example, you can compile a program named *prog.c* that makes use of the vecLib framework as follows:

```
$ gcc -framework Accelerate prog.c
```

## PART III

Working with Packages

There are a good number of packaging options for software you compile, as well as software you obtain from third parties. This part of the book covers software packaging on Mac OS X.

Chapters in this part of the book include:

## CHAPTER 12

Fink

Fink is essentially a port of the Debian Advanced Package Tool (APT) with some frontends and its own centralized collection site, which stores the packaged binaries, source code, and patches you need to build software on Mac OS X. The Fink package manager allows you to install a package (a ported Unix software application or library) and lets you choose whether to install it from source or a binary package file. Consistent with Debian, binary package files are in the *dpkg* format with a *.deb* extension and are managed with the ported Debian tools *dpkg* and *apt-get*.

Fink also provides tools that create a *.deb* package from source. It maintains a database of installed software that identifies packages by a combination of name, version number, and revision number. Moreover, Fink understands dependencies, uses *rsync* to propagate software updates, supports uninstallation, and makes it easy to see available and installed packages. You can use Fink to install over a thousand freely available Unix packages that will run on Mac OS X. Fink also recognizes and supports Apple's X11 implementation, based on the X.Org X Window System, for running X11 applications.

Fink installs itself and all of its packages (with the exception of X11) in a directory named */sw*, thus completely separating itself from the main */usr* system directory. If problems occur with Fink-installed packages, you can simply delete the entire */sw* directory tree without affecting your system.

Installing Fink

Before installing Fink, you must install the Xcode tools. As discussed in Chapter 10, these can be installed from the Mac OS X Install DVD or downloaded from the Apple Developer Connection web site at *http://developer.apple.com/tools/xcode/*. Alternatively, on a new Mac, the Xcode tools installer is located in */Applications/Installers/Developer Tools/*. You'll also need X11 and the X11

SDK. The latter is included with Xcode; X11 is installed by default in Leopard but is an optional installation in previous versions of Mac OS X.

You can install Fink from binary, from a source tarball, or from source in CVS.

Installing Fink from a Disk Image

The binary installation involves the following steps:

1. Download the binary installer disk image (a *.dmg* file) from *http://fink .sourceforge.net/download/*.

   Binary installers are available for both the PowerPC and Intel architectures. Be sure to download the one that matches your hardware.

2. The disk image should mount automatically and show up in the Finder's sidebar. If the disk image does not mount after it has downloaded, locate and double-click the *.dmg* file to mount it.

3. Open the mounted disk image and double-click the Fink installer package inside. At the time of this writing, the name of the installer package is *Fink 0.8.1-Intel-Installer.pkg* for Intel (and *Fink 0.8.1-Intel-Installer.pkg* for PowerPC), though it was not yet available for Leopard.

4. Follow the instructions on the screen.

5. As Fink installs, it will launch the Terminal application and check to see whether you have a *.profile* file in your home directory. If you don't, Fink asks you if you want it to create one. At the prompt, type Y and hit Return; Fink will create this file and add the `. /sw/bin/init.sh` line to it. After creating the *.profile* file, Fink automatically logs you out of the Terminal session; you may need to close the Terminal window by typing ⌘-W.

After Fink has completed its installation, unmount the disk image and drag the *.dmg* file to the Trash.

> The disk image also includes FinkCommander, a graphical frontend to using Fink. For more information, see the "Fink-Commander" section later in this chapter.

Installing Fink from Source

To install the latest release of Fink from source, perform the following steps:

1. Open *http://www.finkproject.org/download/srcdist.php* in your web browser. After you select the link for the tarball, you must choose a mirror

site from which to download it. If your web browser downloads this file to your Desktop, move it to a working directory, such as ~/tmp:

```
$ mv ~/Desktop/ fink-0.28.1.tar.gz ~/tmp/
```

 Do not use StuffIt to unpack the tarball, as some versions of StuffIt may corrupt some files; instead, unpack the tarball from the command line. If your browser automatically turned StuffIt loose on the tarball, you may be left with a *.tar* file and a directory. If this is the case, you will have to *mv* the *fink-0.28.1.tar* instead of the *.gz* file.

2. Extract the archive:

```
$ tar xvzf fink-0.28.1.tar.gz
```

3. Change into the top-level directory and run the *bootstrap* script:

```
$ cd fink-0.28.1
$ ./bootstrap
```

4. Follow the instructions on the screen.

Installing Fink from CVS

You can also install the latest version of Fink via CVS:

1. Change to a temporary directory (one that doesn't contain a subdirectory named *fink*), and log into the Fink CVS server:

```
$ cd ~/tmp
$ cvs -d :pserver:anonymous@cvs.sourceforge.net:/cvsroot/fink login
```

When prompted for a password press, press Return to enter an empty password.

2. Download the package descriptions:

```
$ cvs -d :pserver:anonymous@cvs.sourceforge.net:/cvsroot/fink co fink
```

3. Change to the *fink* subdirectory and run the *bootstrap* script to install and configure Fink:

```
$ cd fink
$ ./bootstrap
```

4. Follow the instructions on the screen.

You must install Fink with superuser privileges and run it with superuser privileges whenever you use it to install, uninstall, or update packages. Whether you install and configure Fink from a downloaded tarball or from CVS, the *bootstrap* script will prompt you to configure Fink to be run with *sudo*, *su*, or *root*. If you choose the default, *sudo*, you won't have to invoke *fink* explicitly with *sudo*. Instead, you'll automatically be prompted for your administrative password.

Post-Installation Setup

When you install Fink, it should configure your shell initialization files to source either */sw/bin/init.sh* (*sh*, *bash*, and similar shells), as follows:

```
. /sw/bin/init.sh
```

or */sw/bin/init.csh* (*csh* or *tcsh*), as shown here:

```
source /sw/bin/init.csh
```

If for some reason it doesn't, or if you need to configure Fink for another user, open a Terminal window and run the script */sw/bin/pathsetup.sh*. When that's finished, close the Terminal window and open a new one to begin using Fink.

You can update Fink later by entering these commands:

```
$ fink selfupdate
$ fink update-all
```

The first command updates Fink itself, including the list and descriptions of available packages, while the second command updates any installed packages. The first time you run *selfupdate*, Fink will prompt you to choose whether to use *rsync* (faster, less bandwidth) or CVS, or to "Stick to point releases":

```
$ fink selfupdate
sudo /sw/bin/fink  selfupdate
Password: ********
fink needs you to choose a SelfUpdateMethod.

(1) cvs
(2) Stick to point releases
(3) rsync

Choose an update method [3] 3
```

"Stick to point releases" means that you'll stay away from the bleeding edge: Fink will be more stable, but you may not get the latest and greatest versions of applications. The third option, *rsync*, is the default option. You can change the *selfupdate* method to CVS by using the command *fink selfupdate-cvs*, and you can switch back to using *rsync* with *fink selfupdate-rsync*. At the time of this writing, you can only select the second option, "Stick to point releases," when you run *fink selfupdate* for the first time. That is, Fink does not support switching to *selfupdate-point* (i.e., option 2) from any other *selfupdate* method.

Using Fink

Once you've installed Fink, you can see what packages are available by entering the command *fink list*. You can install a package from source with the following command:

```
$ fink install package
```

The *fink* command is used from the command line to maintain, install, and uninstall packages from source. Table 12-1 lists some examples of its usage.

Table 12-1. Various fink commands

Command	Description
fink apropos foo	Lists packages matching the search keyword, *foo*.
fink build foo	Downloads and builds the package *foo*. No installation is performed.
fink cleanup	Deletes obsolete and temporary files.
fink configure	Reruns the configuration process.
fink describe foo	Describes the package *foo*.
fink fetch foo	Downloads the package *foo*, but doesn't install it.
fink fetch-all	Downloads source files for all available packages.
fink fetch-missing	Like *fetch-all*, but fetches only source code that's not already present.
fink index	Forces a rebuild of the package cache.
fink install foo	Downloads source, then builds and installs the package *foo*.
fink list	Lists available packages, placing an "i" next to installed packages. This command takes many options: for example, *fink list -i* lists only installed packages. Execute *fink list --help* for a complete set of options.
fink plugins	Lists available plug-ins for *fink*.
fink purge foo	Same as *remove*, but also removes all configuration files. Use *apt-get remove* instead.
fink rebuild foo	Downloads and rebuilds the package *foo*. Installation is performed.
fink reinstall foo	Reinstalls the package *foo* using *dpkg*.
fink remove foo	Deletes the package *foo*.
fink scanpackages	Updates the *apt-get* database.
fink selfupdate	Updates Fink along with the package list. Uses the latest officially released Fink source. Do this first unless you're updating via CVS.
fink selfupdate-cvs	Updates Fink along with the package list using CVS.
fink selfupdate-rsync	Updates Fink along with the package list using *rsync*.

Command	Description
fink show-deps foo	Reveals both compile-time and runtime dependencies of the package *foo*.
fink update foo	Updates the package *foo*.
fink update-all	Updates all installed packages.
fink validate foo	Runs various checks on *.info* and *.deb* files associated with the package *foo*.

FinkCommander

The FinkCommander application provides a free graphical user interface for Fink's commands. FinkCommander is distributed with Fink on the Fink installer disk image, but you can also download it directly from the Fink-Commander site (*http://finkcommander.sourceforge.net*).

 At the time of this writing, FinkCommander had not been updated since 2005, but it still works as advertised. Phynch-ronicity, a newer GUI for Fink, is available from *http://www .codebykevin.com/phynchronicity.html*. Unlike the free Fink-Commander, Phynchronicity is shareware. You can run a 30-day demo of Phynchronicity to try it out before purchasing it for $24.95.

To install FinkCommander, simply drag and drop the application from the disk image into your */Applications* folder (or */Applications/Utilities*, depending on what your preferences are).

You can use FinkCommander's search field, located in the upper-right corner of the main window, to find packages you are interested in. By default, the menu to the left of the search field is set to search package names. However, by clicking and holding down the (left) mouse button in the search field, you can set it to something else (Description, Category, Binary, Stable, Unstable, Local, Status, or Maintainer) before you search. Figure 12-1 shows the main window of FinkCommander with a search in progress for packages whose category includes "sci".

To install a package with FinkCommander, select it in the main window and select Binary→Install for a binary package, or Source→Install to install that package from source. You can remove a package by selecting it in the list and clicking Source→Remove or Binary→Remove.

FinkCommander also lets you run its commands in a Terminal window so you can interact directly with Fink. Use Source→Run in Terminal→*Command* or

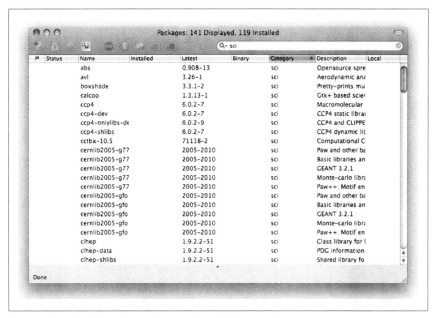

Figure 12-1. Searching for packages with FinkCommander

Binary→Run in Terminal→*Command* to run the selected command in a new Terminal window, as shown in Figure 12-2.

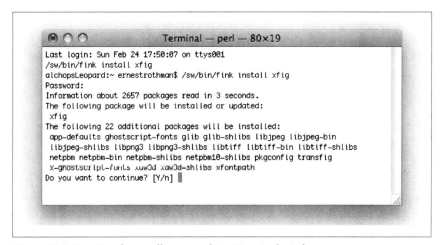

Figure 12-2. Running the install command in a Terminal window

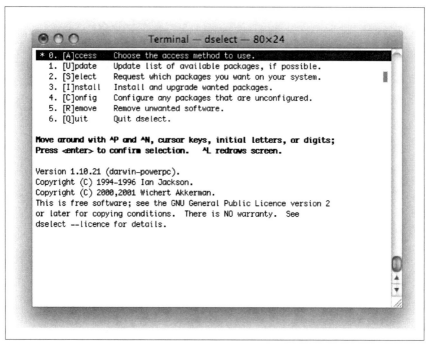

Figure 12-3. The dselect program's main menu

Installing Binaries Using Command-Line Utilities

You can download and install binaries via *dselect* (shown in Figure 12-3), a console-based frontend to *dpkg*, which is installed as part of Fink (*dselect* and *dpkg* are just two of the utilities that Fink borrows from Debian GNU/Linux). To use *dselect*, you must have superuser (or administrator) privileges, so you'll need to run *sudo dselect* in the Terminal.

Once *dselect* has started, you can use the following options to maintain, install, and uninstall packages:

[A]ccess
    Allows you to choose the access method to use.

[U]pdate
    Downloads the list of available packages from the Fink site. This option is equivalent to running *apt-get update*. Table 12-2 lists the *apt-get* and *dpkg* command-line options.

You must run *[U]pdate* at least once after installing Fink.

[S]elect

Displays the package listing, which you can use to select and deselect the packages you want on your system.

[I]nstall

Installs, upgrades, and configures selected packages. Also removes deselected packages.

[C]onfig

Configures any packages that are unconfigured. Not actually needed, since [I]nstall does this after you've installed a package.

[R]emove

Removes unwanted software. Not actually needed, since [I]nstall will do this.

[Q]uit

Quits *dselect*.

Table 12-2. Some apt-get and dpkg commands

Command	Description
apt-get update	Updates the list of available packages. Do this first.
apt-get upgrade	Installs the newest versions of all installed packages.
apt-get install foo	Downloads and installs the package foo.
apt-get remove foo	Deletes the package foo.
dpkg --list	Lists all installed packages.
dpkg --listfiles foo	Lists all the files from the package foo.
dpkg --install foo	Installs the package foo.
dpkg --remove foo	Deletes the package foo. Leaves configuration files.
dpkg --purge foo	Deletes the package foo and its configuration files.
dpkg -S /path/to/file	Tells you which package owns a file.

Mixing Binary and Source Installations

Using Fink, you can mix binary and source installations. That is, you can install some packages from their precompiled *.deb* files and install others from source. If you do this, you must first use *apt-get* to update the available binaries and then use *fink selfupdate* followed by *fink update-all* to update packages installed from source.

## CHAPTER 13

MacPorts

The MacPorts project (*http://www.macports.org*), formerly known as Darwin-Ports, is a package management system that is similar to Fink and the FreeBSD ports collection (*http://www.freebsd.org*) and is hosted by Apple, Inc. Written primarily in Tcl (which is bundled with Mac OS X), MacPorts automates the installation of open source Unix- and Aqua-based software on Mac OS X.

MacPorts provides a way to both install and remove packages, called *ports*, from its collection, as well as a way to track package dependencies. This means that if you attempt to install package A, and package A depends on package B, MacPorts finds and installs package B first and then goes back and installs package A. Similarly, if you attempt to uninstall package B but you have installed another package that depends on package B, MacPorts warns you about this dependency and gives you the option to remove other packages that depend on the one you're attempting to remove.

MacPorts installs Unix-based packages in */opt/local* by default, ensuring that your Mac OS X-installed system files in */usr* won't be affected. You can also use MacPorts to build from source several Aqua-based applications, which MacPorts installs in */Applications/MacPorts*. Additionally, required libraries are installed in */Library/Tcl/macports1.0*. If problems occur with MacPorts-installed packages, you can delete the entire */opt/local* directory tree without affecting your system. In that case, you should also delete the */Library/Tcl/ macports1.0* and */Applications/MacPorts* directories, as well as */Library/ LaunchDaemons/org.macports.** and */Library/Receipts/MacPorts*.pkg*, to completely remove MacPorts.

Unlike Fink and some earlier versions of DarwinPorts, Mac-Ports does not divide ports into stable and unstable ports. On the other hand, you can install either the stable point release of the MacPorts base itself or a prerelease development version of MacPorts via the MacPorts anonymous subversion repository.

When you install a package with MacPorts, it is installed both in the */opt/local* (or whichever directory you choose to install MacPorts in) and */opt/local/var/macports/software* directories, via */usr/bin/install*. For example, if you use MacPorts to install *rxvt*, it will be installed in */opt/local/var/macports/software*, and a hard link will be created in */opt/local* so that any user whose $PATH includes */opt/local/bin* will be able to use the MacPorts-installed *rxvt*.

As an alternative to installation via */usr/bin/install*, you can use MacPorts to produce a *.pkg* (or *.mpkg*, to include dependencies) package that can be subsequently installed on a Mac OS X system via the Mac OS X Installer. You can also use MacPorts to create an Internet-enabled disk image (*.dmg*) containing a package installer, or to create packages in the Red Hat Package Manager (RPM) format. Packages produced by MacPorts in both the *.pkg* and *.dmg* formats can be installed on any Mac OS X systems, even if MacPorts has not been installed on those systems.

Installing MacPorts

You'll find detailed documentation, written by Michael A. Maibaum, on the installation and use of MacPorts on the MacPorts website. Although you should check the MacPorts site for the most up-to-date information, we'll provide a brief description of its installation and usage here.

Before installing MacPorts, you must install the Xcode tools. As noted in Chapter 7, these can be installed from the Mac OS X Install DVD or downloaded from the Apple Developer Connection website at *http://developer.apple.com/tools/xcode/*; alternatively, on a new Mac, the Xcode tools installer is located in */Applications/Installers/Developer Tools/*. You'll also need X11, which is installed by default in Leopard but is an optional installation in earlier versions of Mac OS X, as well as the X11 SDK, which is included with Xcode. Installation of MacPorts is built around *rsync*, which is also installed with Mac OS X by default.

Possible Conflicts Between MacPorts and Fink

MacPorts and Fink can coexist on the same system, but if you've already installed Fink (say, in its default location, /sw), there is a chance that the configuration phase (described later) will identify the Fink-installed version of the required software. For example, if you've installed Tcl/Tk with Fink, MacPorts may use the version of Tcl in /sw, rather than the Mac OS X-bundled Tcl in /usr/bin. If this happens and you later decide to remove Fink, you'll mess up your MacPorts installation.

To avoid this potential problem, you should temporarily remove /sw/bin from your path when installing MacPorts (or, if you've added it to your .bashrc file, comment out the line . /sw/bin/init.sh).

To install MacPorts, you must be logged in as an administrative user. You can install the latest point release of MacPorts either from source or using a binary installer. To install MacPorts using the binary installer, download the .dmg file from the MacPorts website to your Desktop, double-click this file to mount the disk image, and double-click the .mpkg installer in the disk image. Then authenticate yourself as an administrative user and follow the directions in the Installer window to install MacPorts.

If you want to install MacPorts in a directory other than the default /opt/local, you'll need to install it from source. To install MacPorts from source, log into Mac OS X as an administrative user and download the source tarball from the MacPorts website into your home directory. Both .tar.gz and .tar.bz2 formats are available for download.

For example, to download and unpack MacPorts-1.6.0.tar.gz, enter the following commands:

```
$ cd
$ curl -O \
  http://snv.macports.org/repository/downloads/MacPorts-1.6.0/\
  MacPorts-1.6.0.tar.gz
$ tar xzvf MacPorts-1.6.0.tar.gz
```

If, on the other hand, you've downloaded MacPorts-1.6.0.tar.bz2 instead of the .gz file, change the last command to the following:

```
$ tar xjvf MacPorts-1.6.0.tar.bz2
```

After entering the preceding commands, you'll be ready to build and install MacPorts on your system:

1. Change to the ~/MacPorts-1.6.0/ directory:

   ```
   $ cd MacPorts-1.6.0
   ```

2. Perform the *configure*, *make*, and *make install* sequence:

```
$ ./configure
$ make
$ sudo make install
```

These commands build and install necessary files in */opt/local*, */Library/Tcl/macports1.0*, and */Library/Receipts*.

If you want to customize your installation, you should enter the *./configure --help* command to see what configure options are available before proceeding with the *configure*, *make*, and *make install* sequence. For example, if you want to install MacPorts in a directory other than */opt/local* (e.g., if you want to install it on an external hard drive or a large-capacity USB flash drive), you can run *configure* with the *--prefix* option and specify the location.

Once you've installed MacPorts, you can safely delete the *~/MacPorts-1.6.0* directory.

Installing MacPorts from SVN

To download the latest developer release of MacPorts, perform the following steps:

1. Change to your home directory, and download and unpack the latest MacPorts developer source and package descriptions from the MacPorts Subversion (SVN) repository into the *~/trunk* directory:

```
$ cd
$ svn checkout http://snv.macports.org/repository/macports/\
  trunk macports-trunk
```

You're now ready to build and install MacPorts on your system.

2. Change to the *~/trunk/base* directory, which contains the MacPorts infrastructure:

```
$ cd macports-trunk/base
```

3. Perform the *configure*, *make*, and *make install* sequence:

```
$ ./configure
$ make
$ sudo make install
```

These commands build and install necessary files in */opt/local*, */Library/Tcl/macports1.0*, and */Library/Receipts*. Once you've installed MacPorts, you can safely delete the *~/macports-trunk* directory, but you should keep it if you want to continue working with the latest developer releases of MacPorts.

The MacPorts installation creates *macports.conf*, *sources.conf*, and *variants.conf* files in the */opt/local/etc/macports/* directory. These files specify various configuration parameters. For example), among others, *macports.conf* contains the *prefix* parameter, which is set to */opt/local* by default. If you want MacPorts to install software in a directory other than */opt/local*, you can edit the file *macports.conf* and change the value of *prefix* from */opt/local* to the directory in which you want packages installed. The *sources.conf* configuration file contains the location of the *ports* directory, which is set to *rsync://rsync.macports.org/release/ports/*, by default. If you'd like to set up a local ports repository, you can enter the appropriate line in the *sources.conf* file (this file contains sufficient documentation on how to add a local ports repository).

The */opt/local/var/macports/sources/rsync.macports.org/ports* directory is where MacPorts stores local copies of the ported software descriptions and related *Portfiles*, which are Tcl scripts needed to build and install the ported software. Though it may be tempting to think of the */opt/local/var/macports/sources/rsync.macports.org/ports* directory as a local *ports* repository, it is not; rather, it's where the ported software descriptions and related *Portfiles* are updated, when you update your installation of MacPorts.

Since MacPorts software is installed in */opt/local*, you should add */opt/local/bin* and */opt/local/sbin* to your $PATH. Additionally, you may want to add */opt/local/share/man* to your $MANPATH. Once you have performed those steps, you'll be ready to use MacPorts.

Using MacPorts

Once MacPorts has been installed, you can see what packages are available with the *port list* command. Since the list is quite long, you may want to pipe that command through the *more* command.

You can also use the *port* command to search for specific packages. For example, the command *port search tightvnc* returns a listing for the *tightvnc* package, whereas the command *port search kde* lists all available packages that contain the string *kde*. The *port* command may also be used to determine which variants of a given package are available. For example, the output from the *port variants gnuplot* command lists the *universal*, *darwin*, *no_x11*, and *wxwidgets* variants of *gnuplot*.

You can install a package from source with the command *sudo port install package*. (The *port* command must be used with *sudo* whenever the directory */opt/local* or */Applications/MacPorts* is modified.) This command actually performs several steps prior to installing the package on your system, including checking dependencies, downloading the necessary source code (including source of dependencies), verifying checksums, configuring packages, building and installing any other required packages, and building the requested package in an intermediate *work* directory within the */opt/local/var/macports/build* directory. For example, if you install *tightvnc* using MacPorts, it is built in */opt/local/var/macports/build/_opt_local_var_macports_sources_rsync.mac ports.org_release_ports_x11_tightvnc*. After the package is built, it is installed temporarily in the *destroot* subdirectory of the *work* directory.

In the last stages of the sequence of events set into motion by the *sudo port install package* command, the requested package is installed into an "image repository" directory and "activated." Activation of a port creates hard links to the files in the image repository directory. For example, if you install *rvxt* using the *sudo port install rxvt* command, *rxvt* and all its related files are installed into the image repository */opt/local/var/macports/software/rxvt/ 2.7.10_1/opt/local/bin* and then activated through the creation of hard links in the *${prefix}* directory */opt/local/bin*.

The image repository can be revealed with the *port location rxvt* command. You can subsequently deactivate *rxvt* by issuing the command *sudo port deactivate rxvt*, which deletes the hard links in */opt/local/bin* while leaving the *rxvt* installation in the image repository intact. You can later reactivate *rxvt* with the *sudo port activate rxvt* command. The chief advantage of this approach, called *Port Images*, is that it allows you to install multiple versions of a package without having to uninstall one to make room for another. Instead, you can simply deactivate one version and activate another version.

 The Port Images approach is particularly helpful when you want to test a new version of some software, because it means you won't need to uninstall and then reinstall the older version if you're not happy with the new version.

As mentioned earlier, MacPorts automatically checks package dependencies and installs any other required packages. Similarly, if you deactivate a package, you are warned if the package you are deactivating is needed by another installed package.

To uninstall a particular port, use the *port uninstall* command. For example, to uninstall *foo*, enter the command:

```
$ sudo port uninstall foo
```

To update a particular port, you can enter the following command:

```
$ sudo port upgrade foo
```

If a new version of *foo* is available, this command will deactivate the currently installed *foo* port and install and activate the newer version. This command will also update all of *foo*'s dependencies. If you want to remove the older version of *foo* at the same time, you should enter the following command:

```
$ sudo port -u upgrade foo
```

You can update all installed ports with this command:

```
$ sudo port upgrade installed
```

Creating and Installing Packages in .pkg Format

Using MacPorts, you can create a *.pkg* package installer using the *port* command with the *pkg* option. For example, to create a *.pkg* installer for *aterm*, enter the command:

```
$ sudo port pkg aterm
```

This downloads the source for *aterm*, builds the application, and creates a double-clickable package installer named *aterm-1.0.0.pkg*. This package is saved in */opt/local/var/macports/build/_opt_local_var_macports_sour ces_rsync.macports.org_release_ports_x11_aterm/work*.

It's worth noting that this command only creates the package; it does not install the package. To install it (in */opt/local*), double-click *aterm-1.0.0.pkg* in the Finder, authenticate yourself as an administrative user, and install the package on your system as you would with any other package. When you install a package in this manner, the MacPorts database won't list it among its installed packages (that is, if you issue the *port installed* command, this package won't show up in the list). If you enter the command *port clean aterm*, the installer *aterm-1.0.0.pkg* will be deleted.

Creating and Installing Packages in RPM Format

If you are planning to create packages in RPM format, the first thing you should do is install *rpm* (via the *sudo port install rpm* command). Once you have installed *rpm*, you can create RPM packages using the *port* command with the *rpm* option. For example, to create an RPM for *foo*, enter the following command:

```
$ sudo port rpm foo
```

This command creates the RPM file in *${prefix}/src/macports/RPMS/${arch}*. You can safely use the *sudo port clean foo* command after the RPM is created, since the *port clean* command won't remove the *.rpm* installer.

Before installing RPM packages, however, you need to create */etc/mnttab*, which is the file that keeps track of which RPM packages have been installed. This can be done with this command:

```
$ touch /etc/mnttab
```

A summary of the use of the *port* command is provided in Table 13-1.

Table 13-1. Various port commands

Command	Description
port search foo	Lists packages matching the search keyword, foo.
sudo port install foo	Downloads, builds, and installs the package foo.
port destroot foo	Downloads, builds, and installs the package foo into an intermediate destination root, called a "destroot." This is useful for developing and testing new ports.
sudo port uninstall foo	Deletes the package foo.
port installed	Lists all the installed packages.
port clean foo	Deletes intermediate files after installation of the package foo.
port contents foo	Lists all files installed with the package foo.
port deps foo	Lists dependencies of the package foo.
port variants foo	Lists variants of the package foo.
port pkg foo	Builds the .pkg package installer for foo. Does not install foo.
port list	Lists available packages.
port dmg foo	Builds an Internet-enabled disk image containing a Mac OS X .pkg package installer for foo. Does not install foo.
port rpm foo	Builds an RPM package for foo. Does not install foo.
sudo port activate foo	Activates foo. If multiple versions of foo are installed, use port activate foo version.
sudo port deactivate foo	Activates foo. If multiple versions of foo are installed, use port activate foo version.
port location foo	Displays the location of the image directory in which foo is installed.
port outdated foo	Determines if your installed port foo is outdated.
port outdated	Lists all of your outdated ports.
sudo port upgrade foo	Updates foo along with its dependencies, while deactivating the currently installed foo. Use the -u option if you want the outdated foo uninstalled.
sudo port upgrade outdated	Updates all outdated ports with their dependencies, deactivating the currently installed outdated ports. Use the -u option if you want the outdated ports uninstalled.

Command	Description
sudo port selfupdate	Updates the MacPorts installation, including the infrastructure and the Portfiles.

MacPorts Maintenance

How you update your MacPorts installation is dependent on how you installed it. If you've installed a point release of MacPorts, all you need to do is enter the following command:

```
$ sudo port selfupdate
```

This command will update your ports tree to the latest revision on the Mac-Ports *rsync* server and will download and rebuild your current MacPorts base if a new point release is available. If, on the other hand, you're working with SVN development releases of MacPorts and you've maintained your *~/macports-trunk* directory, you can update your MacPorts installation in two steps: the first step is to update the MacPorts infrastructure, and the second step is to update your collection of Portfiles, which contain instructions for building ports.

To update your MacPorts infrastructure, change to the *~/macports-trunk* directory and enter the following commands:

```
$ cd ~/macports-trunk
$ svn update
$ cd base
$ make clean
$ ./configure
$ make
$ sudo make install
```

To update only your Portfiles, enter the command:

```
$ sudo port sync
```

Connecting to the MacPorts SVN Repository

If you'd like to browse the MacPorts subversion repository, you have three options:

1. Point your web browser to the Trac source code browser at *http://trac .macports.org /browser/*.

2. Point your web browser directly to the Subversion repository at *http://svn .macosforge.org/repository/macports/*.

3. Point your WebDav client to directly to the Subversion repository. For example, using the Mac OS X Finder, select Go→Connect to Server (or

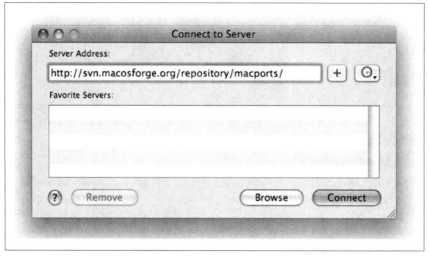

Figure 13-1. Connecting to the MacPorts SVN repository in the Finder

press ⌘-K) and enter the address *http://svn.macosforge.org/repository/mac ports/*, as shown in Figure 13-1.

MacPort GUIs

Here are three GUI frontends to MacPorts that can help you maintain your MacPorts installation:

1. Pallet is included with the MacPorts distribution, so after you've installed MacPorts, you should be able to install *pallet* with the following command:

   ```
   $ sudo port install pallet
   ```

   At the time of this writing, however, *pallet* fails to build.

2. Porticus (*http://porticus.alittledrop.com*) is a freeware application that is, at the time of this writing, under development by Richard Laing.

3. PortAuthority (*http://www.codebykevin.com/portauthority.html*), for-merly freeware, is a $20 shareware application developed by Kevin Walzer.

You'll need to have a working installation of MacPorts in order to use any of the GUI frontends. Though we weren't able to take Pallet for a whirl, we tried out Porticus and PortAuthority.

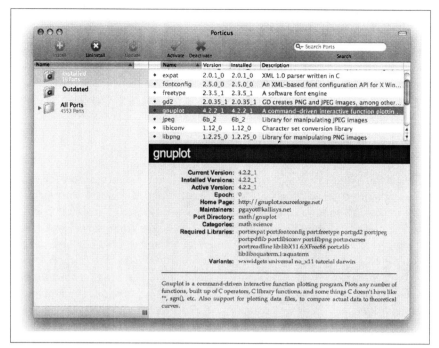

Figure 13-2. The Porticus freeware GUI frontend to MacPorts

Porticus

Porticus makes use of RBSplitView (*http://www.brockerhoff.net/src/rbs.html*), Sparkle (*http://sparkle.artworkapp.com/*), CTGradient (*http://blog.oofn.net/2006/01/15/gradients-in-cocoa/*), DBPrefsWindowController (*http://www.mere-mortal-software.com/blog/details.php?d=2007-03-11*), and Growl (*http://www.growl.info*) to provide an easy-to-use GUI for maintaining your existing MacPorts installation. To install Porticus, download the *.dmg* file from the Porticus website, mount the disk image, and drag the Porticus icon to a convenient location, such as the */Applications* folder. To run the Porticus application, double-click its icon in the Finder, and authenticate yourself as an administrative user. When launched, Porticus gathers information on your MacPorts installation and then, depending on what you've selected in the left part of the Porticus window, lists either your installed ports, your outdated ports, or all ports. Figure 13-2 shows a list of installed ports, with one of them, *gnuplot*, selected to reveal its details.

You can use Porticus to update outdated ports, install new ports, activate and deactivate ports, uninstall ports, and update your MacPorts installation. At the time of this writing, one important thing that Porticus does not do is check for dependencies when uninstalling ports. That feature, however, is planned for a future release. Once that feature has been added and its other quirks have been ironed out, this free GUI frontend to MacPorts may very well be worth a place in your */Applications* folder.

PortAuthority

Though PortAuthority is not free, it has several years' head start on the other GUI frontends to MacPorts, and it can be used to perform most common tasks associated with maintaining your MacPorts installation. To install PortAuthority, download the *PortAuthority.dmg* disk image from its website. If the disk image does not mount automatically, locate and double-click the downloaded *PortAuthority.dmg* file to mount it. Then drag the PortAuthority icon to a convenient location, such as the */Applications* folder. Finally, double-click its icon in the Finder to launch the PortAuthority application. If you haven't purchased a license for PortAuthority, you can try it out for 30 days without charge. As advised on the PortAuthority website, you should try it out first before purchasing it, because no refunds are available.

With PortAuthority, you can perform most common MacPorts maintenance and usage tasks. For example, you can update your MacPorts installation, your collection of Portfiles, and all of your installed ports, as well as installing new ports and selectively uninstalling installed ports. Nevertheless, PortAuthority has its limitations, too. For example, PortAuthority has no menu option to deactivate ports without uninstalling them. Overall, in both functionality and design, PortAuthority is similar to Porticus (and FinkCommander, for that matter). Figure 13-3 shows the PortAuthority revealing information on an installed *gnuplot* port.

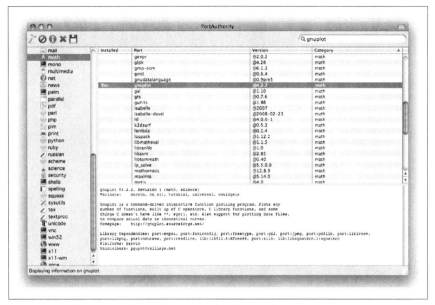

Figure 13-3. The PortAuthority shareware GUI frontend to MacPorts

Though MacPorts is quite easy to use, it has some potential gotchas. At the top of our MacPorts gotcha list: be careful to update all of your installed ports with the *sudo port upgrade installed* command rather than *sudo port upgrade all*. The latter will install all available ports, in addition to updating your installed ports. Next on our list: make sure you update your installed ports before installing a new port. Though MacPorts checks dependencies and will attempt to install required dependency software, the installation of a new port can sometimes fail if you have outdated dependencies installed. For example, *sudo port install gimp* will fail because of dependency problems if your installed *gtk* and *glib* are outdated.

## CHAPTER 14

Creating and Distributing Installable Software

In Chapters 12 and 13, we discussed installing packages with Fink and Mac-Ports, respectively. This chapter shows you how to create packages using tools provided with Mac OS X, as well as with Fink and MacPorts.

The following options for distributing software are supported on Mac OS X by default:

gnutar and gzip
> The Unix tape archive tool *gnutar* is used to bundle the directories and resources for distribution. (The *tar* command is provided as a hard link to *gnutar*.) GNU Zip (*gzip*) is used to compress the *tar* archives to make file sizes as small as possible. Using these tools is generally the simplest way to copy a collection of files from one machine to another.

 Mac OS X supports archiving files and directories in the *.zip* format directly from the Finder by Control/right-clicking on a file or directory and selecting "Compress" from the contextual menu.

Disk Utility
> One of the easiest ways to distribute an application is to use the Disk Utility (*/Applications/Utilities*) to create a disk image. You can use Disk Utility to create a double-clickable archive that mounts as a disk image on the user's computer. From there, the user can choose to mount the disk image each time the application is run, copy the application to the hard drive (usually to */Applications*), or burn the image to a CD. Disk Utility has a command-line counterpart, *hdiutil*, which we'll cover in the later section "Creating a Disk Image from the Command Line."

PackageMaker

PackageMaker (*/Developer/Applications/Utilities*) can be used to create packages (*.pkg* files), which are bundles consisting of all the items that the Mac OS X Installer (*/Applications/Utilities*) needs to perform an installation. PackageMaker can also create metapackages (*.mpkg* files), which can be used to install multiple packages at the same time, and distributions, which specify entire customized installation processes involving one or more packages.

In Leopard, support has been added for "flat" packages, which are single-file packages in the *xar(1)* format. When such a package is installed, a *.bom* file is installed in */Library/Receipts/boms* and the package database file in */Library/Receipts/db* is updated. When an older-style package is installed, a "receipt" for the package is placed in the */Library/Receipts* folder. These receipts are named with a *.pkg* extension and appear in the Finder as packages, even though they are not.

These *.bom* and *.pkg* files maintain a record of which packages have been installed on your system. This is how, for example, System Update knows not to install a package (or knows to update a package) that you've already installed.

In Mac OS X 10.5 (Leopard) and above, you can use the command-line utility *pkgutil* to read and manipulate package receipts and flat packages. To list all installed packages that are in the package database, use *pkgutil --pkgs*. You can also use *pkgutil* to list all files that were installed by a package. (See the *pkgutil* manpage for details.) You can list and extract the contents of flat packages using the *xar* command. (See the *xar* manpage for details.)

Each of these approaches is discussed separately in the following sections.

Using GNU tar

The *gnutar* and *gzip* command-line utilities can be used to create *.tar.gz* or *.tgz* tarballs. These tarballs preserve paths, permissions, symbolic links, compression, and authentication details. Tools to uncompress the tarball are available for many platforms.

The automated creation of such a tarball can be worked into the same makefile that is used to build the software. Preservation of resource forks is tricky, but possible, with this method. For example, the following command (where *foo/* is a directory) preserves Macintosh resource forks:

```
$ tar -pczf foo.tgz foo/
```

If you don't want resource forks preserved, prior to executing the preceding *tar* command, set the environment variable with the command *export COPYFILE_DISABLE=true*. (In releases of Mac OS X prior to Leopard, you would enter *export COPY_EXTENDED_ATTRIBUTES_DISABLE=true*.)

Every good tarball creates a single top-level directory that contains everything else. You should not create tarballs that dump their contents into the current directory. To install software packaged this way, use the following command:

```
$ tar -pxzf foo.tgz
```

This simply unpacks the tarball into the file and directory structure that existed prior to packaging. Basically, it reverses the packing step. This method can be used to simply write files to the appropriate places on the system, such as */usr/local/bin*, */usr/local/lib*, */usr/local/man*, */usr/local/include*, and so on.

 When creating packages, you should keep your package contents out of directories such as */etc*, */usr/bin*, */usr/lib*, */usr/include*, or any top-level directory reserved for the operating system, since you have no way of knowing what a future software update or Mac OS X upgrade will include. For example, the MacPorts project stays out of Mac OS X's way by keeping most of its files in */opt/local*, while the Fink project uses */sw*. We suggest that you use */usr/local* for the packages that you compile.

This packaging method can also be arranged so that the unpacking is done first in a temporary directory. The user can then run an install script that relocates the package contents to their final destination. This approach is usually preferred, since the install script can be designed to do some basic checking of dependencies, the existence of destination directories, the recataloging of libraries, etc. You can also include an uninstall script with your distribution.

The disadvantages of the tarball method of distributing software are:

- There is no built-in mechanism for keeping track of which files go where.
- There is no built-in method for uninstalling the software.
- It is difficult to list what software is installed and how the installed files depend on each other or on other libraries.
- There is no checking of dependencies and prerequisite software prior to the installation.

These tasks could be built into install and uninstall scripts, as we've already mentioned, but there is no inherently uniform, consistent, and coherent method for accomplishing such tasks when installing multiple software packages using *tar* files.

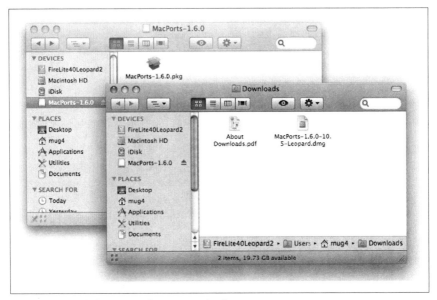

Figure 14-1. A disk image and its mounted volume

Creating Disk Images

Many applications in Mac OS X do not require special installers. Often, an application can be installed by simply dragging its folder or icon to a convenient location in the directory structure (usually the */Applications* folder). Applications that are distributed this way are typically packaged as *disk images*. A disk image is a file that, when double-clicked, creates a virtual volume that is mounted as shown in Figure 14-1.

Inside Applications

An application, represented in the Finder by its icon, is actually a folder with the extension *.app*, which is typically hidden from the user. This folder contains all of the application's resources.

To view the contents of an application bundle, Control/right-click on the application icon and select Show Package Contents from the contextual menu; this opens the application's *Contents* folder in the Finder.

Disk images can be created either with Disk Utility (found in */Applications/ Utilities*) or via the command line (using the *hdiutil* command). There are several types of disk images. In this section we'll briefly discuss how to create Apple disk images, which end with a *.dmg* extension and are commonly used to distribute software packages for Mac OS X.

The Unix command *df* reveals a disk image as a mounted volume that appears in the */Volumes* directory. When you are done with the mounted volume, unmount it by clicking on the volume (in Figure 14-1, the mounted volume is named *MacPorts-1.6.0*) to select it and choosing File→Eject (⌘-E). Alternatively, you can Control/right-click and select Eject Disk from the contextual menu, drag the mounted volume to the Trash, or unmount it using either of the following commands:

```
$ hdiutil unmount /Volumes/MacPorts-1.6.0
$ umount /Volumes/SampleVol/
```

Creating a Disk Image with Disk Utility

To create a disk image using Disk Utility, perform the following steps:

1. Launch Disk Utility (*/Applications/Utilities*).

2. Either select File→New→Blank Disk Image or click the New Image icon in the toolbar. Either way, as shown in Figure 14-2, Disk Utility prompts you for a name, location, volume name, volume size (the maximum size is limited by available disk space, but in Leopard the minimum size is 10 MB), volume format (Mac OS Extended Journaled, Mac OS Extended, Mac OS Extended Case-sensitive, Mac OS Extended Case-sensitive and Journaled, Mac OS Standard, or MS-DOS FAT), encryption options (128-bit AES or 256-bit AES), partitions (hard disk; CD/DVD; no partition map; or single partition selected from Apple, master boot record, GUID, CD/DVD, or CD/DVD with ISO data), and image format (read/write disk image, sparse disk image, or sparse bundle disk image). If you choose to enable encryption, Disk Utility will prompt you for a passphrase.

3. Make your selections, naming the new image "MyDiskImage" and choosing the Desktop as the location. Then click the Create button. The new image will be created as *MyDiskImage.dmg* and mounted as *SampleVol*, or whatever you entered for the volume name when you created the disk image. You can change this volume name in the Finder, if you'd like.

4. Double-click on the disk icon to open the empty volume in a Finder window, as shown in Figure 14-3.

5. Select File→New Finder Window (or press ⌘-N) to open a new Finder window where you can select the files you want to place in the disk image, as shown in Figure 14-4.

6. To copy the files to the mounted volume, select the items and then drag them into the empty *SampleVol* window.

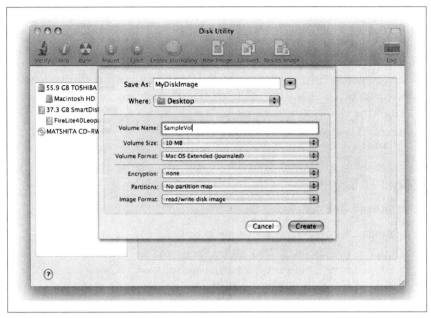

Figure 14-2. Creating a new blank image with Disk Utility

7. Once you've placed the files into the disk image, eject this disk (press ⌘-E, click the Eject icon next to the *SampleVol* in the left column of the Finder, or drag *SampleVol* to the Trash).

8. Return to the Disk Utility application, highlight *MyDiskImage.dmg* in the left column, and either select Images→Convert or click the Convert icon in the toolbar, as shown in Figure 14-5.

9. In the Convert Image window, enter either a new name or the same name in the Save As field, and then select "read-only" from the Image Format pull-down menu. (You can also compress the disk image from this menu, as shown in Figure 14-6.)

10. Click the Save button. If you've given the disk image the same filename as the original image you created, an alert window will appear, asking you to confirm whether you want to replace the older file with the new one. Click Replace to finish the process, then quit Disk Utility with ⌘-Q.

Creating a Disk Image from the Command Line

Here is the procedure for creating a disk image at the command line:

1. Change (*cd*) to the directory where you want to create the disk image:

Figure 14-3. A mounted blank disk image, ready to be loaded up with files

```
$ cd ~/Documents
```

2. Create the disk image using *hdiutil*, specifying the size (10 MB in this example) and the volume name and filename:

```
$ hdiutil create -megabytes 10 -fs HFS+ -volname SampleVol Sample.dmg
```

3. Mount the image as a volume. Since you named it *SampleVol* when you issued the *hdiutil create* command, it will be mounted as *SampleVol* and will be available in */Volumes/SampleVol*:

```
$ hdiutil mount Sample.dmg
```

4. Use the Finder or command-line tools to write to the volume *SampleVol*.

5. When you are done writing to the volume, you can eject it with *hdiutil unmount*:

```
$ hdiutil unmount /Volumes/SampleVol/
```

6. Copy the disk image to a compressed, read-only image named *Ready4Dist.dmg*:

```
$ hdiutil convert -format UDZO Sample.dmg -o Ready4Dist.dmg
```

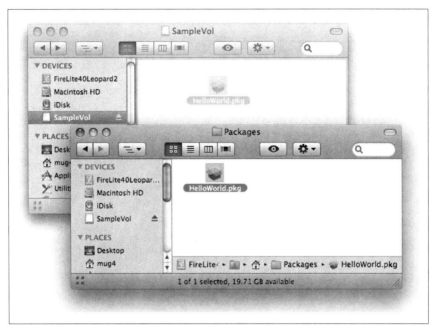

Figure 14-4. Copying a file to the disk image

The *UDZO* format option is used to create a UDIF *zlib*-compressed image. Other formats can be chosen instead: for example, UDIF *bzip2* is available for Mac OS X 10.4+ and can be selected with the *UDBZ* format option. For a complete list of format options, see the manpage for *hdiutil*.

Whenever you want to mount this volume again, double-click the file *Ready4Dist.dmg* in the Finder. Note that the writable disk image *Sample.dmg* is not destroyed in this process.

Distributing Your Image

Once you've created a disk image, you can share it with the world. Put the image up on a web server or FTP server for others to enjoy, share it on your iDisk, or burn it to a CD using Disk Utility (either select Images→Burn or press ⌘-B).

Internet-enabled disk images

An Internet-enabled disk image is a read-only disk image that cleans up after itself, leaving only the software and no by-products of the download. If you

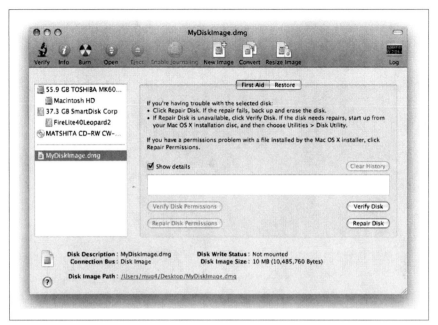

Figure 14-5. Choosing the image to convert in Disk Utility

distribute your software as an Internet-enabled disk image, the user just needs to perform these steps:

1. Download the *.dmg* file to the Desktop (i.e., *~/Desktop*) using a web browser.

2. When the download completes, the following sequence of events happens automatically:

   a. The *.dmg* file is mounted.

   b. Its contents are copied to the user's default download folder (e.g., *~/Desktop*).

   c. The disk image is unmounted.

   d. The *internet-enable* flag of the *.dmg* file is set to *no*.

   e. The *.dmg* file is moved to the Trash.

3. Locate the software and move it to its appropriate location (e.g., */Applications*).

The disk image is mounted in a hidden location until its contents are copied to the user's default download folder, which is typically the *~/Downloads* folder. If the disk image contains a single file, only this file is copied. On the other hand, if the disk image contains more than one file, a new folder is created

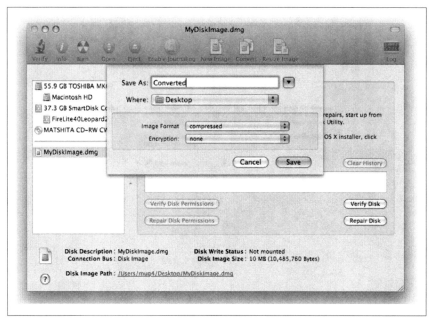

Figure 14-6. Converting an image in Disk Utility

in the download folder bearing the root name of the *.dmg* file. Files contained in the disk image are then copied to this folder. For example, if the Internet-enabled disk image containing multiple files is named *Sample.dmg*, a folder named *Sample* will be created in the download folder and the files contained in the disk image will be copied to the *Sample* folder.

In this scheme, the user does not deal directly with the *.dmg* file (other than initiating the download). This is in contrast to the situation before Internet-enabled disk images were supported, in which the user had to manually un-mount the disk image and drag it to the Trash.

To create an Internet-enabled disk image, first create a read-only *.dmg*-format disk image, as described earlier (neither read/write disk images nor the older *.img/.smi* formats can be Internet-enabled), and then set the *internet-enable* flag with the *hdiutil* command:

```
$ hdiutil internet-enable -yes Ready4Dist.dmg
```

If you want to disable the *internet-enable* flag, enter this command:

```
$ hdiutil internet-enable -no Ready4Dist.dmg
```

If you are not sure whether a disk image has its *internet-enable* flag set, the following command reveals this information:

```
$ hdiutil internet-enable -query Ready4Dist.dmg
```

As noted earlier, Internet-enabled disk images are moved to the Trash after they are downloaded and acted upon by Mac OS X. Although their *internet-enable* flags are set to *no* during the process, you can still rescue *.dmg* files from the Trash in case you want to reinstall the software later.

Using PackageMaker

Apple's native tool for packaging and distributing software is Package-Maker, which can create two types of packages: product packages and component packages. A product package consists of an entire product and contains one or more component packages. A component package consists of one component, which is typically part of a product package. Packages created with PackageMaker have a *.pkg* extension. When a user double-clicks on a package, the Installer application (*/Applications/Utilities*) is invoked and the installation process begins. The package itself is a bundle that contains all of the items Installer needs.

You can also use PackageMaker to create *metapackages* for installing multiple packages. Metapackages contain metainformation, files, and libraries associated with a given application. Packages can also contain multiple versions of an application: for example, both Mac OS X 10.4 and 10.5 versions.

PackageMaker documentation is available in Help Viewer, which is accessible from PackageMaker's Help option in the menu bar. In this chapter, we'll give only a brief description of how to create a package with PackageMaker.

Setting Up the Directory

To demonstrate how to create a package, we'll create a short C program and a manpage for it. Example 14-1 shows *hellow.c*, and Example 14-2 shows its manpage, *hellow.1*.

Example 14-1. The Hello, World sample program

```
/*
 * hellow.c - Prints a friendly greeting.
 */

#include <stdio.h>

int main()
{
  printf("Hello, world!\n");
  return 0;
}
```

Example 14-2. The manpage for hellow.c

```
.\" Copyright (c) 2005, O'Reilly Media, Inc.
.\"
.Dd April 15, 2002
.Dt HELLOW 1
.Os Mac OS X
.Sh NAME
.Nm hellow
.Nd Greeting generator
.Sh DESCRIPTION
This command prints a friendly greeting.
```

PackageMaker expects you to set up the files using a directory structure that mirrors your intended installation. So, if you plan to install *hellow* into */usr/bin* and *hellow.1* into */usr/share/man/man1*, you must create the appropriate subdirectories under your working directory. However, you can use a makefile to create and populate those subdirectories, so to begin with, your *hellow* directory may look like this:

```
$ find hellow
hellow
hellow/hellow.1
hellow/hellow.c
hellow/Makefile
```

Suppose that your *hellow* project resides in *~/src/hellow*. To keep things organized, you can create a subdirectory called *stage* that contains the installation directory. In that case, you'd place the *hellow* binary in *~/src/hellow/stage/bin* and the *hellow.1* manpage in *~/src/hellow/stage/share/man/man1*. The makefile shown in Example 14-3 compiles *hellow.c*, creates the *stage* directory and its subdirectories, and copies the distribution files into those directories when you run the command *make prep*.

Example 14-3. Makefile for hellow

```
hellow:
        cc -o hellow hellow.c

prep: hellow
        mkdir -p -m 755 stage/bin
        mkdir -p -m 755 stage/share/man/man1
        cp hellow stage/bin/
        cp hellow.1 stage/share/man/man1/
```

To get started, you need only *hellow.c*, *hellow.1*, and *Makefile*. When you run the command *make prep*, it compiles the program and copies the files to the appropriate locations in the *stage* directory. After you've run *make prep*, the *hellow* directory will look like this:

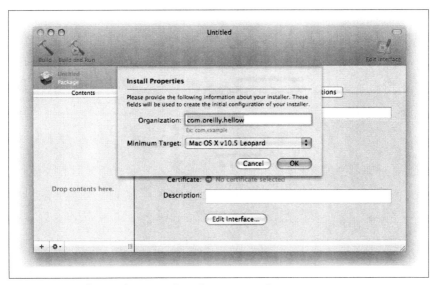

Figure 14-7. PackageMaker's initial configuration window

```
$ find hellow
hellow
hellow/hellow
hellow/hellow.1
hellow/hellow.c
hellow/Makefile
hellow/stage
hellow/stage/bin
hellow/stage/bin/hellow
hellow/stage/share
hellow/stage/share/man
hellow/stage/share/man/man1
hellow/stage/share/man/man1/hellow.1
```

The next step is to launch PackageMaker and bundle the application.

Creating the Package

When you run PackageMaker, you must enter values in the Organization and Minimum Target (the lowest version of Mac OS X that the package can be installed on) fields, as shown in Figure 14-7. Both of these are used to create the initial configuration of your installer.

For the minimum target, you can select from Mac OS X v10.5 Leopard, Mac OS X v10.4 Tiger, or Mac OS X v10.3 Panther.

The next step is to locate the components to be installed in the package and add them to the left part of the PackageMaker Project window, under Contents. You can do this by either dragging the contents from the Finder or

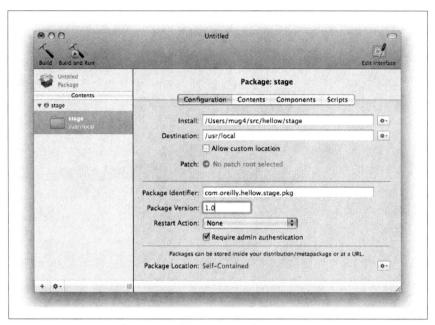

Figure 14-8. Setting configuration values in the Configuration pane

selecting Projects→Add Contents. In this example, you'll drag the *~/src/hellow/ stage* directory to the Contents pane in the Project window. With the contents selected, as shown in Figure 14-8, you must then configure the package in the Configuration pane of the Project window:

- Specify a destination (i.e., the location where the package will be installed). In our example, we selected */usr/local*.
- Check the "Allow a custom location" box if you want to allow the user installing the package to install the package somewhere other than in the specified destination.
- Indicate the package version number.
- Specify a restart action (select from None, Logout, Restart, or Shutdown).
- Check the "Require admin authentication" box, if necessary.

Next, in the Contents pane of the Project window, you'll need to adjust the ownership and permissions of each file to be installed. It is important to bear in mind that the Installer will use the ownership and permissions that you set here when it installs the package on another system. For this example, set the owner to *root* and the group to *admin*, as shown in Figure 14-9.

Typically, the next step would be to move to the Components pane and specify whether each component is relocatable (that is, can be moved after it is

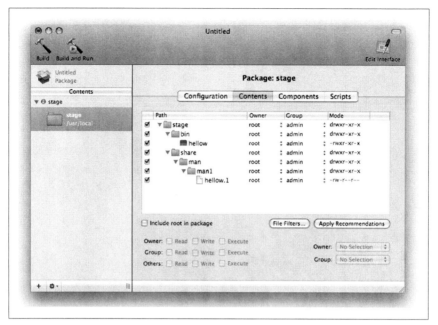

Figure 14-9. Setting ownership and permissions in the Contents pane

installed) and downgradable (that is, if the component can be replaced with an earlier version). Then you would go to the Scripts pane to enter a scripts directory and indicate which scripts must be run before (pre-install) and after (post-install) the installation of the component. Apple advises package developers to consider pre- and post-install actions on the package, rather than on individual components, if possible.

After you've configured the installation options for the components, you must configure the installation options for the package as a whole. To configure installation options for the entire package, click the Package icon at the top of the left part of the Project window. Then set the package options in the configuration pane, as shown in Figure 14-10.

Here are the steps you must perform:

- Enter a title.
- In the User Sees drop-down list, select from "Easy and Custom Install," "Easy Install Only," and "Custom Install Only." The custom install options are useful for enabling users to select only those optional components of a package that they wish to install.
- Select the Install Destination option from the checkboxes "Volume selected by user," "System volume," and "User home directory." Specify

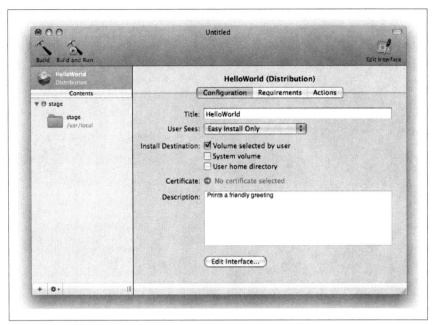

Figure 14-10. Configuring package options

"System volume" if the package must be installed on the boot volume. If, on the other hand, it makes no difference which volume houses the package, you can provide the user with the choice to install on nonsystem volumes. Similarly, you can give the user the option to install the package in his or her home directory. This means it can be installed on a per-user rather than a system-wide basis.

- Select a certificate to be used to sign the package.
- Enter a description of the package.

Clicking the Edit Interface button at the bottom of the Configuration pane opens the Interface Editor, shown in Figure 14-11. You can use the Interface Editor to customize the following interface properties that the user will see when installing your package: background image, introduction or welcome message, Read Me, license, and concluding message.

The next step is to set any prerequisites for the package installation, such as the minimum amount of hard drive space and/or memory that must be available. This is done in the Requirements pane of the Project window, shown in Figure 14-12.

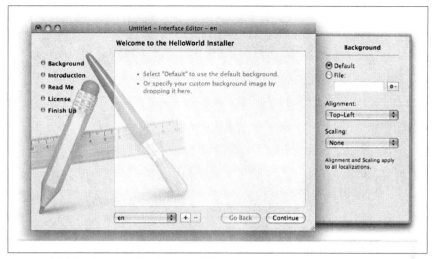

Figure 14-11. Package installer Interface Editor

To add a requirement, click the plus sign (+) at the bottom of the right part of the Project window. You can then select from several available options, as shown in Figure 14-13.

Finally, in the Actions pane (shown in Figure 14-14), you can configure the package installer to perform pre- and post-install actions by clicking on the appropriate Edit button.

The available pre- and post-install actions are shown in the Actions box on the left in Figure 14-15.

After you have filled in the package settings, you'll be ready to build the project. To create the *.pkg* package installer file, click the Build icon in the title bar or select Project→Build from the menu bar. Alternatively, you can click the Build and Run icon in the title bar (or select Project→Build and Run from the menu bar) to create the *.pkg* file and install the package. If all goes well, the *.pkg* file will be created wherever you elected to save it, and you'll be presented with a window (shown in Figure 14-16) in which you can choose to open the *.pkg* file in the Installer, view it in the Finder, or return to editing to adjust the package's installation options.

When you quit PackageMaker, you'll be prompted to save the PackageMaker session with its currently filled-in values as a *.pmdoc* document. If you save the session and subsequently double-click your *.pmdoc* document, PackageMaker will open with the values that were saved in the *.pmdoc* file.

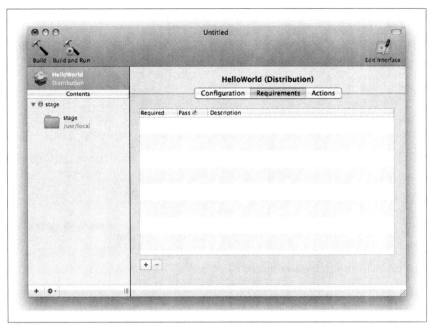

Figure 14-12. Requirements pane

An alternative to PackageMaker is Stéphane Sudre's *Iceberg*,
available at *http://s.sudre.free.fr/Software/Iceberg.html*.

The process we've just described creates a package installer file named
HelloWorld.pkg. To install the package on a Mac OS X system, double-click it
in the Finder to launch the Mac OS X Installer application. In releases of Mac
OS X earlier than Leopard, such *.pkg* installers were actually created as directories, which could be navigated in the Unix shell with *cd* and whose contents
could be listed with *ls*. (Alternatively, you could Control/right-click on such
a *.pkg* installer and select Show Package Contents in the contextual menu.)
Beginning with Leopard, *.pkg* installers are created as single (flat) files in the
xar archive format. You can view the contents of *.pkg* installers created in
Leopard with the *xar* command:

```
$ xar -tf HelloWorld.pkg
stage.pkg
stage.pkg/PackageInfo
stage.pkg/Bom
stage.pkg/Payload
```

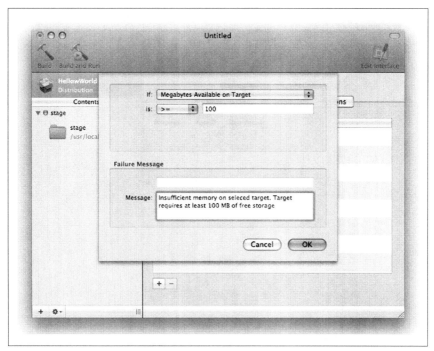

Figure 14-13. Adding a requirement

After you've installed the package, it will show up in the list produced by the *pkgutil --pkgs* command as *com.oreilly.hellow.helloworld.stage.pkg*, and you'll be able to see all the files that were installed with the *pkgutil* command:

```
$ pkgutil --files com.oreilly.hellow.helloworld.stage.pkg
usr/local/.
usr/local/bin
usr/local/bin/hellow
usr/local/share
usr/local/share/man
usr/local/share/man/man1
usr/local/share/man/man1/hellow.1
```

Creating Fink Packages

You can create your own Fink package—which, in this context, is a ported Unix software application or library that can be installed on a user's computer via the Fink package management system—by identifying a source archive and creating an *.info* file in your */sw/fink/dists/local/main/finkinfo* directory.

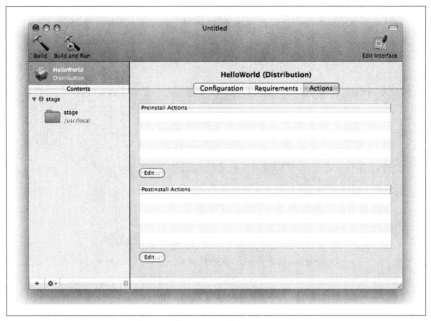

Figure 14-14. Actions pane for specifying pre- and post-install actions

Creating and Publishing the Tarball

To illustrate how to create a Fink package, let's again use the *hellow-1.0* program (see "Using PackageMaker," earlier in this chapter). In this case, you can use the makefile shown in Example 14-4, which is a little simpler than the one used in Example 14-3.

Example 14-4. Makefile for hellow

```
all:
        cc -o hellow hellow.c
```

Before you proceed, create a tarball named *hellow-1.0.tar.gz* with the following contents, and move it to the */Users/Shared/hellow/src* directory:

```
hellow-1.0/
hellow-1.0/hellow.1
hellow-1.0/hellow.c
hellow-1.0/Makefile
```

The *curl* utility can download this file using the following URL: *file:///Users/Shared/hellow/src/hellow-1.0.tar.gz*. (You can host your own files on a public web server or FTP server, or, as in this example, on the local filesystem with a *file:URL*.)

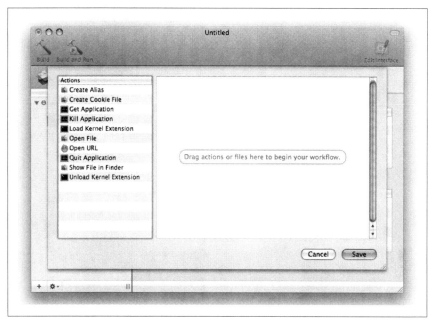

Figure 14-15. Adding pre-install (or post-install) actions

Creating the .info File

Next, create an *.info* file to tell Fink where to download the package from and how to install it. Fink uses this information to download, extract, and compile the source code, and then to generate and install a Debian package (a *.deb* file). This file must be in */sw/fink/dists/local/main/finkinfo*, so you'll need superuser privileges to create it (use the *sudo* utility to temporarily gain these privileges). Example 14-5 shows */sw/fink/dists/local/main/finkinfo/hellow-1.0.info*.

Example 14-5. The hellow-1.0 info file

```
Package: hellow
Version: 1.0
Revision: 1
Source: file:///Users/Shared/hellow/src/%n-%v.tar.gz
Source-MD5: 4ca04528f976641d458f65591da7985c
CompileScript: make
InstallScript: mkdir -p %i/bin
  cp %n %i/bin
  mkdir -p %i/share/man/man1
  cp %n.1 %i/share/man/man1/%n.1
Description: Hello, World program
DescDetail: <<
Prints a friendly greeting to you and your friends.
<<
```

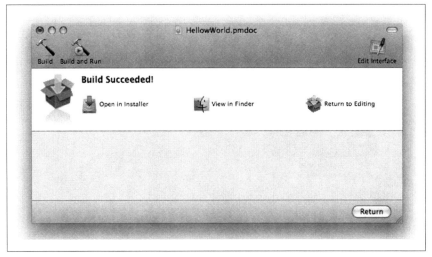

Figure 14-16. Build Succeeded!

```
License: Public Domain
Maintainer: Brian Jepson <bjepson@oreilly.com>
```

The *hellow-1.0.info* file includes several entries, described in the following list (see the Fink Packaging Manual at *http://fink.sourceforge.net/doc/packaging/* for more details):

Package
    The name of the package.

Version
    The package version number.

Revision
    The package revision number.

Source
    The URL of the source distribution. You can use percent expansion in the name. (In this example, %n is the name of the package and %v is the package version; see the Fink Packaging Manual for more percent expansions.)

Source-MD5
    The MD5 checksum for the file. You must calculate this using the *md5sum* command (*/sw/bin/md5sum*) that comes with Fink. Unless your files are identical to the ones we used, your checksum will be different from what's shown in Example 14-5.

CompileScript

The command (or commands) needed to compile the source package. The command(s) may span multiple lines but must begin after the colon.

InstallScript

The command (or commands) that install the compiled package. The command(s) may span multiple lines but must begin after the colon.

Description

A short description of the package.

DescDetail

A longer description of the package, enclosed in double angle brackets (<<).

License

The license used by the package. See the Fink Packaging Manual for information on available licenses.

Maintainer

The name and email address of the maintainer.

Installing the Package

To install *hellow*, use the command *sudo fink install hellow*. This command downloads the source to a working directory and then extracts, compiles, and packages it, generating the file */sw/fink/dists/local/main/binary-darwin-pow erpc/hellow_1.0-1_darwin-powerpc.deb*.

 If */sw/etc/fink.conf* contains the entry `MirrorOrder: MasterFirst` (the default), it will try to find the *.tar.gz* file on the server designated as `Mirror-master`. Since it is unlikely that *hellow-1.0.tar.gz* is hosted on that server, it will fail, and you'll be presented with several options, including "Retry using original source URL," which means download the file from the location specified in *hellow-1.0.info*. You could avoid this by changing the `MirrorOrder` to `MasterLast`, but we do not recommend changing the default behavior of Fink because it could have unpredictable results down the road.

After Fink creates this file, it installs it using *dpkg*. After you've installed *hellow*, you can view its manpage and run the *hellow* command:

```
$ man hellow

HELLOW(1)        BSD General Commands Manual        HELLOW(1)

NAME
```

```
       hellow - Greeting generator

DESCRIPTION
       This command prints a friendly greeting.

Mac OS                   April 29, 2005                   Mac OS
$ hellow
Hello, world!
```

This example illustrates only a portion of Fink's capabilities. For example, Fink can also be used to download and apply patches to a source distribution. For more information on Fink and detailed instructions on how to build a *.deb* package and contribute it to the Fink distribution, see the Fink Packaging Manual (*http://fink.sourceforge.net/doc/packaging/index.php*).

Creating MacPorts Packages

As readily as you can create Fink packages, you can also create your own MacPorts packages (i.e., ports). Like Fink packages, MacPorts packages are not to be confused with packages created with PackageManager: they are simply ported Unix (or Aqua) software applications or libraries ready to be installed on a user's computer via the MacPorts package management system. To create a port in MacPorts, you must first identify a source archive and create a *Portfile* file in the appropriate subdirectory of the *dports* directory. For example, the Portfile for a game named *foo* would be placed in *~/darwinports/dports/games/foo*, assuming that the MacPorts infrastructure has been installed in *~/darwinports*. A Portfile is actually a Tcl script that is similar in purpose to an *.info* file in Fink. The remainder of this chapter is devoted to illustrating the process of creating a MacPorts package.

Creating and Publishing the Tarball

The initial procedure for creating a package in MacPorts is similar to creating a package in Fink. To illustrate how to create a MacPorts package, we'll use the same program, *hellow-1.0*, that we used to illustrate how to create a Fink package in the preceding section. As in Fink, start by creating a tarball named *hellow-1.0.tar.gz* with the following contents:

```
hellow-1.0/
hellow-1.0/hellow.1
hellow-1.0/hellow.c
hellow-1.0/Makefile
```

Then, move this file to the */Users/Shared/hellow/src* directory. The *curl* utility will now be able to download it using the following URL: *file:///Users/Shared/hellow/srcs/hellow-1.0.tar.gz*. (As noted in our discussion of Fink, you can also host your own files on a public web server or FTP server. Hosting the tarball on your local system, however, is useful for testing your port.)

Creating the Portfile

Once the tarball has been placed in *file:///Users/Shared/hellow/src/* you'll need to establish a local ports repository, which can reside in your own user directory (for example, in */Users/mug4/MacPorts/ports*). Then, edit the *sources.conf* file in *${prefix}/etc/macports*. Locate the following line:

```
rsync://rsync.macports.org/release/ports
```

and add a line below it to point to the local repository:

```
file://Users/mug4/MacPorts/ports
```

Next, you'll need to create a file named *Portfile* in */Users/mug4/MacPorts/ports/games/hellow*. The Portfile lists the attributes of the package needed by MacPorts: for example, the name, version, maintainer(s), where to download the package from, and how to install it. MacPorts uses this information to download, extract, and compile the source code. Information on patchfiles, special *configure* or compilation flags, and installation or post-installation configuration instructions may also be included in a Portfile. Example 14-6 shows a Portfile for the *hellow* port. (Be sure to replace the MD5 checksum shown here with the actual checksum of the *hellow-1.0.tar.gz* file; you can generate this with the *md5* utility.)

Example 14-6. The hellow-1.0 Portfile

```
# $ID:  $
PortSystem 1.0
name            hellow
version         1.0
categories      games
maintainers     myemail@mac.com
description     "hello program"
long_description "Classic hello program.  Prints: Hello,\
                World."
master_sites    file:///Users/Shared/hellow/src
homepage        file:///Users/Shared/hellow
distname        ${portname}-${portversion}
platforms       darwin
checksums       md5 4ca04528f976641d458f65591da7985c
configure {}

set instprog    "/usr/bin/install -m 755"
set instman     "/usr/bin/install -m 644"
destroot        {
   system "${instprog} -d ${destroot}${prefix}/bin"
   system "${instprog} -d ${destroot}${prefix}/share/man/man1"
```

```
system "${instprog} ${worksrcpath}/hellow ${destroot}${prefix}/bin"
system "${instprog} ${worksrcpath}/*.1 ${destroot}${prefix}/share/man/man1" }
```

The *Portfile* file includes several items, described in the following list (the list includes a few additional items that weren't needed in our simple example):

$ID: $
> A commented-out RCS ID tag. All Portfiles begin with this string.

Portsystem 1.0
> The Portsystem version declaration.

name
> The package name.

categories
> Used for organization of packages into categories (mail clients, editors, games, etc.).

maintainers
> The email addresses of the folks maintaining the port.

description
> A short description of the package.

long_description
> A more detailed description of the package.

master_sites
> The URL of the software's source distribution.

homepage
> The URL of the software's website.

distname
> The name of the distribution (e.g., *hellow-1.0*).

platform
> The platform on which the port is to be built.

checksums
> A required command that verifies the MD5 checksum.

extract.suffix
> Used if the source file does not have the default suffix *.tar.gz*.

distfile
> The combination of *name, version,* and *extract.suffix*. The default is *${name}-${version}.tar.gz*. This option can be used to override the default if the name of the source file on the server is not in the default form.

depends_lib
> Used to specify additional libraries or binaries required by the port.

patchfiles

A list of patch files needed for the package to compile or run. Patch files are placed in a *files/* subdirectory of the directory that contains the Portfile.

configure{}

The brackets are left empty if there is no autoconf *configure* script to run, as in this simple example. If there is a *configure* script, DarwinPorts passes it the argument *-prefix=${prefix}*. After the *configure{}* line in the sample Portfile, there are installation instructions to ensure that the program and its manpage get installed into the correct directory.

The variables *instprog* and *instman* are used to specify exactly which commands are to be used to install the binary and manpage, respectively. The *destroot* key is included to specify exactly what the system should do when the *destroot* option is used with the *port* command.

 For more details on Portfile contents, see Michael A. Maibaum's MacPorts User Guide (*http://guide.macports.org*), the sample Portfile at */opt/local/var/macports/sources/rsync.macports.org/release/base/doc/exampleport*, and the *portfile(7)* manpage.

Once the Portfile has been created, you'll need to change to the top-level local ports repository and enter the *portindex* command:

```
$ cd /Users/mug4/MacPorts/ports
$ portindex
Creating software index in /Users/mug4/MacPorts/ports
Adding port games/hellow

Total number of ports parsed:  1
Ports successfully parsed:     1
Ports failed:                  0
```

Building and Installing a Port

Once the Portfile is ready, you can build the port. This involves a sequence of *port* commands, each invoked with the *-v* (verbose) and *-d* (debug) options. To begin this process, you must change to the directory that contains the *hellow*-related Portfile and verify the MD5 checksum of the tarball:

```
$ cd /Users/mug4/MacPorts/ports/games/hellow
$ sudo port -d -v checksum
```

Since no explicit port name was provided in the preceding command, MacPorts obtains (from any Portfile in the current directory) the information that is needed to download and verify the MD5, SHA1, and RMD160 checksums of the source file. The source tarball file *hellow-1.0.tar.gz* is downloaded into */opt/local/var/macports/distfiles/hellow*, and a *work/* directory is created in */opt/local/var/macports/build/_Users_mug4_MacPorts_ports_games_hellow*.

Next, extract the source with the following command:

```
$ sudo port -d -v extract
```

This command unpacks *hellow-1.0.tar.gz*, creating the */opt/local/var/mac ports/build/_Users_mug4_MacPorts_ports_games_hellow/work/hellow-1.0* directory. Once the source code has been unpacked, you can build the package with the following command:

```
$ sudo port -d -v build
```

If the build goes well, you can test the installation by first installing the port in the *destroot* directory:

```
$ sudo port -d -v destroot
```

This produces a large number of warning messages, but in the end (if all goes well) both the binary *hellow* and the manpage *hellow.1* will be installed in the *~/darwinports/dports/games/hellow/work/destroot/opt/local* directory. After you've tested the binary and manpage in this *destroot* directory, you can install the *hellow* port system-wide—that is, in */opt/local*. To do this, enter the following command:

```
$ sudo port -d -v install
```

This command installs the *hellow* port in */opt/local/var/macports/software/hel low/1.0_0/opt/local* and activates it by creating hard links to the installed files in */opt/local*. It also removes the work directory, */opt/local/var/macports/build/ _Users_mug4_MacPorts_ports_games_hellow/*. You can check that *hellow* has been installed properly by entering the *port installed* command, and by trying to run *hellow* and viewing its manpage. You can uninstall *hellow* as you would uninstall any other port, with the following command:

```
$ sudo port uninstall hellow
```

As with Fink, this example illustrates only a small portion of MacPorts's capabilities. For more information, see the sources noted earlier, which contain detailed instructions on how to build a port and contribute it to the MacPorts distribution.

## PART IV

Serving and System Management

This part of the book talks about using Mac OS X as a server, as well as system administration.

Chapters in this part of the book include:

## CHAPTER 15

Using Mac OS X As a Server

Although most people think of Mac OS X as a client system only, you can also run Mac OS X as a server. If you need Apple's advanced server administration tools, you can purchase Mac OS X Server (*http://www.apple.com/server/macosx/*), but if you're comfortable with the command line, the client version can easily be configured to run as a server. The services that power the Sharing System Preferences pane are based on the same servers that provide the foundation for everything from private networks to the Internet:

- OpenSSH for remote login
- Samba for Windows file sharing
- Apache for web publishing

However, the System Preferences are limited in what they will let you do. While the tools available to configure the Sharing preferences received a nice upgrade in Leopard, to unleash the full power of Mac OS X as a server, you'll need to install your own administrative tools or edit the configuration files by hand. Once you've unleashed the server lurking inside your Mac, there are many services you can set up. Here are some of the possibilities:

Secure mail server

If your email provider isn't reliable, or doesn't support the way you want to access your email, you can forward all your email to your personal server and retrieve it from there—whether you're in your home office or on the road.

SSH server

When you're on the road, there might be some things you want to access back at the home office. Or perhaps you want to help a family member troubleshoot a computer problem while you're away. At the same time, you don't want to leave your local network wide open for malicious attacks from outside. Your SSH server can be configured to allow you to connect to your local network securely, while keeping out unwanted pests.

VNC/Remote Desktop/X11

One step up from a VPN or SSH connection is a remote connection that lets you completely take over the desktop of a computer in your home. This takes remote access and troubleshooting to the next level.

Built-in Services: The Sharing Preference Pane

Mac OS X includes many built-in services that are based on common open source servers such as Samba, Apache, and OpenSSH. In earlier versions of Mac OS X, there wasn't much configuration you could do through the Sharing preference pane (System Preferences→Sharing), other than enabling and disabling the individual services.

Leopard introduced dramatic changes to this preference pane. Gone are the separate Personal File Sharing, Windows File Sharing, and FTP Access options; these have been replaced by a single File Sharing option. The Apple Remote Desktop option has been renamed Remote Management, and it's joined by a new option called Screen Sharing that provides similar functionality. This section describes each of these services and what you can do under the hood to customize them to your liking.

 Something to realize when you use the Sharing preference pane is that checking (or unchecking) the checkbox next to a service name enables (or disables) that service, but highlighting the line containing the service name is what makes that service "active" in the preference pane. So, use the checkboxes to enable and disable the services, but select the line containing the service name to configure service options. In the sample figures that follow, we show each service highlighted with its checkbox checked.

File Sharing

With the advent of Leopard, the separate options on the Sharing preference pane for Personal File Sharing, Windows File Sharing, and FTP Access have been replaced by a single option that is simply called File Sharing (Figure 15-1).

In pre-Leopard environments:

- Enabling the Personal File Sharing option started the Apple Filing Protocol (AFP) service, which corresponds to the AFPSERVER entry in */etc/hostconfig* (see Chapter 4 for more information on */etc/hostconfig*). When this option was enabled, your Mac shared your home directory and

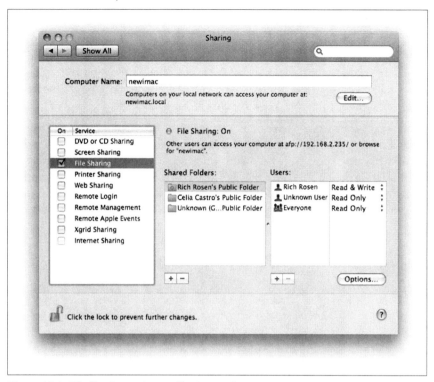

Figure 15-1. File Sharing option on Sharing preference pane

any mounted volumes (including external drives) with the connected machine.

- Enabling the Windows File Sharing option started the Samba service, removing the `Disabled` key in both */System/Library/LaunchDaemons/ nmbd.plist* (the NetBIOS name server for resolving Windows server names) and */System/Library/LaunchDaemons/smbd.plist* (the server that handles Windows file sharing).

- Enabling the FTP Access option started the File Transfer Protocol (FTP) service, removing the `Disabled` key in */System/Library/LaunchDaemons/ ftp.plist* as *launchd* enabled the FTP server.

In Leopard, the single File Sharing option controls access to AFP, SMB, and FTP shares, but it offers more control over access than was available with Tiger. You can list specific directories as *share points* and control access to them at a granular level, specifying read-only or read and write permissions on a per-user or per-group basis. By default, the list of shared folders contains all of your users' *Public* folders (*~user/Public*) and those folders are readable by everyone (including the guest account) and writable by the owner, as shown in the Users list on the righthand side of the pane.

You can add share points to this list by clicking the "+" button under the list of Shared Folders, which opens up a file browser dialog allowing you to choose other folders or disks. (If desired, you can remove any share point, including any user's *Public* folder, by clicking the "–" button.)

When you create a new share point this way, the permissions default to read/write access for administrators and read-only access for everyone else. You can customize these permissions to your liking, adding new users by clicking the "+" button (a dialog appears listing known users on your Mac as well as entries in your address book), removing unwanted users by clicking the "–" button, and altering the level of access given to any of these users ("Read & Write," "Read Only," "Write Only," or "No Access").

Certain user entries ("System Administrator" and "Everyone") cannot be removed, but you can modify their access levels. For example, you can set access for "Everyone" (meaning anyone not explicitly named in the list) and Unknown Users (remote users who don't match up to users on your computer) to "No Access."

If you want to restrict access only to specific users, you must take the steps just outlined; otherwise, *everyone* will have read access!

Clicking the Options button gives you access to even finer controls, as shown in Figure 15-2: you can selectively enable or disable access to a share via AFP (enabled by default), SMB, and FTP.

Prior to Leopard, a third-party preference pane called *SharePoints* from Hornware (*http://www.hornware.com/share points/*) was the only mechanism available for exercising control over AFP and SMB shares, apart from manually editing the Samba configuration file. If you have been using SharePoints, and you upgrade to Leopard, you will need to switch to using the File Sharing option in the Sharing preference pane to configure your shares.

Manual Samba configuration

You can still exercise manual control over SMB shares in the classic fashion—by editing */etc/smb.conf*. For example, you could share your */Applications* directory by adding this entry:

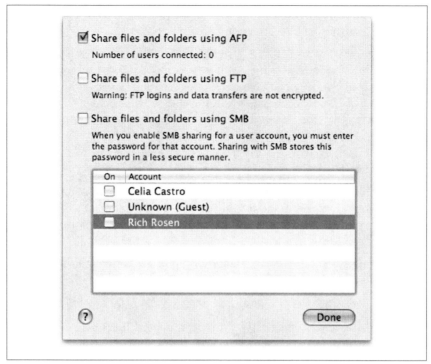

Figure 15-2. Advanced options for File Sharing

```
[Applications]
path = /Applications
read only = yes
```

At a more sophisticated level, you could create an entry that shares a folder more selectively, and limit which files are displayed:

```
[Shared]
path = /Users//Shared
valid users = @admin
writable = yes
public = no
browsable = no
veto files = /.DS_Store/._*/
delete veto files = yes
```

This shares the content of the */Users/Shared* directory only with users in the *admin* group, allowing them both read and write access. The share is marked as *not* "public," meaning that only authorized users can see its contents, and *not* "browsable," meaning that it will be hidden from remote users who are just browsing the network searching for Windows file shares. It also hides files named *.DS_Store* and files whose names begin with ._ (these are "dot" files that Mac OS X creates within a folder whenever it is viewed from the Finder).

Read the Samba documentation and the manpage for *smb.conf* to learn more about the available configuration options.

Use the command *sudo killall -HUP smbd nmbd* to restart Samba so that it uses your updated configuration file, without closing any existing connections. (Stopping and restarting File Sharing would terminate active connections for both AFP and SMB. Although Windows clients will usually reconnect to shared resources without complaining, they will get an error if a file transfer is in progress when you interrupt the connection.)

Manual FTP configuration

The capabilities of the FTP server that comes with Mac OS X are limited. We suggest that you bypass it and install PureFTPd via Fink or MacPorts. (Fink users may need to use the unstable repositories. For more information, see Chapter 12.)

To install PureFTPd, issue the command *sudo fink install pure-ftpd* or *sudo port install pureftpd* and follow the prompts (if any).

To switch Mac OS X over to PureFTPd, follow these steps:

1. Make sure that File Sharing is disabled in System Preferences→Sharing.

2. Back up your existing */System/Library/LaunchDaemons/ftp.plist* file (be sure to add `<key>Disabled</key><true/>` if you decide to back it up to a file in the */System/Library/LaunchDaemons* directory; otherwise, *launchd* may activate both FTP servers and you will end up with the applications having competing access to the port). Replace its contents with the following (if you are using Fink, change the program location to */sw/sbin/pure-ftpd*):

```
<?xml version="1.0" encoding="UTF-8"?>
<!DOCTYPE plist PUBLIC "-//Apple Computer//DTD PLIST 1.0//EN"
        "http://www.apple.com/DTDs/PropertyList-1.0.dtd">
<plist version="1.0">
  <dict>
    <key>Disabled</key>
    <true/>
    <key>Label</key>
    <string>org.pureftpd.ftpd</string>
    <key>Program</key>
    <string>/opt/local/sbin/pure-ftpd</string>
    <key>ProgramArguments</key>
    <array>
      <string>pure-ftpd</string>
      <string>-A</string>
      <string>-lpuredb:/opt/local/etc/pureftpd.pdb</string>
    </array>
    <key>Sockets</key>
```

```
<dict>
  <key>Listeners</key>
  <dict>
    <key>Bonjour</key>
    <true/>
    <key>SockServiceName</key>
    <string>ftp</string>
  </dict>
</dict>
<key>inetdCompatibility</key>
<dict>
  <key>Wait</key>
  <false/>
</dict>
</dict>
</plist>
```

3. You'll now need to add users to the PureFTPd password file, */sw/etc/pureftpd.passwd*. To create a user, use *pure-pw*. Specify an FTP username as well as the UID (*-u*), GID (*-g*), and home directory (*-d*) of a real user to map that FTP user to. You'll be prompted for a password (we suggest you use something different from your login password):

```
$ sudo pure-pw useradd bjepson -u 501 -g 501 -d /Users/bjepson/ftpfiles
Password: ********
Enter it again: ********
```

This way, the insecure FTP password can be different from the login password.

 Make sure you create the directory specified with the *-d* option and that it is owned by the username you specified. Here, we've used a subdirectory of the user's home directory. Used in conjunction with the *-A* argument (which *chroots* the FTP sessions so that the referenced directory appears to be the root directory of the accessible filesystem), this is an acceptable compromise given the insecurity of FTP, which passes usernames and passwords in clear text.

After you set the user's password, you must create the password database (*pureftpd.pdb*) with *pure-pw mkdb*.

4. Next, use System Preferences→Sharing to restart File Sharing, then click Options and enable FTP sharing.

Now, when you log in as a remote user, you're trapped in the *ftpfiles* subdirectory. As far as you're concerned, it's the root of the filesystem. Thus, even if an attacker obtains your FTP password, the damage he can do is limited. For example:

```
$ ftp bjepson@BCJ.local
Trying ::1...
Connected to BCJ.local.
220---------- Welcome to Pure-FTPd ----------
220-Local time is now 16:05. Server port: 21.
220 You will be disconnected after 15 minutes of inactivity.
331 User bjepson OK. Password required
Password: ********
230-User bjepson has group access to:   501
230 OK. Current directory is /
Remote system type is UNIX.
Using binary mode to transfer files.
ftp> ls
229 Extended Passive mode OK (|||8195|)
150 Accepted data connection
226-Options: -l
226 0 matches total
ftp> cd /
250 OK. Current directory is /
ftp> ls
229 Extended Passive mode OK (|||61258|)
150 Accepted data connection
226-Options: -l
226 0 matches total
```

FTP logins and data transfers are not encrypted, so FTP is inherently insecure. Where possible and where necessary, FTP service should be replaced with the more secure *SFTP*, which is essentially FTP over SSH. This does not require additional server software (SFTP is bundled with OpenSSH) or additional configuration (users authorized to connect through SSH simply do so and request that remote SFTP processes be started for their connections). SSHFS, the MacFUSE-based filesystem described in Chapter 8, is another viable replacement for vanilla FTP.

Web Sharing

The Apache web server is activated when you enable Web Sharing (formerly called Personal Web Sharing) in the Sharing preference pane, as shown in Figure 15-3 (it is disabled by default). Apache's main configuration file is */etc/apache2/httpd.conf*, and the local path to the primary website is stored in */Library/WebServer/Documents*. Individual users' sites' configuration files can be found in */etc/apache2/users*, although the sites themselves are stored under the users' home directories. Apache keeps its log files in */var/log/apache2*.

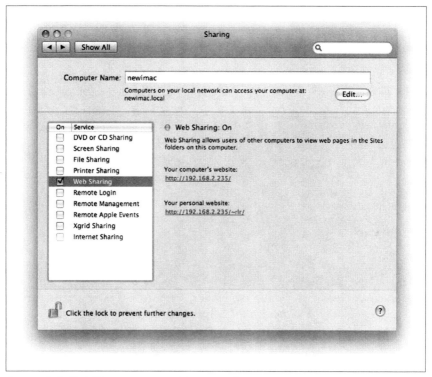

Figure 15-3. Web Sharing option on Sharing preference pane

The Apache server that comes with Mac OS X 10.5 (Leopard) is based on Apache 2.2 and includes several optional modules, which you can enable or disable by uncommenting/commenting the corresponding LoadModule directives in */etc/apache2/httpd.conf*. These modules are described in the following sections.

After you've made any changes to these modules, you should test the changes to the configuration with the command *sudo apachectl configtest* and then have Apache reload its configuration files with *sudo apachectl graceful*.

 You can browse the source code for Apple's version of Apache, as well as the optional modules, by visiting *http://www.open source.apple.com/darwinsource/*.

dav_module (mod_dav)

This is the WebDAV (Web-based Distributed Authoring and Versioning) module, which lets you export a website as a filesystem (this is how Apple's iDisk is exported, for example).

If you enable this module by uncommenting the associated LoadModule directive, as described earlier, you can turn on WebDAV sharing by including the directive DAV on within a <Directory> or <Location> element in *httpd.conf* or one of the user configuration files in */etc/httpd/users*. You will also need to specify the lockfile that *mod_dav* will use. For example, you can enable Web-DAV for your web server root by changing *httpd.conf*, as shown here in bold:

```
DAVLockDB /tmp/DAVLock
<Directory />
  Options FollowSymLinks
  DAV on
  AllowOverride None
</Directory>
```

After you make this change and restart Apache, you'll be able to mount your computer's website by opening the Finder, selecting Go→Connect to Server, and specifying *http://localhost* in the Server Address field.

See *http://www.webdav.org/mod_dav/install.html* for complete information on configuring this module.

ssl_module (mod_ssl)

This module allows you to serve documents securely using the HTTPS (TLS/ SSL) protocol. To properly configure HTTPS, you need to obtain a server certificate signed by a Certificate Authority (CA). However, after you've enabled *mod_ssl* in *httpd.conf*, you can whip up something for testing pretty quickly using the following steps:

1. Create and change to a working directory for creating and signing your certificates:

   ```
   $ mkdir ~/tmp
   $ cd ~/tmp
   ```

2. Create a new CA. This is an untrusted CA, so you'll be able to sign things, but browsers won't trust you implicitly (meaning that visitors will see a warning that there is a certificate for your site that does not come from a known trusted authority):

   ```
   $ /System/Library/OpenSSL/misc/CA.sh -newca
   CA certificate filename (or enter to create)

   Making CA certificate ...
   Generating a 1024 bit RSA private key
   ```

```
.....................................++++++
..++++++
writing new private key to './demoCA/private/./cakey.pem'
Enter PEM pass phrase: ********
Verifying - Enter PEM pass phrase: ********
-----
You are about to be asked to enter information that will be
incorporated into your certificate request.
What you are about to enter is what is called a Distinguished Name
or a DN.
There are quite a few fields but you can leave some blank.
For some fields there will be a default value,
If you enter '.', the field will be left blank.
-----
Country Name (2 letter code) [AU]: US
State or Province Name (full name) [Some-State]: Rhode Island
Locality Name (eg, city) []: Providence
Organization Name (eg, company) [Internet Widgits Pty Ltd]:
Gold and Appel Transfers
Organizational Unit Name (eg, section) []:
Common Name (eg, YOUR name) []: Hagbard Celine
Email Address []: hagbard@jepstone.net
```

3. Next, create a certificate request. This generates an unsigned certificate that you'll have to sign as the CA you just created:

```
$ /System/Library/OpenSSL/misc/CA.sh -newreq
Generating a 1024 bit RSA private key
................++++++
.............................................................++++++
writing new private key to 'newreq.pem'
Enter PEM pass phrase: ********
Verifying - Enter PEM pass phrase: ********
-----
You are about to be asked to enter information that will be incorporated
into your certificate request.
What you are about to enter is what is called a Distinguished Name
or a DN.
There are quite a few fields but you can leave some blank.
For some fields there will be a default value,
If you enter '.', the field will be left blank.
-----
Country Name (2 letter code) [AU]: US
State or Province Name (full name) [Some-State]: Rhode Island
Locality Name (eg, city) []: Kingston
Organization Name (eg, company) [Internet Widgits Pty Ltd]: Jepstone
Organizational Unit Name (eg, section) []:
Common Name (eg, YOUR name) []: Brian Jepson
Email Address []: bjepson@jepstone.net

Please enter the following 'extra' attributes
to be sent with your certificate request.
A challenge password []:
```

```
An optional company name []:
Request (and private key) is in newreq.pem
```

4. Now you must sign the key. The passphrase you must enter in this step should be the passphrase you used when you created the CA:

```
$ /System/Library/OpenSSL/misc/CA.sh -sign
Using configuration from /System/Library/OpenSSL/openssl.cnf
Enter pass phrase for ./demoCA/private/cakey.pem:  ********
Check that the request matches the signature
Signature ok
Certificate Details:
        Serial Number: 1 (0x1)
        Validity
            Not Before: Nov 11 19:34:22 2003 GMT
            Not After : Nov 10 19:34:22 2004 GMT
        Subject:
            countryName               = US
            stateOrProvinceName       = Rhode Island
            localityName              = Kingston
            organizationName          = Jepstone
            commonName                = Brian Jepson
            emailAddress              = bjepson@jepstone.net
        X509v3 extensions:
            X509v3 Basic Constraints:
            CA:FALSE
            Netscape Comment:
            OpenSSL Generated Certificate
            X509v3 Subject Key Identifier:
            1C:AA:2E:32:15:28:83:4B:F4:54:F1:97:87:12:11:45:7C:33:47:96
            X509v3 Authority Key Identifier:
            keyid:DC:C0:D7:A5:69:CA:EE:2B:1C:FA:1C:7A:8A:B2:90:F1:EE:
            1E:49:0C
            DirName:/C=US/ST=Rhode Island/L=Providence/O=Gold and Appel
            Transfers/CN=Hagbard Celine/emailAddress=hagbard@jepstone.
            net
            serial:00

Certificate is to be certified until Nov 10 19:34:22 2004 GMT (365 days)
Sign the certificate? [y/n]: y

1 out of 1 certificate requests certified, commit? [y/n] y
[... output truncated ...]
Signed certificate is in newcert.pem
```

At this point, you have two files for use: the signed certificate (~/tmp/newcert.pem) and the request file, which also contains the server's private key (~/tmp/newreq.pem). The private key is protected by the passphrase you supplied when you generated the request. To configure your server for HTTPS support:

1. Convert the server key so that it doesn't require a passphrase to unlock it (you'll need to supply the passphrase you used when you generated the request):

```
$ sudo openssl rsa -in newkey.pem -out serverkey.pem
Enter pass phrase for newkey.pem: ********
writing RSA key********
```

This removes the protection of the passphrase, but it's fine for testing. If you don't do this, you'll need to supply a passphrase each time Apache starts up (see *http://www.modssl.org/docs/2.8/ssl_reference.html* for documentation on the SSLPassPhraseDialog, which allows you to send the passphrase to Apache in a variety of ways).

2. Copy these files to a location on your filesystem that's outside of the web server's document tree:

```
$ mkdir /Library/WebServer/SSL
$ cp ~/tmp/serverkey.pem /Library/WebServer/SSL/
$ cp ~/tmp/newcert.pem /Library/WebServer/SSL/
```

3. If it's not already enabled, enable the LoadModule directive for *mod_ssl*, and add the following lines to *httpd.conf*:

```
<IfModule ssl_module>
  SSLCertificateFile    /Library/WebServer/SSL/newcert.pem
  SSLCertificateKeyFile /Library/WebServer/SSL/serverkey.pem
  SSLEngine on
  Listen 443
</IfModule>
```

4. Stop and restart the web server (it is not enough to use *apachectl graceful* when you install a new certificate):

```
$ sudo apachectl stop
$ sudo apachectl start
```

Now try visiting *https://localhost* in a web browser. You should get a warning that an unknown authority signed the server certificate. It's OK to continue past this point.

For more information about configuring *mod_ssl* for Mac OS X, see "Using mod_ssl on Mac OS X" at *http://developer.apple.com/internet/serverside/modssl.html*. The *mod_ssl* FAQ at *http://www.modssl.org/docs/2.8/ssl_faq.html #cert-real* includes information on getting a server certificate that's been signed by a trusted CA.

php4_module (mod_php4)

This module lets you serve PHP 4 documents from your Macintosh. After you enable this module and restart Apache, you'll be able to install PHP scripts ending with *.php* into your document directories. As an example, save the following script as *hello.php* in */Library/WebServer/Documents*:

```
<html>
<head><title>PHP Demo</title></head>
<body>
<?
  foreach (array("#FF0000", "#00FF00", "#0000FF") as $color) {
    echo "<font color=\"$color\">Hello, World<br /></font>";
  }
?>
</body>
</html>
```

Next, open *http://localhost/hello.php* (use *https://* if you still have SSL enabled from the previous section) in a web browser. The phrase "Hello, World" should appear in three different colors. If it does not, consult */var/log/httpd/error_log* for messages that might help you diagnose what went wrong.

bonjour_module (mod_bonjour)

This module is enabled by default. However, *mod_bonjour* does not automatically advertise all user sites; it advertises only those user sites whose *index.html* pages have been modified from the default.

If you are using PHP for the index document (*~/Sites/index.php*), Apache may not register your site as changed and thus won't advertise it over Bonjour. For *mod_bonjour* to notice that such a file has changed, you must restart Apache (*sudo apachectl restart*) after modifying the page for the first time.

If you want to override the default *mod_bonjour* settings and advertise all user sites on your server, add the following configuration for *mod_bonjour* to *httpd.conf*:

```
<IfModule bonjour_module>
   RegisterUserSite all-users
</IfModule>
```

You can also enable Bonjour advertising of the primary site by specifying the RegisterDefaultSite directive. Sites that are advertised on Bonjour appear automatically in Safari's Bonjour bookmark list (Safari→Preferences→Bookmarks→Include Bonjour).

Remote Login

When you enable Remote Login, the OpenSSH server is activated, allowing authorized users to connect securely to your Macintosh over SSH. This option removes the Disabled key in */System/Library/LaunchDaemons/ssh.plist*. In

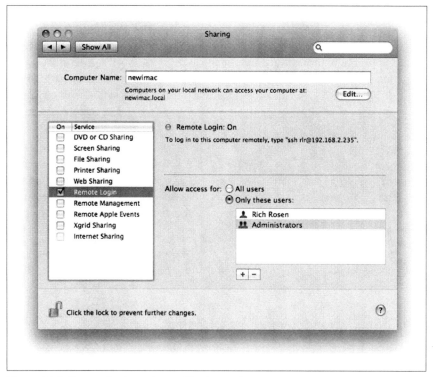

Figure 15-4. Remote Login option on Sharing preference pane

Leopard, the Sharing preference pane allows you to specify which users are allowed to connect using SSH (Figure 15-4).

You can also manually configure the OpenSSH server by editing */etc/sshd_config*. For example, you can configure OpenSSH to allow remote users to request X11 forwarding by uncommenting this line:

```
#X11Forwarding yes
```

so it looks like this:

```
X11Forwarding yes
```

Other options worth examining in this file are:

`PermitRootLogin`
> For security reasons, this should always be explicitly set to "no".

`AllowUsers`
> To restrict SSH access to only certain users, set this option to the list of users who should have access.

```
PasswordAuthentication
```
Assuming you have public key authentication enabled and have set up public and private keys for all your users both on the server and on their remote machines, you may want to disable password authentication on your SSH server. Unlike password authentication, public key authentication does not cause sensitive information (e.g., passwords) to be transmitted during the authentication process, making it inherently more secure.

```
Port
```
Normally SSH runs on TCP port 22, but if you're vigilant about your system's security, or if your ISP blocks port 22 for some reason, changing this setting will add an extra layer of protection. (Note that if you choose to do this, all SSH connections to your Mac must specify the custom port number.)

Changes you make to *letc/sshd_config* will take effect the next time a user logs in via SSH and do not require that you restart the daemon (it's all handled by *launchd*, which we covered in Chapter 4).

Screen Sharing and Remote Management

Before Leopard, there was only one option in the Sharing preference pane that enabled remote control of your Macintosh: Apple Remote Desktop (ARD). Enabling this option started the ARD service, which corresponded to the ARDAGENT entry in *letc/hostconfig*; this allowed someone with an ARD client (or, for that matter, any VNC client) and the proper credentials (i.e., a password if using a VNC or a username and password if using ARD) to connect to your Macintosh and, depending on your settings, potentially take control of the screen, observe it, run reports against it, or even send shell commands to the system.

Leopard replaced this option with two new options, Screen Sharing and Remote Management. Both seem to perform the same function: allowing remote users to connect to and exercise control over your Mac.

 The Sharing preference pane will allow you to enable either Screen Sharing or Remote Management, but not both.

What's the difference? The Remote Management option (shown in Figure 15-5) can lay some claim to being the direct descendant of the old Apple Remote Desktop service. It's intended specifically for use with ARD clients on

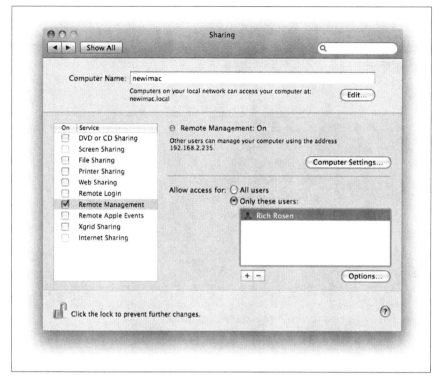

Figure 15-5. Remote Management option on Sharing preference pane

remote machines, providing more fine-grained control over what connecting users can do (see Figure 15-6). If you are interested in using Remote Desktop to control the system, this is the option you will want to use.

Screen Sharing, on the other hand, is geared toward more casual personal usage, particularly through iChat and the new "Back to My Mac" feature. As you can see on the Screen Sharing pane (Figure 15-7), its controls are limited to declaring which users should have access to this feature.

Other systems on the network will automatically register a system with Screen Sharing enabled in their Finder sidebars, and you will be able to use the Share Screen button from within any Finder window to control target systems (except, of course, your own). By default, for security purposes the Screen Sharing feature is Kerberized.

Both Screen Sharing and Remote Management also allow access via standard VNC clients to other users not explicitly listed on the respective service panes, provided they know the VNC password. This is an option that must be enabled explicitly by clicking the "Computer Settings" button under either Screen Sharing or Remote Management and checking the "VNC viewers may control

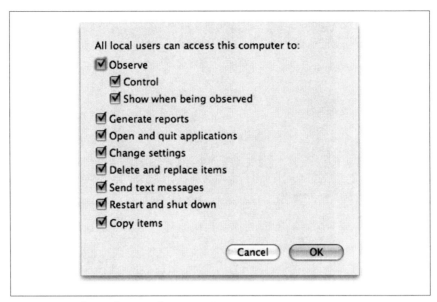

Figure 15-6. Advanced options for Remote Management

screen with password" checkbox, supplying the password of your choice. Figure 15-8 shows the Computer Settings dialog for Screen Sharing; the Remote Management version of this dialog presents additional options.

Another option available in the Computer Settings dialog is "Anyone may request permission to control screen." Checking this box causes a dialog box to be displayed on your Macintosh whenever someone attempts to connect to it via a remote VNC client. When this dialog appears, you can accept or refuse the request to connect.

Leopard also introduced a built-in VNC client for Mac OS X, the Screen Sharing application (found at */System/Library/CoreServices/Screen Sharing.app*). It can be invoked in a number of different ways, including directly from Finder windows that display remote systems available for Screen Sharing connections, and through iChat. It can also be invoked by entering a URL containing the *vnc://* protocol either in Safari, using the Finder's Go→Connect to Server menu option, or in an *open* command entered via the Terminal application:

```
$ open vnc://192.168.2.235
```

The built-in client provides a number of features not available in most VNC clients, including window scaling (useful if the Mac you're connecting to has a screen size equal to or larger than your own), an image quality slider that lets you improve speed on slow network connections by accepting lower-quality

Figure 15-7. *Screen Sharing option on Sharing preference pane*

Figure 15-8. *Computer Settings dialog for Screen Sharing*

screen rendering, and the ability to exchange clipboard contents between local and remote systems.

 Information on more advanced uses of VNC can be found in Chapter 7.

A great usage of this functionality is for management of *headless servers*: that is, servers that lack the standard array of input devices (namely, a keyboard, a mouse, and a monitor). The only way to manage such a server is via some sort of remote connection. While you could certainly connect via SSH to get a command-line shell on the remote machine, having access to another system via its GUI interface provides a great deal more power.

It should be noted that Quartz Extreme requires that you have a real monitor attached to your Mac. Thus, systems with dedicated video-capture devices will not operate on a headless server.

The Mac Mini is an ideal candidate for use as a headless server: it is compact, has a small footprint, and comes without a keyboard, mouse, or monitor, as if begging to be used for this purpose. Initial setup of the Mac Mini does require that those input devices be at least temporarily connected, but once setup is complete you can disconnect them. From that point on, assuming you have enabled Remote Login (for SSH connections), Screen Sharing or Remote Management (for VNC access), and File Sharing, the Mini can run in headless mode as a file server, web server, and so on.

One thing to be aware of when connecting to another Mac that is running as a server is that presumably you don't want to shut down the server when you disconnect (i.e., you want to leave the server running), but you probably do want to log yourself out. The problem is that the key sequence ⌘-Shift-Q (the keyboard shortcut for Log Out) is not intercepted by the Screen Sharing client program: it is recognized by your local system, so instead of logging out of the remote system, you would accidentally log yourself out of your own Mac. Use the Log Out option directly from the menu bar on the remote Mac to ensure that you disconnect properly.

Additionally, bear in mind that if your target system is an Apple Xserve and the lock is in the locked position, you will not have a keyboard or mouse available when you control the system.

Printer Sharing

When you turn on Printer Sharing (Figure 15-9), the *cups-lpd* server is enabled. This option toggles the `Disabled` key in */System/Library/LaunchDaemons/printer.plist*. For more information, see "Printer Sharing" in Chapter 6.

Figure 15-9. Printer Sharing option on Sharing preference pane

Internet Sharing

Prior to Leopard, the Internet Sharing option was found in a separate "tab" within the Sharing pane (System Preferences→Sharing→Internet). In Leopard, however, Internet Sharing is simply another option in the list of sharing services (Figure 15-10).

 There are no longer separate "tabs" on the Sharing preference pane. In Tiger there were three "tabs" on the Sharing System Preferences pane: Sharing (which is analogous to what exists in this pane today), Firewall (now found at System Preferences→Security), and Internet (which corresponds to Internet Sharing—now simply a checkbox item in the services list). Firewall options will be covered later in this chapter.

When you turn on Internet Sharing (System Preferences→Sharing→Internet Sharing), Mac OS X executes */usr/libexec/InternetSharing*, which does quite a bit under the hood: it uses *ifconfig* to configure the network interfaces, *ipfw*

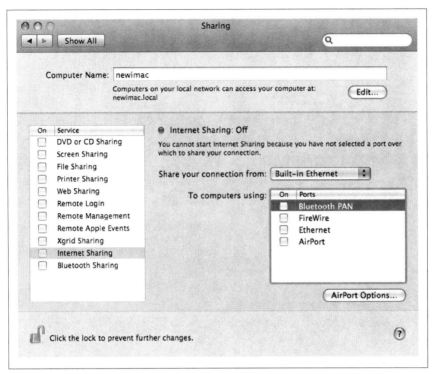

Figure 15-10. Internet Sharing option on Sharing preference pane

and *natd* to handle port redirection, *bootpd* to offer the DHCP service to client machines, and *named* to handle DNS lookups.

ifconfig

ifconfig configures network interfaces. If you're sharing a connection over a port, such as the first Ethernet port (*en0* on most systems), it probably has a self-assigned (APIPA) IP address. Internet Sharing sets this to the first host on whatever subnet it is using (the default is 192.168.2.1).

ipfw/natd

ipfw is the firewall control program, and *natd* is the Network Address Translation (NAT) daemon. Mac OS X adds a firewall rule with a high priority (00010), which diverts any traffic coming into port 8668 on *en1* (the AirPort adapter on many systems):

```
$ sudo ipfw add 00010 divert 8668 ip from any to any via en1
```

It also sets the *net.inet.ip.forwarding sysctl* to 1, which enables IP forwarding.

The Network Address Translation Daemon (*natd*) listens on this port. Internet Sharing starts it with this command, where *IP_ADDRESS* is the IP address you want to share, *INTERFACE* is the network interface (both the IP address and the interface here correspond to the "Share your connection from" settings in the Internet Sharing preference pane), and *INTERFACE2* is the interface to which you're sharing the connection:

```
$ /usr/sbin/natd -alias_address IP_ADDRESS -interface INTERFACE \
  -use_sockets -same_ports -unregistered_only -dynamic -clamp_mss \
  -enable_natportmap -natportmap_interface INTERFACE2
```

So, if your AirPort adapter (*en1*) was assigned the IP address 192.168.254.150, and you shared that connection to another computer plugged into your Ethernet port (*en0*), *natd* would be invoked like so:

```
$ /usr/sbin/natd -alias_address 192.168.254.150 -interface en1 \
  -use_sockets -same_ports -unregistered_only -dynamic -clamp_mss \
  -enable_natportmap -natportmap_interface en0
```

bootpd

bootpd is a combined BOOTP and DHCP server. You can find the *bootpd* configuration in */etc/bootpd.plist*.

To allocate addresses in a different subnet, you'd need to change each occurrence of 192.168.2 to a private subnet that conforms to the rules in RFC 1918 (*ftp://ftp.rfc-editor.org/in-notes/rfc1918.txt*) and load those into Directory Services. Then you'd need to start *bootpd* with this command:

```
$ sudo /usr/libexec/bootpd -P
```

named

named is the BIND (Berkeley Internet Name Domain) server, which provides DNS services to client machines. When you start Internet Sharing, a configuration file is created for *named* in */etc/com.apple.named.conf.proxy*, and *named* runs with that as its configuration file. Here is a trimmed-down version (comments and whitespace removed) of that file:

```
controls { };
options {
        directory "/var/named";
        listen-on { 192.168.2.1;  };
        forward first;
        forwarders { 192.168.254.1;  };
};
zone "." IN {
        type hint;
        file "named.ca";
};
zone "localhost" IN {
```

```
        type master;
        file "localhost.zone";
        allow-update { none; };
};
zone "0.0.127.in-addr.arpa" IN {
        type master;
        file "named.local";
        allow-update { none; };
};
acl can_query {any;};
```

 For more information, see the respective manpages for these commands, as well as the Advanced Networking section of the *FreeBSD Handbook* (*http://www.freebsd.org/doc/en_US .ISO8859-1/books/handbook/*).

Xgrid Sharing

The Xgrid service supports the sharing of processing power among multiple Macs in a local network. Apple's Logic Pro audio application supports Xgrid as a means of pooling the power of multiple processors to perform the CPU-intensive tasks of synthesizing, mixing, and recording music.

DVD/CD Sharing

This service was added to Mac OS X in Leopard primarily to support the MacBook Air, which lacks an optical drive of its own. Enabling this feature on your desktop Mac (or a non-Air laptop that has an optical drive) will allow a MacBook Air to make use of the remote CD/DVD drive as if that optical drive were locally attached.

The Email Server

Apple has given up on the aging and clunky *sendmail*, and is instead using Postfix, which is much easier to configure. (Postfix does include a *sendmail*-compatibility wrapper in */usr/sbin/sendmail*.) The following sections describe how to configure Postfix.

Configuring Postfix to Send Email

By default, Mac OS X runs a program called *master* that monitors the outgoing mail queue, and runs Postfix on the queue as needed. The Postfix daemon is controlled by the *launchd* script */System/Library/LaunchDaemons/org.post fix.master.plist*.

If you want to use Postfix on a standalone server, you must configure two settings in *letc/postfix/main.cf*. The first is the hostname (`myhostname`). This should be a real hostname, something that can be found in a reverse DNS lookup against your IP address. The second is your origin (`myorigin`), which is the domain name from which email you send appears to originate. This can be the same as your hostname (this is probably the case for small sites), but if it isn't, be sure to specify the correct hostname. For example, here are the settings for a computer named *ip192-168-0-1.ri.ri.cox.net* with all email originating from that machine appearing to come from *username@cox.net*:

```
myhostname = ip192-168-0-1.ri.ri.cox.net
myorigin = cox.net
```

If you don't have a permanent domain name for your Mac OS X server, we suggest configuring Postfix to use a *relay host* (most likely your ISP's SMTP server). To configure Postfix to use a relay, add an entry for `relayhost` in *letc/postfix/main.cf*. For example, we use the following setting:

```
relayhost = smtp-server.oreilly.com
```

 If your ISP's network is configured to block outgoing SMTP to all but its own SMTP server, using your ISP's SMTP server as a relay host may be the only way you can configure Postfix to deliver mail.

Along the same lines, you should configure Postfix to masquerade as the appropriate host using the `myorigin` setting in *letc/postfix/main.cf*. In the case of the previous example, the origin is *oreilly.com* (as in *bjepson@oreilly.com*):

```
myorigin = oreilly.com
```

Configuring Postfix to Receive Email

To enable Postfix to act as a legitimate email destination (that is, to allow mail for *username@yourhost* to go directly to your Macintosh), you must create a startup script that runs the commands *postfix start* upon startup and *postfix stop* upon shutdown. For more details, see "Creating Programs that Run Automatically" in Chapter 4.

To receive email at your host, you need a Mail Exchange (MX) record pointing to your machine. The MX record is a DNS entry that identifies the mail servers for a particular domain. If your ISP provides you with a static IP address and supports the use of hostnames (this is typically a given if your Mac is co-located), contact a representative about setting up the appropriate MX record. If you have residential (or low-end business) broadband, it's very likely that your ISP does not support this, and what's more, it probably blocks access to port 25 within its network as a security precaution.

If your system can support the use of port 25, you must change the setting for `inet_interfaces` in */etc/postfix/main.cf*. By default, it listens only on 127.0.0.1 (*localhost*), so you must add the IP address on which you want it to listen. For example, we've set up a server behind a firewall but configured the firewall to forward port 25 to the server (see "Serving from Behind a Firewall," later in this chapter). The private network address of the server is 192.168.254.104, and because traffic on port 25 is going from the outside world to the private network, we must configure `inet_interfaces` to listen on the 192.168.254.104 interface as well as *localhost*:

```
inet_interfaces = localhost 192.168.254.104
```

After you make this change, stop and restart Postfix with *postfix stop* and *postfix start* (it may not be enough to use the command *postfix reload*).

The Mac OS X Firewall

Leopard introduced a number of changes to the firewall built into every Mac. Prior to Leopard, Mac OS X used FreeBSD's *ipfw2* (IP Firewall, version 2) facility to control how incoming and outgoing packets were routed through the system. In Leopard, *ipfw* is still in place as the underlying *network* firewall service, but Apple has also introduced its own homegrown *application* firewall. The application firewall uses application signing to grant each application access to specific ports, rather than simply opening a port and allowing any incoming traffic to pass through it. The Firewall preference pane, which has moved from its position as a tab on the Sharing System Preferences pane to being a tab on the Security System Preferences pane (Figure 15-11), now serves to configure this Apple application firewall, rather than *ipfw*.

Figure 15-11 shows how the application firewall can be configured through the Security preference pane. Notice that you can select from three general modes of operation:

Allow all incoming connections
> Use this mode only if you are very, very trusting, or if your computer is sufficiently protected by an external firewall.

Allow only essential services
> This mode lets Apple make the decision about which services are "essential," enabling them to get through the firewall.

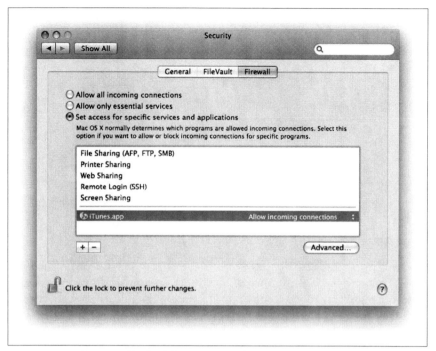

Figure 15-11. The Firewall tab of the Security preference pane

Set access for specific services and applications
This mode lets you decide which applications and services are essential to you, by selectively choosing which applications to allow through the firewall and which ones to block.

When using the "Set access for specific services and applications" option, the list of allowed connections automatically includes whichever services have been enabled in the Sharing preference pane. (This is not unreasonable, since you did explicitly enable these services. If you want them to be removed from this list, go back to the Sharing pane and turn them off.) Individual applications can be added and removed using the "+" and "–" buttons, telling the firewall to allow or block connections initiated by or directed at those applications.

Clicking the Advanced button brings up a dialog (shown in Figure 15-12) that offers two additional options: Enable Firewall Logging and Enable Stealth Mode. Checking these boxes has essentially the same effect as performing the steps described in the following section to configure these options manually.

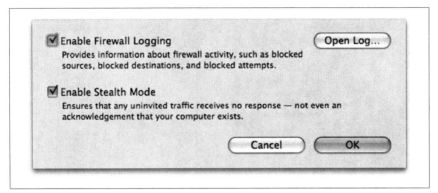

Figure 15-12. Advanced firewall preferences

Manually Configuring ipfw

The *ipfw* firewall is a rule-based filtering system. The default rule, which can be overridden via the *ipfw* utility, allows all traffic from any location to come into your computer (65535 is the priority level of the rule, the lowest priority possible):

```
65535 allow ip from any to any
```

To define this rule yourself, you'd issue the following command:

```
$ ipfw add 65535 allow ip from any to any
```

When you enable the firewall (System Preferences→Security→Firewall), Mac OS X uses its own application firewall to control access. If an *ipfw* rule blocks access to a particular service, the Mac OS X firewall will never even see the connection attempt. For more information, see *http://support.apple.com/kb/HT1810*.

Enabling firewall logging

Enabling firewall logging in the advanced settings causes Mac OS X to do the equivalent of:

```
$ sudo sysctl -w net.inet.ip.fw.verbose=2
```

Enabling stealth mode

This option renders your server somewhat invisible, by setting the following *sysctl*s to 1:

```
net.inet.tcp.blackhole
net.inet.udp.blackhole
net.inet.tcp.log_in_vain
net.inet.udp.log_in_vain
```

This sets both the blackhole (don't reply at all to connections; act as if there's not even a server there) and log_in_vain (log all those rejections in */var/log/ipfw.log*) options for UDP and TCP traffic. It also sets the following firewall rule to deny ICMP echo requests:

```
33300 deny icmp from any to me in icmptypes 8
```

Adding your own rules

You can add your own packet filter rules by clicking the New button on the Firewall tab and filling in the rule information. You can also add your own firewall rules using the *ipfw* utility.

For example, you could add a custom firewall rule such as this one, which permits Telnet connections from only one host (192.168.254.150):

```
$ sudo ipfw add 02075 allow tcp from 192.168.254.150 to any dst-port 23 in
```

You can get things back to normal by deleting the rule:

```
$ sudo ipfw delete 02075
```

Free Database Servers on Mac OS X

There are some great binary distributions for open source databases such as MySQL and PostgreSQL, both of which build out of the box on Mac OS X. This section describes how to install these databases from source and get them set up so you can start playing with them. You can also install MySQL or PostgreSQL via MacPorts or Fink.

SQLite

SQLite is a public domain embeddable database that's implemented as a C library. In Mac OS X, it's also one of several backends used by the Core Data framework, which uses XML and binary formats for storing persistent data.

You can find documentation, source code, and other SQLite resources at *http://www.sqlite.org*. However, Mac OS X Tiger and later ship with SQLite3 pre-installed. You'll find the header file and library in the usual places (*/usr/include/sqlite3.h* and */usr/lib/libsqlite3.dylib*) and the command-line interface in */usr/bin/sqlite3*. Interfaces are available for many programming languages as well.

To use SQLite, simply start *sqlite3* with the name of a database file. If the file doesn't exist, it will be created. You can use standard SQL statements to create, modify, and query data tables. There are also a number of non-SQL commands that start with a dot (.), such as the indispensable *.help* and *.quit*:

```
$ sqlite3 mydata.db
SQLite version 3.1.3
```

```
Enter ".help" for instructions
sqlite> CREATE TABLE foo (bar CHAR(10));
sqlite> INSERT INTO foo VALUES('Hello');
sqlite> INSERT INTO foo VALUES('World');
sqlite> SELECT * FROM foo;
Hello
World
sqlite> .quit
```

You can also issue SQL commands in one-liners from the shell prompt:

```
$ sqlite3 mydata.db 'SELECT * FROM foo;'
Hello
World
```

MySQL

To get the source distribution of MySQL, download the latest tarball from
http://dev.mysql.com/downloads/.

Compiling MySQL

To compile MySQL from source:

1. Extract the tarball:

   ```
   $ cd ~/src
   $ tar xvfz ~/Downloads/mysql-5.0.51b.tar.gz
   ```

2. Change to the top-level directory that *tar* created and run the *configure*
   script. We suggest specifying a prefix of */usr/local/mysql* so it stays out the
   way of any other binaries you have in */usr/local*:

   ```
   $ cd mysql-5.0.51b/
   $ ./configure --prefix=/usr/local/mysql
   ```

3. Type *make* to compile MySQL, and go get a few cups of coffee (compiling
   could take 15 minutes or more).

Installing MySQL

If the compilation succeeded, you're ready to install MySQL. If it didn't suc-
ceed, you should first search the MySQL mailing list archives (*http://lists.mysql
.com*) to see whether anyone has reported the same problem you experienced
and whether a fix is available (if not, you should submit a bug report). If you're
having a lot of trouble here, you may want to install one of the binary packages.

The MySQL installation procedure is as follows:

1. Run *make install* as *root*:

   ```
   $ sudo make install
   ```

2. Install the default configuration file and databases:

```
$ sudo cp support-files/my-medium.cnf /etc/my.cnf
$ cd /usr/local/mysql
$ sudo ./bin/mysql_install_db --user=mysql
```

3. Set permissions on the MySQL directories:

```
$ sudo chown -R root  /usr/local/mysql
$ sudo chown -R mysql /usr/local/mysql/var
$ sudo chgrp -R mysql /usr/local/mysql
```

4. Now you're ready to install a startup script for MySQL. (See "Creating Programs that Run Automatically" in Chapter 4 for a sample MySQL startup script.) After you've created the startup script, start MySQL:

```
$ sudo launchctl start org.mysql.mysqld
```

Configuring MySQL

Next, you need to configure MySQL. At a minimum, set the *root* user's password and create a user and a working database for that user. Before using MySQL, add the following line to your *.bash_profile* and start a new Terminal window to pick up the settings:

```
export PATH=$PATH:/usr/local/mysql/bin
```

To set the *root* password and create a new user:

1. Use *mysqladmin* to set a password for the *root* user (qualified as *root@localhost* and just plain old *root*). When you enter the second line, there will be a *root* password in place, so you need to use *-p*. You'll be prompted for the password you created in the first line:

```
$ mysqladmin -u root password 'password'
$ mysqladmin -u root -p -h localhost password 'password'
Enter password: ********
```

2. Create a database for your user (you'll be prompted for the *mysql root* user's password):

```
$ mysqladmin -u root -p create dbname
Enter password: ********
```

3. Log into the *mysql* shell as *root*, and grant full control over that database to your user, qualified both as *user@localhost* and as the username alone (the -> prompt indicates that you pressed return without completing the command, and the *mysql* shell is waiting for more input):

```
$ mysql -u root -p
Enter password: ********
Welcome to the MySQL monitor.  Commands end with ; or \g.
Your MySQL connection id is 4
Server version: 5.0.51b-log Source distribution
```

```
Type 'help;' or '\h' for help. Type '\c' to clear the buffer.

mysql> GRANT ALL PRIVILEGES ON dbname.* TO username@localhost
    -> IDENTIFIED BY 'password';
Query OK, 0 rows affected (0.08 sec)

mysql> GRANT ALL PRIVILEGES ON dbname.* TO username
    -> IDENTIFIED BY 'password';
Query OK, 0 rows affected (0.00 sec)

mysql> quit
Bye
```

Using MySQL

You should now be able to log into MySQL as the user defined in the previous section and do whatever you want within your database:

```
$ mysql -u username -p dbname
Enter password: ********
Welcome to the MySQL monitor.  Commands end with ; or \g.
Your MySQL connection id is 5
Server version: 5.0.51b-log Source distribution

Type 'help;' or '\h' for help. Type '\c' to clear the buffer.

mysql> CREATE TABLE foo (bar CHAR(10));
Query OK, 0 rows affected (0.06 sec)

mysql> INSERT INTO foo VALUES('Hello');
Query OK, 1 row affected (0.00 sec)

mysql> INSERT INTO foo VALUES('World');
Query OK, 1 row affected (0.01 sec)

mysql> SELECT * FROM foo;
+-------+
| bar   |
+-------+
| Hello |
| World |
+-------+
2 rows in set (0.00 sec)
mysql> quit
Bye
```

PostgreSQL

To get the source distribution of PostgreSQL, download the latest tarball from *http://www.postgresql.org/download/*. At the time of this writing, the latest release is 8.3.3, so we downloaded *postgresql-8.3.3.tar.bz2*.

Compiling PostgreSQL

To compile PostgreSQL from source:

1. Extract the tarball:

    ```
    $ cd ~/src
    $ tar xvfj ~/Downloads/postgresql-8.3.3.tar.bz2
    ```

2. Change to the top-level directory that *tar* created and run the *configure* script. We suggest specifying a prefix of */usr/local/pgsql* so it stays out the way of any other binaries you have in */usr/local*:

    ```
    $ cd postgresql-8.3.3/
    $ ./configure --prefix=/usr/local/pgsql
    ```

3. Type *make* to compile PostgreSQL, and go take a walk around the block while you wait (compiling could take 15 minutes or more).

Installing PostgreSQL

If everything went OK, you're ready to install. If it didn't go OK, check the PostgreSQL mailing list archives (*http://www.postgresql.org/community/lists/*) to see whether anyone has reported the same problem you experienced and whether a fix is available (otherwise, you should submit a bug report). Here's the installation procedure:

1. Run *make install* as *root*:

    ```
    $ sudo make install
    ```

2. Create the *postgres* group and user (this is the PostgreSQL superuser). Be sure to choose an unused group ID and user ID:

    ```
    $ sudo dscl . create /Users/postgres uid 1001
    $ sudo dscl . create /Users/postgres gid 1001
    $ sudo dscl . create /Users/postgres shell /bin/bash
    $ sudo dscl . create /Users/postgres home /usr/local/pgsql
    $ sudo dscl . create /Users/postgres realname "PostgreSQL"
    $ sudo dscl . create /Users/postgres passwd \*
    $ sudo dscl . create /Groups/postgres gid 1001
    $ sudo dscl . create /Groups/postgres passwd \*
    ```

3. Create the *data* subdirectory and make sure that the *postgres* user is the owner of that directory:

    ```
    $ sudo mkdir /usr/local/pgsql/data
    $ sudo chown postgres /usr/local/pgsql/data
    ```

4. Use *sudo* to get a shell as the *postgres* user (supply your own password at this prompt):

    ```
    $ sudo -u postgres -s
    Password: ********
    $
    ```

5. Run the following commands to initialize the PostgreSQL installation:

```
$ /usr/local/pgsql/bin/initdb -D /usr/local/pgsql/data
```

6. You can now log out of the *postgres* user's shell.

Adding the startup item

Now you're ready to create a startup script for PostgreSQL (see "Creating Programs that Run Automatically" in Chapter 4). We'll use a SystemStarter-style startup item, because PostgreSQL requires that a script be run in order for it to shut down properly. First, create the script shown in Example 15-1, save it as */Library/StartupItems/PostgreSQL/PostgreSQL*, and mark it as an executable.

Example 15-1. Startup script for PostgreSQL

```sh
#!/bin/sh

# Source common setup
#
. /etc/rc.common

# Set to -NO- to disable
#
PGSQL=-YES-

StartService()
{
    # Don't start unless PostgreSQL is enabled in /etc/hostconfig
    if [ "${PGSQL:=-NO-}" = "-YES-" ]; then
        ConsoleMessage "Starting PostgreSQL"
        sudo -u postgres /usr/local/pgsql/bin/pg_ctl \
          -D /usr/local/pgsql/data \
          -l /usr/local/pgsql/data/logfile start
    fi
}

StopService()
{
    ConsoleMessage "Stopping PostgreSQL"
    su postgres -c \
      "/usr/local/pgsql/bin/pg_ctl -D /usr/local/pgsql/data stop"
}

RestartService()
{
    # Don't restart unless PostgreSQL is enabled in /etc/hostconfig
    if [ "${PGSQL:=-NO-}" = "-YES-" ]; then
        ConsoleMessage "Restarting PostgreSQL"
        StopService
        StartService
    else
```

```
        StopService
    fi
}

RunService "$1"
```

Next, create the following file as */Library/StartupItems/PostgreSQL/Startup
Parameters.plist*:

```
{
  Description     = "PostgreSQL";
  Provides        = ("PostgreSQL");
  Requires        = ("Network");
  OrderPreference = "Late";
}
```

Now PostgreSQL will start automatically when you reboot the system. If you
want, you can start PostgreSQL right away with this command:

```
$ sudo SystemStarter start PostgreSQL
```

Configuring PostgreSQL

Before you proceed, add the following line to your *.bash_profile* and start a
new Terminal window to pick up the settings:

```
export PATH=$PATH:/usr/local/pgsql/bin
```

By default, PostgreSQL comes with weak permissions; any local user can connect to the database without authentication. Before making any changes, start
a shell as the *postgres* user with *sudo* (you'll stay in this shell until the end of
this section):

```
$ sudo -u postgres -s
Password: ********
postgres$
```

Now you can start locking things down and set up a nonprivileged user:

1. Set a password for the PostgreSQL superuser:

   ```
   postgres$ psql -U postgres -c \
       "alter user postgres with password 'password' ;"
   ```

2. Under the default permissions, any local user can impersonate another
   user. So even though you've set a password, it's not doing any good! You
   should edit */usr/local/pgsql/data/pg_hba.conf* to require MD5 passwords,
   give the *postgres* user control over all databases, and change the configuration so users have total control over databases whose names match their
   usernames. To do this, change *pg_hba.conf* to read:

   ```
   # TYPE DATABASE USER      IP-ADDR   IP-MASK              METHOD
   local  all      postgres                                 md5
   local  sameuser all                                      md5
   ```

```
host   all       postgres 127.0.0.1 255.255.255.255                              md5
host   sameuser all         127.0.0.1 255.255.255.255                            md5
host   all       postgres ::1 ffff:ffff:ffff:ffff:ffff:ffff:ffff:ffff md5
host   sameuser all       ::1 ffff:ffff:ffff:ffff:ffff:ffff:ffff:ffff md5
```

3. Once you've made this change, reload the configuration with *pg_ctl* (from here on in, you'll be prompted for a password when you run *psql* as the *postgres* user):

```
postgres$ pg_ctl -D /usr/local/pgsql/data reload
```

4. Now you're ready to add a normal user. Use the *psql* command to create the user and a database. Because the username and database name are the same, that user will be granted access to the database:

```
postgres$ psql -U postgres -c "create database username ;"
Password for user postgres: ********
CREATE DATABASE
postgres$ psql -U postgres -c \
    "create user username with password 'password' ;"
Password for user postgres: ********
CREATE USER
```

To give more than one user access to a database, create a group with the same name as the database (*create group databasename*), and create users with the *create user* command. Then, add each user to the group with this command:

```
postgres$ psql -U postgres -c \
    "alter group databasename add user newuser ;"
```

Using PostgreSQL

After configuring PostgreSQL's security and setting up an unprivileged user, you can log in as that user and play around with the database:

```
$ psql
Password: ********
Welcome to psql 8.3.3, the PostgreSQL interactive terminal.

Type:  \copyright for distribution terms
       \h for help with SQL commands
       \? for help on internal slash commands
       \g or terminate with semicolon to execute query
       \q to quit

username=> CREATE TABLE foo (bar CHAR(10));
CREATE TABLE
username=> INSERT INTO foo VALUES('Hello');
INSERT 0 1
username=> INSERT INTO foo VALUES('World');
INSERT 0 1
username=> SELECT * FROM foo;
      bar
```

```
     -----------
     Hello
     World
     (2 rows)
     username-> \q
```

For more information on building and using PostgreSQL, see *Practical PostgreSQL* by John C. Worsley and Joshua D. Drake (O'Reilly). *Practical PostgreSQL* covers installing, using, administrating, and programming PostgreSQL.

Database Support in PHP and Perl

On Mac OS X, MySQL support is built into PHP. However, if you want PostgreSQL support, you must reinstall PHP from source.

You can install general database support in Perl by installing the *DBI* module with the *cpan* utility. After that, you can install the *DBD::mysql* module for MySQL-specific support and *DBD::Pg* for PostgreSQL-specific support. Because there are some steps to these installations that the *cpan* utility can't handle, you should download the latest builds of these modules from *http://www .cpan.org/modules/by-module/DBD/* and install them manually. Be sure to check the *README* files, since some aspects of the configuration may have changed.

The *DBD::mysql* module requires a database in which to perform its tests (you can use the database and username/password that you set up earlier in "Configuring MySQL"). To install *DBD::mysql*, you must first generate the *Make file*, compile the code, and test it, and then install the module if the test run is successful. For example:

```
$ perl Makefile.PL --testdb=dbname --testuser=username --testpassword=
password
$ make
$ make test
$ sudo make install
```

Like *DBD::mysql*, the *DBD::Pg* module needs a working directory in which to perform its tests. Again, you can use the database, username, and password that you set up earlier when configuring PostgreSQL.

To begin, generate the *Makefile*, compile the code, and set up environment variables that specify the database, username, and password. Then run the tests. If the tests run successfully, you can install *DBD::Pg*:

```
$ perl Makefile.PL
$ make
$ export DBI_DSN=dbi:Pg:dbname=username
$ export DBI_USER=username
```

```
$ export DBI_PASS=password
$ make test
$ sudo make install
```

The Outside World

If only other computers in your home network or your business's local area network are connecting to your Mac, your work is done. However, if you want your Mac to be accessible to users outside your local network, there's still a bit of work to do. Those outside users will need to know the IP address or DNS name associated with your Mac. And, assuming that your router/gateway is running a firewall, you will need to configure that firewall to allow only the appropriate kinds of connections, originating from only the appropriate places, and initiated by only the appropriate people.

If your intent is to use your Mac as a production server, you are probably either co-locating it at your hosting provider's facility or bringing a dedicated line into your home or office. In that case, your ISP or hosting provider should be taking care of all the details: setting up Domain Name System (DNS) records, providing an IP address, and possibly physically hosting your computer in a rack somewhere.

 Most hosting providers will take care of setting up DNS entries so that you're in the database. However, you will still be responsible for registering the name you want with a domain registrar.

If you're running a Mac on a non-business-grade network, you can approximate the same setup, but there are two configuration issues you need to consider:

DNS

If you're using a residential broadband service, or even the lower tiers of some business-class broadband services, your fully qualified domain name (FQDN) is probably something terrible like *host130.93.41.216.conver sent.net*. If you go to your ISP and ask to be set up with a real name, chances are you will either be greeted with a blank stare or steered toward some service that costs hundreds of dollars a month.

IP address

Residential broadband and low-tier business class broadband users are likely to be assigned dynamic IP addresses. If you have this kind of service, your IP address could change as often as every couple of hours (or possibly every few days, weeks, or months). In some cases, your IP address may be effectively permanent, but without the guarantee that it will remain static, you never know when you'll have to deal with the hassle. You could ask your ISP for a static IP address, but this may cost extra money, or you may have to move up to a higher tier of service.

 Some ISPs, such as Speakeasy, Inc. (*http://www.speak easy.net*), offer commercial-class services for well under $100 a month. If you're interested in running services out of your small office or home office (SOHO), check them out.

If you're running a Mac as a server for personal use (for example, remote access via SSH), you can probably get away with plugging into a residential broadband connection and opening a hole in your firewall. However, if you want others to be able to access services such as a web browser, you'll need to solve the DNS and IP address problems. A dynamic DNS service such as Dynamic Network Services (*http://www.dyndns.org*) can help with this.

Dynamic DNS

Dynamic Network Services, Inc. has been offering dynamic DNS services for many years and has long been a favorite of dial-up and SOHO broadband users who need permanent domain names even when their IP addresses are constantly changing. For this service to work, you must update the *dyndns.org* servers every time your IP address changes. The open source DNSUpdate utility (*http://www.dnsupdate.org*) can detect your public IP address and update the *dyndns.org* servers with that address, rather than your private address. You must select External as the interface type when you add a host to DNSUpdate in order for it to detect and register your public IP address, as shown in Figure 15-13.

That's only half the battle, though; if your Mac resides behind a firewall router (such as the Apple AirPort Base Station), you'll need to configure it to make your network services visible to the outside world. Otherwise, all incoming traffic will be stopped in its tracks at your firewall. In the next section, we discuss solutions to this problem.

Serving from Behind a Firewall

If you have a SOHO router (such as an Apple AirPort Base Station) between your Internet connection and your Mac, the router probably has a built-in firewall that protects your Mac from the outside world. Since most access points and routers have firewalls that block incoming network traffic, you'll

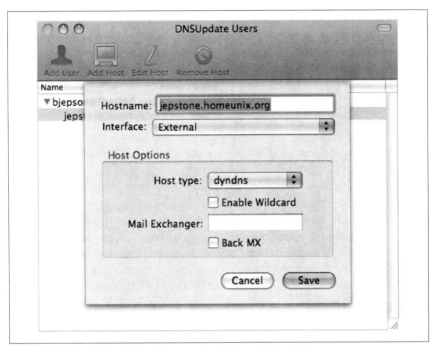

Figure 15-13. Configuring dynamic DNS with DNSUpdate

need to open a hole in the firewall for each service you want to use. The list that follows describes our recommendations for exposing a server to the outside world on a SOHO network:

Use a wired connection

If you have a wireless access point, such as an AirPort Base Station, that's doing double-duty as your wired Ethernet router, we suggest plugging your Mac server into one of the LAN ports on your access point (or one of the LAN ports on an Ethernet switch that's plugged into your access point's LAN port).

Although Wi-Fi speeds typically exceed broadband speeds by quite a lot, actual speeds are often half that of the quoted speed of Wi-Fi networks, and bandwidth is shared among all computers on a given network. So, an 802.11b Wi-Fi network with a raw speed of 11 Mbps is more likely to share 5 to 6 Mbps among its connected machines, and an 802.11g Wi-Fi (AirPort Extreme) network is more likely to have 20 to 25 Mbps available than the advertised 54 Mbps raw speed of the network. This is because Wi-Fi networks have a significant amount of overhead, are susceptible to interference from consumer electronics and microwave ovens, and can experience a sharp drop-off in speeds as the distance between the computer and the base station increases.

Be aware of your ISP's Terms of Service

If your ISP does not permit you to run servers on your network, consider asking them whether it offers another tier of service that does. As an added bonus, those tiers of service often include one or more static IP addresses. On the downside, they tend to cost quite a bit more than the consumer offerings. ISPs that have restrictive policies in place will often also block certain ports. For example, the Cox cable Internet service that we use does not permit inbound or outbound connections on port 25 (SMTP), or inbound connections on port 80 (HTTP). Since these restrictions were implemented when the Windows-based worms that used these ports were at their height, we believe the restrictions are there primarily to protect against such worms. Prior to that, the only reports we had of Cox actually enforcing its "no servers" rule was in cases where customers were using large amounts of bandwidth.

 Although we can't prove that Mac OS X is inherently more secure than Microsoft systems, there are fewer exploits that affect it. If you are diligent about applying security updates, understand the risks and consequences of opening a service (such as a web or IMAP server) to the outside world, and are comfortable monitoring your network for intrusions, you can sleep a little easier while your servers hum away in the night.

Consider nonstandard ports

If your ISP's Terms of Service do not explicitly prohibit running services, but your ISP is still blocking ports to protect against worms, you could choose to run the services on alternate ports that are not blocked. You can do this by either reconfiguring the server or using your router to handle the redirection.

Open your ports

One thing a firewall is really good at is keeping traffic out. However, if you want to run a server on your network, you need to selectively let traffic in. This is called *port mapping*, and it's described in the next section.

 Non-Apple wireless access points may have similar functionality to the AirPort Base Station. Look in your access point's documentation for information on port mapping (sometimes referred to as *forwarding*).

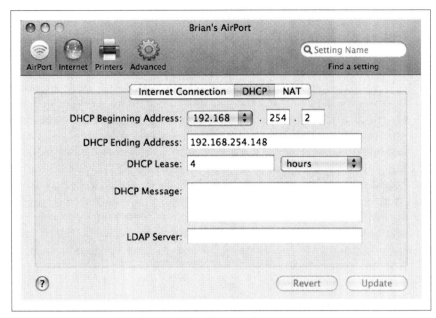

Figure 15-14. Setting the subnet and IP address pool size

Port mapping with an AirPort Base Station

To configure an AirPort Base Station to direct traffic to a Mac that's acting as a server, you should first make sure that the server has a static IP address on your local network. An AirPort Base Station will dynamically assign addresses in the range of 10.0.1.2 to 10.0.1.200 by default, but this range will be different if you've specified a different subnet and pool size. (In the AirPort Admin Utility, choose Internet→DHCP, and set the values as shown in Figure 15-14.)

You must choose your static IP address from outside your DHCP range (known as a *pool*), or you risk there being a conflicting computer with the same address. If you're using the default AirPort configuration, for instance, 10.0.1.201 would be an acceptable choice, as it falls after the ending address of the default range. If you're using the settings shown in Figure 16-2, anything over 192.168.254.148 but below 192.168.254.254 would be OK (we'll use 192.168.254.201 in the next example). Once you have chosen your static IP address, configure your Macintosh server to use this address in System Preferences→Network. This ensures that your server always has the same IP address, and you can then configure your base station to reliably forward traffic to it.

To configure port mapping, open the AirPort Admin Utility (*/Applications/ Utilities*), select your Base Station, and choose Advanced→Port Mapping. Figure 15-15 shows an AirPort Base Station configured to forward traffic coming

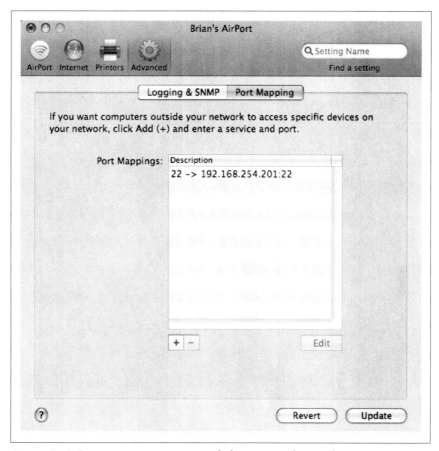

Figure 15-15. Setting up a port mapping with the AirPort Admin Utility

in from the outside world on port 22 (SSH) to a machine inside the network with the private address 192.168.254.201 on port 22.

This means that people can connect via SSH to *PUBLIC_IP_ADDRESS* and be directed to the machine at 192.168.254.201 inside the firewall. You can find the value for *PUBLIC_IP_ADDRESS* by selecting the Airport→Summary from within the AirPort Admin Utility and looking at the IP address.

## CHAPTER 16

System Management Tools

Mac OS X comes with many tools for tweaking and spying on various aspects of your system, including memory, kernel modules, and kernel state variables. Some of these tools come directly from BSD, while others are unique to Mac OS X. Most of the BSD-derived utilities have been filtered through Mach and NeXTSTEP on their way to Mac OS X.

For more details on any of these utilities, see their respective manpages.

Diagnostic Utilities

Mac OS X includes many diagnostic utilities, which you can use to monitor your system and investigate problems.

top

The *top* utility displays memory statistics and a list of running processes. It is divided into two regions: the top region contains memory statistics, and the bottom region contains details on each process.

You can specify the number of processes to show by supplying a numeric argument. By default, *top* refreshes its display every second and sorts the list of processes by process ID (PID) in descending order. You can set *top* to sort by CPU utilization with *-u*, and you can specify the refresh delay with the *-s* option. Figure 16-1 shows the output of *top -u 16* (if you wanted to refresh the output every three seconds, you could run *top -s3 -u 16*).

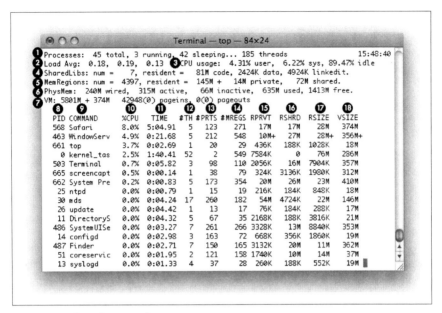

Figure 16-1. Sample output from top

Table 16-1 describes the values shown in the top region, and Table 16-2 describes the columns in the bottom region (process information).

Table 16-1. Memory information displayed by top

Item number	Item	Description
1	Processes	Number of processes and threads. A running process is currently using CPU time, whereas a sleeping process is not.
2	Load Avg.	Average system load (the number of jobs vying for the CPU's attention) over the last 1, 5, and 15 minutes.
3	CPU usage	Breakdown of CPU usage, listing time spent in user mode, kernel (sys) mode, and idle time.
4	SharedLibs	Number of shared libraries in use, along with their memory utilization.
5	MemRegions	Number of Mach virtual memory regions in use, along with memory utilization details.
6	PhysMem	Physical memory utilization. Memory that is wired cannot be swapped to disk. active memory is memory that's currently being used, inactive memory is memory that Mac OS X is keeping "on deck" for processes that need it, and free memory is memory that's not being used at all.
7	VM	Virtual memory statistics, including the total amount of virtual memory allocated (the sum of the VSIZE in the process list), as well as paging activity (data paged in and out of physical memory).

Table 16-2. Process information displayed by top

Item number	Item	Description
8	PID	Process ID
9	COMMAND	Program's name
10	%CPU	Percentage of the CPU that this process is using
11	TIME	Total amount of CPU time this process has used
12	#TH	Number of threads in this process
13	#PRTS	Number of Mach ports
14	#MREGS	Number of memory registers
15	RPRVT	Resident private memory
16	RSHRD	Resident shared memory
17	RSIZE	Resident memory
18	VSIZE	Process's total address space, including shared memory

The GUI-based Activity Monitor application, shown in Figure 16-2, provides much of the same functionality as *top*, plus additional capabilities (for example, it allows you to kill processes from within the application). The Activity Monitor is located in */Utilities*.

fs_usage

The *fs_usage* utility shows a continuous display of filesystem-related system calls and page faults. You can use it to monitor filesystem activity at the system-call level, which can help you identify unusual or unexpected filesystem access. You must run *fs_usage* as *root*. By default, it ignores anything originating from *fs_usage*, *Terminal*, *telnetd*, *sshd*, *rlogind*, *tcsh*, *csh*, or *sh*.

Figure 16-3 shows the output of *fs_usage* monitoring the startup of a new *bash* shell and displaying the following columns:

- Timestamp
- System call
- Filename
- Elapsed time
- Name of process

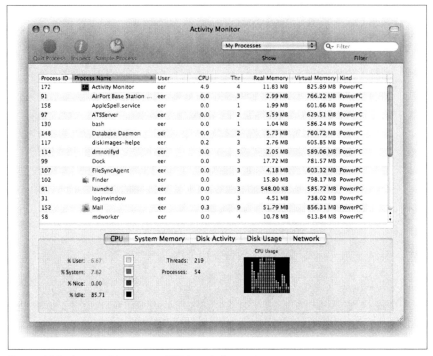

Figure 16-2. Activity Monitor, a GUI-based alternative to top

lsof

The *lsof* utility shows information about open files, including regular files, directories, block special files, character special files, executing text references, libraries, streams, and network files. You can use the *-F* option with *lsof* to produce output that can be used by other programs or utilities such as Perl, Awk, and C programs. If you enter the *lsof* command without options, it will list all open files associated with all active processes, as shown in Figure 16-4. See the manpage for more details.

latency

latency measures the number of context switches and interrupts and reports on the resulting delays, updating the display once per second. Since this tool monitors the behavior of the kernel, it is likely that you will need it only to investigate suspected bugs in the kernel or kernel drivers. This utility must be run as *root*. Example 16-1 shows a portion of its output.

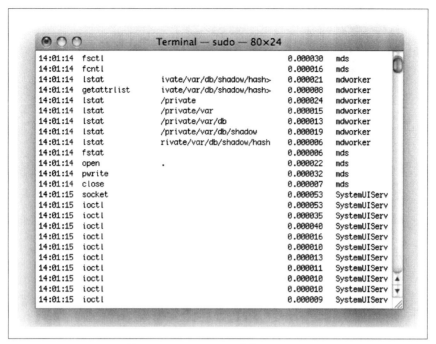

```
    ● ○ ○                    Terminal — sudo — 80×24
    14:01:14  fsctl                                          0.000030  mds
    14:01:14  fcntl                                          0.000016  mds
    14:01:14  lstat        ivate/var/db/shadow/hash>         0.000021  mdworker
    14:01:14  getattrlist  ivate/var/db/shadow/hash>         0.000008  mdworker
    14:01:14  lstat        /private                          0.000024  mdworker
    14:01:14  lstat        /private/var                      0.000015  mdworker
    14:01:14  lstat        /private/var/db                   0.000013  mdworker
    14:01:14  lstat        /private/var/db/shadow            0.000019  mdworker
    14:01:14  lstat        rivate/var/db/shadow/hash         0.000006  mdworker
    14:01:14  fstat                                          0.000006  mds
    14:01:14  open           .                               0.000022  mds
    14:01:14  pwrite                                         0.000032  mds
    14:01:14  close                                          0.000007  mds
    14:01:15  socket                                         0.000053  SystemUIServ
    14:01:15  ioctl                                          0.000053  SystemUIServ
    14:01:15  ioctl                                          0.000035  SystemUIServ
    14:01:15  ioctl                                          0.000040  SystemUIServ
    14:01:15  ioctl                                          0.000016  SystemUIServ
    14:01:15  ioctl                                          0.000010  SystemUIServ
    14:01:15  ioctl                                          0.000013  SystemUIServ
    14:01:15  ioctl                                          0.000011  SystemUIServ
    14:01:15  ioctl                                          0.000010  SystemUIServ
    14:01:15  ioctl                                          0.000010  SystemUIServ
    14:01:15  ioctl                                          0.000009  SystemUIServ
```

Figure 16-3. Monitoring filesystem operations with fs_usage

Example 16-1. Partial output from latency

```
Thu May 29 16:40:25                        0:04:28
                        SCHEDULER    INTERRUPTS
        ----------------------------------------------
        total_samples       241470        303806

        delays <  10 usecs       3        209332
        delays <  20 usecs    2722         10049
        delays <  30 usecs    7184         11609
        delays <  40 usecs    8516          7597
        delays <  50 usecs   12959          6283
        delays <  60 usecs   10902          2972
        delays <  70 usecs    7031          1123
        delays <  80 usecs    5632           716
        delays <  90 usecs    2770         16163
        delays < 100 usecs    1735         22647
        total   < 100 usecs   59454        288491
```

The SCHEDULER column lists the number of context switches, and the INTERRUPTS column lists the number of interrupts.

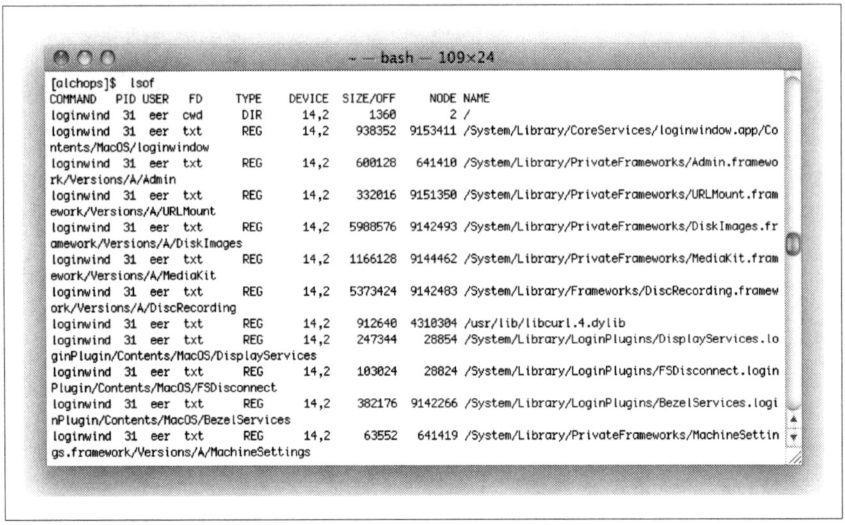

Figure 16-4. Partial output from lsof

sc_usage

The *sc_usage* utility samples system calls and page faults and displays them onscreen, updating the display once per second. You can use it to take a close look at the behavior of an application. You must run *sc_usage* as *root* or a user with superuser privileges. Specify a PID, a program name, or a program to execute (with the *-E* switch). For example, to monitor the Finder, use *sudo sc_usage Finder*. Figure 16-5 shows the output of running *sc_usage* on the Finder. Table 16-3 explains *sc_usage*'s output.

Table 16-3. Information displayed by sc_usage

Item number	Row	Description
1	TYPE	System call type
2	NUMBER	System call count
3	CPU_TIME	Processor time used by the system call
4	WAIT_TIME	Absolute time that the process spent waiting
5	CURRENT_TYPE	Current system call type
6	LAST_PATHNAME_WAITED_FOR	Last file or directory that resulted in a blocked I/O operation during a system call
7	CUR_WAIT_TIME	Cumulative time spent blocked
8	THRD#	Thread ID
9	PRI	Scheduling priority

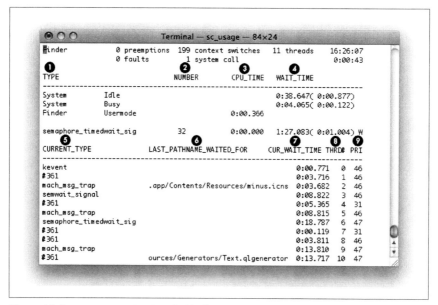

Figure 16-5. sc_usage monitoring the Finder

vm_stat

The *vm_stat* utility displays virtual memory statistics. Unlike implementations on other Unix systems, on Mac OS X *vm_stat* does not default to continuous display; instead, it displays accumulated statistics.

To obtain a continuous display, specify an interval argument (in seconds), as in *vm_stat 1*. Figure 16-6 shows the output of *vm_stat* with no arguments.

Figure 16-7 shows the output of *vm_stat 1*. Table 16-4 describes the information that *vm_stat* displays (the item numbers correspond to the callouts in both figures).

Table 16-4. Information displayed by vm_stat

Item number	Accumulated mode	Continuous mode	Description
1	Pages free	free	Total free pages
2	Pages active	active	Total pages in use that can be paged out
3	Pages inactive	inac	Total inactive pages
4	Pages wired down	wire	Total pages wired into memory (cannot be paged out)
5	Translation faults	faults	Number of times *vm_fault* has been called

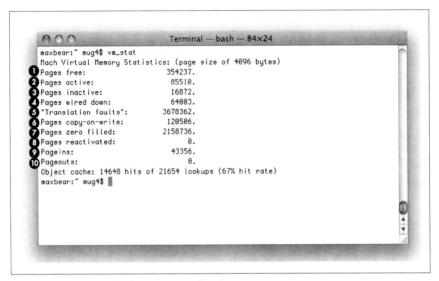

Figure 16-6. vm_stat displaying accumulated statistics

Item number	Accumulated mode	Continuous mode	Description
6	Pages copy-on-write	copy	Number of faults that resulted in a page being copied
7	Pages zero filled	zerofill	Number of pages that have been zero-filled
8	Pages reactivated	reactive	Number of pages reclassified from inactive to active
9	Pageins	pageins	Number of pages moved into physical memory
10	Pageouts	pageout	Number of pages moved out of physical memory

Kernel Utilities

Mac OS X includes various utilities that interact with the kernel. With these utilities, you can debug a running kernel, load and unload kernel modules or extensions, or set kernel variables.

ddb

The *ddb* utility can debug a running kernel. It is not included with the current version of Mac OS X, but if you want to use *ddb*, you can find its source code

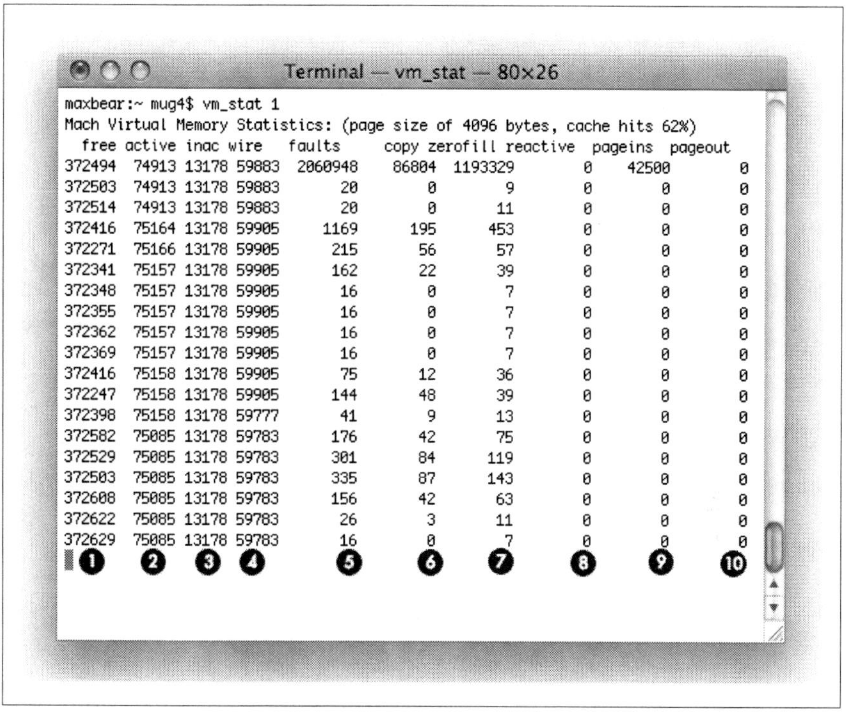

```
● ○ ○              Terminal — vm_stat — 80×26
maxbear:~ mug4$ vm_stat 1
Mach Virtual Memory Statistics: (page size of 4096 bytes, cache hits 62%)
  free active inac wire    faults    copy zerofill reactive  pageins  pageout
372494 74913 13178 59883  2060948   86804 1193329        0    42500        0
372503 74913 13178 59883       20       0       9        0        0        0
372514 74913 13178 59883       20       0      11        0        0        0
372416 75164 13178 59905     1169     195     453        0        0        0
372271 75166 13178 59905      215      56      57        0        0        0
372341 75157 13178 59905      162      22      39        0        0        0
372348 75157 13178 59905       16       0       7        0        0        0
372355 75157 13178 59905       16       0       7        0        0        0
372362 75157 13178 59905       16       0       7        0        0        0
372369 75157 13178 59905       16       0       7        0        0        0
372416 75158 13178 59905       75      12      36        0        0        0
372247 75158 13178 59905      144      48      39        0        0        0
372398 75158 13178 59777       41       9      13        0        0        0
372582 75085 13178 59783      176      42      75        0        0        0
372529 75085 13178 59783      301      84     119        0        0        0
372503 75085 13178 59783      335      87     143        0        0        0
372608 75085 13178 59783      156      42      63        0        0        0
372622 75085 13178 59783       26       3      11        0        0        0
372629 75085 13178 59783       16       0       7        0        0        0
   ❶      ❷    ❸    ❹        ❺       ❻       ❼        ❽        ❾        ❿
```

Figure 16-7. vm_stat's continuous output

in the *xnu* (Darwin kernel) source code (*http://www.opensource.apple.com/dar winsource/*).

DTrace

Beginning with Leopard, *ktrace* is no longer available; it has been replaced by the more powerful utility, *DTrace*. Developed by Sun Microsystems, *DTrace* is a powerful open source utility that can be used to monitor running programs, including the kernel. *DTrace* is used to instrument programs dynamically, enabling runtime inspection of user-owned processes as well as the kernel; has zero overhead when not in use; and is scriptable using its own D programming language. You can interact with *DTrace* either via the command-line *dtrace* generic frontend to *DTrace* or via the GUI *Instruments* (*/Developer/Applica tions/Instruments*), a sophisticated graphical tool for gathering and analyzing *DTrace* data that is included with Xcode. You can see a list of *DTrace*-based utilities that ship with Leopard via the *apropos dtrace* command.

In Tiger and earlier releases of Mac OS X, you can use *ktrace* to perform kernel tracing (tracing system calls and other operations) on a process. To launch a program and generate a kernel trace (*ktrace.out*, which is not human-readable), use *ktrace* `command`, as in *ktrace emacs*. Kernel tracing ends when you exit the process or disable tracing with *ktrace -cp pid*. You can get human-readable output from a *ktrace* file with *kdump -f ktrace.out*.

For more information on *DTrace* see *http://www.sun.com/bigadmin/content/dtrace/*, *http://www.opensource.apple.com/darwinsource/10.5/dtrace-48/*, and */usr/share/examples/DTTk*.

Kernel Module Utilities

The following list describes utilities for manipulating kernel modules (for more information, see the kernel-related tutorials available at *http://developer.apple.com/documentation/Darwin/Kernel-date.html*):

kextload
    Loads an extension bundle. Requires superuser privileges.

kextunload
    Unloads an extension bundle. Requires superuser privileges.

kextstat
    Displays the status of currently loaded kernel extensions.

Figure 16-8 shows some sample *kextstat* output, and Table 16-5 describes the output.

Table 16-5. Information displayed by kextstat

Item number	Column	Description
1	Index	Index number of the loaded extension. Extensions are loaded in sequence; gaps in this sequence signify extensions that have been unloaded.
2	Refs	Number of references to this extension from other extensions.
3	Address	Kernel space address of the extension.
4	Size	Amount of kernel memory (in bytes) used by the extension.
5	Wired	Amount of *wired* kernel memory (in bytes) used by the extension.
6	Name (Version)	Name and version of the extension.
7	<Linked Against>	Index of kernel extensions to which this extension refers.

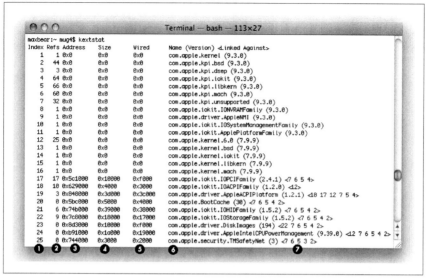

Figure 16-8. Partial output of kextstat

sysctl

sysctl is a standard BSD facility for configuring kernel state variables. Use *sysctlname* to display a variable name, as in *sysctl kern.ostype*. Use *sysctl -a* to display all variables. If you have superuser privileges, you can set a variable with *sysctl -wname=value*.

Table 16-6 lists many of the *sysctl* variables on Mac OS X. See the *sysctl(3)* manpage for a description of the *sysctl* system call and more detailed information on the kernel state variables.

Table 16-6. sysctl's kernel state variables

Name	Type	Writable	Description
debug.*	Various	Yes	Flags used to enable various debugging options.
hw.activecpu	Int	No	Number of CPUs currently active (may be affected by power management settings).
hw.availcpu	Int	No	Number of available CPUs.
hw.busfrequency	Int	No	Bus frequency in hertz. Divide by one million for a megahertz figure.
hw.busfrequency_max	Int	No	Maximum bus frequency in hertz.
hw.busfrequency_min	Int	No	Minimum bus frequency in hertz.

Name	Type	Writable	Description
hw.byteorder	Int	No	Variable that returns 4321 on the PowerPC platform and 1234 on the Intel platform, in each case showing the ordering of four bytes on the given platform.
hw.cacheconfig	Array	No	Reports how the logical processors share caches in the system. The first item reports the number of logical processors sharing RAM, the second reports the number of logical processors sharing a level-1 cache, and the third reports the number of processors sharing a level-2 cache.
hw.cachelinesize	Int	No	Cache line size in bytes.
hw.cachesize	Array	No	Reports the size of various caches. The first item reports the size of RAM, the second reports the size of the level-1 cache, and the third reports the size of the level-2 cache.
hw.cpu64bit_capable	Int	No	Indicates whether the CPU is 64-bit-capable.
hw.cpufamily	Int	No	Integer corresponding to the CPU family: PowerPC G4=2009171118, PowerPC G5=3983988906, Intel Core Solo/Duo=1943433984, Intel Core 2 Duo=1114597871.
hw.cpufrequency	Int	No	CPU frequency in hertz. Divide by one million for a megahertz figure.
hw.cpufrequency_max	Int	No	Maximum CPU frequency in hertz.
hw.cpufrequency_min	Int	No	Minimum CPU frequency in hertz.
hw.cpusubtype	Int	No	Mach-O subtype of the CPU (see /System/Library/Frameworks/Kernel.framework/Versions/A/Headers/mach/machine.h).
hw.cputype	Int	No	Mach-O type of the CPU.
hw.epoch	Int	No	Variable that indicates whether your hardware is "New World" or "Old World." Old World Macintoshes (pre-G3) have a value of 0.

Name	Type	Writable	Description
hw.l1dcachesize	Int	No	Level-1 data cache size in bytes.
hw.l1icachesize	Int	No	Level-1 instruction cache size in bytes.
hw.l2cachesize	Int	No	Level-2 cache size in bytes.
hw.l2settings	Int	No	Level-2 cache settings.
hw.l3cachesize	Int	No	Level-3 cache size in bytes.
hw.l3settings	Int	No	Level-3 cache settings.
hw.logicalcpu	Int	No	Number of logical CPUs.
hw.logicalcpu_max	Int	No	Maximum number of available logical CPUs.
hw.machine	String	No	Machine class (*PowerMacintosh* or *i386*).
hw.memsize	Int	No	Memory size.
hw.model	String	No	Machine model.
hw.ncpu	Int	No	Number of CPUs.
hw.optional.altivec	Int	No	Indicates whether AltiVec is enabled.
hw.optional.datastreams	Int	No	Indicates whether the CPU supports PowerPC data stream instructions.
hw.optional.dcba	Int	No	Indicates whether the CPU supports the PowerPC DCBA instruction.
hw.optional.floatingpoint	Int	No	Indicates whether the CPU supports floating-point operations.
hw.optional.graphicsops	Int	No	Indicates whether the CPU supports graphics operations.
hw.optional.mmx	Int	No	Indicates whether the CPU supports the Intel MMX instruction set.
hw.optional.sse	Int	No	Indicates whether the CPU supports the Intel SSE instruction set.
hw.optional.sse2	Int	No	Indicates whether the CPU supports the Intel SSE2 instruction set.
hw.optional.sse3	Int	No	Indicates whether the CPU supports the Intel SSE3 instruction set.

Name	Type	Writable	Description
hw.optional.sse4_1	Int	No	Indicates whether the CPU supports the Intel SSE4_1 instruction set.
hw.optional.sse4_2	Int	No	Indicates whether the CPU supports the Intel SSE4_2 instruction set.
hw.optional.stfiwx	Int	No	Indicates whether the CPU supports the PowerPC STFIWX instruction set.
hw.optional.supplementalsse3	Int	No	Indicates whether the CPU supports the Intel Supplemental SSE3 instruction set.
hw.optional.x86_64	Int	No	Indicates whether the CPU supports the Intel 64-bit instruction set.
hw.packages	Int	No	Number of processor packages on the system (for example, a single dual-core CPU will report 1).
hw.pagesize	Int	No	Software page size in bytes.
hw.physicalcpu	Int	No	Number of physical CPUs.
hw.physicalcpu_max	Int	No	Maximum available physical CPUs.
hw.physmem	Int	No	Physical memory in bytes.
hw.tbfrequency	Int	No	Base frequency used by Mac OS X for its timing services.
hw.usermem	Int	No	Nonkernel memory.
hw.vectorunit	Int	No	Variable that indicates whether you are running on an AltiVec-enabled CPU.
kern.affinity_sets_enabled	Int	Yes	If set to zero, disables thread affinity hinting.
kern.affinity_sets_mapping	Int	Yes	Configures the cache distribution policy.
kern.aiomax	Int	No	Maximum AIO requests.
kern.aioprocmax	Int	No	Maximum AIO requests per process.
kern.aiothreads	Int	No	Maximum number of AIO worker threads.

Name	Type	Writable	Description
kern.always_do_fullfsync	Int	Yes	Indicates whether *fsync(2)*s should be full *fsyncs*.
kern.argmax	Int	No	Maximum number of arguments supported by exec ( ).
kern.bootargs	String	Yes	Kernel boot arguments.
kern.bootsignature	String	N/A	Unknown or undocumented.
kern.boottime	struct timeval	No	Time when the system was booted.
kern.clockrate	struct clockinfo	No	System clock timings.
kern.copyregionmax	Int	N/A	Unknown or undocumented.
kern.coredump	Int	Yes	Determines whether core dumps are enabled.
kern.corefile	String	Yes	Location of core dump files (%P is replaced with the process ID).
kern.delayterm	Int	Unknown	Unknown or undocumented.
kern.dummy	N/A	N/A	Unused.
kern.exec.archhandler.powerpc	String	Yes	Used on Intel Macs to determine which program to use for running Power PC applications.
kern.flush_cache_on_write	Int	Yes	Determines whether to always flush the drive cache on writes to uncached files.
kern.hibernatefile	String	Yes	Unknown or undocumented.
kern.hibernatemode	Int	Yes	Unknown or undocumented.
kern.himemorymode	Int	No	Unknown or undocumented
kern.hostid	Int	Yes	Host identifier.
kern.hostname	String	Yes	Hostname.
kern.ipc.*	Various	N/A	Various IPC settings.
kern.job_control	Int	No	Variable that indicates whether job control is available.
kern.lctx.*	Various	Unknown	Variables related to login contexts.
kern.low_pri_delay	Int	Yes	Set/reset throttle delay in milliseconds.
kern.low_pri_window	Int	Yes	Set/reset throttle window in milliseconds.
kern.lowpagemax	Int	No	Unknown or undocumented.

Name	Type	Writable	Description
kern.maxfiles	Int	Yes	Maximum number of open files.
kern.maxfilesperproc	Int	Yes	Maximum number of open files per process.
kern.maxnbuf	Int	Yes	Maximum size of the filesystem buffer.
kern.maxproc	Int	Yes	Maximum number of simultaneous processes.
kern.maxprocperuid	Int	Yes	Maximum number of simultaneous processes per user.
kern.maxvnodes	Int	Yes	Maximum number of *vnodes*.
kern.msgbuf	Int	No	Size of the *dmesg* message buffer.
kern.nbuf	Int	No	Size of the filesystem buffer.
kern.netboot	Int	No	Variable that indicates whether the system booted via NetBoot.
kern.ngroups	Int	No	Maximum number of supplemental groups.
kern.nisdomainname	String	Yes	NIS domain name.
kern.nx	Int	Yes	Indicates whether no-execution protection is enabled.
kern.osrelease	String	No	Operating system release version.
kern.osrevision	Int	No	Operating system revision number.
kern.ostype	String	No	Operating system name.
kern.osversion	String	No	Operating system build number.
kern.posix.sem.max	Int	Yes	Maximum number of POSIX semaphores.
kern.posix1version	Int	No	Version of POSIX 1003.1 with which the system attempts to comply.
kern.proc_low_pri_io	Int	Yes	Unknown or undocumented.
kern.procname	String	Unknown	Setup process program name.
kern.rage_vnode	Int	Yes	Unknown or undocumented.
kern.safeboot	Int	No	Indicates whether the system was booted in safe mode.
kern.saved_ids	Int	No	Set to 1 if saved set-group and set-user IDs are available.
kern.secure_kernel	Int	No	Unknown or undocumented.

Name	Type	Writable	Description
kern.securelevel	Int	Increment only	System security level.
kern.shreg_private	Int	No	Indicates whether shared memory regions can be privatized.
kern.singleuser	Int	No	Indicates whether the system was booted in single-user mode.
kern.sleeptime	String	No	Amount of time for which the system slept last.
kern.speculative_reads_disabled	Int	Yes	Indicates whether speculative reads are disabled.
kern.sugid_coredump	Int	Yes	Determines whether SUID and SGID files are allowed to dump core.
kern.sugid_scripts	Int	Yes	Determines whether to permit SUID and SGID scripts.
kern.sysv.*	Various	N/A	System V semaphore settings.
kern.tfp.policy	Int	Yes	Policy for Mach's Task for PID function.
kern.tty.ptmx_max	Int	Yes	Limits on cloned *ptys* (pseudoterminals).
kern.usrstack	Int	No	Address of USRSTACK.
kern.usrstack64	Int	No	Address of 64-bit USRSTACK.
kern.version	String	No	Kernel version string.
kern.waketime	String	No	Time at which the system last woke from sleep.
kern.wq_*	Various	N/A	Settings used by *pthread(3)*.
machdep.cpu.*	Various	N/A	Assorted information about the CPU.
machdep.pmap.*	Various	N/A	Physical address map management settings.
net.appletalk.routermix	Int	Yes	Unknown or undocumented.
net.ath*	Various	N/A	Settings for Atheros-based AirPort adapters.
net.inet.*	Various	N/A	IPv4 settings.
net.inet6.*	Various	N/A	IPv6 settings.
net.key.*	Various	N/A	IPSec key management settings.
net.link.ether.inet.*	Various	N/A	Ethernet settings.
net.link.generic.*	Various	N/A	Generic interface settings.

Name	Type	Writable	Description
net.local.*	Various	N/A	Various network settings.
net.pstimeout	String	No	Unknown or undocumented.
security.mac.*	Various	N/A	Unknown or undocumented.
user.bc_base_max	Int	No	Maximum ibase/obase available in the *bc* calculator.
user.bc_dim_max	Int	No	Maximum array size available in the *bc* calculator.
user.bc_scale_max	Int	No	Maximum scale value available in the *bc* calculator.
user.bc_string_max	Int	No	Maximum string length available in the *bc* calculator.
user.coll_weights_max	Int	No	Maximum number of weights that can be used with LC_COLLATE in the locale definition file.
user.cs_path	String	No	Value for PATH that can find all the standard utilities.
user.expr_nest_max	Int	No	Maximum number of expressions you can nest within parentheses using *expr*.
user.line_max	Int	No	Maximum length in bytes of an input line used with a text-processing utility.
user.posix2_c_bind	Int	No	Variable that returns 1 if the C development environment supports the POSIX C Language Bindings Option; otherwise, the result will be 0.
user.posix2_c_dev	Int	No	Variable that returns 1 if the C development environment supports the POSIX C Language Development Utilities Option; otherwise, the result will be 0.
user.posix2_char_term	Int	No	Variable that returns 1 if the system supports at least one terminal type specified in POSIX 1003.2; otherwise, the result will be 0.
user.posix2_fort_dev	Int	No	Variable that returns 1 if the system supports the POSIX FORTRAN Development Utilities Option; otherwise, the result will be 0.

Name	Type	Writable	Description
user.posix2_fort_run	Int	No	Variable that returns 1 if the system supports the POSIX FORTRAN Runtime Utilities Option; otherwise, the result will be 0.
user.posix2_localedef	Int	No	Variable that returns 1 if the system allows you to create locale; otherwise, the result will be 0.
user.posix2_sw_dev	Int	No	Variable that returns 1 if the system supports the POSIX Software Development Utilities Option; otherwise, the result will be 0.
user.posix2_upe	Int	No	Variable that returns 1 if the system supports the POSIX User Portable Utilities Option; otherwise, the result will be 0.
user.posix2_version	Int	No	Variable that returns the POSIX 1003.2 version with which the system attempts to comply.
user.re_dup_max	Int	No	Maximum repeated occurrences of a regular expression when using interval notation.
user.stream_max	Int	No	Maximum number of streams a process may have open.
user.tzname_max	Int	No	Maximum number of types supported for a time zone name.
vfs.*	Various	N/A	Various VFS settings.
vm.*	Various	N/A	Settings related to virtual memory.
vm.loadavg	String	No	Current load average.
vm.swapusage	String	No	Current swap file usage.

System Configuration Utilities

Although you can perform most system configuration tasks through the System Preferences program, the *scutil* and *defaults* commands let you poke around under the hood. You can get even further under the hood (perhaps further than most people will need or want to get) with the *nvram* command. These commands are described in the sections that follow.

scutil

Mac OS X stores network configuration data in a database called the *dynamic store*. You can get at this database using *scutil*, the system configuration utility. Before you can do anything else, you must connect to the configuration daemon (*configd*) with the *open* command:

```
Chez-Jepstone:~ bjepson$ sudo scutil
Password: ********
> open
```

To list the contents of the configuration database (a collection of keys), use the *list* command. The following shows abbreviated output from this command:

```
> list
  subKey [0] = Plugin:IPConfiguration
  subKey [1] = Plugin:InterfaceNamer
  subKey [2] = Setup:
  subKey [3] = Setup:/
  subKey [4] = Setup:/Network/BackToMyMac
  subKey [5] = Setup:/Network/Global/IPv4
  subKey [6] = Setup:/Network/HostNames
  subKey [7] = Setup:/Network/Interface/en1/AirPort
```

You can show the contents of a key with the *show* command. The contents of a key are stored as a dictionary (key/value pairs). For example, here are the default proxy settings for built-in Ethernet on Mac OS X (to verify that service shows a *UserDefinedName* of *Ethernet*, you should use *show Setup:/Network/Service/130C954F-6B67-429B-94C7-29AE2A562D2C/Interface*; you will probably need to replace *130C954F-6B67-429B-94C7-29AE2A562D2C* with a value obtained from the *list* command shown earlier):

```
> show Setup:/Network/Service/130C954F-6B67-429B-94C7-29AE2A562D2C/Interface
<dictionary> {
  UserDefinedName : Ethernet
  Type : Ethernet
  Hardware : Ethernet
  DeviceName : en0
}
```

Here are the proxy settings for an adapter that's been configured to use an HTTP proxy server:

```
> show Setup:/Network/Service/130C954F-6B67-429B-94C7-29AE2A562D2C/Proxies
<dictionary> {
  HTTPPort : 8080
  FTPPassive : 1
  HTTPEnable : 1
  HTTPProxy : 192.168.254.201
}
```

When you're done, close the session with the *close* command, and exit *scutil* with *quit*.

defaults

When you customize your Mac using System Preferences, most of your changes and settings are stored in what's known as the *defaults* system. Nearly everything that you do to make your Mac your own is stored as a property list (or *plist*). The property lists are, in turn, stored in *~/Library/Preferences*.

Every time you change a setting, the associated property list value is updated. You can also alter the property lists by using either the Property List Editor application (*/Developer/Applications/Utilities*) or the *defaults* command in the Terminal. Regardless of which method you use, any changes you make to the property lists affect the current user.

 Using the *defaults* command is not for the foolhardy. If you manage to mangle your settings, the easiest way to correct the problem is to go back to the Preferences pane for the application in question and reset your preferences. In some cases you can use *defaults delete*, which will cause your defaults to be reset when you next log in. Since the *defaults* command affects only the current user, another option is to create a user just for testing random *defaults* tips you pick up on the Internet.

Here are some examples of what you can do with the *defaults* command (for more information, see the manpage):

View all of the user defaults on your system

```
$ defaults domains
```

This command prints a listing of all the domains in the user's defaults system. The list you'll see is run together with spaces in between—not quite the prettiest way to view the information.

View the settings for the Dock

```
$ defaults read com.apple.dock
```

This command reads the settings from the *com.apple.dock.plist* file, found in *~/Library/Preferences*.

Change your Dock's default location to the left side of the screen

```
$ defaults write com.apple.dock orientation left
```

This command moves the Dock from the bottom to the left side of the screen. After changing this setting, you'll need to log out from the system and then log back in to see the Dock in its new position.

nvram

The *nvram* utility modifies firmware variables, which control the boot-time behavior of your Macintosh. How you interact with *nvram* depends on whether you're using a PowerPC-based Mac or an Intel-based Mac. PowerPC-based Macs use Open Firmware, developed by Sun Microsystems, as the interface with the computer's firmware. Intel-based Macs, on the other hand, use the Extensible Firmware Interface (EFI), developed by Intel, as the interface to the computer's firmware.

You can use *nvram* to modify Open Firmware variables on PowerPC-based Macs and to work with a small set of EFI settings on Intel-based Macs. To list all variables, use the *nvram -p* command.

To change a variable, you must run *nvram* as *root* or as a user with superuser privileges. To set a variable, use *variable=value*. For example, to configure Mac OS X to boot verbosely, use *nvram boot-args=-v*. (Booting into Mac OS 9 or earlier will reset this variable.) Table 16-7 lists *nvram* variables. Some variables use the Open Firmware Device Tree notation (see the Technotes available at *http://developer.apple.com/technotes/tn/tn1061.html*).

Be careful when using the *nvram* utility, since incorrect settings can turn a Mac into an expensive doorstop. If you render your computer unbootable, you can reset the firmware by zapping the PRAM. To do this, hold down Option-⌘-P-R as you start the computer, and then release the keys when you hear a second startup chime. (If your two hands are busy holding down the other buttons and you have trouble reaching the power button, remember that you can press it with your nose.) On PowerPC-based Macs, you can boot into an Open Firmware shell by holding down Option-⌘-O-F as you start the computer. If you need to reset *nvram*, you can boot into the Open Firmware shell and enter *reset-nvram* and then *reset-all* at the prompt.

Table 16-7. nvram variables

Variable	Platform	Description
aht-results	Intel	The results of the last Apple Hardware Test run.
auto-boot?	PowerPC	The automatic boot settings. If true (the default), Open Firmware will automatically boot an operating system. If

Variable	Platform	Description
		`false`, the process will stop at the Open Firmware prompt. Be careful using this with Old World (unsupported) machines and third-party graphics adapters, since the display and keyboard may not be initialized until the operating system starts (in which case, you will not have access to Open Firmware).
`boot-args`	PowerPC, Intel	The arguments that are passed to the boot loader.
`boot-command`	PowerPC	The command that starts the boot process. The default is *mac-boot*, an Open Firmware command that examines the `boot-device` for a Mac OS startup.
`boot-device`	PowerPC	The device to boot from. The syntax is *device*: [*partition*],*path*:*filename*, and a common default is hd:,\\:tbxi. In that path, \\ is an abbreviation for /*System/Library/CoreServices* and tbxi is the file type of the *BootX* boot loader. (Run /*Developer/Tools/GetFileInfo* on *BootX* to see its type.)
`boot-file`	PowerPC	The name of the boot loader. (This is often blank, since `boot-command` and `boot-device` are usually all that are needed.)
`boot-image`	PowerPC, Intel	Contains information about where hibernation data is stored.
`boot-screen`	PowerPC	The image to display on the boot screen.
`boot-script`	PowerPC	Can contain an Open Firmware boot script.
`boot-volume`	PowerPC	Unknown or undocumented.
`console-screen`	PowerPC	Specifies the console output device, using an Open Firmware Device Tree name.
`default-client- ip`	PowerPC	An IP address for diskless booting.
`default-gateway- ip`	PowerPC	A gateway address for diskless booting.
`default-mac- address?`	PowerPC	Unknown or undocumented.
`default-router- ip`	PowerPC	A router address for diskless booting.
`default-server- ip`	PowerPC	An IP address for diskless booting.
`default-subnet- mask`	PowerPC	A default subnet mask for diskless booting.
`diag-device`	PowerPC	A private variable; not usable for security reasons.
`diag-file`	PowerPC	A private variable; not usable for security reasons.
`diag-switch?`	PowerPC	A private variable; not usable for security reasons.
`efi-apple-payload0`	Intel	Undocumented.
`efi-apple-payload0-data`	Intel	Undocumented.
`efi-boot-device`	Intel	The device used to boot the system.

Variable	Platform	Description
efi-boot-device-data	Intel	Information about the device used to boot the system.
fcode-debug?	PowerPC	A variable that determines whether the Open Firmware Forth interpreter will display extra debugging information.
input-device	PowerPC	The input device to use for the Open Firmware console.
input-device-1	PowerPC	A secondary input device (so you can have a screen and a serial console at the same time). Use scca for the first serial port.
little-endian?	PowerPC	The CPU endianness. If true, initializes the PowerPC chip as little-endian. The default is false.
load-base	PowerPC	A private variable; not usable for security reasons.
mouse-device	PowerPC	The mouse device using an Open Firmware Device Tree name.
nvramrc	PowerPC	A sequence of commands to execute at boot time (if use-nvramc? is set to true).
oem-banner	PowerPC	A custom banner to display at boot time.
oem-banner?	PowerPC	The oem banner settings. Set to true to enable the oem banner. The default is false.
oem-logo	PowerPC	A 64-by-64-bit array containing a custom black-and-white logo to display at boot time. This should be specified in hex.
oem-logo?	PowerPC	The oem logo settings. Set to true to enable the oem logo. The default is false.
output-device	PowerPC	The device to use as the system console. The default is screen.
output-device-1	PowerPC	A secondary output device (so you can have everything go to both the screen and a serial console). Use scca for the first serial port.
pci-probe-mask	PowerPC	A private variable; not usable for security reasons.
platform-uuid	Intel, PowerPC	The machine's UUID.
prev-lang:kbd	Intel, PowerPC	The keyboard type.
ram-size	PowerPC	The amount of RAM currently installed. For example, 256 MB is shown as 0x10000000.
real-base	PowerPC	The starting physical address that is available to Open Firmware.
real-mode?	PowerPC	The address translation settings. If true, Open Firmware will use real-mode address translation. Otherwise, it uses virtual-mode address translation.
real-size	PowerPC	The size of the physical address space available to Open Firmware.

Variable	Platform	Description
screen-#columns	PowerPC	The number of columns for the system console.
screen-#rows	PowerPC	The number of rows for the system console.
scroll-lock	PowerPC	Set to true to prevent Open Firmware text from scrolling off the top of the screen.
selftest-#megs	PowerPC	The number of MB of RAM to test at boot time. The default is 0.
SystemAudioVolume	Intel	A representation of the system audio volume (not human-readable).
use-generic?	PowerPC	The device node naming settings. Specifies whether to use generic device node names such as "screen," as opposed to Apple hardware code names.
use-nvramrc?	PowerPC	The command settings. If this is true, Open Firmware uses the commands in nvramrc at boot time.
virt-base	PowerPC	The starting virtual address that is available to Open Firmware.
virt-size	PowerPC	The size of the virtual address space available to Open Firmware.

Third-Party Applications

Although you can perform system administration tasks through the utilities supplied with Mac OS X, several third-party applications provide convenient frontends to these utilities:

Cocktail
> Kristofer Szymanski's Cocktail (*http://www.maintain.se/cocktail/*) is a shareware application that provides a GUI frontend to a wide range of system administration and interface configuration tasks.

MacPilot
> MacPilot (*http://www.koingosw.com/products/macpilot.php*) is a shareware GUI that can be used to enable and disable various features in Mac OS X and to perform numerous maintenance functions.

Onyx
> Onyx (*http://www.titanium.free.fr/pgs/english.html*) is a freeware GUI that can be used to enable and disable various features in Mac OS X and to perform numerous maintenance functions.

rEFIt
> rEFIt (*http://refit.sourceforge.net*) is a freeware boot menu and maintenance utility for EFI-based computers, including Intel-based Macs. Among other things, it provides an EFI-based shell environment.

TinkerTool System

Marcel Bresink's TinkerTool System (*http://www.bresink.com/osx/Tinker ToolSys.html*) is a freeware application that can be used for various tasks, including running the periodic jobs mentioned earlier, managing log files, changing umasks, and tuning the network configuration.

Xupport

Laurent Muller's Xupport (*http://www.applicorn.com*) is another multi-purpose freeware application for system maintenance, backup, and Mac OS X customization.

## CHAPTER 17

Other Programming Languages: Perl, Python, Ruby, and Java

This chapter covers some of the programming languages supported in Mac OS X: namely Perl, Python, Ruby, and Java.

As far as Perl and Python are concerned, Mac OS X is just another Unix. But Mac OS X versions of these packages have some niceties and some quirks that make things a little different from the developer's perspective. In particular, many of Mac OS X's non-Unix APIs, such as Carbon and Cocoa, are accessible through extension modules in both languages.

We suggest limiting your customization of the versions of Perl and Python that come with Mac OS X, since they are both fair game for modification during an upgrade or patch. You might unintentionally modify something that the system depends on, or end up with a partially broken installation the next time Software Update performs a big Mac OS X update.

It's fine to install whatever modules you want, but if you choose to install customized or newer versions of either Perl or Python, install them in */usr/local* so they don't interfere with the ones in */usr*. Check the documentation (*INSTALL* or *README* files) that came along with the source code for any information specific to Mac OS X, and for instructions for specifying an alternate installation prefix.

Java has been a part of Mac OS X from its very early days, but Ruby is a more recent addition, first bundled with Mac OS X 10.2 (Jaguar). Rails, the increasingly popular web application framework written in Ruby, makes its first appearance with the advent of Leopard.

Perl for Mac OS X Geeks

The following sections list a few of the Perl-related extras that come with Mac OS X. You can find these in */System/Library/Perl/Extras*, which is among the paths that the bundled version of Perl searches for modules.

Mac::Carbon

This module comes by way of *MacPerl* (*http://www.macperl.org*), a distribution of Perl for Mac OS 9 and earlier. *Mac::Carbon* (which is included with Mac OS X) gives Perl programmers access to the Carbon APIs. Although its roots go deep into Mac OS 9, Carbon is a supported API on Mac OS X, and these modules work fine on Mac OS X. One of the many modules included with *Mac::Carbon* is *MacPerl*. Here's an example that pops up a dialog box and asks a question:

```
#!/usr/bin/perl -w

use strict;
use MacPerl qw(:all);
my $die_in_the_vacuum_of_space = 0;
my $answer = MacPerl::Ask("Tell me how good you thought my poem was.");
if ($answer =~
    /counterpoint the surrealism of the underlying metaphor/i) {
  $die_in_the_vacuum_of_space = 1;
}
print $die_in_the_vacuum_of_space, "\n";
```

For more information, you can access the *Mac::Carbon* documentation with *perldoc Mac::Carbon*.

PerlObjCBridge.pm

This module gives you a way to call into the Objective-C runtime on Mac OS X. Given an Objective-C call of the form:

```
Type x = [Class method1:arg1 method2:arg2];
```

You can use the equivalent Perl code:

```
$x = Class->method1_method2_($arg1, $arg2);
```

You can also create an **NSString** and display it with the following script:

```
#!/usr/bin/perl -w

use strict;
use Foundation; # import Foundation objects

my $string = NSString->stringWithCString_("Hello, World");
```

```
print $string, "\n";       # prints NSCFString=SCALAR(0x858398)
print $string->cString() , "\n"; # prints Hello, World
```

You can read the documentation for this module with *perldoc PerlObjCBridge*.

Mac::Glue

This module lets you invoke Apple events from Perl. To use it with an application, you'll need to create a layer of glue (code used to connect or interface components of different software) between this module and the application with the *gluemac* utility, which is installed along with *Mac::Glue*.

 Before you use *Mac::Glue*, be sure to run (as *root*) both the *gluedialect* and *gluescriptadds* scripts in */usr/bin*. These scripts create supporting files and OSA bindings for *Mac::Glue*.

For example, to create the glue for the Terminal application, do the following:

```
$ sudo /usr/bin/gluemac /Applications/Utilities/Terminal.app/
Password: ********
What is the glue name? [Terminal]:
Created and installed App glue for Terminal.app, v1.5 (Terminal)
```

This also creates documentation for the module. To read it, use *perldoc Mac::Glue::glues::appname*, as in *perldoc Mac::Glue::glues::Terminal*.

Here's a short example that uses the Terminal glue to open a Telnet session to the Weather Underground website:

```
#!/usr/bin/perl -w

use strict;
use Mac::Glue;
my $terminal = new Mac::Glue 'Terminal';
$terminal->get_url("telnet://rainmaker.wunderground.com");
```

You can read the documentation for this module with *perldoc Mac::Glue*.

Python for Mac OS X Geeks

The following sections list a few of the Python extras that are available for or come with Mac OS X.

Carbon

As with Perl, you can access Carbon APIs from within Python. You can find a list of Carbon APIs with *pydoc Carbon*. Short-named modules (such as *CF*) are usually the APIs you're interested in; the corresponding long-named modules (such as *CoreFoundation*) will be the constants you need for the APIs. You can read documentation for a specific module with *pydoc Carbon.MODULE*, as in *pydoc Carbon.CF*.

Python also includes a number of other modules (look in */System/Library/Frameworks/Python.framework/Versions/2.3/lib/python2.3/platmac*), including EasyDialogs, which you can use to produce a Python version of the Perl example we showed earlier:

```
#!/usr/bin/pythonw

import EasyDialogs
import re

die_in_the_vacuum_of_space = 0
answer = \
  EasyDialogs.AskString("Tell me how good you thought my poem was.", "")
s = "counterpoint the surrealism of the underlying metaphor"
if re.compile(s).search(answer):
  die_in_the_vacuum_of_space = 1
print die_in_the_vacuum_of_space
```

Appscript

Appscript (*http://appscript.sourceforge.net*) is a bridge between Python and Apple events that lets you write Python scripts in a very AppleScript-esque fashion. For example, consider the following snippet of AppleScript:

```
tell app "Finder" to get name of every folder of home
```

Using Appscript, you could write this as the following Python script:

```
#!/usr/bin/pythonw

from appscript import *
print app('Finder').home.folders.name.get()
```

PyObjC

PyObjC (*http://pyobjc.sourceforge.net*) is a bridge between Python and Objective-C that includes access to Cocoa frameworks, support for Xcode, and extensive documentation and examples. To install PyObjC, you can either download an installer from its website, or grab the source code and run the command *sudo python setup.py bdist_mpkg --open*, which builds a metapackage and launches the Mac OS X installer on it.

Here's a very simple example that creates an NSString and prints it out:

```
#!/usr/bin/python

from Foundation import *
```

```
import objc

string = NSString.stringWithString_(u"Hello, World")
print string # prints Hello, World
```

Once you've installed PyObjC, check out the documentation in */Developer/ Python/PyObjC/Documentation* and the examples in */Developer/Python/ PyObjC/Examples*.

Ruby and Rails for Mac OS X Geeks

Mac OS X has included Ruby in its distribution since Release 10.2 (Jaguar), but the version supplied was insufficient for installing and using Rails, the popular framework for rapid development of web applications. It wasn't too difficult to upgrade Ruby to facilitate installation of Rails, but there was still some pain involved.

Leopard comes with Ruby 1.8.6, which is the latest distribution of the Ruby language interpreter and its associated tools. It also includes Rails 1.2.6, which was supplanted early in 2008 by Rails 2.0. The Apple Developer Connection site provides instructions for upgrading both Rails and the support tools needed to download and install it (see *http://developer.apple.com/tools/developon railsleopard.html*).

 The Macintosh seems to be the development environment of choice for people who work with Rails. The original Rails development team all use Macs, and *TextMate* (an extensible Macintosh-only text editor) has long been the preferred editor for Rails developers.

Ruby uses its own package management software, called *RubyGems*. Normally, you would simply use the *gem* command to retrieve and install Ruby modules (such as Rails) from the command line. However, first you need to bring both Ruby and Rails up to date, using the *gem* command:

```
$ sudo gem update --system
$ sudo gem install rails --include-dependencies
$ sudo gem update rake
$ sudo gem update mongrel
$ sudo gem update sqlite3-ruby
$ gem list
```

This sequence of commands tells *gem* to:

1. Update itself to the latest version.

2. Retrieve the latest version of Rails and install it along with any dependent modules.

3. Update its versions of Rake (Ruby's analog to *make* or *Ant*), Mongrel (a small web server written in Ruby that supports Rails applications), and SQLite3 (an extremely lightweight self-configuring database system for use in Rails application development).

4. List all installed RubyGems packages.

A big selling point for Rails is its usage of automated scaffolding to create working web application skeletons that conform to the MVC (model-view-controller) paradigm. Simply entering *rails application_name* on the command line causes a project directory tree to be built, organized into folders that will ultimately contain log files, configuration files, unit tests, static resources, scripts, and Ruby code (organized into model, view, and controller components), as can be seen here:

```
$ mkdir -p Projects/rails
$ cd Projects/rails
$ rails example
      create
      create  app/controllers
      create  app/helpers
      create  app/models
      create  app/views/layouts
      create  config/environments
        ...
```

After performing this initial scaffolding, to confirm that everything is set up properly, you can start up the Mongrel web server that comes bundled with Rails. To do this, run the *server* startup script found in the *script* folder:

```
$ cd example
$ ./script/server
=> Booting Mongrel (use 'script/server webrick' to force WEBrick)
=> Rails application starting on http://0.0.0.0:3000
=> Call with -d to detach
=> Ctrl-C to shutdown server
** Starting Mongrel listening at 0.0.0.0:3000
** Starting Rails with development environment...
** Rails loaded.
** Loading any Rails specific GemPlugins
** Signals ready. TERM => stop.  USR2 => restart.  INT => stop (no
restart).
** Rails signals registered.  HUP => reload (without restart).  It
might not work well.
** Mongrel 1.1.4 available at 0.0.0.0:3000
** Use CTRL-C to stop.
```

The server runs on port 3000, so you can point your browser at *http://localhost:3000/*. You should see the page shown in Figure 17-1.

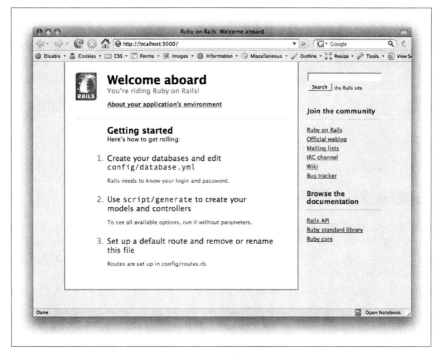

Figure 17-1. The home page presented by a Rails application

If you want your Rails application to start up as your Mac is booting up, you can accomplish this using the services of *launchd*. An example of how this goal can be achieved for another application server, Tomcat, can be found at the end of the section on Java later in this chapter. Simply follow the instructions there, substituting appropriate program arguments and environment variables to execute the *~/Projects/rails/example/script/server* script and an appropriate label and description.

Once you've confirmed that the server comes up, you can execute the *./script/generate* command, which will generate skeletal Ruby classes for model, view, and controller functions. Good material on the subject of building your own Rails applications can be found at the aforementioned link on the Apple Developer Connection website (*http://developer.apple.com/tools/developonrailsleopard.html*) and at the Ruby on Rails wiki (*http://wiki.rubyonrails.org*).

The Mongrel server provided with Rails is not a viable stand-alone production web server. For this reason, most installations frontend their Rails applications with the Apache web server. Starting with Apache 2.2 (which is the web server that comes with Leopard), you can use Apache's *mod_proxy_bal ancer* module to configure automated routing of requests from Apache to your Rails applications. Information on how to do this can be found at *http://httpd.apache.org/docs/2.2/mod/mod _proxy_balancer.html* and *http://www.redhat.com/magazine/ 025nov06/features/ruby/*, among other places.

Java for Mac OS X Geeks

The Java environment in Leopard can be found in the */System/Library/Frame works/JavaVM.Framework* folder. Leopard was introduced with Java SE 5.0 but now supports Java SE 6.0 (*http://www.apple.com/support/downloads/java formacosx105update1.html*). Check for software updates from Apple to make sure your Java environment is current.

Multiple versions of Java can be supported on the same machine, but only one can be the default version. The Java Preferences application (*/Applications/ Utilities/Java/J2SE 5.0/Java Preferences.app* for Java SE 5.0) enables you to set that default. The separate versions can be found in the */System/Library/Frame works/JavaVM.Framework/Versions* folder. The default version is symlinked to *CurrentJDK* within this folder.

Downloading and installing the Java SE 6.0 package will add 1.6.0 as a new version in the Java environment, but it will not automatically change the default version to 1.6.0. You can choose to refer to this new version manually in scripts that run Java programs, or you can use *Java Preferences.app* to set it as the new default.

Each installed version of Java has a *Home* folder. */System/Library/Frameworks/ JavaVM.Framework/Home* is a symlink to the *Home* folder of the current version (*/System/Library/Frameworks/JavaVM.Framework/Versions/Cur rentJDK/Home*), and */Library/Java/Home* is symlinked to */System/Library/ Frameworks/JavaVM.Framework/Home*. So, if you were wondering what value to use for your JAVA_HOME environment variable, that would be */Library/Java/ Home*, assuming you want the system default Java version. Alternatively, you could set JAVA_HOME to point to the *Home* folder of any of the available Java versions.

A lot more information on Java for Mac OS X can be obtained from the Apple Developer Connection site (starting with *http://developer.apple.com/java/java leopard.html*) and from Bill Iverson's book *Mac OS X for Java Geeks* (O'Reilly).

Java Enterprise Edition (Java EE)

The Java EE specification (formerly known as J2EE) defines a coordinated set of functional Java APIs for building sophisticated enterprise applications. Resting on top of the core Java Standard Edition (SE), it includes support for relational database access (JDBC), directory services (JNDI), messaging (JMS), transactionality (JTA), distributed processing (Enterprise JavaBeans), and of course, web applications (the Servlet API and Java Server Pages). Recent additions with the advent of Java EE 5 include the new Java Persistence API (JPA), which simplifies the mapping of Java entities to relational database tables, and Java Server Faces (JSF), which provides a UI-component-driven approach to web application design.

A number of options are available for Java EE servers that can be used with Mac OS X. Java's "write once, run anywhere" philosophy means that if a Java runtime environment (JRE) is present on a computer, any Java program should be executable on it. This includes open source Java EE servers such as Tomcat, JBoss (which comes bundled with Leopard's Server edition), and GlassFish. In this section, we will cover installation of Tomcat 6.0 in the Leopard environment.

Tomcat is a web application container, not a full-fledged Java EE server. This means that it implements the web application facets of the Java EE specification—namely, the Servlet API and JSP—but not the full Java EE specification. It does include support for JDBC DataSources, JNDI directory services, and Java Management Extensions (JMX).

 A common strategy is to frontend a Tomcat application server with the Apache web server, allowing Apache to serve static content and Tomcat to serve the dynamic content produced by Java EE web applications. Several mechanisms are available for doing this, including the use of Tomcat Connectors (*mod_jk*) and the simpler *mod_proxy* approach. More information on how to do this can be found at *http://httpd .apache.org/docs/2.2/mod/mod_proxy.html*, *http://tomcat .apache.org/tomcat-6.0-doc/proxy-howto.html*, and *http://tom cat.apache.org/connectors-doc/webserver_howto/apache.html*.

The steps for installing Tomcat on Mac OS X are straightforward; the steps for configuring it to run as a service that executes at system startup are just a little more complicated. Here they are (these instructions are derived in part from Eric Rank's blog post at *http://blog.lo-fi.net/2008/01/leopard-for-web-de veloper-running.html*):

1. First, download Tomcat 6.0 (the latest version at the time of this writing) from the Apache website (*http://tomcat.apache.org/download-60.cgi*). For Mac OS X, pick the *tar.gz* version of the "core" download.

2. Unzip and unpack the downloaded archive into */usr/local*, which will pro- duce the new directory */usr/local/apache-tomcat-6.0.xx* (the exact name of the archive and of the newly created directory will differ depending on which release of Tomcat is available when you download):

   ```
   $ cd /usr/local
   $ sudo tar xzvf ~/Downloads/apache-tomcat-6.0.xx.tar.gz
   ```

3. Symlink this new directory to */usr/local/tomcat*:

   ```
   $ sudo ln -s /usr/local/apache-tomcat-6.0.xx /usr/local/tomcat
   ```

4. Establish environment variable values for $JAVA_HOME and $CATALINA_HOME:

   ```
   $ export JAVA_HOME=/Library/Java/Home
   $ export CATALINA_HOME=/usr/local/tomcat
   ```

5. Run the Tomcat startup script:

   ```
   $ sudo /usr/local/tomcat/bin/catalina.sh run
   ```

   (Supplying the *run* argument, as shown here, directs console output to your Terminal window; the *start* argument would direct it to a log file.)

6. Open *http://localhost:8080/* in your browser to see the default Tomcat home page.

7. Stop Tomcat by typing Control-C in the Terminal window.

8. Create an *org.apache.tomcat.tomcat6.plist* file containing options for run- ning Tomcat using *launchd*:

   ```
   <?xml version="1.0" encoding="UTF-8"?>
   <!DOCTYPE plist PUBLIC "-//Apple//DTD PLIST 1.0//EN"
             "http://www.apple.com/DTDs/PropertyList-1.0.dtd">
   <plist version="1.0">
     <dict>
       <key>Disabled</key>
       <false/>
       <key>EnvironmentVariables</key>
       <dict>
         <key>JAVA_HOME</key>
         <string>/Library/Java/Home</string>
         <key>CATALINA_HOME</key>
         <string>/usr/local/tomcat</string>
       </dict>
       <key>Label</key>
       <string>org.apache.tomcat.tomcat6</string>
   ```

```
<key>ProgramArguments</key>
<array>
  <string>/usr/local/tomcat6/bin/catalina.sh</string>
  <string>start</string>
</array>
<key>RunAtLoad</key>
<true/>
<key>ServiceDescription</key>
<string>Tomcat 6 Server</string>
  </dict>
</plist>
```

9. Copy this file into the */Library/LaunchDaemons* folder:

```
$ sudo cp ~/org.apache.tomcat.tomcat6.plist /Library/LaunchDaemons
```

10. Tell *launchd* about this new service by invoking *launchctl*:

```
$ sudo launchctl load /Library/LaunchDaemons/org.apache.tomcat.tomcat6.plist
```

To prevent the Tomcat server from showing up super-fluously as one of the active applications, you can ⌘-Tab through on the Desktop, or include *-Djava.awt.head less=true* as an argument to the *java* command invoked by the startup script. This can be done simply by ap-pending this string to the JAVA_OPTS shell variable in */usr/local/tomcat/bin/catalina.sh*:

```
JAVA_OPTS="${JAVA_OPTS} -Djava.awt.headless=true"
```

You can also place this setting in the *.plist* file:

```
<key>EnvironmentVariables</key>
<dict>
  <key>JAVA_HOME</key>
  <string>/Library/Java/Home</string>
  <key>CATALINA_HOME</key>
  <string>/usr/local/tomcat</string>
  <key>JAVA_OPTS</key>
  <string>-Djava.awt.headless=true</string>
</dict>
```

Mac OS X GUI Primer

If you're a Unix geek new to Mac OS X, some of the terminology may not be that obvious. Although you know what most things do, you probably haven't connected them with their street names. This appendix first provides an overview of the Mac OS X desktop environment, and then continues with a more detailed account of how to make the most out of your limited desktop space.

Overview of the Aqua Desktop

Figure A-1 shows Mac OS X's Desktop.

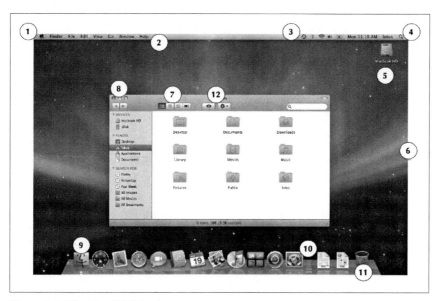

Figure A-1. The Mac OS X Desktop

The numbered items are explained in the following list:

1. Legend has it that the Apple menu almost didn't survive the transition from the classic Macintosh operating system into Mac OS X, but the cries of the faithful kept it there. This menu leads to information about your Mac and quick access to the Software Update utility, Dock Preferences, and System Preferences, as well as the ability to "force quit" running applications and view recently opened documents. Finally, at the bottom of the menu are options for putting the system to sleep, restarting, logging out, and shutting down.

2. The menu bar is where the frontmost application's menus appear. Unlike Windows and Linux desktops such as GNOME and KDE, whose menus are attached to individual windows, Mac OS X's menu bar's appearance and function changes based on which application is in the foreground. The active foreground application is listed as the second item in the menu bar, right after the Apple menu. Underneath that menu item, you will typically find options for the application's preferences and for quitting the application, among other things. If your active application is the Finder, notice the options available under the Finder menu item.

3. Some parts of the operating system, including Bluetooth networking, AirPort, VPN, and your battery options, install menu "extras" at the rightmost side of the menu bar. Use these to check the status of these items, and click on them for menus that let you adjust aspects of how each item operates. ⌘-drag to rearrange the ordering of your menu extras on the menu bar, or ⌘-drag an item off of the menu bar to consign it to oblivion. (To bring it back, you'll need to poke around in System Preferences to find the appropriate option.) Notice that the username appears at the far right if you have more than one user on the system. If you've enabled Fast User Switching (System Preferences→Accounts→Login Options), you will be able to click on the username to log in as another user while keeping your session active.

4. Also on the far right of the menu bar, Spotlight awaits your moment of need. For more information on Spotlight, see Chapter 2.

5. By default, all mounted volumes appear on the Desktop, starting with your system's main hard drive (named *Macintosh HD* by default). You can unmount a volume (other than your main hard drive) by dragging it to the Trash (located at the far right edge of the Dock), or you can hide all of them by selecting Finder→Preferences→General→"Show these items on the Desktop" and choosing which items you want or don't want displayed on the Desktop. But don't worry; if you choose to hide volumes from the Desktop, you will still be able to access and unmount them using the sidebar.

6. The Finder is how you view the filesystem. Finder windows display the contents of folders, like Explorer windows on a Microsoft Windows system. On the left edge of a Finder window is the sidebar, which has changed significantly in Leopard. It now includes lists of mounted volumes (Devices), commonly used folders (Places), and other computers with shared resources, including VNC access (Shared). You can add your own favorite files and folders into the Places list by dragging and dropping them there.

7. Finder windows have four view modes: icon view (⌘-1), list view ⌘-2), column view (⌘-3), and the new cover flow view (⌘-4). Use this widget to select which of the four views to use on a given window, or use the keyboard shortcuts to quickly switch views without using the mouse.

8. All Finder windows have three buttons in the upper-left corner:
   • The red button closes windows (⌘-W).
   • The yellow button minimizes windows to the right side of the Dock (⌘-M).
   • The green button zooms windows, expanding or reducing their size depending on their previous state.

   The oblong grey button in the upper-right corner toggles the display of the sidebar on and off.

9. The Dock contains shortcuts to the applications you need to use the most. The leftmost icon is always the Finder. You can rearrange the others as you see fit, and you can drag new items onto the Dock. To remove an icon from the Dock, simply drag it off toward the Desktop and the icon disappears in a puff of smoke. (To view an item opening in slow motion, you can hold down the Shift key while clicking on it.)

10. Drag the Dock separator up and down to resize the Dock. Control-click (or right-click) on it to adjust the Dock's options, such as where it sits on the Desktop, the magnification level, and auto-hiding.

11. The right side of the Dock contains icons for open documents and for the Trash. Drag files to the Trash to delete them (⌘-Delete); drag volumes to the Trash to unmount or eject them, as in the case of optical or floppy disks (⌘-E); and Control-click (or right-click) the Trash when you want to empty it. You can add other documents or folders to the right side of the Dock separator by dragging them there.

12. Clicking on the eye button here allows you to interact with Quick Look and Slideshow (accessed by clicking on the eye button while holding down the Option key). The gear menu allows you to perform many of the actions that would be available as contextual menu items for the folder you are viewing, such as creating a new folder, viewing additional file or folder information on the folder, and burning selected items to CD or DVD.

Figure A-2. Mac OS X's Dashboard

 The Finder's application menu also contains an Empty Trash option, as well as a Secure Empty Trash option that, when selected, overwrites files in the Trash so many times that they're practically impossible to recover.

There's a predefined keyboard shortcut for Empty Trash (Shift-⌘-Delete), but not for Secure Empty Trash. If you find yourself using Secure Empty Trash enough, you can add a keyboard shortcut for it in System Preferences→Keyboard & Mouse→Keyboard Shortcuts.

Click the Dashboard icon in the Dock (or press F12) to bring up the Dashboard, an alternate universe that lurks under your Mac's Desktop. Here, you'll find a set of "widgets" that provide you with quick access to information such as the time and date, weather forecasts, and a calculator. The Dashboard is shown in Figure A-2.

The numbered items are explained in the following list:

1. The Calculator widget is one of four widgets visible on the screen right now. If you hover the mouse over a widget and a little *i* appears in the lower-right corner, you can click it to customize the settings for that widget.

2. This disclosure button shows and hides the list of additional widgets. When this list is active, a circled *x* appears in the upper-left corner of each of your current widgets; click this *x* to remove the widget.

3. Choose a widget from this list, and it immediately appears on the Dashboard.

4. Clicking Manage Widgets will display the Widget Manager.

5. You can use the Widget Manager to find more widgets available online (see *http://www.apple.com/downloads/dashboard/*); click this button to display Apple's list of additional Dashboard widgets in your browser.

6. If you've installed more widgets than can appear on the screen at once, click on the left and right arrows to see them. Bear in mind that although you can add as many available widgets as you'd like, if you select a large number of widgets to open when Dashboard is activated, it may take a while for all of them to load.

Dashboard lets you keep frequently required information at your fingertips without cluttering up your Desktop. If there's a widget you want that doesn't already exist, all you need is a little JavaScript and HTML skill to build it. For more information on how to create your own Dashboard widgets, see *http://developer.apple.com/macosx/dashboard.html*.

Making the Most of Your Desktop Space

The desktop-real-estate-saving features of Aqua are provided by options on the application menu (the leftmost menu that has the same name as the frontmost application), Exposé, and Spaces, described in the following sections.

The Application Menu

The ability to *hide* an application is particularly useful for applications that you want to keep open but don't frequently need to interact with, such as the Vine VNC server. The Hide option, found in the application menu of most Mac OS X applications (for example, Word→Hide Word), can usually be invoked with the ⌘-H keyboard shortcut to hide the currently running application.

To unhide the application, simply click on its Dock icon or use the application switcher (⌘-Tab) to locate the application. Using the application switcher will always switch applications from left to right, unless you hold down the Shift key while switching (then it moves from right to left). Pressing the H, M, or Q keys when an application is highlighted in the application switcher will hide, move, or quit the application, respectively. The Hide Others menu selection (depending on the application, this is usually available with the keyboard shortcut Option-⌘-H) continues to show you the active application but hides all other open applications.

Finally, the Show All option in the application menu brings all running applications out of hiding.

Exposé

Exposé found its way into Mac OS X 10.3 (Panther) as a nifty hack by one of the Apple engineers. It was previewed and quickly added to Mac OS X's code base as a must-have for the Panther release and has been retained in the subsequent releases. Exposé uses Quartz rendering to quickly give you access to all of the display windows for your open applications, or to scoot windows out of the way so you can quickly see what's on your Desktop.

Exposé can be activated in four ways:

- Function keys
- Double-clicking its icon in the Finder (in */Applications*)
- Hot corners (as defined in System Preferences→Exposé & Spaces→Exposé)
- Programming the buttons of a multibutton mouse (as defined in System Preferences→Exposé & Spaces→Exposé)

By default, F9 tiles all open windows (as shown in Figure A-3), F10 tiles all open windows of the current application, and F11 forces all open windows out of the way so you can see what's on the Desktop. In each case, pressing the given function key a second time reverses the effect of pressing it the first time. For example, if you press F11 to hide all open windows, pressing F11 again will undo this action and return all open windows to the Desktop.

Other tricks you can try with Exposé include the following:

- If you hold down the Shift key and press the F9, F10, or F11 key, Exposé works in slow motion.
- If you've pressed F9 to separate all the open windows, you can use the arrow keys on your keyboard to highlight a particular window. The window is shaded light blue, and its filename is superimposed on the window.
- If you've pressed F10 to separate the windows for the current application, you can hit the Tab key to switch to another application and bring its windows—again, separated by Exposé—to the front. Shift-Tab cycles backward through the window stack, so if you've gone too far with the Tab key, you can press Shift-Tab to return to the application you need.
- If you've done the previous trick, combine that with the trick before it and use the arrow keys to highlight a window; pressing Return brings that window to the front of the stack.

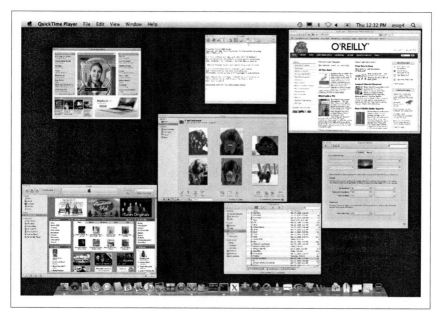

Figure A-3. An Exposé-tiled Desktop

- If you've used F11 to push the windows out of the way so you can see the Desktop, the window that previously had the focus is still active, even though it isn't really visible (F9 and F10 take the focus away). For example, if you have a Terminal window open and you hit F11, try typing "ls" on the keyboard and pressing the Enter key, then hitting F11 again to bring the windows back; you should see the output of the *ls* command in the Terminal window.

Spaces

One desktop feature that has long been a staple of the Unix world is the virtual desktop. For example, if you've used GNOME or KDE, you are probably accustomed to having multiple workspaces in which to run various applications or open different sets of windows. Nearly all Unix/Linux desktop environments have this feature, and beginning with Leopard, Mac OS X is no exception: Mac OS X users can enjoy a multiple workspace feature too, through the Mac OS X Spaces application. The Exposé feature is still available, and Spaces adds features to the Mac OS X desktop rather than replacing them.

Before you can use Spaces, you'll need to set it up. In the Spaces preference pane (System Preferences→Exposé & Spaces→Spaces), select Enable Spaces and, if you'd like, Show Spaces in Menu bar. Though the default number of virtual desktops (or "spaces") is four, you can add more spaces in the Exposé

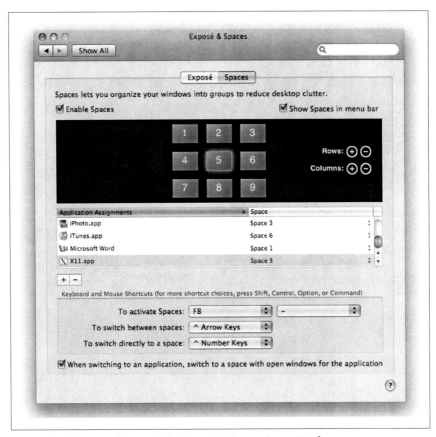

Figure A-4. Setting up Spaces in the Exposé & Spaces System Preferences pane

& Spaces System Preferences pane, where you can also assign various applications to different spaces, as shown in Figure A-4.

Any application can be assigned either to one specific space or to all spaces. By default, the F8 key is configured to activate Spaces. You can assign that task to another F-key and to a mouse button of a multibutton mouse. When you activate Spaces with the F8 key, you get a tiled view of all the spaces you've established in the Exposé & Spaces preference pane, as shown in Figure A-5.

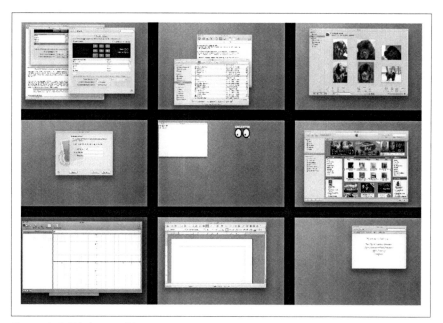

Figure A-5. Tiled view of Spaces

You can switch between adjacent spaces by holding down the Control key and pressing the arrow keys, and you can switch directly to a given space by pressing Control-*number*, where *number* is the number assigned to the given space in the Exposé & Spaces preference pane. Spaces and Exposé are designed to work together to allow the user to make the most out of limited desktop real estate. Figure A-6 shows a tiled view of Spaces, in which the individual spaces show tiled Exposé views.

Figure A-6. Tiled Spaces and tiled Exposé

If you're not satisfied with Spaces, a more fully featured commercial virtual desktop application may soon be available from CodeTek Studios, Inc. (*http://www.codetek.com*). At the time of this writing, Codetek VirtualDesktop is not available for Leopard.

 If you double-click the Spaces icon in the Finder (in */Applications*), you'll be prompted to set up Spaces in the Exposé & Spaces System Preferences pane.

Index

We'd like to hear your suggestions for improving our indexes. Send email to *index@oreilly.com*.

I

iChat, screen sharing via VNC, 143
iconv.h header file, 220
ifconfig utility, 320
image-editing tools, 166
imake utility, 211
importers
    installed on system, listing, 40
    Spotlight, 33
.info file, creating for Fink package, 289
initialization in Mac OS X startup, 69
inline assembly code, 210
input devices, X11 interaction with, 125
InputManager, 5
installation disk image, getting for Linux, 181
instprog and instman variables (Portfile), 295
Instruments, 193
Intel-based Macs, 171
    binaries, 207
    modifying EFI settings with nvram, 364
Interface Builder, 193
Internet Sharing, 319
Internet-enabled disk images
    creating and using for software distribution, 276
    creating with MacPorts, 256
IP addresses
    Mac server on non-business-grade network, 336
    managing, 89
    network computers, assigned using Bonjour, 22
    static IP address for server on Mac OS X, 340
IP printer, adding, 98
ipfw (IP Firewall), 320, 324
    configuring manually, 326
iPhoto, using GIMP as default image editor, 166
ISP policies on running servers on your network, 339
iTerm, 23
    background images in windows, 27
    contextual menu, 27

profiles and bookmarks, 23

J

Java, 376
    Java EE (Enterprise Edition), 377

K

KDE desktop environment
    connecting to printer shared from a Mac, 110
    remote Mac, displayed by Screen Sharing VNC viewer, 138
    versions, installed via MacPorts or Fink, 127
kernel extensions, loading during boot, 68
kernel utilities, 350–361
    ddb, 350
    DTrace, 351
    sysctl, 353–361
    utilities to manipulate kernel modules, 352
kextload utility, 352
kextstat utility, 352
kextunload utility, 352
keyboard
    single, for multiple Mac OS X and X11 desktops, 130
    X11 system, customizing, 125
ksh (Korn shell), 3

L

latency utility, 346
LaTeX, 150
LaTeXiT, 155
launchctl utility, 70
launchd, 70
    launching MySQL, 77
LDAPv3, 83
Leopard
    64-bit computing, 208, 209
    changes to Sharing preference pane, 300
    launching X11 applications, 29
    saving Terminal settings, 15
    Terminal application features, 27
    Terminal contextual menu, 10

libraries
    building a shared library, 223–227
    important Mac OS X libraries, 235
    loading dynamically, 227
    for numerical computing, 240
    shared, versus loadable modules, 222
    significant libraries not included with
        Mac OS X, 238
    static, creating and linking, 230
    versions, 229
    X11-based, 126, 211
/Library directory, 64
libstdc++, 222
libSystem, 221
limits.h header file, 220
linking static libraries, 231
Linux
    avahi package (Bonjour services), 22
    GNOME desktop environment,
        connecting to shared Mac
        printer, 108
    KDE desktop environment, connecting
        to shared Mac printer, 110
    manual printer configuration, 111
    printing to Mac shared printer, 112
    running on Mac hardware, 174
        installing and configuring Ubuntu
            8.04 on Mac, 176
        older Macs, 178
    support for HFS+ filesystem, 48
Linux-PAM (Pluggable Authentication
        Modules for Linux), 92
little-endian ordering, 210
loadable modules versus shared libraries,
        222
LoadModule directive for mod_ssl, 311
Local plug-in (Directory Utility), 83
logging (firewall), enabling, 326
login preferences, 72
look and feel, configuring for X11 system,
        125
LPD (Line Printer Daemon) protocol, 98
lsof utility, 346

M

Mac OS X
    emulators on, 181

running different operating systems
        under, 171
    software releases, xiv
    VersionTracker, xiv
Mac OS X 10.4 (see Tiger)
Mac OS X 10.5 (see Leopard)
Mac-on-Linux hardware virtualizer, 180
Mac::Carbon module (Perl), 370
Mac::Glue module (Perl), 371
MacFUSE, 148
Mach, 67
Mach bootstrap services, 71
Mach-O, 222
MacOSXHints, xiii
MacPerl, 370
MacPilot, 367
MacPorts, xiii, 211, 255–266
    connecting to SVN repository, 263
    creating and installing in RPM format,
        261
    creating and installing packages in .pkg
        format, 261
    creating packages (example), 292–296
        building and installing a port, 295
        Portfile, 293
        tarball, 292
    customizing installation, 258
    gotchas, 267
    GUI frontends, 264
        PortAuthority, 266
        Porticus, 265
    installing additional window
        managers, 123
    installing from source, 257
    installing from SVN, 258
    installing packages from source, 260
    installing X11-based applications and
        libraries, 126
    listing available packages with port list
        command, 259
    possible conflicts with Fink, 257
    prerequisites for installation, 256
    revealing image repository with port
        location rxvt, 260
    searching for specific packages with
        port search command, 259
    summary of port commands, 262

of Accelerate framework, 240
sudo command, 5
    editing motd file, 6
Summarize service, 21
SuperDuper!, 175
SVN
    connecting to MacPorts SVN
        repository, 263
    installing MacPorts from, 258
symbolic links
    for libraries in libSystem, 221
    pointing to current version of a library,
        229
sysctl utility, 353–361
/System/Library directory, 62
system alert sounds, X11 system, 126
system library (libSystem), 221
system management tools, 343–368
    diagnostic utilities, 343–350
    kernel utilities, 350–361
    system configuration utilities, 361–
        367
    third-party applications, 367
System Preferences, launching AddPrinter,
    95
SystemStarter, 69, 71, 72–77
    daemons starting automatically at boot
        time, 72
    invoking from command line to start or
        stop MySQL, 77

T

tab completion, 19
tabs, creating and arranging in Terminal
    window, 8
tar command, 269
tarballs, 196
    created with GNU tar, 270
    creating and publishing for Fink
        package, 288
    creating and publishing for MacPorts
        package, 292
    disadvantages for software
        distribution, 271
    installing software packaged as, 271
tcsh (TENEX C shell), 3
.term files, 14
    exporting Terminal settings to, 16

Terminal, 3–31
    alternative applications, 23
    Bonjour, 22
    changing default shell, 20
    comparison with xterm, 4
    contextual menu, 10
    creating and arranging tabs in a
        window, 8
    customizing, 10
        exporting and importing settings,
            14
        Preferences, 10
        using shell scripts, 13
    customizing startup options for
        windows, 8
    cycling between open windows, 8
    launching, 5
    launching AddPrinter, 96
    launching windows, 7
        using executable shell scripts, 9
    launching X11-based applications,
        128
    managing users and passwords from,
        85
    open command, 27
    running FinkCommander commands,
        250
    Services menu, 20
    shells, 3
    xterm command, 5
    xterm window versus, 119
.terminal files, 8
    exporting settings in, 16
    importing without launching, 17
Terminator, 27
TeX, 150
    installing MacTeX, 151
    LaTeXiT, 155
    TeXShop, 153
text and graphics rendering, 5
TextEdit, 22
    opening files in, 28
third-party applications for system
    management, 367
3D modeling, 167
Tiger
    64-bit computing, 209
    saving Terminal settings, 14

W

wchar.h header file, 220
-Wconversion compiler flag, 210
web applications, development with Ruby
and Rails, 373
Web Sharing, 306–312
(see also Apache web server)
WebDAV (Web-based Distributed
Authoring and Versioning)
module, 308
website for this book, xvi
Wi-Fi network speed, 338
wide character data types, 220
window groups (Terminal), 12
window managers, installing with
MacPorts, 123
Windows systems
Active Directory plug-in for Directory
Utility, 82
Bonjour for Windows, 22
running Windows applications on
Mac, 173
Samba file and printer sharing solution,
50
VNC clients and servers, 142
wireless access points, 338

X

X Window System, 5, 117–131
connecting Mac OS X to other X
Window systems, 128
connecting to Mac OS X VNC server,
137
installing X11, 119
interactions between X11 and Mac OS
X, 128
opening applications in X11
environment, 29
osx2x application, 130
running X11, 119
standard X11 Unix versions of VNC,
132
using AquaTerm instead of X11
libraries, 212
using X11 graphics with R, 160
X11 customizations, 121–126

dot-files, desktops, and window
managers, 122
preferences, Applications menu,
and Dock menu, 124
X11-based applications and libraries,
126, 211
X11-based video applications, 164
X11 forwarding, 313
xclock application, displaying on Mac OS
X desktop, 129
Xcode tools, 191
installing, 211, 245
installing before MacPorts, 256
Xgrid sharing, 322
.xinitrc script, 122
xmkmf script, 211
XML property lists (plist), 14, 16
MySQL startup parameters, 75
XML schema, 40
for Spotlight-collected metadata, 40
xterm
comparison with Terminal, 4
setting window title, 13
xterm window
copying between Mac OS X
applications and, 128
opening, 119
Xupport, 368

Y

Yellow Dog Linux, 179

Z

ZeroConf standard, 22
.zip files, 269
zsh (Z shell), 3

About the Authors

Brian Jepson is a programmer, author, and executive editor for MAKE's book series. He's also a volunteer system administrator and all-around geek for AS220, a nonprofit arts center in Providence, Rhode Island. AS220 gives Rhode Island artists uncensored and unjuried forums for their work. These forums include galleries, performance space, and publications. Brian sees to it that technology, especially little blinky bits of technology, supports that mission.

Ernest E. Rothman is a professor of mathematical sciences at Salve Regina University (SRU) in Newport, Rhode Island. Ernie holds a Ph.D. in applied mathematics from Brown University and a B.S. in mathematics from Brooklyn College, CUNY. Before accepting a full-time faculty position at SRU in 1993, he held the positions of research associate and scientific software analyst at the Cornell Theory Center at Cornell University in Ithaca, New York. His professional interests are scientific computing, applied mathematics and computational science education, and the Unix underpinnings of Mac OS X. Ernie lives in southern Rhode Island with his wife Kim and Newfoundland dog Joseph. You can keep abreast of his latest activities at *http://homepage.mac.com/samchops*.

Rich Rosen's career began at Bell Labs, where his work with relational databases, Unix, and the Internet prepared him well for the world of web application development. He's been a Macintosh user for over 20 years, and is currently using a Mac Mini as his home server, an iMac as the centerpiece of his home recording studio, and a MacBook for live musical performance and writing. He is the coauthor of *Web Application Architecture: Principles, Protocols & Practices* (Wiley), a textbook on advanced web application development. Rich currently works at Interactive Data Corporation writing software for the Fixed Income Systems group. He holds an M.S. in computer science from Stevens Institute of Technology, and he lives in New Jersey with his wife, Celia. His website can be found at *http://www.neurozen.com*.

Colophon

The animal on the cover of *Mac OS X for Unix Geeks*, Fourth Edition, is a leopard (*Panthera pardus*). The leopard is the fifth largest of all the big cats, behind the lion, tiger, jaguar, and mountain lion. It weighs between 70 and 200 pounds and has a body length of four to six feet and a tail length of three to four feet. Leopards are strongly built, with a large head and powerful jaws, so they are able to kill prey much larger than themselves. They are nimble and stealthy hunters.

Leopards stalk their quarry and attack with a fatal bite to the neck. They feed on a wide variety of animals, including wildebeest, monkeys, rodents, insects, fish, snakes, and birds. They often store their larger kills in trees to protect them from scavengers and other cats. Extremely agile climbers, leopards can haul prey up to three times their body weight into a tree.

Leopards are the most widespread feline in the world; they can be found in Africa, India, China, and Central Asia. They are highly adaptable and live in open savannah, jungles, forests, and mountains. Leopards are nocturnal and spend their days resting in trees, where their spotted coats provide good camouflage. Most leopards have a tawny base coat with a black rosette (spot) pattern. The shade of their base coat depends on their environment: lighter colored leopards tend to live in warm, dry areas and open plains, and darker colored leopards tend to live in dense forests, as the darker coat helps them stay hidden.

The cover image was drawn by Lorrie LeJeune. The cover font is Adobe ITC Garamond. The text font is Linotype Birka; the heading font is Adobe Myriad Condensed; and the code font is LucasFont's TheSansMonoCondensed.